The Population of Peninsular Malaysia

The **Institute of Southeast Asian Studies (ISEAS)** was established as an autonomous organization in 1968. It is a regional centre dedicated to the study of socio-political, security and economic trends and developments in Southeast Asia and its wider geostrategic and economic environment.

The Institute's research programmes are the Regional Economic Studies (RES, including ASEAN and APEC), Regional Strategic and Political Studies (RSPS), and Regional Social and Cultural Studies (RSCS).

ISEAS Publishing, an established academic press, has issued almost 2,000 books and journals. It is the largest scholarly publisher of research about Southeast Asia from within the region. ISEAS Publishing works with many other academic and trade publishers and distributors to disseminate important research and analyses from and about Southeast Asia to the rest of the world.

Saw Swee-Hock

The Population of Peninsular Malaysia

Institute of Southeast Asian Studies
Singapore

This Reprint Edition published in Singapore in 2007 by
ISEAS Publishing
Institute of Southeast Asian Studies
30 Heng Mui Keng Terrace
Pasir Panjang
Singapore 119614

E-mail: publish@iseas.edu.sg
Website: <http://bookshop.iseas.edu.sg>

This book is published under ISEAS Malaysia Study Programme funded by Professor Saw Swee-Hock.

© Reprint Edition 2007 Institute of Southeast Asian Studies, Singapore
First Edition 1988 (Singapore University Press)

ISEAS Library Cataloguing-in-Publication Data

Saw Swee-Hock, 1931–
    The population of Peninsular Malaysia.
    1. Demography—Malaysia—Malaya.
    2. Malaya—Population.
    I. Title
HB3644.6 A3S37   2007

ISBN: 978-981-230-427-8 (hard cover)
ISBN: 978-981-230-730-9 (PDF)

Printed in Singapore by Markono Print Media

CONTENTS

LIST OF TABLES

LIST OF APPENDIX TABLES

LIST OF FIGURES

PREFACE

In preparing the manuscript I have been constantly guided by a desire to produce a comprehensive and up-to-date book by covering all the major topics which ought to be included in such a study and by going as far back in time as the availability of data permits. In doing this in the various chapters and appendices, special emphasis has also been placed on ethnic differences in view of the profound influence of ethnicity in determining demographic trends and patterns in the country. It is hoped that this approach adopted to prepare the manuscript has resulted in a more interesting and meaningful study. The book is the product of many years of research effort, interrupted, however, by my diversion into other research projects and by my regular duties in the university and other professional activities. The timing in the completion of the manuscript also depended on the necessary statistics being made available from the latest population census conducted in 1980. Intensive writing could only be carried out in the mid-1980s when the results of this census required to prepare the various sections of the book began to be released. The timing has turned out to be quite fortuitous in that it coincided with my sabbatical leave spent in the Centre for Population Studies, London University, during the second half of 1985.

I would like to acknowledge the assistance of numerous institutions and individuals. For helping me to gather the research materials, my thanks go to the University of Malaya Library, the Malaysian Department of Statistics, the National University of Singapore Library, the British Museum Library, and the London School of Economics Library. The late Professor D.V. Glass and the late Mr. Norman Carrier, both of the London School of Economics, were responsible for stimulating my interest in the study of this multi-racial population. I wish to thank Professor W. Brass, Director of the Centre for Population Studies, for his hospitality and assistance, and Mr. Kwok Kwan Kit of the Malaysian Department of Statistics for helping me to obtain some of the census data. My thanks also go to Miss Patricia Tay, Editor/Manager of the Singapore University Press, for her tireless effort in the production of the book. I am greatly indebted to my wife, Cheng Siok Hwa, for her kind support and valuable comments on the various versions of the manuscript. Needless to say, any opinions and shortcomings in the book are entirely my own.

September 1986   **Saw Swee-Hock**

PREFACE TO THE REPRINT EDITION 2007

Since this book on *The Population of Peninsular of Malaysia* was published in the mid-eighties and became out-of-print quite some years ago, there has been many enquiries concerning the availability of the book from various quarters. The opportunity was taken to reprint the book under the Malaysia Study Programme in the Institute of Southeast Asian Studies, which has brought out a series of books on Malaysia in recent years. The reprint of this book has been made possible by the Singapore University Press kindly assigning the copyright of the book to the author, and for this I would like to express my grateful thanks.

January 2007   **Saw Swee-Hock**

1

Introduction

Geographical Setting

The long narrow peninsula of Peninsular Malaysia extends from latitude 1°20′ north to latitude 6°40′ north, and from longitude 99°35′ east to longitude 104°20′ east. It is situated in a central position within Southeast Asia, being an extension of the Asian land mass as well as part of the island world of the Malay archipelago. Beyond Peninsular Malaysia's northern land border lies Thailand, and its immediate neighbour in the south is the small island state of Singapore joined to it by the 1,056 metre rail-and-road causeway cutting through the narrow Straits of Johore. A little further southwards is the vast multi-island Republic of Indonesia. Across the South China Sea in the east is the huge island of Borneo which contains the two eastern Malaysian states of Sarawak and Sabah, and in the west just across the vital Straits of Malacca is the large elongated island of Sumatra.

Peninsular Malaysia extends some 740 kilometres in length from Perlis state in the north to Johore Bahru town in the south, and about 322 kilometres in width at its widest point. The total land area approximates 132,090 square kilometres, slightly larger than England without Wales. It has a coastline of nearly 1,931 kilometres, covered in many places with mangrove swamps, sand bars and sandy beaches. The western side has a few natural harbours but the eastern coastline is rather shallow, sandy and without good harbours. The country comprises a series of mountain ranges running from the northwest in the Thai border to southwest into the state of Negri Sembilan. To the west of this central range is the Bintang Range extending from the northern border to the Taiping region, while to the east is an area of highland in Kelantan and Trengganu. These main mountain masses determine the drainage system which is well served by a multiplicity of rivers, somewhat shorter and more numerous in the west. The rivers are narrow and swift in their upper reaches but become sluggish and meandering once they enter the coastal plains. They have been the chief means of communication and important factors in the growth of settlements and towns.

The country, being in the equatorial zone, has nearly two-thirds of its land area covered with dense tropical rain forests and mangrove swamps. The mangrove forests, occupying some 1,425 square kilometres, are strung along the west coast, varying in width from tens of metres to twenty kilometres. In the east coast the strong waves and sandy soil restrict the growth of mangrove trees to small patches around river mouths. Between the central highlands and the coastal swamps is the belt of cultivated vegetation, dominated by rubber, oil palm, cocoa, coconut and padi landscape. Beyond the agricultural zone are the dense forests which stretch from the cultivated fringe to the hillslopes of the central ranges. Below the level of 760 metres in general are the lowland rain forests interspersed by secondary forests or *belukar*, and above this height are the hill forests and the mountain forests with less dense and shorter trees.

The climate of the country is equatorial, with uniform and high temperatures, abundant rainfall and high humidity. Temperatures are constantly high throughout the year, with only slight changes in the average monthly temperatures. Somewhat greater variations are shown by the daily temperatures which may fluctuate between 20 to 30 degrees centigrade inland. The rainy seasons are very much influenced by the southwest and the northeast monsoons. During the northeast monsoon in October to March, the east coast is exposed to heavy rain, while the west coast has its wettest period in April to September when the southwest monsoon prevails. Fairly frequent convectional rain occurs during the two inter-monsoon periods; thunderstorms are frequent all the year round. The average rainfall for the whole country reaches 250 centimetres a year, though the amount varies among the different parts of the country.

Historical Background

Before the coming of the Europeans in the early sixteenth century, the territory now known as Peninsular Malaysia was under the rule of various Malay sultanates established at different periods in the west coast, especially around Malacca. Prior to this the country was under the sway of the Majapahit Empire centred in Java which had earlier replaced the Sri Vijaya Empire in the fourteenth century. The first European incursion into the country occurred in 1511 when the Portuguese captured Malacca and held sway until it was in turn captured by the Dutch in 1641. The Dutch ruled Malacca until the late eighteenth century when the British took over. In 1786 Francis Light occupied the island of Penang on behalf of the East India Company, and the island together with the hinterland of Province Wellesley were ceded to the company. A decade later in 1795, Malacca was surrendered by the Dutch to the British and, though returned on two occasions, was eventually given to the British in 1825 in exchange for Bencoolen. Further south the settlement of Singapore was established by Stamford Raffles for the East India Company in 1819.

In 1826 the three British possession of Penang, Malacca and Singapore were combined into one administrative unit known as the Straits Settlements, which was subsequently transferred from the control of the East India Company to the Colonial Office in 1867. British influence did not stop here. The increasing interest of the British in the affairs of the hinterland Malay States resulted in the four central states of Perak, Selangor, Negri Sembilan, and Pahang accepting British control and coming together to form the Federated Malay States in 1895. This larger political unit had a centralised form of government, with a British Resident in each state. In theory the British Residents were supposed to advise the Rulers, but in practice their advice must be accepted if it had nothing to do with Malay customs and religion. The other five states, Perlis, Kedah, Kelantan, Trengganu and Johore, remained outside the two larger political groupings, and were frequently referred to, rather accusingly, as the Unfederated Malay States. They were each administered with the aid of a British Adviser as a separate political entity. This broad political framework continued to exist right up to the outbreak of war in December 1941, culminating in the Japanese occupation of the country from February 1942 to September 1945.

The early postwar period saw some swift and profound political changes. The first government to take control of the country after the war was the British Military Administration whose prime task was to restore law and order. This temporary military administration was replaced by the creation of the Malayan Union on 1 April 1946, incorporating all the states, except Singapore, under a Governor and a strong central government. Since the new constitution deprived the Rulers of all their important powers, it evoked the resentment of the people, especially the Malays. The Malayan Union was thus abandoned in favour of the Federation of Malaya on 1 February 1948. Under this new constitutional framework the Malay Rulers remained sovereign in the nine Malay states, while Penang and Malacca were administered as British territo ries. Singapore was excluded from the Federation and was governed as a separate British colony. A significant feature of the new agreement is that, with the censensus of the British Crown and the Malay Rulers, provisions for progress towards eventual self-government were included.

On 1 August 1957 the Federation of Malaya became a free and independent country under a Yang Di-Pertuan Agong elected every five years from among the nine Rulers. Each state has an elected state legislature, while the federal legislature consists of a senate and a house of representatives which had fully elected members. In the election held after independence the Alliance, which

FIGURE 1.1
MAP OF PENINSULAR MALAYSIA

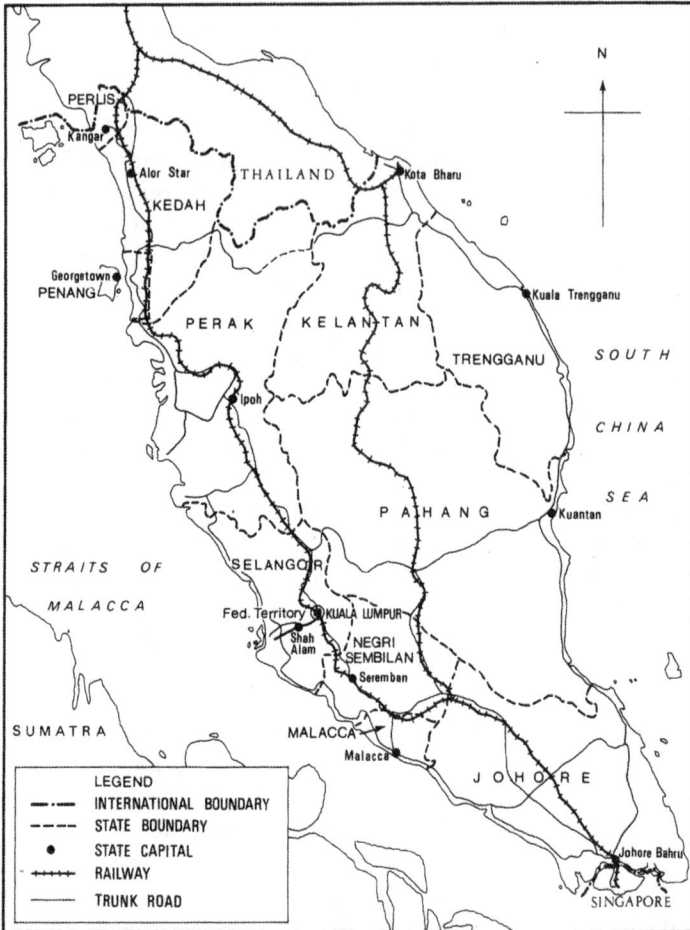

N

PERLIS
Kangar
Alor Star
THAILAND
KEDAH
Kota Bharu
Georgetown
PENANG
Kuala Trengganu
PERAK   KELANTAN
TRENGGANU
SOUTH
Ipoh
CHINA
SEA
PAHANG
Kuantan
STRAITS OF
SELANGOR
MALACCA
Fed. Territory KUALA LUMPUR
Shah NEGRI
Alam SEMBILAN
Seremban
SUMATRA
MALACCA
Malacca
JOHORE
Johore Bahru
SINGAPORE

LEGEND
—·—· INTERNATIONAL BOUNDARY
- - - - STATE BOUNDARY
● STATE CAPITAL
+++++ RAILWAY
——— TRUNK ROAD

National University of Singapore

comprised the United Malay National Organisation (UMNO), the Malayan Chinese Association (MCA), and the Malayan Indian Congress (MIC), was voted into power. The Alliance, under the premiership of Tengku Abdul Rahman, formed the first independent government. The Alliance, subsequently enlarged to include other political parties and renamed the National Front, has been ruling the country ever since.

The Federation of Malaya was expanded on 16 September 1963 with the formation of Malaysia notwithstanding the opposition from Indonesia and the Philippines. The larger political unit of Malaysia includes the eleven states in the former Federation of Malaya as well as the internally self-governing colony of Singapore and the two colonies of Sarawak and North Borneo (now Sabah). By participating in this new political development, the three colonies achieved their independence within Malaysia. The larger political partnership did not function smoothly, and, because of irreconcilable differences, the membership of Singapore in Malaysia came to an abrupt end on 9 August 1965 when it was forced to secede and thus became an independent country by itself. Since then Malaysia comprises the eleven states in Peninsular Malaysia (formerly known as West Malaysia) and the two states of Sarawak and Sabah in the island of Borneo. Four states, Penang, Malacca, Sarawak and Sabah have an appointed Governor and a Chief Minister heading the elected state legislative council, while the other nine states have a hereditary Sultan and a Mentri Besar as head of the elected state legislature.

Economic Structure

The economic structure of Peninsular Malaysia is now quite diversified and broadly based, with agriculture, livestock, forestry and fishing accounting for 20 per cent of the gross domestic product in 1984. Another 20 per cent was contributed by manufacturing; and wholesale and retail trade, hotels and restaurants contributed 12 per cent. In terms of land area and export earning, rubber is by far the most important crop. The estimated total cultivated area devoted to rubber was about 1.67 million hectares, and of these one-fourth are in estates and the other three-fourths in smallholdings of less than 4 hectares each. The proportion of rubber land in estates has dropped in recent years as a result of the fragmentation of some estates and the substitution of rubber trees with oil palm in many estates. Most of the cultivated rubber land is situated along the western coastal belt. Rubber occupies nearly one-half of the entire cultivated area in the country and accounts for about one-tenth of the domestic export earnings. Peninsular Malaysia is of course well known as the largest rubber producer, supplying slightly more than one-third of the total world production.

Padi cultivation, the traditional occupation of the rural Malays, now occupies some 0.47 million hectares or 13 per cent of the total cultivated land in the country. Padi is grown entirely in smallholdings, located chiefly in the fertile plains of Perlis, Kedah, Kelantan and Trengganu. Strenuous efforts are being made by the government to increase the output of rice so as to raise the standard of living of the rural padi farmers. Some of the most notable measures are huge irrigation and drainage schemes, new strains of high-yielding seeds, mechanisation, subsidised fertilisers and credit facilities. Such measures, coupled with more double-cropping and new padi land converted from virgin jungle and swampland, have resulted in a marked rise in the production of rice. Rice does not fetch any important export earning since almost all of the annual harvest is consumed within the country. What is significant is that the aim of self-sufficiency in rice has been nearly achieved and a decreasing amount of rice need to be imported to meet the overall requirements.

Oil palm is one of the cash crops introduced as part of the agricultural diversification programme aimed at moving away from rubber as the prime source of export earnings. The cultivation of oil palm has proved to be successful, and the land area occupied by this crop amounts to 1.24 million hectares or slightly less than one-third of the total cultivated area. Palm oil, both crude and processed, now contributes about one-tenth of the total export earnings. A less important cash crop introduced in recent years is cocoa which is planted on some 59,000 hectares of land. Coconut is one of the crops that are cultivated to meet local requirements as well as foreign demand. Some 0.25 million hectares are devoted to coconut cultivation, and of these nearly 90 per cent are in smallholdings. Coconut produce is a negligible foreign exchange earner as copra and coconut oil form less than 1 per cent of the total export value. The other minor crops are pineapple, tea, tobacco, vegetable and fruit grown mostly in smallholdings.

The mining economy has been dominated by the production of tin since its discovery in the middle of the nineteenth century, but in recent years the petroleum industry has been growing in importance. The tin mines were operated and owned by the Chinese in the early days, but by the interwar years European mines worked by dredges dominated in terms of production. Almost all the tin mines are located along the western coastal belt, particularly in the Kinta Valley and Klang Valley. As the export sector of the economy became more diversified, the share of tin products in the total domestic export earnings has decreased over the years to less than 5 per cent. Peninsular Malaysia is still the largest tin producer in the world supplying about one-third of the total tin production. Oil exploration in the offshore areas of both the east and west coasts began in the mid-1970s, and not too long afterwards oil discoveries and natural gas strikes were made. Since then the petroleum industry under the control of the national petroleum corporation, Petroleum National Berhad (Petronas), has overtaken tin mining in terms of export earnings. The eight offshore oilfields produced about 0.21 million barrels of crude petroleum per day.

Immediately after gaining independence, Peninsular Malaysia embarked on an industrialisation programme in order to diversify the economy and to provide jobs for the growing labour force. Among the more important measures taken by the government to promote industrialisation were the establishment of industrial estates with all the basic manufacturing facilities and the introduction of tax relief in various forms to local and foreign investors. The manufacturing sector is now quite broadly based, producing a wide range of light to heavy products. Nearly one-fifth of the gross domestic product is contributed by the manufacturing sector.

The economy of Peninsular Malaysia has been greatly transformed in recent years by the New Economic Policy introduced in 1970 to eradicate poverty by raising income levels and increasing employment opportunities for all Malaysians irrespective of race and to accelerate the process of restructuring Malaysian society to correct economic imbalance so as to eliminate the identification of race with economic function. The people of Peninsular Malaysia being the principal component of the larger political unit of Malaysia, have benefited from the economic progress recorded by the whole country. In the seventies and early eighties, Malaysia has recorded an annual economic growth of some 5 to 9 per cent as measured in terms of the increase in the real gross domestic product. In 1984 the per capita income for Malaysia was US$2,155 which compared favourably with the corresponding figures of US$832 for Thailand, US$615 for the Philippines and US$610 for Indonesia but less so with the US$6,842 for Singapore and the US$20,450 for Brunei.

Demographic Data

The taking of a census in Peninsular Malaysia has its origins in the beginning of the nineteenth century when the inhabitants of the newly established Straits Settlements of Penang, Malacca and Singapore were first separately counted in 1801, 1928 and 1824 respectively. Thereafter, counts were made almost every year and later at longer intervals, and by 1836 eight were held in Penang, seven in Malacca and eleven in Singapore. The crude statistics of these counts were collected and published by T.J. Newbold (see Appendix D). After 1836 it appears that three further counts were conducted in the Straits Settlements in 1840, 1849 and 1860, and the results classified by sex and race were reproduced by T. Braddell in his book. The statistics produced from these counts completed prior to 1871 were not only extremely narrow in scope but also seriously in error in many respects. Very limited demographic value can be placed on these early population statistics though they are of some historical interest.

The first proper census as understood in the modern form was conducted in the Straits Settlements in 1871 as part of the overall colonial census programme implemented throughout the British Empire. In each of these settlements of Penang, Malacca and Singapore a committee of government officials was in charge of the census and each committee produced a report consisting of a brief administrative account and about twenty pages of basic tables. Another census in the same format was held in 1881 in the Straits Settlements. The year 1891 saw the Federated Malay States inaugurating the first proper census and the Straits Settlements conducting the third one under, not committees, but a single superintendent of census. A decade later similar censuses were held in the Straits Settlements and in the Federated Malay States. The year 1911 was of special significance in that it witnessed not only the continuation of the decennial censuses in these two regions, but also the launching of census taking in the Unfederated Malay States. Population statistics for the whole territory now known as Peninsular Malaysia were thus made available for the first time in 1911. This delay in the availability of population statistics for the whole of the Peninsula may be attributed to the varying degrees of British influence and hence the different systems of government among the various parts of the country.

In 1921 a population census for the combined territory of Peninsular Malaysia and Singapore was undertaken by a single superintendent who was also responsible for bringing out the census report. The next decennial census was conducted on the same scale in 1931. A census was planned for April 1941 but the increasing difficulties arising from the imminence of war led to the abandonment of the project and to a break in the long series of decennial censuses. After the war plans were immediately drawn up to enumerate the population and a common census for the whole of Peninsular Malaysia and Singapore was finally completed in 1947. The next postwar census taken in 1957 was a departure from the three previous ones in that Peninsular Malaysia, being a distinct political unit at that time, was separately enumerated under one single superintendent. With the formation of Malaysia in 1963, the next census held in 1970 covers Peninsular Malaysia as well as the two eastern states of Sarawak and Sabah. In the latest decennial census conducted in 1980 Peninsular Malaysia was again enumerated as part of the overall census of Malaysia.

It is apparent that the population statistics for the region now known as Peninsular Malaysia for the period under study are not available from individual census reports covering this region. More often than not the statistics have to be collated from separate reports for different political units or extracted from parts of reports for larger political units. This naturally requires much care and effort in obtaining the required statistics for the territory known as Peninsular Malaysia.

The other major set of statistics required for our study refers to those generated from the vital registration system. Compulsory registration of births and deaths were introduced in 1872 in the Straits Settlements, and vital statistics for this region was made available from 1886. But the registration system in the other parts of the Peninsula took many more decades to be introduced on account of the late penetration of British influence in these states. It was only in 1920 that vital registration was legally enforced in the Federated Malay States. As for the Unfederated Malay States, each had its own ordinance governing vital registration initiated at about the same time. However, it was not till 1934 that complete sets of birth and death statistics for all the eleven states within the Peninsula were made available annually. This necessarily implies that an analysis of mortality, fertility and other demographic aspects requiring reliable birth and death statistics cannot go back beyond 1934.

In addition to the above two major sources of demographic statistics, our study also utilises data from other sources and these are dealt with in the appropriate parts of the chapters concerned or in Appendix D. This appendix has been included for the benefit of readers who would like to have a comprehensive discussion of the development of demographic statistics in the Peninsula. Our intention in presenting the brief account of the demographic data used in this study in this section is to complete the task of this introductory chapter in furnishing the essential background information for a better appreciation of our study of the demography of Peninsular Malaysia in the chapters that follow. It should also be mentioned that the details of the publications containing these demographic statistics are cited in full in the bibliography included at the end of the book. Unless otherwise stated, the sources of the data given in all the tables in this book are from these publications.

In studying the demography of Peninsular Malaysia, our main focus of attention will be on the changing character of the population over the years insofar as the availability of statistics permit us to do so. The analysis of population trends in the various chapters will be supplemented by an investigation of patterns and differentials particularly among the various regions and races. The Peninsula is a good example of a multiracial country with little racial integration and hence an appraisal of the interesting differentials among the three principal races would constitute an important component of our study. The Peninsula's population that we are concerned with in this study was estimated to number some 12.64 million in the middle of 1984 or 84 per cent of the total population of 15.09 million in the whole of Malaysia.

2

International Migration

Introduction

The Malay Peninsula has been one of the most important areas of migration ever since the establishment of British colonial rule in Penang in 1786 and in other parts of the Peninsula in the nineteenth century. The large and sustained immigration was mainly due to the demand for labour in the public works and primary production sectors, the excellent prospects for trade and commerce, and the law and order attendant on British rule. Such forces of attraction coupled with liberal immigration policies, were reinforced by equally strong repelling forces in the immigrants' countries of origin. Natural calamities, political upheavals, population pressure, and lack of economic opportunities induced the immigrants to leave their countries for Peninsular Malaysia at a time when the supply of labour from the indigenous Malays was neither adequate nor forthcoming.

In the early days the immigrants would usually leave their families behind in their own countries and come to Peninsular Malaysia not as permanent settlers but as 'bird-of-passage'. With their earnings, quite a number were able to send regular remittances to their families, make occasional visits home, and eventually return to their countries after acquiring some wealth or on retirement. In the course of time, however, an increasing proportion of immigrants brought their families along, sent for their families or married local residents and remained in the country permanently. But their numbers did not alter the generally transient character of the population, which persisted until the outbreak of war in Peninsular Malaysia in December 1941. The Japanese Occupation, the increasing supply of local labour in the postwar period, and the strict immigration control from the 1950s have put an end to large-scale immigration. At the same time an increasingly significant proportion of the prewar immigrants have come to regard Peninsular Malaysia as their permanent home.

During the prewar period there were essentially three main streams of migration into Peninsular Malaysia: the northern stream from China, the western stream from India, and the relatively less important stream from the then Dutch East Indies in the south. In view of the pronounced differences in magnitude, composition, mode of entry, and government regulations, it is perhaps more convenient to consider each stream separately. It should be mentioned that in official matters concerning migration, Peninsular Malaysia and Singapore have until very recently been treated as a single unit governed by common law and regulations. In fact, up to the 1960s persons disembarking at one territory could proceed without hindrance to the next through the rail-and-road causeway, where movement between the two was completely free and unrestricted. It is therefore inevitable that the official statistics compiled during this period and presented in the various tables that follow refer to this combined area.

Another feature of migration in Peninsular Malaysia is that until the out-break of the Second World War the emigration of permanent residents to foreign countries has always been extremely insignificant. What this means is that the emigration figures presented in the various tables refer to persons who had in the first place migrated into Peninsular Malaysia and were making short visits home or returning permanently to their motherland. In recent years migration appears to have assumed a new character, with some emigration from the minority races to foreign countries and secondly perceptibly more immigration from Indonesia than before.

Chinese Migration

Chinese contacts with the *Nanyang* or the Southern Ocean could be traced back to ancient times when Chinese pilgrims, travellers and good-will missions visited the region. As for the Malay Peninsula the Chinese appeared to have frequented the place from about the early fourth century, but it was only in the mid-fourteenth century that they were known to have first settled there at *Temasik* or Old Singapore. In the fifteenth century Chinese merchants and emissaries visited the Malay Kingdom in Malacca, and during the later years there were probably Chinese staying there as merchants and traders. Under the control of the Portuguese and later the Dutch in the sixteenth and seven-teenth centuries, Malacca witnessed the founding of a Chinese community.[1] But

---

1. Victor Purcell, "Chinese Settlement in Malacca", *Journal of Malayan Branch of the Royal Asiatic Society* XX, Part 1 (1974): 115-25.

the Portuguese and the Dutch were somewhat passive in their attitude towards the immigration and permanent settlement of the Chinese in the colony.

The establishment of British rule in Penang, Malacca and Singapore at the turn of the century marks the beginning of a long period of continuous Chinese migration. It was mainly the good employment opportunities in the tin-mining industry and agricultural enterprises and the bright prospects for business that attracted the Chinese newcomers. Motivated by the desire to expand trade and develop the primary-producing industries, the British placed no restriction on the movement of the Chinese. But for several reasons, the Chinese Government on its part was definitely against the emigration of its nationals to foreign territories.[2] Still, thousands of Chinese managed to come to Peninsular Malaysia during the first half of the nineteenth century. By far the largest group were those who came to work as labourers in the tin mines, pepper and tapioca farms, and gambier and sugar-cane plantations.[3]

By mid-nineteenth century the immigration of Chinese had developed into a well-organised system.[4] Potential immigrants were recruited in South China, particularly Kwangtung and Fukien provinces, by a returned emigrant known as *kheh thau* or headman or by a professional recruiter. The *kheh thau* usually carried out the recruiting in his own village among persons known to him. He accompanied his *sin kheh* or new recruits to their final destination in Peninsular Malaysia and handed them over to a particular employer for whom he acted as an agent. Sometimes the *kheh thau* was also the recruits' headman or overseer in the tin-mines or plantations, and in more recent times, as a labour contractor, he became their employer.

As for the professional recruiter, he accompanied or sent his recruits to lodging-houses at the Chinese ports from which they were shipped to Peninsular Malaysia. On arrival in the Malaysian ports the recruits were met by an agent of the lodging-houses, and then dispatched to employers or labour contractors. The lodging-house owners acted as brokers, reaping a handsome profit out of the recruitment, dispatch and distribution of Chinese immigrant labourers. It would be surprising if the lodging-houses did not in fact account for the major proportion of Chinese immigration in the nineteenth century, but statistical evidence on this is not available.

---

2. Victor Purcell, *The Chinese in Southeast Asia* (London: Oxford University Press, 1951), pp. 33–36.
3. P. C. Campbell, *Chinese Coolie Emigration to Countries Within the British Empire* (London: P. S. King and Son, 1923), p. 5.
4. A more detailed account of the method of Chinese immigration at this time may be obtained from W. L. Blythe, "Historical Sketch of Chinese Labour in Malaya", *Journal of the Malayan Branch of the Royal Asiatic Society* XX, Part I (June 1947): 64–125.

Regardless of which of the two channels the immigrants came through, they had their passages and other expenses paid for them and were therefore already in debt on arrival. The total cost was included in the price paid by the employer who recovered the sum from their monthly wages. On the whole, the system of Chinese immigration at that time was known to suffer from many undesirable practices, the most serious being ill-treatment and exploitation. Until 1877 no laws were enacted to protect the immigrants especially those employed as labourers, but this also implied that throughout this period their entry into Peninsular Malaysia was completely free and unrestricted.

The British colonial government's attempt at protecting and regulating Chinese immigrants was first instituted on 23 March 1877 with the passing of the *Chinese Immigration Ordinance, 1877*. A Chinese Protectorate Office under the charge of a Protector of Chinese Immigrants was established in 1887 under the provision of this ordinance. Conditions on board junks and steamers were improved, depots for the reception of immigrants were set up, and recruiters were licensed.[5] A more important result was the emergence of Chinese indentured immigrants who signed formal contracts according to the provisions of the ordinance and thus received protection from the law. Each labourer and employer would receive a copy of the contract numbered according to the Registration Books kept in the office. The terms of the contract were explained to the immigrant, and he was told that while the employer would not be allowed to defraud or ill-treat him in any way, he himself would be punished according to the law for any breaches of the engagement. However, a large number of immigrants preferred not to sign contracts, remaining legally free but in practice under the clutches of their employers as long as their debts were not paid up. A third category was the really free and independent immigrants who came on their own to seek a livelihood as businessmen, shopkeepers, hawkers, artisans and others.

Separate figures for indentured immigrants or passengers whose fares were paid for by persons with whom they entered into formal contracts for service on arrival are presented in Table 2.1. The gradual decline in the proportion of indentured immigrants may be attributed partly to the preference of some immigrants not to sign formal contracts and partly to the few real advantages to be gained by employers in hiring indentured immigrants.[6] The original aim of introducing formal contracts was therefore only partially achieved, and a

---

5. R. N. Jackson, *Immigrant Labour and the Development of Malaya* (Kuala Lumpur: Government Printer), p. 72.
6. C. W. C. Parr, *Report of Commission Appointed to Enquire into the Conditions of Indentured Labour in the Federated Malay States*, 1910, pp. 10–12.

TABLE 2.1
ANNUAL CHINESE INDENTURED IMMIGRANTS, 1881–1914

Year	Chinese Indentured Immigrants	% of C.I.I. to Total Chinese Immigrants	Year	Chinese Indentured Immigrants	% of C.I.I. to Total Chinese Immigrants
1881	32,316	36.0	1898	16,536	12.4
1882	28,415	28.1	1899	19,525	13.0
1883	26,446	24.2	1900	25,533	12.7
1884	24,871	23.3	1901	21,121	11.8
1885	26,391	23.7	1902	22,545	10.9
1886	39,192	27.1	1903	20,588	9.3
1887	42,400	25.3	1904	16,930	8.3
1888	34,607	21.2	1905	14,864	8.6
1889	21,213	14.1	1906	18,675	10.6
1890	14,335	11.2	1907	24,089	10.6
1891	15,136	12.0	1908	13,604	8.9
1892	15,710	11.3	1909	13,379	8.8
1893	29,134	13.6	1910	23,935	11.1
1894	15,544	10.1	1911	24,345	9.0
1895	23,249	12.2	1912	13,600	9.0
1896	24,019	13.7	1913	14,197	5.9
1897	13,799	12.0	1914	2,648	1.8

Source: Annual Reports of the Protector of Chinese.

considerable number of Chinese immigrants was still susceptible to exploitation. By the early 1910s public opinion against the indentured system was gathering momentum in China and Peninsular Malaysia, culminating in the colonial government passing the *Labour Contracts Ordinance, 1914* by which Chinese indentured immigration was abolished from 30 June 1914.[7] This, according to some employers, might adversely affect the supply of labour through the damping effect on the flow of Chinese immigrants. This fear was unfounded as the prohibition had only a minor effect on the volume of immigration be-

7. Straits Settlements, *Report of the Protector of Chinese, 1914* (Singapore: Government Press), p. 46.

cause the Chinese could still come under the old system whereby their passages were paid for by the employers. However, the banning of Chinese indentured labour was the final factor that ended the large-scale estate cultivation of tapioca and sugar.[8]

The banning of indentured Chinese labour in 1914 left the government with almost no legislation to deal with Chinese immigration, and for a long period the Chinese were free to enter the country unhampered by any legal hindrance. It was in 1928 that the *Immigration Restriction Ordinance, 1928* was enacted by the colonial government to equip itself with the necessary powers to regulate or prohibit immigration whenever the influx of immigrants threatened to bring about employment, economic distress, or other situations which were not in the public interest.[9] The ordinance appeared to have been prompted also by the government's desire to exercise a stricter control with the view to excluding criminals and other undesirable elements. However, the powers conferred by the ordinance were not enforced until a few years later.

With the growth of widespread unemployment that followed the closure of some tin mines and rubber estates and the general worsening of the economy during the World Depression of the early 1930s, the government used the *Immigration Restriction Ordinance* to proclaim a monthly quota on adult Chinese male immigrants from August 1930 onwards.[10] From an initial figure of 6,016 per month, the quota was eventually reduced to 1,000 per month during the last five months of 1932, but no restriction was placed on the immigration of Chinese women and children under 12 years of age.

Though the ordinance resulted in a considerable reduction of Chinese immigrants, the experience of the past years showed that it was not entirely satisfactory because it could be resorted to only in emergencies and did not provide any control over immigrants once they had landed. Moreover, it was generally felt that the time had come to introduce quantitative and qualitative control on the admission of aliens according to the political, social and economic needs of the country. The ordinance was thus replaced by the *Aliens Ordinance, 1933* which came into force on January 1933, and almost all functions concern-

---

8. R. N. Jackson, op. cit., p. 155. "When in 1911 the Government announced that all indentured Chinese labour contracts would lapse and become illegal on the 1st July 1914 — which meant the end of cheap labour under complete year-long control — the death knell of these two estate crops, the cultivation of which depended upon abundant and dependable supply of very cheap labour, was sounded for all time."

9. Norman Parmer, *Colonial Labour Policy and Administration*, Monograph of the Association for Asian Studies No. IX (New York, 1960), p. 30.

10. Straits Settlements, *Report of the Protector of Chinese, 1930* (Singapore: Government Press), p. 65.

ing Chinese immigration were transferred from the Chinese Protectorate Office to the new Immigration Department.[11] The new Ordinance was designed not only to regulate the entry of aliens but also to register and control alien residents in Peninsular Malaysia. But Indian immigrants from British India, being British subjects, were not affected by this *Aliens Ordinance* which was meant to control the alien (or non-British subject) immigrants from China.

From April 1933 the quota system of restricting adult Chinese male immigrants was continued under the *Aliens Ordinance* until the outbreak of the Second World War in Peninsular Malaysia in December 1941. The monthly quota varied from 500 to 6,000, though remaining constant at 4,000 from August 1934 to January 1937. At the beginning of 1933 unemployment and economic distress still prevailed and most of the monthly quotas were not fully utilised. Nevertheless, employers' criticism of the ordinance for its possible adverse effects on the supply of labour caused the government to introduce an amendment in December 1933 to solve any likely shortage of labour in the future.[12] The amendment, affecting Section 12a, allowed employers who could give adequate reasons to obtain official permits to recruit labour abroad and bring them to Peninsular Malaysia outside the quota. During 1934 and 1935 some Chinese male immigrants were permitted to enter by means of these permits, but the primary aim of the amendment was not achieved and relatively few permits were issued after mid-1935.[13]

The immigration of Chinese women and children continued to be exempted from any restriction under the *Aliens Ordinance*; the government was anxious to encourage the immigration of women in order to improve the sex ratio. But by 1938 Peninsular Malaysia had suffered a reduction in the exports of tin and rubber, and the demand for Chinese labour had fallen sharply. In order to ease the unemployment situation, the government cancelled the exemption of alien women from the ordinance and proclaimed a monthly quota of 500 on the immigration of alien women on 1 May 1938, thus for the first time controlling the movement of Chinese women.[14] Immigration of Chinese was of course at a complete standstill on account of the Pacific War, from about December 1941 to September 1945.

11. Straits Settlements, *Report of the Immigration Department, 1933* (Singapore: Government Press), p. 23.
12. Straits Settlements, *Report of the Immigration Department, 1933* (Singapore: Government Press), p. 32.
13. Straits Settlement and Federated Malay States, *Report of the Immigration Department, 1935* (Singapore: Government Press), p. 32.
14. Straits Settlement and Federated Malay States, *Report of the Immigration Department, 1938* (Singapore: Government Press), p. 61.

In the immediate postwar years Chinese immigration continued to be regulated by the prewar *Aliens Ordinance*, but by the 1950s two new developments had emerged to make the colonial government adopt a new attitude towards immigration in general. The overall demand for labour was not increasing at such a rapid rate as in the prewar days, and there was now an adequate supply of labour from the indigenous Malays and from the earlier immigrants and their descendants. It became increasingly necessary to exercise a tight control on all immigrants and to allow permanent entry only to those who could contribute to the social and economic development of the country. With this in view the old *Aliens Ordinance* was replaced with the more comprehensive *Immigration Ordinance, 1953* which came into force on 1 August 1953.[15] The ordinance in the first place restricts permanent entry to the following:

(a)   persons who can contribute to the expansion of commerce and industry,
(b)   persons who can provide specialised services not available locally,
(c)   families of local residents, and
(d)   others on special compassionate grounds.

After attaining independence on 1 August 1957, the whole question of immigration was under the constant review of the independent government whose main objective was to look after the interests of its citizens.

In 1959 the old ordinance was replaced by the *Immigration Ordinance, 1959* which came into force on 1 May 1959. This new ordinance was meant to tighten entry under (c) by prohibiting the entry of wives and children of local residents who have been living separately from their husbands for five continuous years after December 1954, and children of citizens who were six years of age and more.[16] In addition, children aged six and more of those persons admitted as specialists under (b) or on grounds of economic benefit under (a) were also prohibited. The principal objectives of the new legislation are to safeguard the employment and livelihood of residents and "to bring about a more balanced and assimilated Malayan population whose ties and loyalty are to this country alone without which the foundation of a true Malayan nation cannot be laid".[17] On the whole, the ordinance has provided a very strict and effective control over the quantity and quality of immigrants of all races entering Peninsular Malaysia during the postwar years.

---

15. Malaya, *Federation of Malaya Annual Report, 1953* (Kuala Lumpur: Government Press), p. 9.
16. Singapore, *Immigration Ordinance, 1959*, No. 12 of 1959 (Singapore: Government Printer, 1959).
17. *The Straits Times*, 3 November 1959. Statement issued to the press by the Malayan Ministry of External Affairs and the Singapore Ministry of Home Affairs in the new immigration orders issued under the amendment ordinance.

Overall Chinese Migration

In Table 2.2 the yearly statistics of Chinese immigration from 1881 and
emigrants, hence also net migrants, from 1916 are laid out. The statistics for
1939 to 1958 refer to arrivals and departures by air, sea and land. The years
1881–1913 were characterised by a gradual upward trend, with some minor
fluctuations, in the number of annual immigrants, increasing from about 90,000
in 1881 to about 250,000 at the end of this period. The next ten years first witnessed a major curtailment in the annual inflow caused by the First World
War and its aftermath, reinforced subsequently by the local slump of 1921–23.
This was followed by a short period, 1924–30, of uninterrupted and greatly
enlarged immigration, with the record number of 359,000 in 1927. Then came
the second and more serious setback in the 1930s when the World Depression
and government restriction took the annual inflow to unprecedented low levels
in the first few years. The slight recovery in the late 1930s was attributable to
the large influx of women. But the enforcement of control on Chinese female
immigration in May 1938 kept the overall volume of inflow relatively low until
the outbreak of war. While a complete cessation of immigration occurred

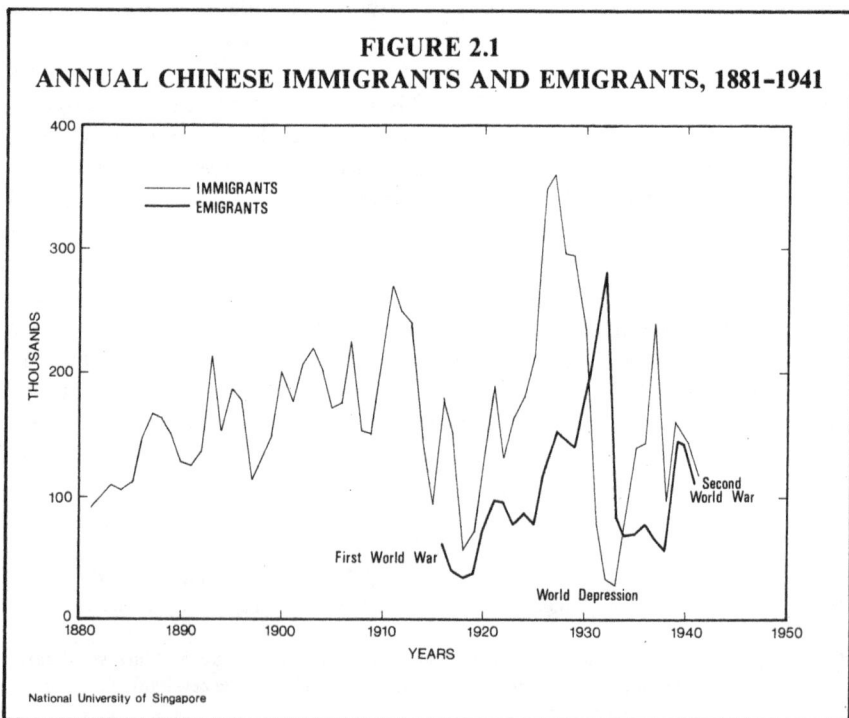

FIGURE 2.1
ANNUAL CHINESE IMMIGRANTS AND EMIGRANTS, 1881–1941

National University of Singapore

TABLE 2.2
ANNUAL CHINESE IMMIGRANTS AND EMIGRANTS, 1881–1958

Year	Immigrants	Year	Immigrants	Emigrants	Net Migrants
1880	—	1916	183,399	61,630	121,769
1881	89,801	1917	155,167	41,282	113,885
1882	101,009	1918	58,421	35,585	22,836
1883	109,136	1919	70,912	37,590	33,322
1884	106,748	1920	126,077	68,383	57,694
1885	111,456	1921	191,043	98,986	92,057
1886	144,517	1922	132,886	96,869	36,017
1887	167,906	1923	159,019	78,121	80,898
1888	164,300	1924	181,430	87,749	93,681
1889	150,809	1925	214,962	77,920	136,772
1890	127,936	1926	348,593	120,308	228,285
1891	126,088	1927	359,262	155,198	204,065
1892	139,448	1928	295,700	149,354	146,346
1893	213,717	1929	293,167	139,967	153,200
1894	153,954	1930	242,149	167,903	74,246
1895	190,901	1931	79,091	213,992	−134,947
1896	175,718	1932	33,543	282,779	−249,245
1897	114,978	1933	27,796	86,555	− 58,759
1898	133,558	1934	98,864	68,129	30,735
1899	149,697	1935	141,892	69,025	72,867
1900	200,947	1936	143,331	80,578	62,753
1901	178,778	1937	239,106	66,502	172,604
1902	207,156	1938	98,863	53,603	44,260
1903	220,321	1939	160,448	146,106	14,339
1904	204,796	1940	147,016	143,694	3,322
1905	173,131	1941	117,426	110,826	6,600
1906	176,587	1947	126,203	130,242	− 4,039
1907	227,342	1948	105,209	110,712	− 5,505
1908	153,452	1949	96,449	128,884	− 32,435
1909	151,752	1950	82,676	87,751	− 5,075
1910	216,321	1951	77,437	113,767	− 36.330
1911	269,854	1952	64,197	77,785	− 13,588
1912	251,644	1953	67,145	73,550	− 6,402
1913	240,979	1954	62,683	67,888	− 5,205
1914	147,150	1955	74,230	70,945	3,285
1915	95,735	1956	98,255	84,727	13,528
		1957	101,145	95,773	5,372
		1958	82,961	75,092	7,869

Note: The figures for 1939–58 refer to total arrivals and departures by air, sea and land. Figures for 1942–46 are not available.

Sources: Annual Reports of the Protector of Chinese, 1881–1932, Annual Reports of the Immigration Department, 1933–38 and the Malayan Statistics Monthly Digest, 1939–58.

during the Japanese Occupation, the postwar years witnessed much reduced immigration, lower than in the nineteenth century, following on tighter government control. In fact, the actual inflow was probably much lower than Table 2.2 suggests because these arrival and departure figures by air, sea and land included short-term visitors.

The number of annual emigrants, mainly persons returning for short visits or for good after a term of employment, also showed a rising trend from 1916 to 1932, but the somewhat high figure for the last three years of this period was in the main contributed by the repatriation of the unemployed at the height of the World Depression. From 1933 to the outbreak of war in 1941, the annual outflow seemed to have been stabilised between 60,000 to 80,000. There is reason to believe that the departure figures shown in Table 2.2 for the early postwar years included an appreciable number of prewar immigrants who would have normally returned to China during 1942–45 except for the war.

It may be noted that the number of annual net migrants displayed a rather indefinite trend with considerable fluctuations throughout. By far the largest gain for Peninsular Malaysia took place in the 1930s, particularly during the second half when about 0.8 million net gain was recorded. In contrast, the net loss during the World Depression amounted to about 0.4 million. Perhaps the most striking feature is that the first ten postwar years witnessed a continuous deficit, though not substantial, as a result of rigid controls on inward movement and the swelling of the outward movement by persons prevented from emigrating earlier.

Sex Ratio of Chinese Immigrants

The immigration of Chinese into Peninsular Malaysia has been very sex-selective, the forces of attraction exerting a far greater influence on men than on women. Even in the case of the married male immigrants, the men found it cheaper and more convenient to leave their wives and children in their homeland, forwarding regular remittances, paying them short visits, and eventually returning to them for good. This practice was to a certain extent looked upon with favour by the Chinese Government who was not quite disposed to the idea of women emigrating overseas because of the desire to maintain a strong hold on the overseas Chinese and to ensure remittances which yielded valuable foreign exchange. In the course of time, however, with the growing tendency to consider Peninsular Malaysia as their permanent home and with the encouragement of the Malaysian Government, an increasing proportion of Chinese women were entering the country, as can be noted in Table 2.3. The sex ratio reflects a steady but gradual fall from about 30 males per female at the beginning of the 1880s to about four males per female at the end of the

TABLE 2.3
SEX RATIO OF CHINESE IMMIGRANTS, 1881–1938
(Males Per 1,000 Females)

Year	Sex Ratio	Year	Sex Ratio	Year	Sex Ratio
1880	—	1900	15,062	1920	3,543
1881	27,773	1901	13,180	1921	4,309
1882	37,131	1902	14,006	1922	4,787
1883	26,469	1903	13,298	1923	4,595
1884	29,326	1904	12,480	1924	4,157
1885	32,093	1905	9,254	1925	4,761
1886	29,657	1906	10,518	1926	4,665
1887	25,775	1907	10,551	1927	3,908
1888	23,618	1908	6,908	1928	3,538
1889	30,308	1909	9,166	1929	4,428
1890	21,475	1910	9,847	1930	3,562
1891	17,236	1911	8,744	1931	2,941
1892	18,017	1912	7,728	1932	2,166
1893	19,840	1913	7,611	1933	1,651
1894	19,715	1914	18,148	1934	1,753
1895	16,630	1915	6,338	1935	2,117
1896	17,113	1916	7,143	1936	1,401
1897	12,299	1917	7,407	1937	1,054
1898	12,919	1918	4,630	1938	429
1899	17,537	1919	2,994	1939	—

Sources: Annual Reports of the Protector of Chinese, 1881–1932 and Annual Reports of
the Immigration Department, 1933–38.

1910s, thereafter remaining around the latter figure through the next decade.

It may be recalled that when the entry of Chinese adult males was rigidly regulated by the quota system in the 1930s, Chinese women were not affected at all and remained so until May 1938. It was indeed the intention of the government to continue allowing women to enter so as to rectify the great imbalance in the sex ratio of the Chinese population already in Peninsular Malaysia. In fact, the sex-discriminatory policy led to a more far-reaching result than was perhaps originally anticipated, as pointed by Blythe in the following quotation:

> But the working of this ordinance had another unforeseen effect. As women were outside the quota, passage for women were far cheaper than for men.

There was no limit to the number of women who could enter Malaya. These factors encouraged women in China to emigrate, but this emigration was stimulated by the action of ticket brokers at the China ports who refused to sell quota tickets unless three or four non-quota tickets were bought by the lodging-houses and ticket agencies for each quota ticket bought. It was therefore to the advantage of the lodging-houses and ticket agents to encourage the emigration of women to take up these non-quota tickets.[18]

The overall effect on the actual sex ratio of immigrants may be observed in Table 2.3 where, after remaining fairly stationary at around four males per female for about ten years, the sex ratio experienced a definite movement towards parity in the 1930s, culminating in a complete reversal of the position in 1938 when only about three males entered the country for every four females.

Indian Migration

Contacts between India and the Malay Archipelago go back far into ancient times when traders from both regions visited one another's seaports. From the early seventh century such trading relations were reinforced by cultural and religious influence from India through the Hindu Empire of Srivijaya in Sumatra (about 600–1000 A.D.).[19] In the meantime the emergence of the Malay Kingdom in Malacca (about 1405–1511 A.D.) witnessed the beginning of Indian settlement in Peninsular Malaysia and the commencement of a more frequent and direct intercourse with India.[20] The movement of traders and settlers between the two regions continued into the periods of the Portuguese and later Dutch rule of Malacca in the sixteenth and seventeenth centuries. But such movements, being mainly personal and voluntary, had so far occurred on a somewhat spasmodic and meagre scale.

Following the establishment of British rule in the Malay Peninsula in the late eighteenth century and the early nineteenth century, a radical change occurred in the pattern of Indian migration which became not only officially countenanced and organised but continuous and sizeable in numbers. The British brought in Indian convicts and indentured immigrants to construct public works, while in the private sector the plantation owners imported both free and indentured immigrants to work in their agricultural estates. In addition, there were, as in the early days, the free immigrants who came on their own to seek trade and commerce, and employment in the domestic and government services. Throughout the nineteenth century Indian migration was fairly steady

---

18. W. L. Blythe, op. cit., p. 103.
19. D. G. E. Hall, *A History of South-east Asia* (London: Macmillan, 1958), pp. 37–57.
20. J. Kennedy, *A History of Malaya, A.D. 1400–1959* (London: Macmillan, 1962), pp. 6–17.

and moderate, but the turn of the century witnessed an increasing flow of migrants engendered mainly by the rapid growth of the rubber industry. This flow was completely stopped during the Japanese Occupation when contacts with India were cut off for about four years, and after the war it resumed but at an insignificant level owing to rigid government control.

Convict Immigration

In the nineteenth century the immigration of Indians gradually evolved into several distinct forms according to the needs and conditions prevailing in the country. One of the earliest forms was the immigration of Indian convicts, introduced soon after the founding of the Straits Settlements by the East India Company with its governing body at Bengal. The convicts constituted a cheap and ready source of labour to the government in the construction of essential public works, such as roads, railways, bridges, canals and wharves. After completing their term of sentence they were repatriated to India but a few were allowed to remain behind to seek new jobs and a fresh start in life. The majority were perhaps not confirmed criminals and had only been involved in crimes through poverty and ignorance.

Convicts immigration was not very substantial, numbering 416 in May 1855, 562 in May 1856 to May 1857, and 148 in May 1859 to May 1860.[21] The total number in Malaya at any one time amounted to a few thousand only, for instance 772 in 1805, 3,802 in 1885, 4,024 in 1857 and 4,063 in 1860. But convict immigration received much publicity and criticism while it lasted; and it was finally prohibited after 1860 and the remaining ones were repatriated to India by 1873.[22]

Indentured Immigration

Indentured immigration appeared to have been introduced also in the early nineteenth century, but it was not until 1872 that it was legalised and controlled by laws enacted by the Indian Government.[23] From 1884 it was brought under the control and protection of the colonial government in Peninsular Malaysia. Immigrants imported under indenture were mainly employed by plantation owners in cultivating tapioca, tea, coffee and sugar cane and by government in constructing railway and public works. Notwithstanding the protection

21. The figures are obtained from the *Annual Report on the Administration of the Straits Settlements*, for the relevant years.
22. Straits Settlements, *Annual Report on the Administration of the Straits Settlements, 1860–1961*, p. 28.
23. J. Geoghegan, *Note on Emigration from India* (Calcutta: Government Press, 1873), p. 64.

TABLE 2.4
ANNUAL INDIAN INDENTURED IMMIGRANTS, 1880–1910

Year	Indian Indentured Immigrants	% of I.I.I. to Total Indian Immigrants	Year	Indian Indentured Immigrants	% of I.I.I. of Total Indian Immigrants
1880	1,298	25.7	1895	1,637	10.2
1881	1,038	15.2	1896	2,810	13.9
1882	1,661	16.7	1897	2,732	13.3
1883	1,626	15.3	1898	3,413	17.9
1884	1,716	10.7	1899	5,078	25.5
1885	1,691	7.9	1900	8,694	22.6
1886	2,992	14.7	1901	3,965	14.0
1887	5,046	29.3	1902	2,736	13.5
1888	5,001	24.0	1903	503	2.3
1889	2,921	16.0	1904	2,783	9.1
1890	3,132	17.0	1905	5,542	14.0
1891	3,736	12.4	1906	3,674	7.1
1892	2,051	11.1	1907	5,499	8.9
1893	2,342	12.9	1908	5,456	10.0
1894	1,801	12.0	1909	4,119	8.3
			1910	2,523	3.0

Source: Annual Reports on Indian Immigration.

accorded by the law, a decreasing proportion of Indians was choosing to immigrate under this system because of the lack of choice and freedom in selecting and changing jobs.

Moreover, by the end of the nineteenth century long contracts were found to be unsuitable in the coffee plantations and in 1899 the period of contract was reduced from three to two years. Even so, the usefulness of the indenture system was beginning to diminish as more Indians preferred to come under the *kangany* system. With the introduction of a new form of assisted immigration in 1908 and the renewed public agitation against the indenture system, the government eventually banned Indian indentured immigrants in June 1910 in the Malay States and in December the same year in the Straits Settlements.[24]

24. Straits Settlements and Federated Malay States, *Report on Indian Immigration, 1910* (Singapore: Government Press), p. 503.

It may be observed from Table 2.4 that during the last three decades prior to the imposition of the ban, the number of indentured immigrants generally oscillated within the range of 1,500–5,500 per year, without any definite sign of a continuous upward trend. At no time did indentured immigrants form a substantial proportion of the total number of Indians entering Peninsular Malaysia, remaining below 15 per cent most of the time.

TABLE 2.5
ANNUAL INDIAN KANGANY-RECRUITED
IMMIGRANTS, 1899–1907

Year	Number	% of Total Indian Immigrants
1899	2,446	12.3
1900	7,828	20.3
1901	4,147	14.7
1902	1,711	8.5
1903	2,125	9.6
1904	3,774	12.3
1905	8,429	21.3
1906	22,467	43.5
1907	26,948	43.4

Kangany-recruited Immigration

It appears that by the 1860s the *kangany* system was introduced by plantation owners who preferred to send their own agent or *kangany* to India to recruit labourers for their estates.[25] The *kangany*, usually a labourer already employed in the estate, undertook to recruit agricultural workers from his village in India in return for a certain fee from his employer. But he had to advance money to defray the expenses of the journey incurred by the recruits who were willing to come but too poor to finance their own passage, recovering the amount from their monthly wages. In most cases, the first month's wage was not sufficient to settle the debt completely so that the immigrants became the *kangany*'s debtors from the very beginning, with all the attendant ill effects such as 'squeezing' or exploitation. Such immigrants, unlike the indentured ones, were legally free and not bound by any contract to serve their employer

25. Geoghegan, op. cit., p. 63.

for a definite period, though they had to sign a promissory note for the advances made to them. Sometimes the expenses of the immigrants' journey were paid by the employer through the *kangany*, and in practice the immigrants had to work for the employer as long as the debt remained unsettled.

Except for complying with certain regulations governing labour conditions, the *kangany* system was almost free from any restrictions until 1884 when *kangany* recruiters were required to be licensed.[26] With the rapid expansion of the rubber industry at the turn of the century, the *kangany* system became extremely popular during its last few years in existence, as may be observed in the figures in Table 2.5. In 1908 the system ceased to exist, having been considerably modified and transformed into the system of recruited immigration.

Assisted Immigration

In the first few years of the present century the supply of immigrant labour was lagging far behind demand in the rapidly expanding rubber industry, resulting in irregular practices such as 'crimping' of labourers whether free or indentured.[27] To solve the unsatisfactory labour situation and to encourage Indian immigration, the government passed the *Tamil Immigration Fund Ordinance, 1907* by which the Indian Committee was constituted to manage a fund, the Indian Immigration Fund, to be compulsorily contributed to by employers of Indian labour and to be used solely for financing the importation of Indian labourers.[28] The main functions of the Committee were to advise the government on matters concerning Indian labour and to regulate the flow of assisted immigrants according to the needs of the country by varying the number of recruiting licences and the amount of recruiting allowance or subsidy.

Under the regulations and supervision of the Committee, immigration evolved into two distinct types — recruited and non-recruited. Except in the first few years when professional recruiters were involved, the recruiting of assisted immigrants was performed through licensed *kanganies* under strict government control.[29] The recruiters received a fee and sometimes even their passage fares from the employers who later claimed back recruiting allowances from the Fund. As for the immigrants, almost all their expenses of the journey from India to the place of work in Peninsular Malaysia were met by the Fund. These

---

26. N. E. Marjoribanks and A. K. G. Ahmad Tambi Marakkaya, *Report on Indian Labour Emigration to Ceylon and Malaya* (Madras: Government Press, 1917), p. 28.
27. Straits Settlements and Federated Malay States, *Report on Indian Immigration, 1907* (Singapore: Government Press), p. 16.
28. J. Norman Parmer, op. cit., p. 39.
29. S. Nanjudan, *Indians in Malayan Economy* (New Delhi: Indian Government Press, 1950), p. 23.

TABLE 2.6
ANNUAL INDIAN ASSISTED IMMIGRANTS, 1908–1939

Year	Indian Assisted Immigrants	% of I.A.I. to Total Indian Immigrants	Year	Indian Assisted Immigrants	% of I.A.I. to Total Indian Immigrants
1908	21,841	40.1	1924	43,147	77.7
1909	21,963	44.1	1925	70,198	77.4
1910	60,347	72.1	1926	149,414	85.5
1911	84,389	77.8	1927	123,826	78.6
1912	79,838	74.7	1928	27,240	42.7
1913	91,236	76.9	1929	82,183	71.7
1914	36,905	72.1	1930	42,671	60.7
1915	54,881	72.9	1931	111	0.5
1916	72,091	75.4	1932	17	0.1
1917	78,407	87.0	1933	20	0.1
1918	55,585	85.1	1934	45,469	50.8
1919	88,021	86.8	1935	20,771	31.3
1920	78,855	82.8	1936	3,754	8.2
1921	15,413	33.7	1937	54,849	44.3
1922	38,336	65.3	1938	4,580	10.2
1923	30,234	61.1	1939	0	0.0

Sources: Annual Reports on Indian Immigration, 1908–1911 and Annual Reports of the Labour
Department, 1912–38.

immigrants, in contrast with the *kangany*-recruited or indentured immigrants, were therefore brought to the country free from any debt and free to change their jobs subject to one month's notice only.

Non-recruited assisted immigrants refer to those who received free passages to Peninsular Malaysia on presenting themselves before the Malayan Immigration Commissioner at Avedi or Negapatam. On arrival in Peninsular Malaysia, they and their families or dependents were provided with free transport and other facilities to enable them to reach their place of employment. In addition, from 1925 an extra bonus were given: $2 for each adult and $1 for each minor under 12 years old. A fairly large proportion of this type of immigrants were Indians who were on short holiday to India and had returned with friends and relatives.

TABLE 2.7
ANNUAL INDIAN ASSISTED IMMIGRANTS
BY TYPE, 1908–1939

Year	Recruited Assisted Immigrants	Non-Recruited Assisted Immigrants	% Recruited to Total Assisted Immigrants
1908	16,293	5,548	74.6
1909	15,888	6,075	72.3
1910	52,440	7,907	86.9
1911	74,867	9,522	88.7
1912	71,266	8,572	89.3
1913	80,528	10,708	88.3
1914	31,140	5,765	84.4
1915	48,969	5,912	89.2
1916	67,902	4,189	94.2
1917	71,318	7,089	91.0
1918	48,064	7,519	86.5
1919	75,690	12,331	86.0
1920	69,767	9,088	88.5
1921	13,371	2,042	86.7
1922	33,848	4,488	88.3
1923	22,772	7,462	75.3
1924	33,506	9,641	77.7
1925	51,401	18,797	73.2
1926	120,796	28,678	80.0
1927	91,524	32,302	73.9
1928	16,260	10,980	59.7
1929	53,266	28,917	64.8
1930	27,650	15,021	64.8
1931	0	111	0.0
1932	0	17	0.0
1933	0	20	0.0
1934	2,067	43,402	4.5
1935	1,862	18,909	9.0
1936	669	3,085	1.8
1937	5,337	49,512	9.7
1938	88	4,492	1.9
1939	0	0	0.0

Sources: Annual Reports on Indian Immigration, 1908–1911 and Annual Reports of the Labour Department, 1921–38.

The size and composition of assisted immigration from 1908 to 1938 are presented in Tables 2.6 and 2.7. The sharp rise in the number of assisted immigrants in 1910 may be attributed to considerable increase in the demand for labour in the rubber plantation industry which was experiencing a period of prosperity and rapid growth.[30] The rise continued until 1914 when the First World War put a complete stop to immigration for about six months commencing from 6 August of the same year. The number soon resumed at slightly below prewar levels but was reduced again to the record low level of about 15,000 in 1921 by a local slump in the rubber industry.[31] Thereafter, it remained moderately low for a couple of years and recovered during the second half of the 1920s, with the highest figure of about 150,000 in 1926.

During the World Depression assisted immigration was suspended on 6 August 1930; only a small number of non-recruited labourers and their dependents who wished to join their families in Peninsular Malaysia were assisted. Assisted immigration, mainly in the form of non-recruited, resumed in May 1934 and came to a final end with the complete ban on the emigration of unskilled labour imposed by the Indian Government on 15 June 1938.[32]

Despite the fluctuations in the total number of assisted immigrants, the recruited class maintained its dominance, generally above 70 per cent, throughout the period prior to 1931. During and after the World Depression the position was just the reverse, with the non-recruited class comprising at least 90 per cent.

Independent Immigration

The movement of independent immigrants dates back to ancient times and prevailed for the longest period, remaining free from any government control throughout the pre-Second World War years. Such immigrants normally came on their own initiative and by their own financial means or arrangements, though some had friends and relatives in Peninsular Malaysia with whose assistance they were able to make all the necessary preparations for their journey and employment.[33] They belonged to a wide range of occupational groups traders, merchants, shopkeepers, money-lenders, clerks, artisans and

30. Straits Settlements, *Annual Report of the Straits Settlements, 1910* (Singapore: Government Press), p. 485.
31. Straits Settlements and Federated Malay States, *Report of the Labour Department, 1921* (Singapore: Government Press), pp. 670–71.
32. Malaya, *Report of the Labour Department, 1938* (Singapore: Government Press), p. 17.
33. S. Nanjudan, op. cit., p. 25.

TABLE 2.8
ANNUAL INDIAN INDEPENDENT IMMIGRANTS, 1880–1939

Year	Indian Independent Immigrants	% of I.I.I. to Total Indian Immigrants	Year	Indian Independent Immigrants	% of I.I.I. of Total Indian Immigrants
1880	3,755	74.3	1910	20,853	24.9
1881	6,769	99.4	1911	24,082	22.2
1882	8,276	83.3	1912	27,090	25.3
1883	8,979	84.7	1913	27,347	23.1
1884	14,365	89.3	1914	14,312	27.9
1885	19,819	92.1	1915	20,442	27.1
1886	17,316	85.3	1916	23,475	24.6
1887	12,156	70.7	1917	7,079	7.9
1888	15,812	76.0	1918	9,708	14.9
1889	15,285	84.0	1919	13,412	13.2
1890	15,341	83.0	1920	16,365	17.2
1891	26,446	87.6	1921	30,260	66.3
1892	16,370	88.9	1922	20,338	34.7
1893	15,899	87.3	1923	19,268	38.9
1894	13,455	90.0	1924	18,905	34.0
1895	14,368	89.8	1925	20,510	22.6
1896	17,340	86.1	1926	25,381	14.5
1897	17,867	86.7	1927	32,306	20.5
1898	15,613	82.1	1928	35,832	56.2
1899	12,935	64.9	1929	32,069	28.0
1900	22,007	57.1	1930	26,343	37.5
1901	20,247	71.6	1931	19,581	94.4
1902	15,795	78.0	1932	17,717	95.1
1903	19,399	88.1	1933	20,222	99.9
1904	24,144	78.6	1934	43,637	47.6
1905	25,568	64.7	1935	44,420	67.0
1906	25,720	49.4	1936	39,437	86.3
1907	29,827	48.0	1937	67,717	54.7
1908	27,174	49.8	1938	39,627	88.4
1909	23,735	47.6	1939	23,961	100.0

Sources: Annual Reports on Indian Immigration, 1880–1911 and Annual Reports of the Labour Department, 1921–39.

many others — all attracted by good commercial and employment ópportunities.

The years following the World Depression witnessed an increasing proportion of labourers coming in as independent immigrants, mainly to avoid the one week's detention at the quarantine camp.[34] However, this form of immigration ceased to exist from 15 June 1938, when the Indian Government's ban on the emigration of unskilled labourers to Peninsular Malaysia was imposed.[35] It may be recalled that at this time too the other forms of Indian immigration had ceased to exist so that the only Indians to continue coming to Peninsular Malaysia after this date were the independent immigrants other than the labouring class. Their movement was for the first time completely stopped by the outbreak of war in Peninsular Malaysia on 8 December 1941, and resumed on a minor scale during the immediate postwar years. Since 1 August 1953 independent immigrants have been rigidly controlled by the *Immigration Ordinance, 1953* and subsequently by the *Immigration Ordinance, 1959*. A detailed analysis of these two legislations has already been presented in the preceeding section on Chinese migration.

The data set out in Table 2.8 seem to indicate a very gradual upward trend in annual volume of independent immigration, without any apparent pronounced fluctuation as experienced by assisted immigrants. In general the annual inflow oscillated slightly below 20,000 during the nineteenth century, below 30,000 during 1900–1926, and below 40,000 during 1926–33, with the highest of about 68,000 in 1937. The proportion of independent immigrants to total immigrants amounted to more than 80 per cent during the nineteenth century, but was progressively reduced during the first three decades of the present century by the popularity of *kangany*-recruited immigrants up to 1907 and subsequently by the success of assisted immigrants. The rise in the proportion to almost pre-1900 levels in the 1930s was caused partly by the severe drop in assisted immigrants and partly by additional Indians coming in as independent instead of assisted immigrants.

Overall Indian Migration

Table 2.9 depicts the long-term trends in Indian migration irrespective of types. It appears that during the last two decades of the nineteenth century, Indian immigration rose steadily in the first few years to about 22,000 in 1886, and thereafter oscillated below this level in general. The initial rise and sustained inflow may be attributed to the continuous demand for immigrant labour in

---

34. Malaya, *Report of the Labour Department, 1938* (Singapore: Government Press), p. 12.
35. Ibid., p. 15.

TABLE 2.9
ANNUAL INDIAN IMMIGRANTS AND EMIGRANTS, 1880–1962

Year	Immigrants	Emigrants	Net Migrants	Year	Immigrants	Emigrants	Migrants
1880	5,053	3,812	1,241	1920	95,220	55,481	39,739
1881	6,807	5,269	1,538	1921	45,673	61,551	−15,878
1882	9,937	5,947	2,990	1922	58,674	45,733	12,941
1883	10,605	9,041	1,564	1923	49,502	42,778	6,724
1884	16,081	10,749	5,332	1924	55,526	37,326	18,200
1885	21,510	13,417	8,093	1925	90,706	43,144	47,564
1886	20,308	18,105	2,203	1926	174,795	65,786	109,009
1887	17,202	12,596	4,606	1927	157,626	93,269	64,357
1888	20,813	13,190	7,623	1928	63,755	91,430	−27,675
1889	18,206	14,099	4,107	1929	114,597	76,854	37,743
1890	18,473	15,276	3,197	1930	70,317	152,231	−81,914
1891	30,182	23,912	6,270	1931	20,734	103,090	−82,356
1892	18,421	17,722	699	1932	18,637	85,051	−66,414
1893	18,220	14,044	4,176	1933	20,242	32,738	−12,496
1894	14,956	13,537	1,419	1934	89,584	28,407	61,177
1895	16,005	12,360	3,645	1935	66,350	38,869	27,481
1896	20,150	12,977	7,173	1936	45,706	40,557	5,149
1897	20,599	14,280	6,319	1937	123,732	45,167	78,565
1898	19,026	11,500	7,526	1938	44,839	76,199	−31,360
1899	19,920	10,766	9,154	1939	23,961	42,724	−18,763
1900	38,529	11,251	27,278	1940	44,177	51,772	− 7,595
1901	28,259	16,204	12,055	1941	41,008	50,283	− 9,275
1902	20,242	18,183	2,059	1942	43,614	54,856	−11,242
1903	22,030	17,832	4,198	1943	23,925	24,189	− 264
1904	30,701	19,550	11,151	1949	31,770	48,033	− 6,263
1905	39,539	19,754	19,785	1950	29,325	21,805	7,520
1906	52,041	21,879	30,162	1951	50,678	44,538	6,095
1907	62,130	30,522	31,608	1952	65,745	44,624	21,121
1908	54,522	30,920	23,602	1953	63,746	38,337	25,409
1909	49,817	31,374	18,443	1954	41,524	46,041	− 4,517
1910	83,723	39,080	44,643	1955	53,397	53,431	− 34
1911	108,471	48,103	60,368	1956	61,451	57,178	− 4,273
1912	106,928	63,885	43,043	1957	58,743	59,294	− 551
1913	118,583	70,090	48,493	1958	55,656	64,697	− 9,041
1914	51,217	63,073	−11,856	1959	58,512	57,494	1,018
1915	75,323	50,320	25,003	1960	56,147	64,616	− 8,469
1916	95,566	54,479	42,087	1961	59,268	66,317	− 7,049
1917	90,077	57,583	32,494	1962	59,103	65,804	− 6,701
1918	65,291	52,132	13,159				
1919	101,433	46,767	54,666				

Note: The figures for 1940–62 refer to total arrivals and departures by air, sea and land. Figures for 1944–48 are not available.

Sources: Annual Reports on Indian Immigration, 1880–1911, Annual Reports of the Labour Department, 1912–38 and Malayan Statistics Monthly Digest, 1940–62.

FIGURE 2.2
ANNUAL INDIAN IMMIGRANTS AND EMIGRANTS, 1880–1941

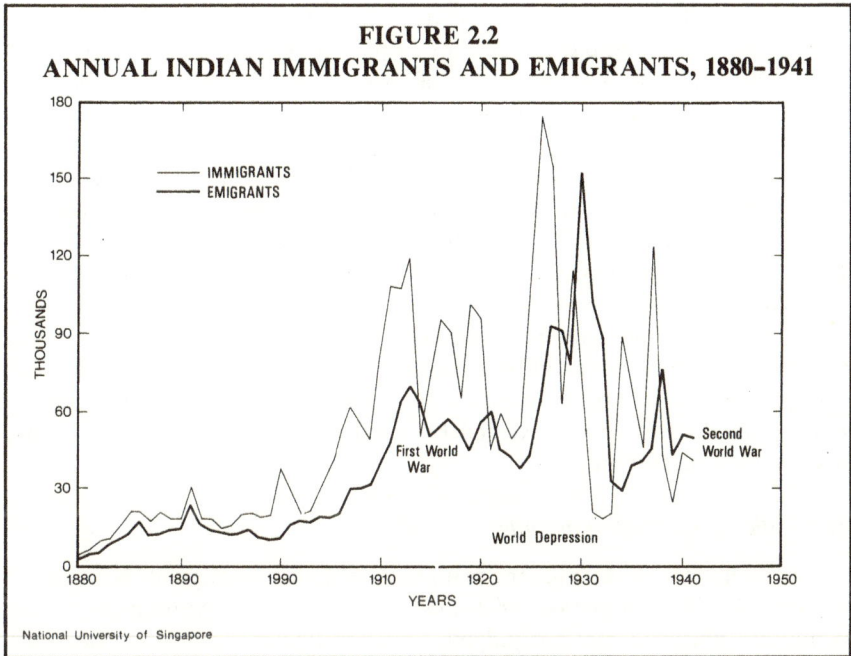

the expanding public works and in the prospering agricultural enterprises. The slight oscillations in the yearly inflow were generated by temporary factors such as bad harvest, famines and epidemic diseases in India and minor economic slumps and booms in Peninsular Malaysia. The annual outflow, consisting mainly of persons on brief visits home or returning permanently after termination of employment, was never greater than the annual inflow so that a net gain for Peninsular Malaysia was always recorded in the nineteenth century.

The first three decades of the present century were characterised by a high volume of Indian migration, with however, rather violent fluctuations in the annual movements. The setting up of new rubber plantations and the operation of those already in existence necessitated a large and continuous supply of labour which was met by the immigration of Indians under the regulation and assistance of the Indian Immigration Committee. The annual fluctuations were primarily caused by short-term movements in the level of employment in the rubber industry arising from changes in price and output of rubber as determined by world demand.

The first setback occurred during the First World War when the drop in rubber exports was the main cause in the reduction of about 50 per cent in the number of immigrants and in a net deficit of about 12,000 in 1914. The second setback was during the local slump in 1921 with a higher deficit of about 16,000 and as the slump continued the surplus in the next few years continued to be relatively low. The net deficit of about 28,000 in 1928 was apparently due to the new passport regulations that came into force with the new Immigration Ordinance. The worst years were during the World Depression when the number of immigrants was drastically reduced to pre-1900 levels and thousands of unemployed Indians were repatriated back to India. The net deficit for the years 1930–33 amounted to no less than 243,000. After 1933 the position recovered somewhat but the four years before the Japanese Occupation again recorded substantial net losses as a result of the Indian government's prohibition on the emigration of unskilled labour in 1938. The postwar years continued to show a deficit in Indian immigrants, all belonging to the independent type of immigrants, as inward movement was strictly controlled and as more Indians, who were prevented by war from returning, were emigrating back to their motherland.

Sex Ratio of Indian Immigrants

The computed sex ratio for the main types of Indian immigrants is presented in Table 2.10 for the period 1908–1938. Statistics for the years prior to this period are not available, but judging from the figures given in the table the overall sex ratio during the late nineteenth century must have exceeded 7,200 males per thousand females in most years, and considering that the immigrants at that time were mainly indentured and independent classes the ratio might even approach 14,000. This disproportionate sex ratio and its likely effects on the Indian settlers attracted some concern in India and Peninsular Malaysia. By and large, the authorities in Peninsular Malaysia were not only in agreement with the Indian Government that the sex composition should be conducive to normal healthy living but also appreciated that any evil emanating from a disproportionate sex ratio would be entirely manifested in Peninsular Malaysia. Insofar as India was concerned, the number of men recruited in any year formed an almost negligible proportion of the total number of men in the regions where emigration originated. Nevertheless, nothing positive seemed to have been done to improve the sex ratio which remained rather uneven throughout the nineteenth century.

The twentieth century, however, witnessed the institution of definite measures to normalise the sex ratio by means of directly fostering female immigration and indirectly encouraging the men to bring their wives and children with them. To mention only the important measure, the Indian Immigration Committee fixed a lower rate of assessment on employers of female labour, gave

TABLE 2.10
SEX RATIO OF INDIAN IMMIGRANTS BY TYPE, 1908–1938
(Males Per 1,000 Females)

Year	Total Immigrants	Recruited Assisted Immigrants	Non-Recruited Assisted Immigrants	Independent Immigrants
1908	7,196	4,734		14,026
1909	7,001	4,725		12,402
1910	5,115	4,246		10,135
1911	5,051	4,142		16,450
1912	4,651	3,860		10,500
1913	4,273	3,746		7,689
1914	4,663	3,970		8,127
1915	4,941	4,128		9,837
1916	3,892	3,328	4,011	6,796
1917	3,781	3,629	4,708	7,718
1918	3,982	2,776	5,514	9,750
1919	3,991	2,950	6,328	8,314
1920	3,837	3,213	5,691	8,267
1921	6,894	4,595	4,249	9,063
1922	4,425	3,680	3,299	7,010
1923	4,124	2,856	3,836	7,711
1924	3,406	2,406	3,622	7,756
1925	3,421	2,451	4,137	9,443
1926	3,229	2,606	4,169	10,030
1927	2,857	2,195	3,383	6,242
1928	3,604	1,541	1,956	8,989
1929	3,413	2,053	3,863	11,843
1930	3,358	1,912	3,377	8,305
1931	9,564	—	1,581	9,753
1932	8,398	—	545	8,444
1933	7,378	—	429	7,419
1934	2,943	1,314	1,704	6,782
1935	3,474	1,282	1,572	5,940
1936	4,369	1,071	1,406	6,488
1937	3,137	1,282	1,913	5,578
1938	6,484	1,378	1,594	8,576

Note: Recruited Assisted Immigrants were completely suspended during 1931–33, and hence no figures for these years.

Sources: Annual Reports on Indian Immigration, 1908–1911 and Annual Reports of the Labour Department, 1912–38.

a higher recruiting allowance to employers who recruited married couples, and paid a bonus of one dollar to each child of a non-recruited immigrant.[36]

The effectiveness of the above measures can be observed in Table 2.10 where the sex ratio of assisted immigrants was far less uneven than that of independent immigrants who were not covered by the measures. Another important effect is that over the years the former sex ratio has undergone a much more pronounced trend towards parity than the latter sex ratio. Between the two types of assisted immigrants, the sex ratio of the recruited was more often than not nearer to parity than that of the non-recruited owing to the greater scope for implementing the measures among the recruited type. While recruited immigration was completely prohibited during 1931–33, most of the non-recruited immigrants allowed to enter Peninsular Malaysia were wives and children of Indians already in the country and this accounts for the excess of females over males in the last two of the three years. Insofar as the sex ratio of the overall Indian immigrants is concerned, there is an apparent connection with the composition of the total immigrants, the ratio being generally more uneven in years when the proportion of assisted immigrants was relatively low.

It would be of some interest to compare the sex ratio of Indian immigrants with that of the Chinese immigrants depicted in Table 2.3. A closer examination reveals that the sex ratio of the Indian immigrants was relatively more uneven during the whole period 1908–1930 except for the three years 1919, 1921 and 1928. But during 1930–38, the Indian figure was far more uneven consequent on a marked normalisation of the Chinese sex ratio and on the Indian sex ratio being more abnormal than usual as a result of the cessation during 1931–33, and subsequent restriction, of assisted immigration.

Malay Migration

Contacts between the Malay Peninsula and the numerous islands in the Indonesian Archipelago date back to ancient times. The earliest recorded contacts were with the Srivijaya Empire (6001–1,000 A.D.) with its capital situated at Palembang in south Sumatra. The Srivijaya rulers held sway over certain parts of Peninsular Malaysia at various periods, and into these regions came Sumatran settlers and traders. This was subsequently followed by Javanese contacts and immigration during the time of the Majapahit Empire (1,293–1,520 A.D.) whose central rule in Java embraced a wide area including a group of territories in Peninsular Malaysia.[37] Movements of people from the Indonesian islands assumed a more definite pattern from the early fifteenth century

---

36. Malaya, *Report of the Labour Department, 1937* (Singapore: Government Press), pp. 548–50.
37. D. G. E. Hall, op. cit., p. 72.

with the founding of the Malay Kingdom of Malacca by Parameswara, a Palembang prince married to a Majapahit princess.

At the time of its founding in 1403, Malacca was just a village inhabited by indigenous Malay fishermen and sea-gypsies, but with the establishment of some law and order and the prospect of trade, a considerable number of settlers and traders were attracted from Palembang.[38] Throughout the fifteenth century, Malacca, which was then the most important commercial centre in the Archipelago, continued to receive immigrants from the islands across the Straits, particularly Sumatra and Java. There was a large community of Javanese, predominantly slaves and merchants who seemed to have monopolised the trade between Malacca and east Java.

In the sixteenth and seventeenth century, while Malacca under Portuguese and later Dutch control received fewer immigrants from the Indonesian islands, other regions of Peninsular Malaysia were receiving Bugis immigrants from the southern portion of the Celebes. The Bugis were mercenary fighters and maritime traders who were prone to wander all over the Archipelago. They were known to have visited Peninsular Malaysia frequently around the mid-1600s, and by 1681 they had established numerous settlements along the Klang and Selangor estuaries. Waves of Bugis immigration continued into the eighteenth century which was characterised by the dominance of Bugis commercial and political activities. They served as mercenary fighters, were involved in the various struggles between rival princes, extended their influence over the tin-states of Kedah, Perak and Selangor, and virtually controlled the trade of the Malay Peninsula during the major part of the eighteenth century.[39]

Another stream of Indonesian immigration was from the Minangkabau region of Sumatra into the territories north of Malacca. This movement had taken place peacefully over a long period and in small groups consisting mainly of skilled agriculturists. By the mid-1600s Minangkabau settlements were established in many parts of Peninsular Malaysia, the principal areas being Naning, Rembau, Sungei Ujong and Klang. The eighteenth century witnessed the founding of the independent state of Negri Sembilan by the Minangkabau settlers under the leadership of one of their royal personages from Sumatra.

While the main features of Chinese and Indian immigration during the nineteenth and twentieth century stand out quite clearly, Indonesian immigration in the same period is less easy to detect and analyse owing largely to the paucity of statistical data and official reports. There is some evidence of Indonesian traders, planters and labourers being engaged in various kinds of employment

---

38. R.O. Windstedt, "A History of Malaya", *Journal of the Malayan Branch of the Royal Asiatic Society* XIII, Part 1 (March 1935): 38.

39. Hall, op. cit., pp. 289–96.

in the late 1890s.[40] Of the two types of immigration — the free and independent type and the indentured category — more is known about the latter.

The movement of Indonesian indentured immigrants into Peninsular Malaysia was governed by regulations of the government of the Netherlands Indies concerning emigration. In 1887 the Netherlands Indies government prohibited the emigration of skilled and unskilled Javanese labour for work outside country. But it appeared that "in special cases and for important reasons, the Governor-General could lift the prohibition on condition that the recruitment always took place in Java and Madura".[41] Permission was at times granted for emigration to the Straits Settlements and other parts of Peninsular Malaysia. In 1909 the *Netherlands Indian Labourers Protection Enactment* came into force; its twofold aim was to regulate the importation of Indonesian indentured labour into Peninsular Malaysia and to protect Indonesian workers from maltreatment and exploitation.[42] The enactment stipulated certain working and living conditions such as the maximum duration of a contract, wages, conditions of work, etc.

The original contracts were in Dutch and signed in the Netherlands Indies. Besides stating that the period of indenture was not to exceed 900 days, the enactment also stipulated that no labourer could be compelled to remain in a place of employment for a period longer than (a) two years where the contract did not exceed 300 days, (b) three years where the contract was for 300–600 days, and (c) four years where the contract was for 600–900 days.[43] The employer was allowed to deduct up to a maximum of two dollars per month from the labourer's pay, the amount was equivalent to the sum of advances given to the labourer at the time of recruiting. Furthermore, the enactment imposed penal sanctions on the labourer as well as the employer. They were liable to be fined and imprisoned for breach of contract or for committing any other offences such as failure to work, refusal to proceed to place of employment, disobedience, desertion and absence during working hours on the part of labour and maltreatment and failure to respect the agreement on the part of the employer.

In Peninsular Malaysia planters who wished to recruit Indonesian indentured labourers had first to make applications to the Governor-General of the Netherlands Indies through the Dutch Consul-General in Penang or Singapore. After the permits were obtained they had to rely on professional

---

40. Norman Parmer, op. cit., p. 108.
41. *Proceedings of the 24th Session of the National Labour Conference* (Geneva, 1937), pp. 57–58.
42. R.N. Jackson, op. cit., p. 127.
43. *Netherlands Indian Labourers Protection Enactment, 1909*, Section 9.

recruiters licensed by the Netherlands Indies Government, the only persons authorised to recruit the labourers in Java. The more usual practice was for the planters to approach one of the European firms in Java to request the professional recruiters to recruit and transport the required number of labourers to Peninsular Malaysia. These licensed recruiters had to comply with strict rules and regulations passed by the Netherlands Indies Government. They had to provide adequate accommodation for the labourers, both at the place of recruitment and at the port of embarkation. Food, medical attention and decent travelling facilities throughout the whole journey were to be provided by the recruiters who were not allowed to charge these expenses to the labourers. The planters paid for not only these expenses but also certain fees to the firms and professional recruiters for services rendered. A lesser number was recruited in Singapore where the assisted labourers proceeding from Java to Sumatra used to spend a few days in the coolie depots. Occasionally, some changed their minds and signed contracts just like the Chinese immigrants before the Protector of the Chinese and remained in Peninsular Malaysia to work in the oil-palm and rubber plantations.[44]

Apart from the high cost of importing labourers through professional recruiters, there was the additional defect of bringing in many unsatisfactory labourers due to the system of paying recruiters by the number of labourers imported. Recruiters were known to use unscrupulous means of luring labourers with rosy pictures of living and working conditions in Peninsular Malaysia; subsequently many labourers were dissatisfied with the actual conditions they found. To some extent it is also true that besides "having to employ a number of disappointed individuals, the employees were often sent unhealthy, anaemic, lazy and inexperienced labourers".[45]

Owing to these serious shortcomings of the indenture system it was only in times of labour shortage resulting from an insufficient inflow from South India that the employers turned to Java to augment their labour force, as was notably the case in 1911 and 1918. In 1911 a sub-committee was appointed by the Planters' Association of Peninsular Malaysia to find ways and means of recruiting labourers directly in order to do away with the middlemen's profits and thus reducing the cost of the imported labour. There was a suggestion that the employers could adopt the newly-introduced system of labour recruitment by which firms in the Netherlands Indies were allowed to recruit Javanese workers direct from the agricultural districts of Java and Madura.

44. Malaya, *Report of the Labour Department, 1938* (Singapore: Government Press), p. 9.
45. Tungku Shamsul Bahrin, "Indonesian Labour in Malaya", *Kajian Ekonomi Malaysia* 2, No. 1 (June 1965): 64.

But the scheme, though favourably regarded by the Dutch, fell through owing to lack of funds.

In 1918 Peninsular Malaysia again experienced a shortage of labour on account of wartime restrictions on shipping facilities, the outbreak of cholera in Madras State, and the prohibition in 1917 by the Madras Government on the emigration of men between the ages of 18 and 25 years to Peninsular Malaysia. The Planters' Association approached the Federated Malay States Government to urge the Netherlands Indies authorities to adopt a more liberal attitude towards Javanese labour emigrating into the country. The matter was referred to London but nothing came of it due to the reluctance of Whitehall to interfere in the colonial administration of another country.

Indonesian indentured immigration outlived Chinese and Indian indentured immigration by a considerable number of years partly because of the preference of the Dutch authorities for this system and partly because the relatively small numbers involved meant that abuses received little or no publicity at the request of the Dutch authorities in 1927 and after some negotiations, Indonesian indentured immigration into Peninsular Malaysia was finally abolished in 1932 when the *Netherlands Indies Labour Protection Enactment, 1909* was abrogated.[46] Figures for the annual number of Indonesian indentured immigrants are not available, but judging from the relatively small number employed at any one time,[47] the yearly volume of inflow was undoubtedly much lower than that of Chinese or Indian indentured immigration.

No government machinery was instituted to organise and promote Indonesian immigration as a whole, though some European planters and British officials were rather keen to encourage this kind of immigration.[48] The relatively low magnitude of overall Indonesian migration may perhaps be deduced from the total arrival and departure figures by sea and air to and from Indonesia given in Table 2.11. In most years there was a net gain for Peninsular Malaysia of about 2,000 which is very low in comparison with the corresponding figure for the Chinese or the Indians. Indonesian immigration was under the regulation of the *Aliens Ordinance* during the immediate postwar years, and since 1953 has been rigidly controlled by the *Immigration Ordinance, 1953* and later the *Immigration Ordinance, 1959*. It should be emphasised that because of racial, religious and cultural similarities, the Indonesian immigrants mix and intermarry freely with the indigenous Malays. This process of assimilation has been in operation all the time so that the distinction between the two groups is

46. Norman Parmer, op. cit., p. 108.
47. Tungku Shamsul Bahrin, op. cit., pp. 56–61.
48. R.N. Jackson, op. cit., p. 127.

TABLE 2.11
ANNUAL MALAY ARRIVALS AND
DEPARTURES TO THE
NETHERLANDS EAST INDIES, 1923–40

Year	Arrivals	Departures	Surplus of Deficit
1923	44,669	43,653	1,016
1924	54,809	55,193	– 386
1925	81,691	81,830	126
1926	85,691	79,120	6,571
1927	71,151	71,250	– 99
1928	61,513	61,249	264
1929	64,658	57,716	6,924
1930	53,453	54,634	– 1,181
1931	35,728	39,293	– 3,566
1932	35,283	34,972	311
1933	34,842	32,922	1,921
1934	33,445	29,178	2,267
1935	30,581	27,586	2,995
1936	35,637	32,234	3,403
1937	62,312	52,209	10,103
1938	38,446	37,094	1,352
1939	31,203	31,295	92
1940	30,528	27,413	3,115

Source: Annual Report of the Statistical Office, Straits Settlements.

becoming less clear cut, and hence both are considered as Malays. It is largely due to this ease of assimilation that a perceptible resurgence of Indonesian immigration has taken place in recent years.

Foreign-Born Population

The analysis of migration incorporated in the previous sections was based on statistics and written statements extracted from numerous special and annual reports of government departments. The other major source of migration statistics is from the series of population censuses which provide data on the country of birth and hence the foreign-born population. These figures indicate the stock position of the immigrants at the various census dates as against the dynamic situation reflected by the annual figures given in the previous sections. The census data are therefore defective to the extent that they do not take in account immigrants who died during the intercensal period as well as those who moved in and out of the country during the period. But the coverage of the census data is more complete and comprehensive since they refer precisely to Peninsular Malaysia without Singapore and can portray the changing size of the immigrant population in the country over the census years. The usefulness of the census data has also been enhanced in the 1970 and 1980 censuses with the introduction of the supplementary question on the duration of residence in Peninsular Malaysia, which provides an idea of the time period during which the immigrants entered the country.

The figures in Table 2.12 show the exact number of foreign-born population residing in the country in the various census years from 1921 to 1980. The data in this and the other tables that follow include those born in Sabah, Sarawak and also Singapore since we are interested in persons born outside Peninsular Malaysia. A total of 1,248,000 foreign-born persons were living in Peninsular Malaysia in 1921, and a decade later the number increased by 22.6 per cent to reach 1,529,900 in 1931. The latter figure does not necessarily represent the peak of the foreign-born population which might have occurred in the intercensal years. As a result of immigration controls in the 1930s and the Japanese Occupation during 1942–45, the number of foreign-born persons dropped by 29.0 per cent to reach 1,086,300 in 1947. Thereafter, the postwar restrictive immigration policies and the emergence of the communist government in China in 1949 continued to hold immigration to an extremely low level. This, coupled with the continuous depletion by deaths, led to a sustained downturn in the foreign-born population in the next three censuses. The number was reduced to 989,600 in 1970, and finally to 529,600 in the latest census held in 1980; the rate of decline was 8.9 per cent during 1947–57, 31.1 per cent during 1957–70 and 22.1 per cent during 1970–80.

The figures for the Chinese and the Indians exhibit the same trend over the years, with however some minor variations in the percentage change. Both races recorded an increase in the foreign-born population during the first intercensal period 1921–31 but a reduction during the subsequent four intercensal periods. Between 1921 and 1931 the foreign-born Chinese recorded an increase of 31.9 per cent, but the foreign-born Indians managed to reach only half the rate of increase, i.e. 16.2 per cent. When the decline set in during 1931–47, the foreign-born Indians suffered a much heavier loss of 42.4 per cent than the foreign-born Chinese which was reduced by only 21.5 per cent. But in the following decade 1947–57 the position was reversed, with the foreign-born Indians experiencing a fall of 5.2 per cent as against the 15.8 per cent registered by the foreign-born Chinese. No significant difference occurred during the

TABLE 2.12
FOREIGN-BORN POPULATION BY RACE, 1921–80

Year	Foreign-Born Population	Intercensal Increase	
		Number	Percentage
All Races			
1921	1,248,020	281,911	—
1931	1,529,931	–443,658	22.6
1947	1,086,273	– 96,636	–29.0
1957	989,637	– 96,636	– 8.9
1970	680,060*	–309,577	–31.3
1980	529,608*	–150,452	–22.1
Malays			
1921	161,928	—	– 9.5
1931	146,592	– 15,336	–30.8
1947	101,444	– 45,148	–12.8
1957	88,483	– 12,961	– 7.4
1970	81,908	– 6,575	– 8.2
1980	116,930	35,022	42.8
Chinese			
1921	682,502	—	—
1931	900,486	217,984	31.9
1947	707,024	–193,462	–21.5
1957	595,326	–111,698	–15.8
1970	410,399	–184,927	–31.1
1980	283,516	–126,883	–30.9
Indians			
1921	387,038	—	—
1931	449,624	62,586	16.2
1947	258,903	–190,724	–42.4
1957	245,430	– 13,473	– 5.2
1970	165,432	– 80,007	–32.6
1980	110,678	– 54,745	–33.1

Note: Persons born in Sarawak and Sabah are included.

two latest intercensal periods, both races experiencing a decline of a shade more than 30 per cent. A completely different trend was delineated by the foreign-born Malays; they recorded a decline during the first four intercensal periods and a large increase of some 42.8 per cent during the latest period 1970–80.

The above diverse changes resulted in some marked shifts in the racial composition of the foreign-born population in the country. In 1921 some 13.0 per cent of the foreign-born population were Malays, 54.7 per cent Chinese and 31.0 per cent Indians. By 1980 the proportion of Malays among the foreign-born population has moved up to 22.1 per cent, while that of the Indians has gone down to 20.9 per cent. For the first time therefore census data show there were more foreign-born Malays (116,900) than foreign-born Indians (110,700). The proportion of foreign-born Chinese was reduced marginally to 53.5 per cent in 1980. These percentages reflect the strong representation of Chinese and Indians among the immigrants into Peninsular Malaysia during the major part of the twentieth century.

The distribution of the foreign-born population by country of birth for the two latest censuses is presented in Table 2.13. Judging from our account of immigration in the previous sections, it is not surprising that most of the foreign-born population in 1970 were born in China and India. However, with no fresh immigration from the two countries and with continuous depletion

TABLE 2.13
DISTRIBUTION OF FOREIGN-BORN POPULATION BY
COUNTRY OF BIRTH, 1970 AND 1980

Country of Birth	Number ('000)		Percentage	
	1970	1980	1970	1980
China	377.9	251.5	55.6	47.5
India	165.5	110.9	24.3	20.9
Indonesia	51.8	53.6	7.6	10.1
Singapore	48.6	50.4	7.1	9.5
Thailand	7.0	17.5	1.0	3.3
Sarawak	2.2	11.8	0.3	2.2
Sabah	1.8	8.2	0.3	1.5
Philippines	0.2	0.4	0.0	0.1
Others	24.9	22.0	3.7	4.2
Unknown	0.1	3.3	0.0	0.6
Total	680.0	529.6	100.0	100.0

due to death, the number born in China declined by 33.4 per cent from 377,900 in 1970 to 251,500 in 1980 and those born in India by 33.0 per cent from 165,500 to 110,900 during the same period. On the other hand, there was an increase in the number born in the ASEAN countries and Sarawak and Sabah. The number born in the two East Malaysian states increased significantly during the intercensal period, from 2,200 to 11,800 in the case of Sarawak and from 1,800 to 8,200 in the case of Sabah. These East Malaysians were attracted by the better economic opportunities in Peninsular Malaysia. A fair increase was also recorded by those born in Thailand, moving up from 7,000 in 1970 to 17,500 in 1980. A greater insight into the pattern of immigration may be

TABLE 2.14

FOREIGN-BORN POPULATION BY DURATION OF RESIDENCE AND COUNTRY OF BIRTH, 1980

Country	Duration of Residence in Years						
	< 3	3 to <6	6 to <11	11 to <20	21 & Over	Unknown	Total
Number							
Total	39,445	18,099	17,148	26,868	396,305	8,443	506,307
China	564	433	879	2,944	243,262	3,433	251,515
India	2,452	1,814	2,724	7,025	95,238	1,634	110,887
Indonesia	14,148	5,575	2,136	1,658	29,278	782	53,577
Singapore	4,629	3,594	7,384	12,655	21,162	1,011	50,435
Thailand	7,480	2,841	1,935	1,362	2,488	408	17,514
Philippines	153	93	60	22	82	14	424
Others	10,019	3,749	2,029	1,202	3,795	1,161	21,955
Percentage							
Total	7.8	3.4	3.4	5.3	78.3	1.7	100.0
China	0.2	0.2	0.3	1.2	96.7	1.4	100.0
India	2.2	1.6	2.5	6.3	85.9	1.5	100.0
Indonesia	26.4	10.4	4.0	3.1	54.6	1.5	100.0
Singapore	9.2	7.1	14.6	24.1	42.0	2.0	100.0
Thailand	42.7	16.2	11.0	7.8	19.9	2.3	100.0
Philippines	36.1	21.9	14.2	5.2	19.3	3.3	100.0
Others	45.6	17.1	9.2	5.5	17.3	5.3	100.0

Note: The figures for Others do not include Sarawak and Sabah; separate figures for these two
      states are not available.

observed in Table 2.14 showing the foreign-born population tabulated by country of birth and duration of residence in Peninsular Malaysia.

In reckoning the total length of time a person has lived in Peninsular Malaysia, temporary absences such as short-term job transfers, study leave, etc. were ignored. However, if the length of stay was interrupted by a long period of living in another country, the time of absence was deducted from the total time.[49] It should also be noted that separate figures for Sarawak and Sabah are not available and are excluded in Table 2.14. Out of a total of 506,307 persons born in foreign countries, no less than 396,305 or 78.3 per cent had lived in Peninsular Malaysia for 21 years and more. This serves to confirm that most of the foreign-born population had migrated to Peninsular Malaysia more than two decades ago. By comparison recent immigration was relatively insignificant; 5.3 per cent had resided in the country for 11 to 20 years and the remaining 16.4 per cent for less than 11 years. Among the last group with less than 11 years duration of residence, 3.4 per cent had stayed for 6 to less than 11 years, 3.4 per cent for 3 to less than 6 years, and 7.8 per cent for less than 3 years. These figures may not however indicate actual immigration. Those persons stating their duration of residence in the country as less than one year could well be visitors, while those with slightly longer residence up to three years could possibly be work permit holders who were engaged to work in the newer industries.

A closer look at the more detailed figures given in Table 2.14 cross-classified by country of birth will reveal a better picture of the nature of past immigration. Among the 251,515 born in China, 96.7 per cent reported a duration of residence of 21 years and more. The small number with short duration of residence did not come directly from China but from other countries though they were born in China. Among those born in the Indian subcontinent, some 85.9 per cent had stayed in the country for 21 years and more, 6.3 per cent for 11 to less than 21 years, and the rest for varying periods of time less than 11 years. It may be observed that the India-born figures for the four periods less than 11 years are larger than the corresponding China-born figures, which seems to suggest that, unlike immigration from China, immigration from India has continued during the postwar period though in extremely small numbers. However, there is no doubt that large-scale immigration from China and India is now a past phenomenon and is unlikely to occur again in the future.

A completely different pattern of duration of residence was displayed by persons born in Indonesia. Some 54.6 per cent of the 53,577 born in this country had stayed in Peninsular Malaysia for 21 years and more. But for the others,

---

49. R. Chander, *1970 Population Census of Malaysia, General Report*, Vol. 1 (Kuala Lumpur: Department of Statistics, 1977).

the proportion becomes larger as the period of residence becomes shorter, 3.1 per cent for 11 to less than 21 years, 4.0 per cent for 6 to less than 11 years, 10.4 per cent for 3 to less than 6 years, and 26.4 per cent to less than 3 years. Another way of looking at the figures given in Table 2.14 is that out of the total of 39,445 foreign-born persons who have been staying in the country for less than 3 years, the Indonesia-born constituted the largest group with 14,148 or 35.9 per cent. They still formed the largest group among the 18,099 with 3 to less than 6 years duration of residence. It is therefore evident that there has been an increasing inflow of persons from Indonesia in recent years, and some of them were known to be illegal immigrants.[50] A predominant proportion, 94.5 per cent of those born in Indonesia were Malays.

Another similar development refers to those born in Thailand with 42.7 per cent of the total of 17,514 having stayed in the country for less than 3 years as against the 19.9 per cent with 21 and more years of residence. Some 77.8 per cent of these Thai-born persons were Malays, the majority of them having moved into the northern part of Peninsular Malaysia in search of better economic opportunities and security from the communist insurgents operating in southern Thailand. The figures for those born in Singapore do not reveal the same extent of increased immigration in recent years, but then there was a fairly sizeable proportion of 46.4 per cent with less than 21 years of stay in Peninsular Malaysia. Moreover, 51.9 per cent of the Singapore-born population were Malays. It would appear that a new pattern of immigration in the form of predominantly Malays from the ASEAN countries moving into Peninsular Malaysia has emerged in recent years.

The large-scale influx of foreign workers in the past has assisted in the development of the tin and rubber industries by supplying the necessary labour that was so badly needed. Other classes of immigrants contributed capital and enterprise to develop these industries and economy as a whole. While the role of the immigrants in the development of the country in the past has been recognised, there is also no denying that they have created certain problems which have come to the forefront in the present-day emphasis on nation building and more equal distribution of wealth among the principal races. By and large, the problems have arisen because of the extremely low level of assimilation among the various races and the concentration of political power in the hands of the Malays and of economic wealth among the immigrant races.

---

50. See, for instance, *Singapore Monitor*, 2 May 1984.

3

Population Growth, Distribution and Structure

O ur preceding account of international migration serves to provide the necessary background information to a better understanding of the subject matter to be discussed in this chapter. The dominant role played by migration in the demographic history of the country prior to the Second World War has exerted a strong influence on the rate of population increase in those days and, more importantly, a lasting impact on the distribution and structure of the population. Indeed, the vestiges of past migration are still unmistakably reflected in the regional distribution of the population, the race composition, the religious composition, the marriage pattern, the age structure and the economic activities of the people. In a way this will make our study of population growth, distribution and structure in this chapter more interesting and rewarding, but we should also bear in mind that past migration has undoubtedly brought with it many intractable problems in relation to the political, economic and social development of the country.

Population Growth

It may be recalled that while some head counts of the inhabitants were held in the early nineteenth century in certain regions of the country, the first proper census as understood in the modern sense was conducted in 1871 in Penang and Malacca as part of the census programme implemented in the Straits Settlements. Twenty years later in 1891 the decennial census was expanded to cover the Federated Malay States of Perak, Negri Sembilan, Selangor and Pahang. The population in the remaining states of Kedah, Perlis, Kelantan, Trengganu and Johore, known collectively as the Unfederated Malay States, was only enumerated another two decades later in 1911, thus making available for the first time population statistics for the whole of the

Malay Peninsula. Even so, the quality of the statistics compiled in the three censuses administered independently in the three political entities is known to have varied from state to state.

It would appear that there is no way in which we can ascertain precisely the nature and magnitude of population growth during the period prior to 1911. All we can say is that various sources mentioned that towards the end of the seventeenth century there were about a quarter million people of primarily Malay descent living in settlements near the coastal regions and river banks, with the densely forested interior inhabited by a few thousand nomadic aborigines known as *Orang Asli*.[1] The establishment of British influence in Penang and Malacca in the late eighteenth and early nineteenth century respectively saw a continuous increase in the population and by the middle of the century the number of inhabitants was estimated to have reached half a million.[2] The second half of the nineteenth century saw a further increase in the population following the greater penetration of British influence and control in the Malay states. Since death rates were extremely high in those days, natural increase could only account for a small portion of the total population increase. Continuous streams of Chinese and Indians had settled in the western coast of region to work, in particular in the tin mines and agricultural plantations.

By the time of the 1911 censuses held in the three different political territories the population as a whole had reached 2,339,051. A decade later a country-wide census was uniformly conducted under a single superintendent of census. The results of the census indicated a population of 2,906,691 as compared with the combined total of 2,339,051 obtained in the three censuses held in 1911. This gives an increase of some 567,640 or an annual growth rate of 2.2 per cent during this first intercensal period. Quite a sizeable proportion of this increase was undoubtedly due to a net surplus of migration considering the large volume of immigration noted for these years in the previous chapter. It is not possible to separate the population increase into natural increase and net migration because the relevant birth and death statistics for the whole country are not available until the first postwar intercensal period.[3]

In 1931 a total population of 3,787,758 was enumerated and this represents an addition of 881,067 over the previous census. The annual rate of increase was somewhat higher, 2.7 per cent per annum. But this rapid rate of growth

---

1. E.H.G. Dobby, *Southeast Asia* (London: London University Press, 1956).
2. J.J. Newbold, *Political and Statistical Account of British Settlements in the Straits of Malacca* (London: John Murray, 1839).
3. As noted in the first chapter, the compulsory registration of births and deaths was put into effect in all states in 1932 and vital statistics for all these states were made available in 1934.

was not maintained in the next intercensal period as can be observed in Table
3.1 The world depression in the early thirties, the imposition of tighter immigration control just before as well as after the Second World War, and the
Japanese Occupation of the country during 1942–45 have contributed to a
slackening of the growth rate to a low of 1.6 per cent during the period 1931–
47. This all-time low was also engendered by the higher death rate and the
lower birth rate during the difficult war years when social and economic conditions deteriorated significantly throughout the country.

In the first postwar intercensal period the annual rate of population growth
recovered and reached its previous level in spite of the sharp reduction in the
volume of migration. The population rose from 4,908,086 in 1947 to 6,278,758
in 1957, giving an increase of 1,370,672 or an annual increase of 2.6 per cent.
The restoration of preventive and curative health facilities brought down the
death rate rapidly during the early postwar years, while the birth rate recovered
and even showed a gentle uptrend. In fact, natural increase has now replaced
migration as the principal factor of population growth; during the period the
number due to natural increase came to 1,624,809 and hence there was a net
migrational deficit of 254,137. By and large, the migrational deficit represents

TABLE 3.1
POPULATION GROWTH, 1911–84

Year	Population	Intercensal Increase	Annual Growth Rate (%)
1911	2,339,051	—	—
1921	2,906,691	567,640	2.2
1931	3,787,758	881,067	2.7
1947	4,908,086	1,120,328	1.6
1957	6,278,758	1,370,672	2.6
1970	8,809,557	2,530,799	2.6
1980	11,426,613	2,617,056	2.7
1984	12,643,000	1,216,387	2.6

the net movement of previous immigrants back to China and India as well as
the rural-urban drift of people from the Peninsula to the highly urbanised
state of Singapore in search of city lights and better job opportunities. It was
estimated that there was a net loss of some 141,700 persons to this island state.[4]

4. Saw Swee-Hock, *Singapore Population in Transition* (Philadelphia: University of Pennsylvania Press, 1970), p. 30.

In the third postwar census conducted in 1970 the population was enumerated as 8,809,557, an increase of 2,550,799 since 1957 or an annual growth rate of 2.6 per cent. During this 13-year period the death rate continued to fall, while the birth rate remained very high. The drift of people southwards into Singapore had abated somewhat towards the end of the period on account of the introduction of immigration control by Singapore after she separated from the Federation of Malaysia on 9 August 1966. But the race riots that flared up on 13 May 1969 in Kuala Lumpur started a fresh movement of people outwards to Singapore and, to a lesser extent, other countries. This accounts for the large net migrational deficit of 511,914 recorded during the intercensal period. Unlike the years prior to the outbreak of war in Peninsular Malaysia on December 1941, the postwar period was characterised by a net movement of people outwards to primarily Singapore, India and China and, in more recent years, other countries as well.

The latest census conducted in 1980 reveals that the population passed the ten-million mark with a figure of 11,426,613. This represents an increase of 2,617,056 over that counted ten years ago in 1970, and the annual rate of increase went up slightly to 2.7 per cent. Since the natural increase was only 2,470,536 during the intercensal period, there was a surplus in net migration amounting to some 146,520. However, it should be pointed out that the 1980 census figure has been adjusted for under-enumeration in the census.[5] The population was estimated to have reached 12,643,000 in 1984, representing an increase of 1,216,387 or an annual rate of 2.6 per cent during the postcensal period. It would appear that this is the level of growth rate that has persisted during the postwar years, quite unlike the scenario in other countries where a slackening in population increase is not uncommon. The explanation lies in the changing age structure favouring high birth rates as well as the shift in migration from a deficit to a surplus position.

A better idea of the relationship between births and deaths within the factor of natural increase as the prime determinant of population growth in recent years is provided by the data laid out in Table 3.2. It should be noted that the crude birth rate, crude death rate, crude natural increase rate, and population growth rate for the years 1971 to 1979 are based on revised intercensal population estimates. Besides, the population figures for these years as well as for

---

5. In this book we have decided to use the 1980 census figure adjusted for under-enumeration because this figure was employed by the Department of Statistics to prepare the revised intercensal estimates for 1971–79 as well as the postcensal estimates for 1981 onwards. This is to ensure that there is consistency in the time series data for these years.

TABLE 3.2

FACTORS OF POPULATION GROWTH, 1970–83

Year	Number			Crude Birth Rate	Crude Death Rate	Crude Natural Increase Rate	Annual Population Growth Rate
	Births	Deaths	Increase Natural				
1970	297,358	64,035	233,323	33.2	6.9	26.3	2.4
1971	309,378	64,304	245,074	32.8	6.8	26.0	3.0
1972	308,347	63,522	244,825	32.0	6.6	25.4	2.3
1973	302,867	65,276	237,591	30.7	6.6	24.1	2.2
1974	312,740	64,000	248,740	31.1	6.4	24.7	2.2
1975	313,741	64,360	249,381	30.5	6.2	24.3	2.3
1976	324,759	63,814	260,945	30.9	6.1	24.8	2.1
1977	322,916	66,217	256,699	30.0	6.2	23.8	2.3
1978	323,541	63,176	260,365	29.5	5.8	23.7	2.0
1979	336,848	64,345	272,503	30.0	5.7	24.3	2.2
1980	347,015	64,212	282,803	30.3	5.5	24.8	2.0
1981	362,585	61,562	301,023	30.8	5.2	25.6	2.6
1982	368,456	64,207	304,249	30.6	5.3	25.3	2.6
1983	368,438	66,032	302,406	29.8	5.3	24.5	2.5

1980 to 1983 have been adjusted for under-enumeration in the 1980 census.[6] Focusing first on the absolute figures, we can see no definite trend in the annual number of deaths since 1970, oscillating between the low of 61,562 and the high of 66,217. On the other hand, the number of births went up steadily from 297,358 in 1970 to 368,438 in 1983. The net outcome is that the number of natural increase moved upwards from the low of 233,323 in 1970 to 302,406 in 1983.

Of greater significance viewed in terms of the annual rate of population growth are the completely different trends underlined by the three rates which are expressed as per thousand mid-year population. The crude birth rate declined from 33.2 in 1970 to 32.0 in 1972 and thereafter remained within the narrow range of 29.5 and 31.1 right up to 1983. A gentle downtrend brought the crude death rate from 6.9 in 1970 to 5.3 in 1983. The combined effect on the crude rate of natural increase is that there was only a slight decline from

6. The revised intercensal estimates for 1971–79 are given in *Peninsular Malaysia: Revised Intercensal Population Estimates, 1971–1979* (Kuala Lumpur: Department of Statistics, 1985). The postcensal estimates for 1981–83 are taken from *Peninsular Malaysia: Current Population Estimates 1984* (Kuala Lumpur: Department of Statistics, 1984).

the initial rate of 26.3 in 1970 for a couple of years, and for the rest of the period the rate stayed almost stationary at about 25 per thousand population. The annual growth rate, which also takes into account net migration, has been exposed to somewhat greater fluctuations from year to year. But what is evidently clear is that in the long haul the trend has not been downwards, and has in fact moved slightly upwards in the early 1980s when the rate even reached 2.6 per cent.

We will now move on to examine the differences in the annual growth rates recorded by the three principal races as indicated in Table 3.3.[7] First of all, let us compare the growth rates between the two dominant races in the country. There is a clear-cut relationship, the Chinese experiencing a higher rate of increase than the Malays during the years prior to the Second World War, and vice versa during the postwar period. During the first three intercensal periods prior to 1947 the Chinese recorded growth rates of 2.1 per cent during 1911–21, 4.2 per cent during 1921–31 and 2.4 per cent during 1931–47. The three corresponding figures for the Malays were 1.4 per cent, 1.8 per cent and 1.7 per cent respectively. After 1947 the Chinese experienced progressively slower population growth than the Malays. During the period 1947–57 the annual growth rate of the Chinese was 2.2 per cent as compared with the 2.6 per cent of the Malays, and by the next intercensal period the two figures were 3.0 per cent and 2.1 per cent respectively. The gap widened slightly to 3.0 per cent and 2.0 per cent during 1980–84.

The growth of the Indian population has been rather erratic, particularly during the prewar period. Due mainly to migration, the Indians registered an exceptionally high growth rate of 6.2 per cent during the period 1911–21. This rapid growth was not sustained, and the rate fell sharply to 2.6 per cent during 1921–31 and even to a negative figure of 0.4 per cent during 1931–47. As noted in the previous chapter, many Indian labourers were repatriated to India during the world depression in the early 1930s, followed by the imposition of more stringent immigration controls by the government. During the Second World War the Indian population was not augmented by fresh immigrants, and instead suffered from very high death rates and the forced transfer of able-bodied men to work on the construction of the Siam-Burma railway. It was estimated that some 60,000 Indians were forcibly recruited to work there and only about a third returned after the war.[8] As the Indian community assumed a more stable and settled character during the postwar years, the

7. It should be reminded that the 1980 and 1984 figures given in this table refer to those adjusted for under-enumeration in the 1980 census.
8. J.M. Gullick, *Malaya* (London: Ernest Benn, 1963), p. 81.

TABLE 3.3
POPULATION GROWTH FOR THREE MAIN RACES, 1911–84

Year	Population	Intercensal Increase	Annual Growth Rate (%)
		Malays	
1911	1,370,000	—	—
1921	1,568,588	198,588	1.4
1931	1,863,872	295,284	1.8
1947	2,427,834	563,962	1.7
1957	3,127,472	697,640	2.6
1970	4,671,874	1,544,402	3.1
1980	6,315,572	1,643,698	3.0
1984	7,111,000	795,428	3.0
		Chinese	
1911	693,000	—	—
1921	855,863	162,863	2.1
1931	1,284,888	429,025	4.2
1947	1,884,534	599,646	2.4
1957	2,333,756	449,222	2.2
1970	3,131,320	797,564	2.3
1980	3,865,431	734,111	2.1
1984	4,172,000	306,569	2.0
		Indians	
1911	239,000	—	—
1921	439,172	200,172	6.2
1931	570,987	131,815	2.6
1947	530,638	−40,349	−0.4
1957	696,186	165,548	2.7
1970	936,341	240,155	2.3
1980	1,171,135	234,794	2.3
1984	1,280,000	108,865	2.2

annual population increase was subject to less violent fluctuations. The growth rate showed a continuous drop from 2.7 per cent during 1947–57 to 2.2 per cent during 1980–84.

The figures given in Table 3.4 provide some idea of the relative importance of natural increase and migration as factors of population growth among the three principal races. Two general features may be observed. Firstly, the postwar growth of the population among these three races began to depend largely on natural increase as migration ceased to be of any real importance. In fact, there was a deficit rather than a surplus of migration. Secondly, migration has continued to play a relatively smaller role as a factor of population growth among the Malays up to 1970, but more importantly a bigger role in recent years. This is illustrated by the figures shown in the last column of the table.

We will proceed to examine the figures laid out in Table 3.4 in greater detail. During the early postwar years 1947–57, the Malays recorded a net migrational deficit of 60,400 on account of the drift of the predominantly rural people from the Peninsula to Singapore which was still part of the wider political unit

TABLE 3.4

FACTORS OF POPULATION GROWTH FOR THREE MAIN RACES,
1947–80

Period	Population Increase	Natural Increase	Net Migration	% of Net Migration
		Malays		
1947–57	697,600	757,900	− 60,400	8.7
1957–70	1,544,400	1,618,700	− 74,300	4.8
1970–80	1,459,800	1,458,200	+ 1,600	0.1
		Chinese		
1947–57	449,200	642,500	−193,300	43.0
1957–70	797,600	1,044,400	−246,800	30.9
1970–80	519,900	775,100	−255,200	49.1
		Indians		
1947–57	165,500	207,800	− 42,300	25.6
1957–70	240,200	343,600	−103,400	43.0
1970–80	156,800	232,800	− 76,000	48.5

generally known as British Malaya. This rural-urban movement continued into the early 1960s, but was considerably reduced after Singapore separated from Malaysia in August 1965. Since then some of these Malays have returned home and some new Malay immigrants have entered the country from Singapore, Indonesia and Southern Thailand, resulting in a conspicuous migrational surplus of 185,498 during the period 1970–80.

A different growth pattern was displayed by the Chinese and the Indians. In the case of the Chinese, the migrational deficit during the years 1947–57 amounted to 193,300. Expressed in terms of the total population increase, this deficit was 43.0 per cent. The deficit rose to 246,800 during 1957–70, but expressed as a percentage of the total increase it fell to 30.9 per cent. The importance of migration was further reduced during 1970–80 when the deficit shrank to 40,989 or 5.6 per cent of the total increase. The Indians appeared to have experienced a different pattern, an increasing importance of migration from 25.6 per cent during 1947–57 to 43.0 per cent during 1957–70 but a sharply reduced role during 1970–80 with only 1.2 per cent. It is also different in the sense that for the first time there was a surplus though small that appeared during the latest intercensal period.

Population Distribution

Since our focus of attention with regard to population distribution will essentially be on the regional distribution of the people among the eleven states, we can only go as far back as the early twentieth century when the relevant statistics for all the states became available. However, historical documents revealed that in the eighteenth century the indigenous Malays lived in settlements strung along the coasts and river banks where they engaged in fishing and farming.[9] The densely forested interior and swampy coastal regions were almost devoid of inhabitants. Towards the middle of the nineteenth century the distribution of the population began to undergo some changes following the development of tin mining in Perak, Selangor and Negri Sembilan by Chinese immigrant settlers. At that time there was also considerable clustering of the population in gambier, pepper, tapioca, sugar and coffee plantations.[10] Late in the century another important event that affected population distribution was the introduction of rubber as a plantation crop with the help of cheap labour from southern India. The rubber plantations sprang up in the western foothills with well-drained terrain and near existing railway lines to

9. J. Kennedy, *A History of Malaya* (Kuala Lumpur: MacMillan, 1964).
10. James C. Jackson, *Planters and Speculators: Chinese and European Agricultural Enterprise in Malaya, 1786–1921* (Kuala Lumpur: University of Malaya Press, 1968).

transport the rubber to the ports for export. By the early twentieth century a more precise picture of population distribution surfaced as statistics from the census held in 1911 were made available.

Data showing the distribution of the population among the eleven states in 1911 and every subsequent census year are presented in Table 3.5. By and large, the population distribution in 1911 and the changes that followed in later years have been determined by the size of states, the geographical configurations, the historical background of early settlements, the extent of British colonial influence, the type of economic activities, and government policies that affect the relocation of people. The varying degree of influence exerted by these factors in different regions has resulted in an uneven spread of the population among the 11 states. It may be observed that in 1911, 21.4 per cent

TABLE 3.5

PERCENTAGE DISTRIBUTION OF POPULATION BY STATE, 1911–80

State	1911	1921	1931	1947	1957	1970	1980
Selangor	12.6	13.8	14.1	14.5	16.2	18.5	21.4
Perak	21.4	21.0	20.7	19.4	19.4	17.8	15.9
Johore	7.7	9.7	13.3	15.0	14.8	14.5	14.4
Kedah	10.5	11.5	11.3	11.3	11.2	10.5	9.9
Penang	11.1	10.1	9.0	9.1	9.1	8.8	8.2
Kelantan	12.2	10.6	9.6	9.1	8.5	7.8	7.9
Pahang	5.1	5.0	4.8	5.1	5.0	5.7	7.0
N. Sembilan	5.6	6.5	6.2	5.5	5.8	5.5	5.0
Trengganu	6.6	5.3	4.7	4.6	4.4	4.6	4.8
Malacca	5.3	5.3	4.9	4.9	4.6	4.6	4.1
Perlis	1.4	1.4	1.3	1.4	1.4	1.4	1.3
Total	100.0	100.0	100.0	100.0	100.0	100.0	100.0

of the total population lived in Perak, 12.6 per cent in Selangor, 12.2 per cent in Kelantan, 11.1 per cent in Penang and 10.5 per cent in Kedah.[11] The remaining six states took in very much less than 8 per cent each, and collectively for only 32 per cent of the total.

11. In this book the data for Selangor include the Federal Territory or Wilayah Persekutuan which was created in 1974 as a separate legal entity from the State of Selangor. From the demographic point of view there is little value in treating them separately and besides continuity with time series figures is necessary.

Over the years a gradual change in the proportionate distribution has taken place as the states recorded diverse rate of population increase. Some states experienced higher birth rates and lower death rates, some attracted more in-migrants than they lost in out-migrants and still others received a larger number of immigrant settlers from overseas. There are four states which registered a regular diminution in their individual share of the total population, Perak from 21.4 per cent to 15.9 per cent, Penang from 11.1 per cent to 8.2 per cent, Kedah from 10.5 per cent to 9.9 per cent and Malacca from 5.3 per cent to 4.1 per cent. Three other states which witnessed a reduction in their proportion — though not continuously — are Kelantan, Trengganu and Negri Sembilan. The fall in the proportion for the whole period 1911–80 was from 12.2 per cent to 7.9 per cent in Kelantan, from 6.6 per cent to 4.8 per cent in Trengganu and from 5.6 per cent to 5.0 per cent in Negri Sembilan. The only state that was not subjected to any visible change is Perlis, the smallest state, where the proportion has remained at about 1.4 per cent.

In contrast, as a result of the phenomenal rates of population increase, the two states of Selangor and Johore made striking gains, the former from 12.6 per cent of total population to 21.4 per cent and the latter from 7.7 per cent to 14.4 per cent. In Selangor the increase in the prewar days was due to the development of the tin-mining and plantation sectors of the economy, accompanied by a substantial rise in the population of Chinese and Indians. The far greater increase in the postwar years may be attributed to the accelerated development of Kuala Lumpur as the capital city, the establishment of the new industrial town of Petaling Jaya, and the rapid growth of the economy of the Klang valley as a whole that together form a predominant area of attraction for settlers of all ethnic groups from every part of the Peninsula.[12] The major change in Johore's share of the total population is seen to have happened during the prewar period when the state received considerable numbers of immigrants from Indonesia as well as from China and India.[13]

The above changes in the proportionate distribution of the population among the eleven states have obviously led to some alteration in the relative position of these states. A more convenient way of depicting the relative position of the states in Table 3.5 is to present the ranking at the various census dates in the form of a diagram as shown in Figure 3.1. It is apparent that Johore has recorded the greatest improvement, moving up quickly from sixth place in

---

12. Manjit S. Sidhu, "Migrants to Kuala Lumpur" in Manjit S. Sidhu and Gavin W. Jones (eds.), *Population Dynamics in a Plural Society: Peninsular Malaysia* (Kuala Lumpur: UMCB Publications, 1981), pp. 131–40.

13. For more details, see Tungku Shamsul Bahrin, "The Pattern of Indonesian Migration and Settlement in Malaya", *Asian Studies*, Vol. 5, Part 2, August 1967.

FIGURE 3.1
CHANGING RANK ORDER OF STATES, 1911–80

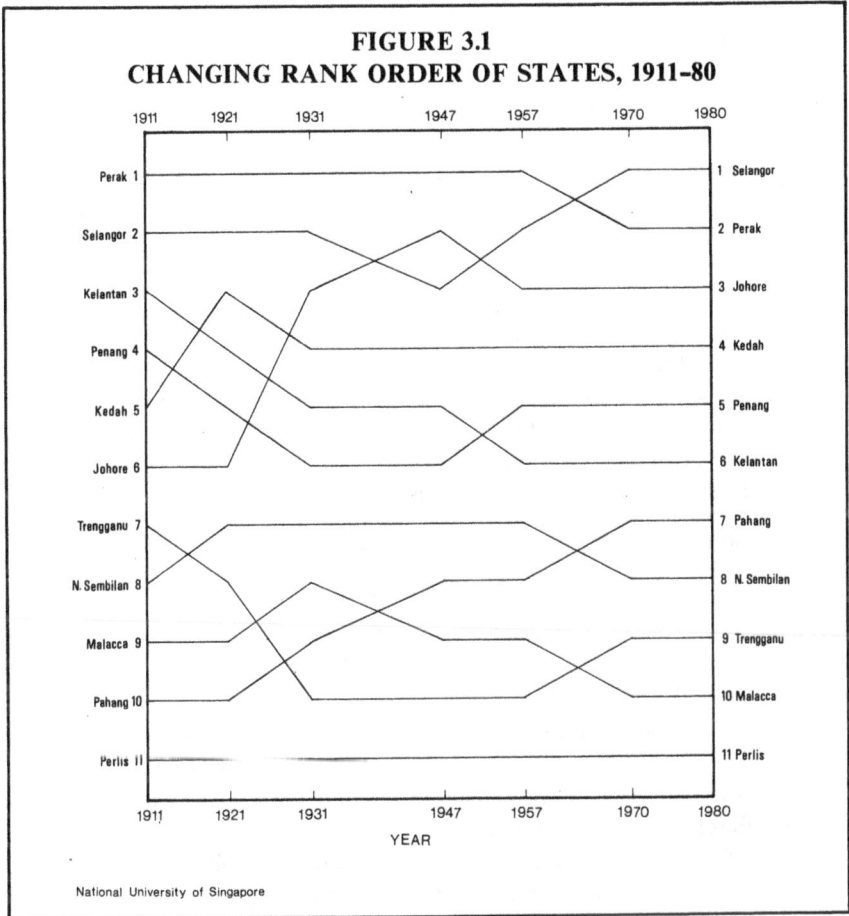

National University of Singapore

1911 to third in 1931 and then to second in 1947. After that it fell back to third place in 1957 and has maintained this position right up to 1980. Another remarkable gain was chalked up by Pahang which rose continuously from tenth place in 1911 to seventh in 1970, and remained so until 1980. Pahang has benefited greatly from land development schemes such as the Jengka Triangle and Pahang Tenggara projects which attracted considerable numbers of settlers from other states.[14] Though constituting the top state nowadays with about

---

14. For example during the period 1976–78 some 198,200 acres out of a total of 647,500 acres of land development projects were in Pahang. See Malaysia, *Mid-Term Review of the Third Malaysia Plan 1976–1980* (Kuala Lumpur: Government Press, 1979).

one-fifth of the total population, Selangor did not undergo very radical change in its ranking over the years. It started as the number two state in 1911 and until 1957 it had altered position only once in 1947 when it dropped to third spot; it attained its present top position only as recently as 1970. Kedah managed to improve its ranking by one place towards the end of the period.

Among the states that lost out in relative importance, Kelantan appears to have suffered the most, falling over the years from third position in 1911 to sixth in 1957, and stayed there until 1980. Its neighbour Trengganu slipped quickly from seventh position to tenth in 1931 and remained so until 1957, but thereafter it recovered by one step to reach ninth position. The other states which ultimately lost by one rank towards the end of the period are Perak, Penang and Malacca. Negri Sembilan, which moved up by one step during the middle of the period, slipped back to its original eighth place in recent years. The tiny northern state of Perlis has not altered its ranking at all, remaining all the time at the bottom position. A summary of the shifts in the ranking of the eleven states over the years is given below:

Alteration	1921	1931	1947	1957	1970	1980
Up	2	3	2	2	3	0
Down	3	4	2	2	3	0
Same	6	4	7	7	5	11

Taking the period as a whole, greater shifts in the ranking of the 11 states appeared to have taken place in early years and surprisingly no change was noted in the 1970s when government policies that directly affected the relocation of the inhabitants were introduced.

Each of the 11 states has never been populated in proportion to the size of its land area because land size is only one of the many factors that eventually determine the regional distribution of the population. This aspect of regional distribution is examined in Table 3.6 which shows the total land area and population density for the 11 states.[15] Pahang stands out as the most typical example of the nil relationship between the size of land area and population as it has the largest land area of 35,964 square kilometres but the smallest population density. Another good example is Penang which has the second smallest land area of only 1,033 square kilometres but the highest density at all times. In fact, the data seem to point to an inverse relationship

---

15. For a detailed account of population distribution, see Chapter 6: "The Pattern of Population Distribution" in Ooi Jin-Bee, *Peninsular Malaysia* (London: Longman, 1976), pp. 133–74.

TABLE 3.6
LAND AREA AND POPULATION DENSITY FOR ELEVEN STATES, 1947–80

State	Area in Square Kilometres	Number of Persons per Sq. Kilometre			
		1947	1957	1970	1980
Penang	1,033	432	554	751	872
Selangor	7,956	89	127	199	485
Malacca	1,650	145	176	245	271
Perlis	795	88	114	152	182
Kedah	9,425	59	74	101	114
Perak	21,005	45	58	75	83
N. Sembilan	6,643	40	40	72	83
Johore	18,984	39	49	67	83
Kelantan	14,931	30	34	46	57
Trengganu	12,955	17	21	31	40
Pahang	35,964	7	9	14	21
Peninsular Malaysia	131,585	37	48	67	83

between land area and population, with the smallest states having higher densities than the bigger states.

Since the land size has been held constant in the computation of the population densities for the latest four censuses, the changes in population densities experienced by the states would be purely a reflection of the rate of population increase. For instance, the increase in population density in every state during the intercensal periods was engendered by continuous population growth in these years. The most remarkable increase in population density occurred in Selangor which saw its density rising five times from only 89 persons per square kilometre in 1947 to 485 persons in 1980. Pahang's density rose by about threefold, and Trengganu's by about two-and-a-half times. In general, a doubling of the density was recorded in the other states.

The ranking of the states according to population density has however not altered at all between 1947 and 1970, and a minor change involving only two states was noticeable in 1980. Selangor has now moved up from third to second position at the expense of Malacca which is now the third instead of the second most dense state. Such comparisons based on total land area do not quite reflect over-population or under-population since areas of land not fit for human habitation are included in the computation. There are large tracts of hilly tropical jungles in the central mountain ranges and considerable mangrove swamps along certain coastal regions that are not habitable.

A glance again at the figures given in Table 3.6 seems to convey a general picture of high density states situated on the west coast of the Peninsula and low density states on the eastern region. Briefly, the population is distributed on both sides of the north-south mountain ranges, with the principal densely populated belt stretching from Perlis in the north to Johore Bahru in the south and the minor belt from Kota Bahru to Dungan along the northeast coast.[16] The factors favouring the settlement of the west coast are the deepwater harbours sheltered from the southwest monsoon by Sumatra and from the northeast monsoon by the central mountain ranges, the richer alluvial soils deposited by the numerous swift-flowing eastwest rivers, the existence of rich tin-deposits, and the superior systems of roads, railways and river communications. The western seaports have served as the main channels of foreign trade and immigration. Since the early nineteenth century the development of the country has proceeded at a faster pace along the west coast where tin-mines and agricultural estates were established with the influx of foreign capital and immigrant labour.

Indeed, all the immigrants landed on the key western seaports and spread along the western coastal plains into the tin-mines, agricultural estates and urban centres.[17] Very few pushed further eastward. Data from the 1911 censuses reveal that nearly 32 per cent of the total foreign-born persons settled in Perak, 25 per cent in Selangor, 13 per cent in Penang and 10 per cent in Johore. This means that in those days some 80 per cent of the immigrant community lived in these four western states. This concentration has persisted practically unchanged despite the inter-state movement that must have taken place among these immigrants: their combined proportion in these states approached 75 per cent in 1980. The eastern states of Kelantan and Trengganu and the northern state of Perlis were consistently avoided by the immigrant settlers so that the proportion of foreign-born has always remained less than 1.5 per cent.

For a better understanding of the present position we should turn to the figures for the three main races laid out in Table 3.7. The foreign-born Chinese

---

16. E.H.G. Dobby, "Settlement Patterns in Malaya", *The Geographical Review*, Vol. 32, No. 2, April 1942.

17. T.E. Smith, "Immigration and Permanent Settlement of Chinese and Indians in Malaya and the Future Growth of the Malay and Chinese Communities" in C.D. Cowan (ed.), *The Economic Development of South East Asia* (London: Allen and Unwin, 1964), pp. 174–85.

TABLE 3.7
PERCENTAGE DISTRIBUTION OF POPULATION BY STATE
FOR THREE MAIN RACES, 1980

State	Malays		Chinese		Indians	
	Total	Foreign-Born	Total	Foreign-Born	Total	Foreign-Born
Selangor	15.5	31.3	27.4	25.4	34.4	35.2
Perak	12.9	6.4	19.4	18.6	22.1	19.2
Johore	14.3	25.2	16.4	19.8	9.4	11.4
Penang	4.9	3.2	13.3	11.4	9.4	9.0
Kedah	12.7	2.9	5.5	4.7	7.4	7.0
N. Sembilan	4.2	3.8	5.4	6.3	8.5	8.2
Pahang	8.5	6.8	5.4	6.5	4.7	4.7
Malacca	3.9	5.9	4.6	4.6	3.0	3.2
Kelantan	13.0	10.2	1.2	1.1	0.6	1.1
Trengganu	8.1	2.2	0.7	1.0	0.2	0.5
Perlis	1.9	2.1	0.6	0.6	0.3	0.3
Total	100.0	100.0	100.0	100.0	100.0	100.0

and Indians are still crowded together in Selangor, Perak, Johore and Penang, which collectively accounted for about three-fourths of foreign-born population of each of these two races in 1980. What is more interesting is that the distribution of the foreign-born Malays was equally lop-sided: 31.1 per cent in Selangor, with 25.2 per cent in Johore, and 10.2 per cent in Kelantan, leaving the other states with a share of less than 7 per cent each. This conforms more to the settlement pattern of the immigrant Chinese and Indians than to that of the indigenous Malays with whom the new Malay arrivals have close ethnic and religious affinities. As immigrants they were primarily attracted by the greater employment and business opportunities in the much more modernised and rapidly developing economies of the western states.

Some important variations in the distribution of the total population of each of the three main races are underlined by the figures shown in Table 3.7. By and large, the dispersion of the Malays over the 11 states was much greater than that of the two immigrant races. The Malays have a fair proportion of their people staying in five states: 15.5 per cent in Selangor, 14.3 per cent in Johore, 13.0 per cent in Kelantan, 12.9 per cent in Perak and 12.7 per cent in Kedah. Even in the other states the proportion was by no means insignificant. The position of the Chinese was somewhat different with 27.4 per cent centred in Selangor, 19.4 per cent in Perak, 16.4 per cent in Johore and 13.3 per cent in Penang. In the other seven states the Chinese population hardly approached more than 5.5 per cent each. A still more lopsided population distribution was exhibited by the Indians who have as many as 34.4 per cent crowded in Selangor and 22.1 per cent in Perak.[18] In some ways the diverse patterns of distribution of these races reflect their economic specialisation in relation to the differences in the economic activities among the 11 states. For one thing, most of the Malays are engaged in padi-farming in areas known as Malay Reserves protected by the Land Enactment of 1913 which prohibits the sale of land in these areas to non-Malays.[19]

Race Composition

In studying the population structure of the Peninsula population, one must examine first the race composition which has a profound influence on almost every aspect of the country's demographics. In analysing the race composition we have followed the traditional practice of grouping the races in four major components, viz. Malays, Chinese, Indians and Others. The definition of Chinese has been somewhat clear-cut, referring to people of Chinese descent regardless of their country of citizenship or birth. The term "Indians" has not been uniformly defined in the past, but now it is used to refer to all persons from the Indian subcontinent such as Indians, Pakistanis, Bangladeshis and Sri Lankans. The term 'Malays' is used to include the indigenous Malays in the Peninsula as well as those Malay immigrants who come from Sabah, Sarawak, Singapore, Indonesia and other countries.

The changes in the race composition according to the four-fold classification are depicted in Table 3.8. Out of the total population of 2,339,051 enumerated in 1911, some 58.9 per cent were Malays, 29.6 per cent Chinese, 10.2 per cent Indians and 1.6 per cent other races. The proportion of Malays fell continuously to 54.0 per cent in 1921 and 49.2 per cent in 1931, and thereafter stayed at slightly below the 50 per cent level right up to 1957. This diminishing Malay proportion was due to immigration of other races, particularly Chinese and Indians. As immigration became negligible, during the postwar years, the Malay proportion started rising to reach 56.2 per cent in 1984.

It is not surprising that the proportion of each of the two major immigrant races moved in the opposite direction during the same period. The proportion

---

18. A detailed analysis is given in Kernial Singh Sandhu, *Indians in Malaya: Immigration and Settlement, 1756–1957* (London: Cambridge University Press, 1969).
19. K.G. Tregonning, *A History of Modern Malaya* (London: University of London Press, 1964).

TABLE 3.8
PERCENTAGE DISTRIBUTION OF POPULATION BY RACE,
1911–84

Year	Malays	Chinese	Indians	Others	Total
1911	58.6	29.6	10.2	1.6	100.0
1921	54.0	29.4	15.1	1.5	100.0
1931	49.2	33.9	15.1	1.8	100.0
1947	49.5	38.4	10.8	1.3	100.0
1957	49.8	37.2	11.1	1.9	100.0
1970	53.1	35.5	10.6	0.8	100.0
1980	56.0	33.4	10.0	0.6	100.0
1984	56.2	33.0	10.1	0.7	100.0

of Chinese rose from 29.6 per cent in 1911 to 36.4 per cent in 1947, and after that took a continuous downturn all the way till it dropped to 33.4 per cent in 1984. The reduction in the Chinese proportion may be attributed to the net migrational deficit in the early period and to the relatively more rapid decline in fertility in recent years. The Indian population rose quickly from 10.2 per cent in 1911 to 15.1 per cent in 1921, and thereafter remained at the latter level. By 1947 the proportion had dropped to 10.8 per cent, and remained at around 10–11 per cent until recently. A special reason for the declining proportion applicable to the Indian only is that some of them returned to their country of origin in the Indian sub-continent. On the other hand, the Chinese found it almost impossible to return to China since October 1949 when the communist People's Republic of China was established.

In order to achieve a better understanding of the various demographic features that are examined in our study according to geographic region, we will compare the race composition among the 11 states as shown in Table 3.9. The race composition of the various states that emerged in the 1980 Census has been determined by the extent of British colonial influence in the past as well as the level of economic development with particular reference to commerce and trade, tin-mining and agricultural plantations.[20] Generally speaking, the proportion of Chinese or Indians tends to be higher in states where British

20. See, for example, W.D. McTaggart, "The Distribution of Ethnic Groups in Malaya, 1947–1957", *Journal of Tropical Geography*, Vol. 26, June 1968.

TABLE 3.9
PERCENTAGE DISTRIBUTION OF POPULATION BY RACE IN
EACH STATE, 31 DECEMBER 1983

State	Malays	Chinese	Indians	Others	Total
Johore	55.5	37.8	6.6	0.2	100.0
Kedah	72.4	18.3	7.7	1.6	100.0
Kelantan	93.2	5.1	0.7	0.9	100.0
Malacca	54.5	37.3	7.6	0.7	100.0
N. Sembilan	46.8	36.0	17.0	0.3	100.0
Pahang	67.5	25.4	6.9	0.2	100.0
Penang	33.3	54.0	11.5	1.2	100.0
Perak	45.5	40.1	14.1	0.2	100.0
Perlis	78.6	15.8	2.8	2.8	100.0
Selangor	40.7	42.4	16.2	0.7	100.0
Trengganu	94.6	4.7	0.5	0.2	100.0

influence had been the greatest and where these economic activities are heavily concentrated. It can be observed that there are proportionately less Chinese and Indians in the former Unfederated Malay States of Perlis, Kedah, Kelantan, Trengganu and Pahang where padi cultivation is the dominant economic activity.

The state with the highest proportion of Malays at the end of 1983 is Trengganu which has 94.6 per cent Malays and only 4.7 per cent Chinese and 0.5 per cent Indians. In the neighbouring state of Kelantan the position is no different with 93.2 per cent Malays, 5.1 per cent Chinese and 0.7 per cent Indians. The most northern state of Perlis has 78.6 per cent Malays, 15.8 per cent Chinese and 2.8 per cent Indians. Its southern neighbour Kedah has basically the same racial mix, the three corresponding proportions standing at 72.4 per cent, 18.3 per cent and 7.7 per cent. In sharp contrast, there is the different type of racial mix in Penang where a predominantly commercial economy evolved on the basis of its past free port status. Here there are only 33.3 per cent Malays as against the 54.0 per cent Chinese and 11.5 per cent Indians. The only other state with a higher proportion of Chinese than Malays is Selangor where the two respective proportions are 40.7 per cent and 42.4 per cent. The other states where the Chinese and the Indians are fairly well represented are Perak, Negri Sembilan, Malacca and Johore.

In recent years considerable attention has been focused on the race composition of the population not only in the country as a whole but also in the urban centres where the immigrant races have traditionally congregated.[21] One of the strategies adopted under the New Economic Policy is aimed at encouraging the Malays to move to the urban areas to benefit from the better and wider range of employment opportunities and the higher standard of living. It is therefore instructive to examine the changes in the race composition of the urban population as revealed by the census data shown in Table 3.10. These data are based on the traditional census definition of urban population enumerated in towns with 10,000 or more inhabitants.

In 1947 the Malays constituted only 19.0 per cent of the urban population though they were the dominant community with about 50 per cent of the total population in the whole country. Since then their share of the urban population has risen slowly in the early years but has gathered momentum in more recent years. Their proportion was raised to 21.0 per cent in 1957, 27.6 per cent in 1970, and then substantially to 37.9 per cent in 1980. The greater changes that took place during the latest intercensal period coincided with the introduction of the New Economic Policy in 1970. As to be expected, the

TABLE 3.10

PERCENTAGE DISTRIBUTION OF URBAN POPULATION BY RACE,
1947–80

Race	1947	1957	1970	1980
Malays	19.0	21.0	27.6	37.9
Chinese	63.1	62.6	58.5	50.3
Indians	14.7	12.8	12.8	11.0
Others	3.2	3.6	1.1	0.7
Total	100.0	100.0	100.0	100.0
	929,928	1,666,969	2,530,433	4,073,105

Chinese share of the urban population was reduced over the years, falling from 63.1 per cent in 1947 to 50.3 per cent in 1980. The Indians too saw their share of the urban population sliced from 14.9 per cent to 11.0 per cent during

---

21. See, for example, Malaysia, *Second Malaysia Plan 1971–1975* (Kuala Lumpur: Government Press, 1971) and Malaysia, *Mid-Term Review of the Second Malaysia Plan 1971–1975* (Kuala Lumpur: Government Press, 1973).

the same period. In spite of these major changes, the Chinese have continued to maintain their dominant place in the urban areas, but the Malays have caught up rather quickly in recent years so that the difference between these two races is no longer that striking.

The immigrant races have contributed to the development of the tin-mining industry and agricultural plantations by supplying the labour that was so badly needed in the early days. Other classes of immigrants have contributed capital and enterprise to build up these industries and the economy of the country in general. Whilst the role of the immigrant races in the development of the country in the past has been recognised, there is no denying that their presence has created certain problems which have come to the forefront during the post-independence period when great emphasis is being placed on nation-building. By and large, the problems emanating in the political, social and economic spheres have persisted because of the extremely low level of assimilation among the various races in the past. Each ethnic group has a strong tendency to hold on to its own religion, language and culture, its own special economic activities, and its own traditions and customs. It may be recalled that the government introduced the New Economic Policy in the Second Malaysia Plan 1971–75 as a means of working towards national unity.

Sex Composition

In a closed population unaffected by migration, the sex composition is determined by the proportion of boys and girls at birth, but this is counter-balanced by the males being subject to higher mortality so that the eventual sex ratio of the general population is very near normal with fairly even numbers of each sex. However, in a country where migration of predominantly males has been a major force of population growth, one can expect the sex ratio to deviate from the normal pattern. This is true in the case of Peninsular Malaysia in the early twentieth century. In the course of time a slow movement towards a more balanced sex ratio occurred first as the proportion of female immigrants increased, then as the volume of natural increase became larger, and latterly as the flow of migration diminished.

In Table 3.11 is depicted the sex composition of the population examined in terms of the sex ratio defined as the number of males per thousand females. It may be observed that the sex ratio of the general population in 1911 was quite abnormal with 1,689 males per thousand females, caused by the immigration of more males than females. In those days, most of the male immigrants had no intention of settling down in the country, and they therefore left their families behind in their own country. This tendency persisted for many decades and the sex ratio was able to improve to a very limited extent only in the prewar

TABLE 3.11
SEX-RATIO BY RACE, 1911–84
(Males Per Thousand Females)

Year	Total	Malays	Chinese	Indians
1911	1,689	*	4,651	3,125
1921	1,543	1,042	2,819	2,358
1931	1,424	1,028	2,059	1,938
1947	1,122	990	1,228	1,456
1957	1,065	987	1,080	1,340
1970	1,010	985	1,013	1,134
1980	999	985	1,005	1,056
1984	1,007	996	1,012	1,048

Note: * Not Available.

days. It was lowered to 1,543 in 1921 and 1,424 in 1931. The promotion of more female immigrants to rectify the sex imbalance in the 1930s and the emergence of natural increase as the dominant factor of population growth in the 1940s led to a significant improvement in the sex ratio which stood at 1,122 in 1947. After that the normalisation of the sex ratio continued though at a slower pace, being lowered to 1,065 in 1957, 1,010 in 1970 and to the almost even position of 999 in 1980. Since then it has become slightly uneven again, reaching 1,007 in 1984. The fairly even sex composition that prevails nowadays may be taken as a sign that the population is now a comparatively settled one and no longer subjected to violent fluctuations in migration.

The figures in Table 3.11 also reveal some interesting differences in the sex composition of the three main races. The sex ratio of the Malays differs from those of the Chinese and the Indians in two respects. In the first place, the Malays, though including some immigrant elements, have constituted a predominantly settled community and have exhibited a near balanced sex ratio at all times. Even in 1921 the Malay ratio was already quite normal at 1,042. Another special characteristic of the sex composition of the Malays refers to the slight excess of females during the whole postwar period. The movement towards a more even ratio from 985 in 1980 to 996 in 1984 was most probably due to the return of male workers from Singapore where the government has made a serious attempt to reduce the number of guest workers.[22]

22. See, for example, "Target: Wholly Singapore Workforce" in The Straits Times, 1 January 1982.

As was noted in the previous chapter, a striking feature of Chinese immigration in prewar days is that for a long time the immigrants did not bring their womenfolk with them. There was a number of contributing causes: being only temporary sojourners the Chinese immigrants preferred to leave their wives and children in China; the majority of them could not afford to bring their families with them; the Chinese government took precautions to discourage women from going overseas in order to maintain a strong hold over overseas Chinese and to ensure remittances from them. As the ban on female emigration was lifted in China, as female immigration was positively encouraged by the British colonial government, and as natural increase became larger, the Chinese sex ratio was propelled towards a more normal position. From an extremely uneven ratio of 4,651 in 1911, the position improved progressively to 2,819 in 1921 and 2,058 in 1931. Though further progress was made in the early postwar years when the ratio was lowered to 1,228 in 1947, 1,080 in 1957 and 1,013 in 1970, it was not until 1980 that the ratio approached the normal position of 1,005. For the same reason advanced to explain the position of the Malays, the Chinese ratio retrogressed in recent years and moved to 1,012 in 1984.

As in the case of the Chinese, the practice within the Indian community has been for the men of working age to migrate into Peninsular Malaysia in search of employment and trade, leaving behind their wives and children in the sub-continent. One important difference is that this practice among the Indians persisted for a longer period of time because they have a lesser tendency to settle for good in the country consequent on the feasibility of returning to their country of origin. The Chinese, on the other hand, have been prevented from returning to China since 1949. By comparison, the normalisation of the Indian sex ratio has therefore proceeded at a much slower pace, having lowered from 3,125 in 1911 to 1,938 in 1931. During the postwar period the Indian ratio has remained the most uneven, improving from 1,450 in 1947 to only 1,048 in 1984.

Another important aspect of the study of the sex composition concerns the changes that have occurred in broad age groups as shown in Table 3.12.[23] Even as early as 1921 the sex ratio in the 0–4 age groups was quite normal and remained so in all subsequent censuses. In this age group the sex ratio at birth and the differential child mortality between the sexes are the two factors that determine the ratio. There are always more male than female babies born — about 1,060 boys to every 1,000 girls — but this is subsequently counterbalanced by a heavier mortality among males than females in this age group.

---

23. The 1984 figures in Tables 3.9, 3.10 and 3.11 are based on the estimates prepared by the Department of Statistics. See *Peninsular Malaysia: Current Population Estimate, 1984,* op. cit.

TABLE 3.12
SEX-RATIO BY BROAD AGE GROUP, 1921–84
(Males Per Thousand Females)

Age Group	1921	1931	1947	1957	1970	1980	1984
0– 4	1,021	1,014	1,034	1,025	1,040	1,051	1,056
5–14	1,083	1,082	1,054	1,053	1,034	1,039	1,045
15–29	1,504	1,455	988	985	973	948	984
30–59	2,108*	2,002*	1,343	1,144	990	1,001	1,001
60 & Over	1,514*	1,399*	1,201	1,252	1,078	963	901

Note: * For age groups 30–54 and 55 & Over.

In 1921 the sex ratio stood at 1,021, and in the postwar period it generally moved upwards to reach 1,056 in 1984. The long-term uptrend may be attributed to the narrowing in the gap between the higher male mortality and the lower female mortality that followed the decline in child mortality during those years.

In the 5–14 age group the sex ratio was less normal than that in the first age group in 1921 with a figure of 1,083. In spite of the exposure of the boys to heavier mortality since birth, the sex ratio was still higher than that at birth, which suggests that there were more boys than girls immigrating into the country in those days. Over the years the ratio improved and by 1970 it reached 1,034, which was more normal than the 1,040 registered in the first age group. More interesting changes in the sex ratio have taken place in the 15–29 age group. There was clearly a substantial excess of males over females in the prewar days, the ratio lingering at 1,504 in 1921 and 1,455 in 1931. But by 1947 the position had completely reversed as the ratio dropped to 988; this diminution of males became progressively more pronounced in the postwar years until it reached the low of 948 in 1980. The explanation lies in the movement of predominantly young male workers to Singapore to seek permanent jobs as potential immigrants or temporary work as guest workers and the larger number of males leaving the country to study in overseas educational institutions. The rise to 984 in 1984 could be due to the return of Malaysian male workers from Singapore in recent years.[24]

In the older 30–50 age group in the prewar days, the sex ratio was in fact most unbalanced with 2,108 in 1921 and 2,002 in 1931, which reflects the

24. *The Straits Times*, 22 June 1983 and 23 February 1984.

large extent to which migration affected the composition of the population in those days. The ratio in the 30–59 age group improved during the postwar period but not to the extent of having more females than males. In the oldest age group, there was still an excess of males in 1921, and this persisted for the next 50 years as the impact of past migration of predominantly males continued to be felt. It was only in 1980 that there were more females in this age group with a ratio of 963, a reflection of the settled character of the population.

Age Structure

In studying the population structure of a country, it is vitally important to examine the age distribution in view of its significant influence on the amount of labour available, the supply of marriageable partners, the level of annual births and deaths, and the extent and type of dependency burden. The age distribution is determined mainly by fertility and to a lesser extent by mortality in a closed population.[25] In such a case the age structure resembles the shape of a pyramid, with the largest number at the youngest age group at the base and tapering off upwards with the advance of old age. If the population is not a closed one, this usual pattern of age distribution will be distorted by migration, the extent of which will depend on the size and type of migrational flow.

The evolution of the age structure over the years 1921–80 is examined in Table 3.13 in terms of five broad age groups. It should be pointed out that similar figures for 1911 are not available, and the age grouping for the last two oldest age groups in 1921 and 1931 is different from that in subsequent censuses. Two general features stand out clearly. First, as a result of the rapid overall population growth the number in every age group recorded an increase in these census years. Second, the population structure experienced a gradual but continuous shift from a predominantly middle-age structure to a relatively young one as evidenced by the changes in the proportionate distribution among the various age groups.

The substantial rise in the proportion of population in the youngest age group 0–4 from 10.7 per cent in 1921 to 17.8 per cent in 1957 is due to the rising crude birth rate, the relatively faster decline in mortality at these infant years, and the lesser under-enumeration of the Chinese in this age group in 1957 resulting from the introduction of the animal-year system of collecting

---

25. United Nations, *The Aging of Populations and Its Economic and Social Implications* (New York: Department of International and Social Affairs, 1956).

TABLE 3.13
POPULATION BY BROAD AGE GROUP, 1921–84

Age Group	1921	1931	1947	1957	1970	1980	1984
	Number ('000)						
0– 4	308.6	450.3	632.1	1,118.3	1,370.4	1,459.8	1,718
5–14	536.5	758.3	1,313.5	1,633.9	2,555.7	2,812.7	3,020
15–29	838.8	1,083.6	1,176.6	1,573.6	2,271.2	3,188.7	3,752
30–59	1,033.6*	1,289.3*	1,508.8	1,663.6	2,137.6	2,843.5	3,409
60 & Over	161.8*	180.6*	247.5	289.8	474.6	640.2	747
Total	2,874.3	3,762.1	4,878.5	6,279.2	8,809.5	10,944.9	12,646
	Percentage						
0– 4	10.7	12.0	13.0	17.8	15.5	13.3	13.6
5–14	18.7	20.1	26.9	26.0	29.0	25.7	23.9
15–29	29.0	28.8	24.1	25.1	25.8	29.1	29.7
30–59	36.0*	34.3*	30.9	26.5	24.3	26.0	26.9
60 & Over	5.5*	4.8*	5.1	4.6	5.4	5.9	5.9
Total	100.0	100.0	100.0	100.0	100.0	100.0	100.0

Note: * For age groups 30-54 and 55 & Over.

Chinese age statistics.[26] Thereafter, the trend was reversed and the proportion dropped to 13.6 per cent in 1984 consequent on the fall in the birth rate from the early 1960s. For essentially the same reasons, the proportion in the schooling age group 5.14 was raised from 18.7 per cent in 1921 to 29.0 per cent in 1970, and following that reduced to 23.9 per cent in 1984. The more prolonged upward movement in this proportion may be attributed to the longer time required for the rising trend in births to take effect in the older age group.

We may regard the third age group 15–29 as constituting the important and active segment of the population viewed in terms of fertility and employment and the 30–59 group as the more mature adults of working age and also past

26. A comprehensive account of this system is given in Saw Swee-Hock, "Errors in Chinese Age Statistics", *Demography*, Vol. IV, No. 2, 1967.

the prime of their reproductive life. The steady reduction in the proportion in the 15–29 age group up to the early postwar years in 1947 was brought about by the growing proportionate importance at the young age groups as well as the diminution of immigration to a negligible level. The sustained rise from 24.1 per cent in 1947 to 29.7 per cent in 1984 was engendered by the high birth rates in the early postwar years. Since the prewar figures for the older age group are for 30–54 rather than 30–59, we can safely conclude that there was also a continuous reduction in the proportion in the 30–59 age group right up to 1970 when it stood at 24.3 per cent. The diminishing importance of migration was undoubtedly the principal cause of this reduction. No significant trend is discernible in the oldest age group 60 and over; the proportion seems to have fluctuated between 4 to 6 per cent. It is perhaps worth mentioning that the enumerated population at these old ages may be affected by the tendency of the old people to overstate their age.[27]

The evaluation of the population's age structure over a long period of time can best be examined in terms of the age pyramid which presents the age statistics in a diagrammatic form. In Figure 3.2 are presented the age pyramids for the four postwar censuses; similar pyramids for the prewar days are not drawn because of the absence of the prerequisite statistics.[28] The age pyramid has evolved from a somewhat irregular one in 1947 to a fairly smooth and normal one in 1980 with the numbers in the different age groups decreasing regularly from the first year of life upwards. The depression of the 1947 age pyramid at ages 0–4 in both the male and female sections was caused by the low birth rate and the high infant mortality prevailing during the Japanese Occupation. Another noteworthy feature of this early age pyramid was the slight bulge at the 40s and early 50s in the male section, which was due to the prewar immigration of more males than females at the working ages. These two features seemed to have disappeared in the 1957 age pyramid which has an extremely broad base on account of the rapid increase in births after the early postwar years. As the rapid increase in births levelled off, the age pyramid evolved into a lesser broad base pyramid in 1970. By 1980 the age pyramid was quite smooth and regular, a reflection of the settled character of the population with natural increase as the prime determinant of population growth. It should be pointed out that the computed percentages of the total

---

27. See "Appendix: A Method of Testing and Correcting Age Overstatement at Old Age Based on Stable Population Theory" in Saw Swee-Hock, ibid., pp. 872–75.

28. The age statistics published in the prewar census reports are given in quinary age groups up to 55 and over; but for the purpose of constructing age pyramids, it is necessary to have the age statistics up to much older age groups.

FIGURE 3.2
AGE PYRAMIDS, 1947–80

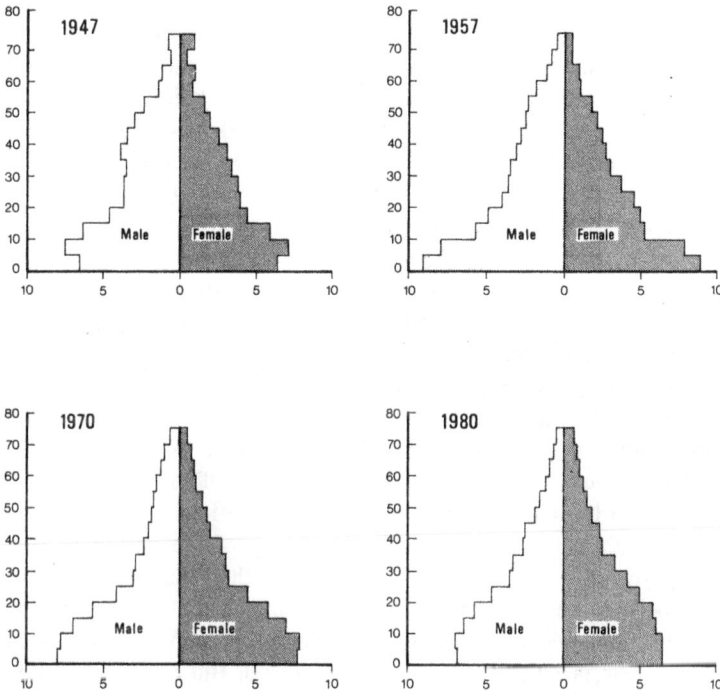

National University of Singapore

population in the quinary age groups were employed to construct the age pyramids, and hence provides a better comparison of the four pyramids.

The data in Table 3.13 have been presented in such an age grouping that they can be utilised to evaluate the dependency burden of the population. The number of persons in the age group 15 to 59 may be taken to represent the working population, while those in the age group 0–14 the young dependents and those aged 60 and over the old dependents. This provides only an approximate measure of the relationship between those persons who bear the responsibility of support in society and those who depend on them for their upbringing, education and old age support. It is of course merely an age-based classification and is not directly related to whether the persons are actually in school, at work or in retirement.

Bearing in mind the above limitation, we see that in 1947 some 55.0 per cent of the population were entrusted with the responsibility of supporting the other 45.0 per cent, broken down into 39.9 per cent young dependents and 5.1 per cent old dependents. The total proportion of dependents was raised to 48.4 per cent in 1957 and 49.9 per cent in 1970, after which it dropped back to 43.3 per cent towards the end of the period in 1984. With the old dependents remaining somewhat stationary between 5 and 6 per cent, it was the young dependency burden that has been changing. The population of young dependents was raised from 39.9 per cent in 1947 to the peak of 44.5 per cent in 1970, after which it was lowered to 37.5 per cent in 1984 as the recent decline in fertility commenced to take effect. The figures seem to suggest that in the prewar years a much smaller proportion of dependents — about 35 per cent — was taken care of by the working-age persons. However, this does not necessarily imply that the dependency problem was lighter in those days owing to the common practice among the immigrant workers of contributing towards the upkeep of their families left behind in China or India.

The changes in the age structure of each of the three major races are analysed in Table 3.14 for the same five age groups. In the 0–4 age group, the Malay proportion remained stable at about 14 per cent from 1921 right up to 1947, after which it jumped to 18.7 per cent in 1957 and then fell to 15.2 per cent in 1984. In contrast, both the Chinese and the Indian proportions in this youngest age group rose by about twofold from the beginning of the period to the peak level of slightly above 17 per cent in 1957 and then decreased towards the end of the period. The extremely low proportions in the prewar days may be attributed to the children of these two immigrant communities being left behind with their families in their home countries. But the lower proportion in the case of the Chinese is also attributable to the Chinese method of reckoning ages which invariably leads to a deficient number in the 0–4 age group.[29]

The practice of leaving their children also affected the proportion in the 5–14 age group for the two immigrant races, with about 13 per cent in 1921 as compared with the 24 per cent for the Malays. Over the years every race experienced a rise in the proportion up to 1947, though at a much faster pace in the case of the Chinese and the Indians. The minor drop in the proportion for every race in 1957 was caused by the smaller cohort aged 12 to 14 born during the Japanese Occupation when fertility was low and child mortality was exceptionally high. By 1970 the proportion for every race had risen again to even higher levels, but there has been a decline in recent years.

The movement in the proportion in the young working age group 15–29

---

29. According to the Chinese method of reckoning age, a person is one year old at birth and another year older on the occasion of the Chinese New Year, hence resulting in the transfer of some persons aged 3 or 4 to the next age group 5–9. For more information see Saw Swee-Hock, op. cit.

TABLE 3.14
PERCENTAGE DISTRIBUTION OF POPULATION BY
BROAD AGE GROUP FOR THREE MAIN RACES, 1921–84

Age Group	1921	1931	1947	1957	1970	1980	1984
Malays							
0– 4	14.0	14.6	14.2	18.7	16.5	14.4	15.2
5–14	23.6	24.7	27.2	25.7	29.4	26.3	24.5
15–29	26.3	26.1	25.6	25.6	25.1	29.1	29.5
30–59	29.2*	28.8*	27.3	23.5	24.0	25.0	25.4
60 & Over	6.9*	5.8*	5.7	6.5	5.0	5.2	5.4
Total	100.0	100.0	100.0	100.0	100.0	100.0	100.0
Chinese							
0– 4	16.2	8.9	12.0	16.7	14.5	11.9	11.0
5–14	12.9	16.2	27.7	27.5	28.3	25.0	23.1
15–29	26.4*	28.7	21.9	24.3	26.9	28.4	29.5
30–59	49.1*	41.3*	32.4	22.7	23.7	27.6	29.5
60 & Over	5.3*	4.9*	5.0	8.8	6.6	7.1	6.9
Total	100.0	100.0	100.0	100.0	100.0	100.0	100.0
Indians							
0– 4	8.3	10.6	11.5	18.7	14.8	12.7	12.9
5–14	12.7	15.1	23.9	23.7	30.2	24.7	23.2
15–29	43.6	37.3	25.8	23.7	25.2	31.9	31.8
30–59	33.6*	35.6*	38.8	28.8	25.6	25.5	26.8
60 & Over	1.8*	1.4*	1.8	5.1	4.2	5.2	5.4
Total	100.0	100.0	100.0	100.0	100.0	100.0	100.0

Note: * For age groups 30–54 and 55 & Over.

varies in nature among the three races. The Malay proportion remained quite
stable at about 26 per cent right up to 1970, and only increased in recent years
to touch 29.5 per cent in 1984. The Indian proportion commenced at a high
level of 43.6 per cent in 1921, and was reduced all the way up to 23.7 per cent
in 1957 and then took an upturn again. The Chinese showed a less clear-cut
movement, going up and down during the early part of the period and rising
regularly in recent years.

In the older working age group 30–59 the Malay proportion followed a
downtrend from 1921 to 1957 and an uptrend up to 1984. The same type of
long-term movement was displayed by the Chinese proportion with, however,
one difference in that the downtrend part has been much steeper. This is because
the proportion of Chinese in this age group started at a much higher base in
1921, certainly more than 50 per cent and consisting primarily of immigrant
male workers. A completely different trend was delineated by the Indian proportion, reducing slowly but steadily from 1921 to as late as 1980. The more
prolonged downtrend was caused by the longer time taken by the Indians to
consider Peninsular Malaysia as their permanent home. It is also to be noted
that the more common practice of retiring to India has resulted in the extremely
small proportion in the last age group 60 and over.

Religious Composition

Though not as important as race which affects almost every aspect of the
demographics of the country, religion deserves some consideration in view of
its direct impact on nuptiality, fertility and the population control programme.
In the Peninsula religious differences have a strong tendency to reinforce racial
and cultural identities of the people and have thus presented serious obstacles
to effective racial integration in the country. Furthermore, the resurgence of
religious fervour in recent years has propelled religion into the forefront as
the key factor that determines the racial and political harmony of the nation.
A study of the religious composition of the population is however handicapped
by the inherent difficulties encountered in the collection of information on
religion which involves a wide range of personal beliefs and attitudes. The
information, if collected, is generally less precise and accurate than other types
of data compiled in a population census, and this should always be taken into
account when interpreting census data on religion.

The major religions in the country have been firmly established and the
religious affiliations of the people have remained essentially unchanged over
the years. In fact, a comparison of past data for the last two censuses has
revealed very minor changes during the latest intercensal period.[30] This leads

30. The information on religion was not collected in the 1947 and 1957 censuses.

us to confine our analysis of religious composition to the latest data collected in the 1980 census shown in Table 3.15. It is clear that the predominant religion in the country is Islam which is being professed by some 56.1 per cent of the total population. A very poor second is Buddhism which can count on only 19.0 per cent of the population to profess it, and this is followed by Confucianism with 12.9 per cent. The other minor religions practised by the people are Hinduism with 8.4 per cent, Christianity with 2.1 per cent and 0.8 per cent professing other religions. The census data seem to suggest that only a very small group, amounting to 0.7 per cent of the population, do not have any religion at all, but this is probably an underestimation of the true position. The dominance of Islam, the state religion, may be enhanced in the future since

TABLE 3.15
DISTRIBUTION OF POPULATION BY RELIGION AND RACE, 1980

Religion	Malays	Chinese	Indians	Others	Total
Number ('000)					
Islam	6,036.0	7.4	58.5	4.2	6,106.1
Buddhism	0.7	2,025.8	6.8	31.7	2,064.9
Confucianism	0.5	1,399.5	1.5	0.3	1,401.7
Hinduism	0.6	4.2	909.9	0.8	915.4
Christianity	4.8	120.2	82.1	26.0	233.0
Others	46.0	16.7	28.1	0.9	92.9
No Religion	13.7	56.8	0.7	0.6	72.7
Total	6,102.3	3,630.6	1,087.6	64.5	10,886.7
Percentage					
Islam	98.9	0.2	5.4	6.5	56.1
Buddhism	0.0	55.8	0.6	49.2	19.0
Confucianism	0.0	38.5	0.1	0.5	12.9
Hinduism	0.0	0.1	83.7	1.2	8.4
Christianity	0.1	3.3	7.5	40.3	2.1
Others	0.8	0.5	2.6	1.4	0.8
No Religion	0.2	1.6	0.1	0.9	0.7
Total	100.0	100.0	100.0	100.0	100.0

increasing proselytising among the non-Malays has resulted in some embracing the religion.

The other figures given in Table 3.15 serve to confirm the close distribution of religion along racial lines. The best example is seen among the Malays with as much as 98.9 per cent of their members professing the Islamic faith, and the vast majority of them are Sunni Muslims belonging to the Islam Shafei school of thought. In fact, Islam is one of the principle criteria used to determine whether a person is classified as a Malay since Article 160(2) of the constitution of the country defines a Malay as a "Person who professes the Muslim religion, habitually speaks the Malay language and conforms to the Malay custom." The influence of Islam on its followers is permanent as there is no provision in the Islamic laws for the conversion of a Muslim to another religion, or for the renunciation of Islam. Under such conditions the Malays will always be identified with Islam. The small number of non-Muslims among this community are mainly *Orang Asli* and Indonesian immigrants who may be Christians or Hindus.

By and large, the Chinese are adherents of two not too dissimilar religious faiths, Buddhism and Confucianism. Some 55.8 per cent of the Chinese profess the Buddhist faith, while another 38.5 per cent are practising Confucianists. An important minority of 3.3 per cent of the Chinese are Christians. In the case of the Indians, a large proportion amounting to 83.7 per cent are Hindus. The two minor religions which they worship are Christianity with 7.5 per cent and Islam with 5.4 per cent. It should be mentioned that some Indian Muslims would declare themselves as Malays to the census enumerators. The figures for Others, which encompass such minority races as Eurasians, Arabs, Japanese and Europeans, exhibit a different and wider combination of religious faiths. Sufficient has been said to show that the population of Peninsular Malaysia is not only multi-racial but also multi-religious in character; there is freedom of worship though Islam is the state religion.

Another way of looking at the figures in Table 3.15 is to examine the racial composition of the people belonging to a particular religion. The most obvious feature is that almost all Muslims are Malays, almost all Buddhists and Confucianists are Chinese, and almost all Hindus are Indians. Only the small Christian community escapes this close identification of race with religion since it has sizeable numbers of Chinese, Indians, Eurasians and even some 5,000 Malays. In view of the strong identification of the major religions with the main races, the distribution of the population by religion in each of the 11 states must necessarily follow closely the racial composition in that state. For instance, Trengganu has 94.2 per cent Malays and 94.5 per cent Muslims and Kelantan has 93.0 per cent Malays and 93.7 per cent Muslims. As a matter of fact, the close overlap of race and religion was cited as a reason for not collecting religious data. The 1947 Census Report states, "No enquiry as to religion was made on this occasion, past experience having shown it to be of little value in Malaya where the entire Malay population is Muhammadan, practically every European and Eurasian is a Christian and the great majority of the Chinese hold to the national religion of China which some describes as Confucianism and others prefer to regard as ancestor-worship."[31]

Citizenship Pattern

The extent to which the population has assumed a settled character can be best viewed in terms of citizenship data which were collected in the two latest population censuses from persons aged 12 and over. This particular age cut-off point was adopted in the census because the collection of citizenship statistics was intrinsically linked to the compilation of information on the colour of identity cards which are compulsory for all permanent residents age 12 and over. In any case one can assume that almost all children below age 12 are citizens by birth or would be able to acquire one when they attain the age of 21. It is of some significance that the item on citizenship was not included until the post-independence era when the great concern for citizenship issues and political enfranchisement became part of the process of nation-building.

Out of a total of 5,579,200 persons aged 12 and over enumerated in 1970, some 5,133,000 or 92.0 per cent considered themselves as Malaysian citizens. The position improved by 1980 when 7,204,900 or 97.8 per cent of the population aged 12 and over were citizens. The corresponding percentages for the three main races are shown below:

	1970	1980
Malays	97.9	98.2
Chinese	91.3	98.1
Indians	68.2	95.7

It is only natural that the citizenship position in 1970 was the best among the Malays with 97.9 per cent, followed fairly closely by the Chinese with 91.3 per cent but way behind by the Indians with only 68.2 per cent. The latter figure goes to demonstrate what we have mentioned on numerous occasions about the Indians being rather hesitant in regarding the Peninsula as their permanent place of abode. But then they had made tremendous progress in the 1970s and

---

31. M.V. Del Tufo, *Malaya: A Report on the 1947 Census of Population* (London: Crown Agents, n. d.), p. 123.

by the next census held in 1980 the proportion of citizens among them had shot up to 95.7 per cent. This coupled with the further progress experienced by the Malays and Chinese constitutes the most positive evidence that the transition of the population into a stable and settled one is almost complete.

TABLE 3.16

DISTRIBUTION OF NON-MALAYSIAN CITIZENS AGED 12
AND OVER BY SEX, 1980

Country of Citizenship	Total	Males	Females
Indonesia	17,002	11,185	5,817
Singapore	10,289	3,892	6,397
Thailand	7,861	3,549	4,312
Philippines	263	123	140
Other Countries	40,616	21,112	19,504

It would be useful to look at the figures in Table 3.16 in respect of the population who were not citizens of Malaysia. The number of Indonesian citizens counted in 1980 was 17,002, with nearly twice as many men as women. Among the 11,185 Indonesian men, no less than 7,219 were enumerated in the rural areas. Many of the Indonesian men were working in the agricultural plantations which have been facing a shortage of labour.[32] The number of Singapore citizens came to only 10,289 with, however, more women than men. This by no means implies that there were more Singapore women working in the Peninsula but rather that many of them were married to Malaysians and have yet to take up their husband's citizenship. Most of the Singaporeans (4,489) were residing in the southern state of Johore. The third largest group of foreigners were Thai citizens numbering some 7,861 with the most balanced sex ratio. Most of these Thai families were found in the border states of Kelantan (4,316) and Perlis (1,308). Among the 40,616 citizens of other countries were those who came from Japan, Europe, America and Oceania. Many of these foreigners belonged to the expatriate business community and would eventually return to their home countries or proceed to another country to take up a new overseas posting.

32. See *Malaysian Business Times*, 1 May 1984; *The Straits Times*, 15 May 1984; and *Malaysian Business*, 1 July 1984.

4

Internal Population Movements

The movement of people within the Peninsula has assumed greater significance in recent years in view of the official concern about the unbalanced
distribution of population among the various parts of the country. This concern was explicitly expressed in the development plans adopted from the
early 1970s onwards, and specific strategies were spelled out to, among other
things, redistribute the population. The plans seek to distribute the population to sparsely settled rural areas with considerable agricultural potential,
to spread out the urban population more evenly throughout the country, and
to rearrange the population with the view of attaining greater economic
balance among the major communities. The underlying purpose of the last
strategy is to free the Malays from their dependence on subsistence agriculture
and to allow them to participate in the "modern rural and urban sectors of
the economy at all levels".[1] By and large, the overall aim of the population
redistribution policies is meant to achieve "economic balance between urban
and rural areas and to eliminate the identification of race with vocation as
well as location".[2]

In studying the movement of population within the country, we will discuss
as many types of movement as the availability of statistics permit us to do so.
The most comprehensive information that goes as far back as 1911 refers to
the census data tabulated according to urban and rural areas which can be
utilised to study urbanisation. Another important source of census data is in
respect of the information collected from place of birth, and tabulated according to state of birth and state of enumeration which can then be employed to
analyse inter-state migration in the country. In the more recent censuses data
on the locality of last previous residence were collected and tabulated accord-

---

1. Malaysia, *Third Malaysia Plan 1976–1980* (Kuala Lumpur: Government Press, 1976), pp. 7–8.
2. Malaysia, *Second Malaysia Plan 1971–1975* (Kuala Lumpur: Government Press, 1971), p. 45.

ing to the various districts in each state, hence enabling us to look at intra-
state migration. Besides, the 1980 Census collected for the first time valuable
particulars regarding the reasons for the inhabitants moving from one place
to another. Sufficient data are therefore at our disposal to secure a thorough
investigation into the various dimensions of population movement within
the Peninsula.

General Pattern of Urbanisation

In studying urbanisation we are immediately confronted with the universal
problem of securing a practical and yet useful definition of an urban population viewed in demographic, occupational, sociological and morphological
terms. The definition of an urban area has varied from one country to another,
and even within a particular country changes in the definition may be introduced. In the early census reports of the Peninsula, urban areas have been
equated to gazetted administrative districts with a population of 1,000 or
more inhabitants.[3] This figure is now regarded as too low and, if utilised,
might overemphasise the extent of urbanisation and distort its character. For
our purpose, we will adopt the more commonly accepted definition of urban
areas as equivalent to gazetted areas with 10,000 or more inhabitants. It is
important to point out that this definition has also been employed in other
parts of this book when an urban-rural classification is applied to analyse
other aspects of the demography of the country.

The data given in Table 4.1 show the level of urbanisation for the seven
census years from 1911 to 1980. The figures in the last column of the table are
derived by taking the difference between the annual average growth rate of
the urban area and that of the rural area.[4] During the whole period the urban
population grew at a much faster pace than the total population. While the
total population increased by about slightly less than fivefold from 2,339,000
in 1911 to 10,944,844 in 1980, the urban population was augmented by no
less than sixteenfold from 250,273 to 4,073,050 during the same time-span.
Indeed, the faster rate of urban growth was consistently recorded during every
intercensal period. Consequently, the share of the urban population to the
total population in the country has risen from 10.7 per cent to 37.2 per cent
at the end of the 70-year period. The speed of urbanisation is in fact faster

---

3. The process of gazetting an area is an essential part of government administration that involves
   the careful mapping of the area to establish the boundaries which are then notified in the
   government gazettes for public information.
4. Another way of expressing this measure of the tempo of urbanisation is the annual rate of
   exponential change in the ratio of urban to total population.

TABLE 4.1
RATE AND TEMPO OF URBANISATION, 1911–80

Year	Total Population	Urban Population	Percentage Urban to Total Population	Tempo of Urbanisation
1911	2,339,000	250,275	10.7	—
1921	2,906,691	406,936	14.0	2.7
1931	3,787,758	571,951	15.1	0.7
1947	4,908,086	929,928	18.9	1.4
1957	6,278,758	1,666,300	26.5	3.4
1970	8,819,928	2,530,433	28.7	0.6
1980	10,944,844	4,073,105	37.2	2.6

than these figures suggest if we take into consideration the drift of some rural people from the country to the city state of Singapore which was part of the political entity of Malaya until 1 April 1946 when it became a separate crown colony.

Between 1911 and 1921 a fairly rapid speed of urbanisation was recorded, with the share of the urban population to total population moving up from 10.7 per cent to 14.0 per cent. The next decade witnessed a marked slackening in the speed of urbanisation, the level having been raised by only 1.1 percentage points by 1931. The tempo of urbanisation fell from 2.7 per cent in the first intercensal period to 0.7 per cent in the second period. During the next one and a half decades the urbanisation of the country gathered speed as evidenced by the tempo of urbanisation going up to 1.4 per cent bringing the proportion of urban population to 18.9 per cent in 1947. The growth of urban population prior to the Second World War was due to overseas immigration, concentrated largely in towns whose formation and growth could be traced to the development of tin, rubber and commerce.[5] Soon after the war ended in August 1945, there was also a drift of people, relocated by the Japanese authorities to the rural areas to grow more food, back to the towns.

A spectacular acceleration in the speed of urbanisation took place during the first postwar intercensal period as evidenced by a sharp rise in the tempo of urbanisation to 3.4 per cent. As a result the proportion urban was raised from 18.9 per cent a decade ago to 26.5 per cent in 1957. This is in the main attri-

5. Hamzah Sendut, "Patterns of Urbanization in Malaya", *Journal of Tropical Geography*, Vol. 16, October 1962.

butable to the declaration of the State of Emergency in June 1948 which for many years caused countless families to leave their homes in the dangerous remote rural districts for new ones in the relative security of towns. Other families were forcefully transplanted to government-organised New Villages protected by barbed-wire fencing under the tight surveillance of security forces.[6] At the same time some rural folk, faced with the lack of worthwhile jobs and a town-life, drifted into the large urban centres in search of better jobs and city lights.

The usual economic and social forces continued to push the rural inhabit-ants to the urban centres during the intercensal years 1957–70, but the rural-urban drift on account of security reasons ceased completely towards the end of the Emergency in 1960. Normalisation of conditions has probably resulted in a minor reversal of the trend as some of the former rural inhabitants returned to their farms in the previously terrorist-infested areas. As for those who were forced to shift to the New Villages, many remained in their adopted homes.[7] An important new factor that affected urbanisation during this period was the introduction of large-scale government development projects in the early 1960s. The various land development schemes established in the poten-tially rich rural areas have diverted the rural inhabitants who might have otherwise moved to the urban centres. All things considered, we should not be surprised therefore that the speed of urbanisation slowed down appreciably as evidenced by the drop in the tempo of urbanisation to the record low of 10.6 per cent during the period 1957–70. The proportion urban managed to be raised marginally from 26.5 per cent to 28.7 per cent in 1970.

The pace of urbanisation recovered and accelerated during the latest inter-censal period 1970–80 when the tempo of urbanisation went up to 2.6 per cent. This resulted in a rise in the proportion of urban population by as much as 8.5 percentage points to the all-time high of 37.2 per cent in 1980. This upsurge was generally brought about by the high economic growth rates in the 1970s which created excellent job opportunities in the construction, manu-facturing, services and government sectors in the urban centres. More balanced regional development and the establishment of new growth centres under the New Economic Policy also led to the more rapid growth of relatively smaller centres. What is significant is that the 37.2 per cent recorded in the 1980 Census exceeded the target of 35.0 per cent set by the government in its develop-ment plans.[8]

---

6. W.C.S. Corry, *A General Survey of New Villages* (Kuala Lumpur: Government Printer, 1954).
7. Kernial Singh Sandhu, "Emergency Resettlement in Malaya", *Journal of Tropical Geography*, Vol. 18, 1964.
8. Malaysia, *Third Malaysia Plan 1976–1980*, op. cit. and Malaysia, *Mid-Term Review of the Third Malaysia Plan 1976–1980* (Kuala Lumpur: Government Press, 1979).

An analysis of the components of urban growth will throw some light on the nature of the process of urbanisation that occurred in recent years. The change in the urban population during a particular period is determined not only by the rate of population growth in the localities but also by alterations in the localities due to their changed status from urban to rural or vice versa, localities being annexed by existing urban areas, etc. A precise estimation of the components of urban population growth by means of the survival ratio method is not feasible owing to the lack of the prerequisite census data. However, the natural growth rate method has been employed to compute the various components for the three latest intercensal periods and the results are summarised in Table 4.2.[9]

TABLE 4.2
PERCENTAGE DISTRIBUTION OF COMPONENTS OF
URBAN POPULATION GROWTH, 1947–80

Components	1947–57	1957–70	1970–80
Natural Increase	34.9	60.6	39.6
Migration	31.7	18.1	29.7
Reclassification	33.4	21.3	30.7
Total	100.0	100.0	100.0

The rapid pace of urbanisation during the intercensal period 1947–57 noted earlier is attributable in almost equal measure to natural increase (34.9 per cent), migration (31.7 per cent) and reclassification (33.4 per cent). A completely different position may be observed during the next intercensal period 1957–70 when migration accounted for only 18.1 per cent of the total urban growth as against the 60.6 per cent contribution made by natural increase and 21.3 per cent by reclassification. This confirms the much reduced rural-urban drift as the main reason responsible for the lower tempo of urbanisation experienced during this period. In the latest intercensal period 1970–80 migra-

9. These estimates of the components of urban population growth were obtained from Dorothy Fernandez, Amos H. Hawley and Silvia Predaza, *The Population of Malaysia*, C.I.C.R.E.D. Series 1975 and Kok Kim Lian, *Levels, Trends and Patterns of Urbanization in Peninsular Malaysia, 1957–1980* (Mimeograph).

tion regained its relative importance. While natural increase continued to be the mainstay of urban growth with a contribution of 39.6 per cent, the role of migration has resumed its previous importance with its percentage raised to 29.7 per cent. Reclassification too has become more important in recent years.

So far we have confined our analysis of urbanisation to the traditional cut-off point of 10,000 persons or more, and it is necessary to proceed to look at the distribution of the urban population according to size of the urban centres so as to provide a good idea of the process of urbanisation. The data for the percentage distribution of the urban population by four sizes of urban areas are presented in Table 4.3. It should be emphasised that these figures refer to the size classes as determined at each census date, and hence allowing the urban centres to change from one class to another over the intercensal period. What it implies is that changes in the urban population may be due to an enlargement or contraction of the boundaries of these centres.

During the intercensal period 1957–70 the urban population in the largest group of towns with at least 75,000 inhabitants registered the highest annual rate of increase, 5.5 per cent, while the second largest group with 50,000–74,999 inhabitants recorded the second highest rate of 3.7 per cent. In the next smaller group of towns with 25,000 to 49,999 persons, the annual growth rate dropped to a negative figure of 0.8 per cent. Besides, the small towns with 10,000–24,999 inhabitants managed to grow by a low rate of 0.3 per cent. The pattern of growth in the more recent period 1970–80 was quite different except for the fact that the largest group of towns continued to record distinctly

TABLE 4.3

PERCENTAGE DISTRIBUTION AND GROWTH OF URBAN
POPULATION BY SIZE OF TOWNS, 1957–80

Size of Towns (Persons)	1957	1970	1980	Annual Growth Rate (%)	
				1957–70	1970–80
75,000 or More	45.8	58.5	74.4	5.2	7.2
50,000–74,999	15.2	16.0	6.1	3.7	–4.8
25,000–49,999	18.5	10.8	6.8	–0.8	0.2
10,000–24,999	20.5	14.7	12.6	0.3	3.2
Total	100.0	100.0	100.0	—	—

the highest rate of increase, 7.2 per cent.[10] This time, however, a moderately high rate of 3.2 per cent was experienced by the smallest group of towns. Another striking difference is that the growth rate in the second largest group of towns shifted from the moderate level in the previous period to a completely negative rate of 4.8 per cent. The shift in the second smallest group of towns was not that radical, the rate moving from a decrease of 0.8 per cent to an increase of 0.2 per cent. The net result of the differential rate of increase among the four groups of towns was that there was a continuous shift in the proportionate distribution of urban population towards the largest group which saw its percentage rising from 45.8 per cent in 1957 to 74.4 per cent in 1980. A reduction in the proportion for each of the three smaller groups was recorded right through the whole period.

Another way of investigating in more detail the process of urbanisation is to examine the growth in the number of towns with at least 10,000 inhabitants and the changing distribution of these towns according to the various sizes. According to the figures in Table 4.4, the number of such towns increased from 8 in 1911 to 58 in 1980, a net gain of 50 during the whole period, with

TABLE 4.4
DISTRIBUTION OF TOWNS WITH 10,000 PERSONS AND MORE
BY SIZE, 1911–80

Size of Town ('000)	1911	1921	1931	1947	1957	1970	1980
400.0–499.9	0	0	0	0	0	1	1
300.0–399.9	0	0	0	0	1	0	0
200.0–299.9	0	0	0	0	1	2	4
100.0–199.9	1	1	2	2	1	2	6
75.0– 99.9	0	1	0	1	2	3	2
50.0– 74.9	0	0	1	1	3	7	4
30.0– 49.9	1	2	2	6	7	4	4
20.0– 29.9	2	1	4	5	6	7	12
15.0– 19.9	1	2	2	2	9	5	4
10.0– 14.9	3	7	5	3	6	18	21
Total	8	14	16	20	36	49	58

10. This phenomenon is apparently common in the experience of countries in Southeast Asia where the large cities have been subjected to more dynamic expansion than the small towns.

12 during the first 36 years and 38 during the next 33 years. During the latter period, there was an increase from 3 to 13 in the number of large towns with at least 75,000 inhabitants, 1 to 4 in the moderately large towns with 50,000 to 74,999 persons, 11 to 16 in the small towns with 20,000–24,999 persons, and 5 to 25 in the smallest towns with only 10,000–19,999 people. During the latest intercensal period 1970–78 a total of 10 small towns crossed the 10,000 threshold as compared with 15 during the preceeding period.

The Emergency as mentioned earlier, exerted a great impact on the growth of small towns during the intercensal period 1947–57. Among these towns which crossed the cut-off point were Raub with an increase from only 3,616 to 15,363, Dungun from 4,256 to 12,515, Temerloh from 5,200 to 12,296, Sungei Siput from 5,967 to 15,337, Bentong from 7,087 to 18,845, Segamat from 7,289 to 18,445 and Kuantan from 8,084 to 23,034. Significantly, these seven towns were the ones that experienced the seven highest annual rates of increase, ranging from 15.3 per cent for Segamat to the high of 32.5 per cent for Raub. These were typical towns situated in the terrorist-infested parts of the country, and had offered a comparatively safe heaven for the rural dwellers from their neighbouring outskirts. In the following period 1957–70 there was a decrease in the population in three of these towns — Temerloh, Sungei Siput and Segamat — with the first two falling below the 10,000 level. Former rural settlers had apparently returned to their original homes in the remote areas.

We will now move on to look at the large towns which played a more vital role in the process of urbanisation in recent years. The figures for the 13 largest towns with at least 75,000 persons in 1980 are given in Table 4.5 for the three latest census years. The general overview is that none of the 13 towns had experienced a doubling of their population during the 13-year period 1957–70. The nearest to doubling was Ipoh which saw its population rise from 125,770 to 247,969. The picture that emerged during the recent ten-year period 1970–80 was entirely different. This time there was clearly a twofold increase of the population in Kuala Lumpur, Johore Bahru and Petaling Jaya, a threefold increase in Kota Bahru, Kuantan and almost so in Taiping, and even a clear fourfold increase in Kuala Trengganu.[11] The policy of redistributing population under the New Economic Policy constitutes a major force in the unprecedented growth of the large towns.

One notable feature of the pattern of urbanisation of Peninsular Malaysia refers to the widely ranging spread of the towns with at least 10,000 persons

---

11. The exceptional growth of Kuala Trengganu may be traced to its absorption of the two gazetted urban areas of Kuala Trengganu Barat and Kuala Trengganu Tengah which appeared as separate urban centres in 1970.

TABLE 4.5
POPULATION OF PRESENT THIRTEEN LARGEST TOWN, 1957–80

Towns	1957	1970	1980
Kuala Lumpur	326,990	451,810	919,610
Ipoh	125,770	247,969	293,849
Georgetown	234,903	269,247	248,241
Johore Bahru	74,909	113,607	246,395
Petaling Jaya	—	93,447	207,805
Klang	75,649	136,290	192,080
Kuala Trengganu	29,446	44,524	180,296
Kota Bahru	38,103	55,124	167,872
Taiping	48,206	54,645	146,002
Seremban	52,091	80,921	132,911
Kuantan	23,034	43,358	131,547
Malacca	69,848	87,160	87,494
Butterworth	42,504	61,187	77,982

all over the country. The key explanation to this characteristic lies in the federal system of government which allows considerable autonomy to the state government under the nine Sultans and two Governors in the case of Penang and Malacca. Each state has its own local urban configuration centred at the state capital. This is already reflected in Table 4.5 where 9 out of the 13 largest towns in 1980 are state capitals. Even Alor Star, the state capital of Kedah and not included in the table, has a sizcable population of 69,435 in 1980. Only Kangar, the capital of the tiny state of Perlis has understandably a small population of 12,949. The implication of the widely ranging spread of the towns is that the urban population is scattered over the length and breadth of the country. In many respects, this pattern of urbanisation is advantageous because the economic, social and political problems associated with rapid urbanisation would be partially dissipated into the various parts of the country, rendering them more manageable than would have been the case if heavily concentrated in a few large urban centres.[12]

Whilst the dispersion of urban population has continued in recent years, we are beginning to witness the greatest concentration of urban people in the

12. Saw Swee-Hock, "Patterns of Urbanization in West Malaysia, 1911–1970", *Malayan Economic Review*, Vol. 17, No. 2, October 1972.

city of Kuala Lumpur. The population of this city was only 1.4 times in 1947 and 1.7 times in 1957 as large as that in the second largest town of Georgetown, but by 1980 it was 3.1 times larger than that in Ipoh, the second biggest town by then. If we add the 207,805 residents for Petaling Jaya to Kuala Lumpur, the combined population in this practically inseparable connurbation will top 1.1 million in 1980. However, the underlying forces that influence dispersed urbanisation are so entrenched in the country that the likelihood of Kuala Lumpur developing into a primate city like Bangkok or Manila is quite remote. Bangkok's population is about 40 times bigger than the second largest town, Chiangmai,[13] and Manila is about 10 times larger than the second biggest town, Cebu.[14]

State Differences in Urbanisation

The preceding analysis of towns provides a better appreciation of urbanisation among the eleven states presented in Table 4.6. At the beginning of the century, a moderate level of urbanisation is noticeable in the three state

TABLE 4.6
PROPORTION OF URBAN TO TOTAL POPULATION BY STATE,
1911–80

State	1911	1921	1931	1947	1957	1970	1980
Johore	—	10.1	10.9	15.4	21.8	26.3	35.2
Kedah	—	3.4	4.3	8.2	13.3	12.7	14.4
Kelantan	4.4	3.5	4.1	5.1	9.8	15.1	28.0
Malacca	17.0	20.0	20.4	22.8	24.0	25.1	23.4
Negri Sembilan	—	9.7	9.2	13.2	17.8	21.5	32.6
Pahang	—	—	—	—	22.2	19.0	26.1
Penang	37.3	41.8	47.7	52.9	56.7	50.9	47.5
Perak	11.0	13.3	14.4	17.1	25.0	27.5	32.2
Perlis	—	—	—	—	—	—	8.9
Selangor	15.9	23.0	24.8	32.7	43.0	45.0	60.0
Trengganu	9.1	8.1	7.8	11.9	19.0	27.0	42.9

13. A detailed account of urbanisation in Thailand is given in Sydney Goldstein, "Urbanization in Thailand, 1947–1967", *Demography*, Vol. 8, No. 2, May 1971.

14. United Nations, *Population of the Philippines*, Country Monograph Series No. 5 (Bangkok: Economic and Social Commission for Asia and the Pacific, 1978).

of Malacca, Perak and Selangor between 11 and 17 per cent in 1911. Penang (including Province Wellesley in the mainland) was the most urbanised state with 37 per cent urban population. All these states are on the west coast of the country where British influence was first established. Most of the other states were predominantly rural in character; five states did not have even a single town of size 10,000 and over. In the course of time as socio-economic progress and modernisation penetrated the country, the process of urbanisation was seen to occur in every state though at varying speeds. During the whole 70-year period, Selangor stands out as the state with the most consistent and rapid rate of urbanisation with the level rising from 15.9 per cent in 1911 to 60.0 per cent in 1980. On the other hand, the slowest rate of urbanisation was experienced in Malacca which has a long history of contact with foreign powers; the level was lifted from 17.0 per cent to 23.4 per cent during the same period.

Confining our analysis to the intercensal period 1947–57, it may be observed that not every state appeared to have experienced the rapid tempo of urbanisation that was seen to have occurred in this period. Malacca and Penang are two states falling within this category; the proportion of urban increased by 1.2 and 3.8 percentage points respectively in these two states. By far the most rapid urbanisation occurred in Pahang where the percentage shot up from zero to 22.2 in 1957. The deep jungles of Pahang were favourite hideouts of the terrorists during the Emergency and the rural dwellers had to seek safety in nearby towns like Raub, Bentong, Temerloh and Kuantan which, as noted earlier, grew at a phenomenal speed. The other two eastern states of Kelantan and Trengganu also recorded a high rate of urbanisation that resulted in almost a doubling of their proportion of urban population.

In line with the general slowdown in the tempo of urbanisation during the period 1957–70, all the states have experienced a lower rate of urbanisation as compared with the preceeding period. Whilst none of the states recorded a reduction in their proportion of urban in the previous decade, the present period did in fact witness a reduction in the proportion of urban population in Pahang, Kedah and Penang. The reversal observed in the first two states can be explained partly in terms of the end of the Emergency in 1960 and the subsequent return of the inhabitants to the rural areas to resume their agricultural activities. Pahang was exposed to an additional factor, viz. the establishment of huge rural land development projects which attracted migrants from within the state as well as from other states. With regard to Penang, it is a question of out-migration to other urban centres in other states, especially Kuala Lumpur and even Singapore.

Apart from the setback noted in the above three states, many other states had recorded only marginal increases in their proportion of urban population.

These states were Malacca with a rise from 24.0 per cent in 1957 to 25.1 per cent in 1970, Selangor from 43.0 per cent to 45.0 per cent, and Perak from 25.0 per cent to 27.5 per cent. Rapid strides in urbanisation continued in Kelantan and Trengganu, the proportion urban increasing from 9.8 to 15.1 per cent in the former and from 19.0 to 27.0 per cent in the latter. The tempo of urbanisation was 3.3 per cent in Kelantan and 2.7 per cent in Trengganu, compared with the national figure of 0.58 per cent noted earlier.

Despite the resurgence of urbanisation during the latest intercensal period 1970–80, there were still two states which suffered a reduction in their level of urbanisation. Penang again saw a reduction in the proportion of urban population from 50.9 per cent in 1970 to 47.5 per cent in 1980, while Malacca for the first time had its proportion of urban population lowered from 25.1 per cent to 23.4 per cent during the same period. It is more than mere coincidence that during a time when government policies affecting population redistribution became prominent that reduced urbanisation happened to take place in two states under the rule of appointed governors rather than hereditary Sultans whose interest in the socio-economic development of their states would naturally be more intense and permanent. Another interesting feature is that the smallest state, Perlis, finally has an urban population in 1980 when its capital town of Kangar crossed the threshold of 10,000 persons. With an urban population of 12,949 in Kangar, the level of urbanisation in the state was 8.9 per cent.

All the other states experienced an increase in their level of urbanisation. As can be observed in Table 4.7, Kelantan and Trengganu continued to have

TABLE 4.7
TEMPO OF URBANISATION BY STATE, 1947–80

State	1947–57	1957–70	1970–80
Kelantan	6.53	3.33	6.18
Trengganu	4.68	2.70	4.63
Negri Sembilan	2.99	1.45	4.16
Pahang	—	-1.20	3.17
Johore	3.48	1.44	2.91
Selangor	2.74	0.35	2.88
Perak	3.80	0.73	1.58
Kedah	4.84	-0.36	1.26
Penang	0.69	-0.83	-0.69
Malacca	0.51	0.34	-0.70
Perlis	—	—	—

the two highest tempo of urbanisation equivalent to 6.2 and 4.6 per cent respectively. These two east coast states appeared to have gained from the government policy of promoting less developed states with the rapid expansion of urban centres. Trengganu had also benefited from off-shore oil exploration which resulted in the rapid growth of its capital, Kuala Trengganu. The speed of urbanisation in the other states can also be seen in Table 4.7. Except Penang and Malacca, all the states have recorded a higher tempo of urbanisation during the latest intercensal period as compared with the preceeding period.

The varying speed of urbanisation among the 11 states in the past has resulted in considerable shifts in the level of urbanisation. The pattern that emerged in 1980 is a fairly moderate level of urbanisation in almost every state, with a narrowing in the differences among them. As noted in Table 4.7, three states now have levels of urbanisation above 40 per cent, another three states above 30 per cent, and still another three above 20 per cent. Only the two small northern states of Kedah and Perlis have relatively low rates of 14.4 per cent and 8.9 per cent respectively. Selangor with 60.0 per cent has finally overtaken Penang with 47.5 per cent as the most urbanised state in the Peninsula. There is no doubt that the introduction of government policies under the New Economic Policy to ensure a balanced distribution of the population has exerted a considerable impact on the level and pattern of urbanisation in recent years.

Race Differences in Urbanisation

The variation in the level of urbanisation among the 11 states is not completely unrelated to the pattern of urbanisation among the main races. For decades, the socio-economic development of the country has progressed in such a manner that a general alignment of ethnic distribution along economic and spatial lines has emerged. We have observed earlier the concentration of Malays in the rural areas and the Chinese and Indians in the urban centres. The significance of this unbalanced distribution is underlined by the wide disparities in the socio-economic conditions between the urban and the rural areas viewed in terms of educational facilities, employment opportunities and social amenities. The uneven distribution of the population of the main races according to urban-rural classification is regarded as not conducive to achieving national unity, and one of the strategies of the New Economic Policy is to "speed up the exposure of the rural inhabitants, particularly Malays and other indigenous people, to the influence of an urban environment".[15] This apparent concern of the government has accorded greater significance to our discussion

---

15. Malaysia, *Second Malaysia Plan 1971–1975*, op. cit., p. 45.

of the differences in the pattern of urbanisation among the major races.

How each of the three main races participated in the postwar urbanisation
process is analysed in Table 4.8. The general picture conveyed by the table
is one where all the races experienced an uninterrupted process of urbanisation
throughout the whole period. It is also apparent that the speed of urbanisation
has varied from race to race as well as from period to period for each race. The
tempo of urbanisation among the Malays has always been faster than that
of the Chinese or the Indians, but the relative position of the last two races
is not so clear-cut. Another noteworthy feature is that over the years, all the
three races displayed the same general trend observed for the total population
earlier, namely, a drop in the tempo of urbanisation from the first period
1947–57 to the second period 1957–70, and then a recovery during the latest
period 1970–80.

TABLE 4.8
PERCENTAGE URBAN AND TEMPO OF URBANISATION FOR
THREE MAIN RACES, 1947–80

Year	Percentage Urban			Tempo of Urbanisation		
	Malays	Chinese	Indians	Malays	Chinese	Indians
1947	7.3	31.1	25.8	—	—	—
1957	11.3	44.7	30.6	4.3	3.6	1.7
1970	14.8	47.0	34.4	2.2	0.4	0.9
1980	25.1	56.1	40.9	5.2	1.7	1.7

Starting from an extremely low urbanisation level of 7.3 per cent in 1947,
the Malays experienced a high tempo of urbanisation equivalent to 4.3 per
cent in the decade that followed. With such a huge pool of rural dwellers, the
potential for rural-urban movement of the Malays in those days must necessarily
be great.[16] These predominantly kampong Malays were also affected by
modernisation tendencies and nationalistic awakening during the years following the Japanese Occupation and were moved by a keen desire to improve
their living conditions by migrating to the urban centres to secure better jobs
and access to education and enjoy the city lights. The reduced tempo of Malay
urbanisation, 2.2 per cent, during 1957–70 was still moderately rapid and

16. J.C. Caldwell, "The Demographic Background" in T.H. Silcock and E.K. Fisk (eds.), *The
Political Economy of Independent Malaya* (Canberra: Australian University Press, 1963).

certainly way ahead of that of the other two races. The moderate tempo of urbanisation coincided with the attaining of independence from British colonial rule on 1 August 1957. Certain privileges for the Malays guaranteed in the Constitution facilitated their movement into the urban centres. Most jobs in the government sector were reserved for the Malays whose numbers increased greatly in district headquarters, state capitals and the Federal Capital where government departments at different levels are located. In the private sector in primarily the urban areas, employers were required to take in 30 per cent Malays on their staff, apart from the assistance in various forms provided by the government to Malay businessmen.

Exceptional progress was made by the Malays in the urbanisation process during the latest intercensal period 1970–80 when the tempo of urbanisation shot up to 5.2 per cent. The beginning of this period also coincided with the introduction of certain government policies in 1970 that affected Malay urban- isation. Numerous measures were instituted by the government to shift the rural poor to existing towns and to new urban centres established in rural areas with growth potential as a means of eradicating poverty among all races and restructuring society in order to achieve national identity and unity under the New Economic Policy. The rural Malays benefited greatly from this new strategy, and indeed the success of the policy even exceeded government expectations. The 25.1 per cent of urban population among the Malays attained in 1980 was larger than the figure of 20 per cent forecasted in the Third Malaysia Plan.[17] The difference in the level of Malay urbanisation as compared with that of the other two races has narrowed considerably in 1980. In 1947 Malay urbanisation prevailed at a level which was 76 per cent lower than that of Chinese urbanisation but by 1980 this disparity was narrowed to 60 per cent.

The Chinese also experienced important changes in their urbanisation but the forces underlying these changes originate from an entirely different set of circumstances. First of all, the Chinese were already quite urbanised in 1947 with 31.1 per cent urban population, and it is not surprising that their tempo of urbanisation in the first intercensal period was lower than that of the Malays. During this period the Emergency resulted in some rural Chinese moving into the relative security of towns, but most of them were relocated into New Villages. The tempo of urbanisation plunged to the low of 0.4 per cent during the years 1957–70 on account of the return of thousands of Chinese to their rural homes after the end of the Emergency in 1960. The tempo went up during the latest intercensal period but managed to reach the moderate rate of only

17. Malaysia, *Third Malaysia Plan 1976–1980*, op. cit.

1.7 per cent. Apart from the sharp drop in Chinese fertility in recent years, there was also considerable emigration of urban Chinese to Singapore and other countries after the riots of 13 May 1969.

In addition to the usual pull-factors of the urban centres, the Indians were affected by the more prolonged practice of returning to India for good when they retire or even before their retirement was due. In the early postwar years, probably more urban than rural Indians, who were prevented from doing so during the Japanese Occupation, returned home to India. At the same time many stayed on or went back to the rural areas to participate in the rehabilitation of the rubber plantations. As compared with the other two races, the tempo of Indian urbanisation was therefore the slowest, only 1.7 per cent, during the period 1947–57. In the late 1950s the increased tendency towards sub-division of some large European estates which were taken over by local syndicates led to the loss of jobs by Indian workers, while the switch from rubber to oil palm in the 1960s also resulted in the retrenchment of Indian tappers as a smaller workforce was now required. Mainly on account of these developments the tempo of Indian urbanisation (0.9 per cent) was higher than that of the Chinese (0.4 per cent) during the second intercensal period 1957–70. Indian urbanisation also picked up after 1970 and, coincidentally recorded the same tempo as the Chinese in the latest decade with 1.7 per cent. Throughout the whole postwar period the level of Indian urbanisation was raised from 25.8 per cent to 40.9 per cent, remaining all the time at an intermediate position between the other two races.

The continuous attention accorded to urbanisation by race in the country necessitates a more detailed analysis of the dynamics of urbanisation within these races. This is attempted in Table 4.9 showing the growth of the urban population according to the size of towns and the shifts in the urban population that followed within these urban centres. Looking first at the figures for the growth rates, some similarities and differences among the three races are noticeable. During the first period 1957–70 every race experienced the most rapid rate of increase in the largest towns with at least 75,000 residents and the second most rapid in the next largest group of towns with at least 50,000 persons. This seems to suggest that the usual pull-factors in the large towns have operated very forcefully in these earlier years among all the races, but more so among the Malays. In the largest towns the Malays registered a growth rate of 8.6 per cent as compared with the 4.6 per cent for the Chinese and 5.1 per cent for the Indians. More significant is the 7.6 per cent recorded by the Malays in the second largest urban area as against the 2.2 per cent for the Chinese and 2.0 per cent for the Indians.

The differences in the growth rates assume greater dimensions in the two smallest urban areas. In the smallest urban area with less than 25,000 in-

TABLE 4.9
PERCENTAGE DISTRIBUTION AND GROWTH OF URBAN
POPULATION BY SIZE OF TOWNS FOR THREE MAIN RACES, 1957–80

Size of Towns (Persons)	1957	1970	1980	Annual Growth Rate (%)	
				1957–70	1970–80
Malays					
75,000 or more	30.3	46.4	75.1	8.6	12.7
50,000–74,999	18.5	24.7	5.8	7.6	–6.5
25,000–49,999	29.4	8.3	5.6	–4.4	4.0
10,000–24,999	21.8	20.6	13.5	4.9	3.7
Total	100.0	100.0	100.0	—	—
Chinese					
75,000 or more	47.7	61.4	73.0	4.6	5.0
50,000–74,999	14.1	13.3	7.0	2.2	–3.1
25,000–49,999	15.4	12.4	7.7	1.0	–1.6
10,000–24,999	22.8	13.0	12.3	–1.7	2.7
Total	100.0	100.0	100.0	—	—
Indians					
75,000 or more	54.6	69.6	78.5	5.1	4.5
50,000–74,999	12.2	10.5	3.3	2.0	–8.1
25,000–49,999	15.2	9.6	7.5	–0.4	0.8
10,000–24,999	18.0	10.3	10.7	–1.1	3.6
Total	100.0	100.0	100.0	—	—

habitants there was an annual growth rate of 4.9 per cent for the Malays but an annual decrease of 1.7 per cent for the Chinese and 1.1 per cent for the Indians. The decrease recorded by the Chinese is consistent with what we mentioned earlier, viz. the reversal of movement to the small towns after the end of the Emergency. The substantial decrease of 4.4 per cent per annum among the Malays in the urban centres with 25,000 to 49,999 persons was

caused by the tremendous growth of the predominantly Malay towns of Kota
Bahru and Kuala Trengganu which were therefore transferred to the next
bigger category of urban centres in 1970.

The strong influence of Kota Bahru and Kuala Trengganu continued unabated into the latest period 1970–80. Their rapid growth led to their upgrading
to the biggest urban area in 1980 and hence the high negative growth of 6.5
per cent in towns with 50,000 to 74,999 persons and the greatest ever growth
rate of 12.7 per cent in the biggest urban area among the Malays. The same
type of phenomenon occurred among the Chinese whose negative growth
rate of 3.1 per cent in the second largest urban area was engendered by the
predominantly Chinese towns of Taiping and Kuantan crossing the 50,000
cut-off point by 1980. Similarly, the tremendous decline of 8.1 per cent per
annum recorded by the Indians in the second largest urban area was caused
by the rapid growth of these two towns and, additionally, Butterworth which
crossed this cut-off point.

The differential growth rates obviously affected the proportionate distribution of the population among the four categories of urban areas. In 1957
the urban Malays were more evenly spread among the four urban areas as
compared with the urban Chinese with 47.7 per cent in the largest towns or
the urban Indians with 54.6 per cent in these towns. By 1970 the distribution
of the urban Malays had already become quite uneven, with 46.4 per cent in
the biggest towns. This movement towards a more uneven distribution continued rapidly in recent years, and by 1980 some three-quarters of the urban
Malays were residing in these big towns. By then the other two races were also
having three-quarters of their urban dwellers clustered in the biggest towns.
Indeed a strikingly similar pattern of distribution of their urban population
among the four categories was displayed by the three races in 1980.

The result of recent urbanisation in relation to the objectives of the New
Economic Policy should be considered in terms of the changes that have
taken place in the ethnic distribution of the population among the four classes
of urban areas. Table 4.10 reveals that satisfactory progress has been made
by the Malays, with a twofold rise in their proportion from 21.2 per cent in
1957 to 40.6 in 1980 in the smallest urban area and a nearly threefold increase
from 14.1 per cent to 38.2 per cent in the largest urban area. The rise in their
representation in the smallest urban area is significant in that this will provide
greater potential for urbanisation in the future. The much bigger inroad
made by the Malays in the largest urban area implied that a sizeable number
of them have benefited by the superior living conditions in the large towns.
Furthermore, as noted earlier the 25.1 per cent overall level of Malay urbanisation in 1980 exceeded the target of 20 per cent set in the development plan.

The success of the New Economic Policy in accelerating Malay urbanisation

TABLE 4.10
PERCENTAGE DISTRIBUTION OF URBAN POPULATION BY RACE
AND SIZE OF TOWNS, 1957–80

Size of Towns (Persons)	Malays	Chinese	Indians	Others	Total
1957					
75,000 and over	14.1	66.1	15.5	4.3	100.0
50,000–74,999	25.9	58.6	10.5	5.0	100.0
25,000–49,999	33.9	52.8	10.7	2.9	100.0
10,000–24,999	21.2	66.1	10.7	2.0	100.0
1970					
75,000 and over	21.9	61.4	15.2	1.5	100.0
50,000–49,999	42.6	48.4	8.4	0.6	100.0
25,000–49,999	21.2	67.0	11.4	0.4	100.0
10,000–24,999	38.8	51.6	9.0	0.7	100.0
1980					
75,000 and over	38.2	49.4	11.6	0.8	100.0
50,000–74,999	36.1	57.5	6.0	0.4	100.0
25,000–49,999	31.2	56.4	12.1	0.3	100.0
10,000–24,999	40.6	49.2	9.3	0.9	100.0

must necessarily affect Chinese representation in the various urban areas. What happened is that the Chinese proportion was reduced during the whole period in the largest and the smallest urban areas, with the two intermediate areas displaying no clear pattern in the shifts. By 1980 the gap between the Malay proportion and the Chinese proportion in the smallest urban area was narrowed from 44.9 percentage points in 1957 to only 8.6 in 1980. The narrowing in this gap was even more remarkable in the largest urban area, from 52.0 percentage points to 11.2, and most of this narrowing took place in the 1970s when government measures aimed at restructuring the urban population were implemented. The changes in the Indian representation in the four urban areas were less spectacular.

Pattern of Inter-State Migration

Internal migration has also attracted considerable attention in recent years in view of the concern and emphasis placed on balanced socio-economic development among the various regions of the country. In general, internal migration may be defined as a change of residence from one community or geographical unit to another within the national boundaries. In this section we will confine our analysis to internal migration that involves the change of residence among the largest geographical units, i.e. the 11 states in the Peninsula. Such changes of residence invariably lead to a complete readjustment of the community affiliation of the individuals consequent on the change of jobs, friends, neighbours and many other social and economic relationships.

There are various methods of estimating the volume and direction of internal migration and we will use the place-of-birth method based on census data on the place of birth of respondents at the census dates to estimate the various dimensions of inter-state migration.[18] An explanation of a few key terms related to this method is necessary. Lifetime in-migrants refer to persons enumerated in a given state at a particular census and born outside the state of enumeration but within the national boundaries, while lifetime out-migrants refer to persons born in a given state and enumerated outside the state but within the national boundaries. Lifetime net migrants would refer to the difference between the number of lifetime in-migrants and the number of lifetime out-migrants at the census date. The term 'lifetime' is used to refer to the cumulative numbers in the past up to the census date. When we deal with internal migration that occurred during intercensal periods, the three corresponding terms, in-migrants, out-migrants and net migrants, would be used.

According to the place-of-birth method the inter-state migration based on the last four population censuses has been estimated. The estimates using the data obtained in the first three censuses have been prepared by the author earlier and are published in full by sex and race in an earlier monograph.[19] A summary of the results together with the estimates computed from the 1980 census are presented in Tables 4.11 and 4.12. Before commenting on the figures, we should bear in mind the inherent shortcomings of the method. Firstly, it does not cover the inter-state movement of foreign-born persons and hence does not reflect the total inter-state movement that has occurred in the country. However, this defect is becoming more negligible as the pro-

---

18. A discussion of the various methods is given in United Nations, *Manual VI: Methods of Measuring Internal Migration* (New York: Departments of International Economic and Social Affairs, 1970).

19. Saw Swee-Hock, *Estimation of Interstate Migration in Peninsular Malaysia, 1947–1970* (Singapore: Institute of Southeast Asian Studies, 1980).

TABLE 4.11
LIFETIME IN-MIGRANTS AND LIFETIME OUT-MIGRANTS
BY STATE, 1947–80

State	1947	1957	1970	1980
	Lifetime In-Migrants			
Johore	27,346	55,943	81,581	133.4
Kedah	35,976	59,977	78,408	90.8
Kelantan	4,618	10,522	19,669	32.9
Malacca	8,946	24,238	47,805	58.1
Negri Sembilan	22,249	52,182	75,163	98.4
Pahang	17,553	41,186	107,113	236.9
Penang	20,897	48,674	91,060	127.3
Perak	34,725	76,597	105,678	136.3
Perlis	5,648	10,793	16,317	19.7
Selangor	42,240	116,807	293,928	617.3
Trengganu	7,596	18,491	36,959	52.3
	Lifetime Out-Migrants			
Johore	11,784	40,497	86,565	159.5
Kedah	18,392	53,925	103,765	198.0
Kelantan	8,972	27,631	67,497	121.3
Malacca	22,031	49,452	88,130	149.8
Negri Sembilan	19,692	49,295	96,762	160.3
Pahang	8,142	23,207	41,315	73.7
Penang	46,887	79,515	111,147	148.7
Perak	49,763	108,003	219,990	388.7
Perlis	2,150	6,690	13,241	26.8
Selangor	32,645	61,372	94,257	140.2
Trenggau	7,336	15,823	31,011	59.9

TABLE 4.12
LIFETIME NET MIGRANTS BY STATE, 1947–80

State	1947	1957	1970	1980
	Number			
Johore	15,562	15,446	– 4,984	– 26.1
Kedah	17,584	6,052	– 25,357	–107.2
Kelantan	– 4,354	–17,109	– 47,828	– 88.4
Malacca	–13,085	–25,214	– 40,325	– 91.7
Negri Sembilan	2,557	2,887	– 21,600	– 61.9
Pahang	9,411	17,979	65,798	163.2
·Penang	–25,990	–30,841	– 20,087	– 20.9
Perak	–15,038	–31,406	–114,312	–252.4
Perlis	3,498	4,103	3,076	– 3.1
Selangor	9,595	55,435	199,671	477.1
Trengganu	260	2,668	5,948	– 7.6
	Rate			
Johore	21.1	16.7	– 3.9	– 16.5
Kedah	31.7	8.6	– 26.6	– 99.5
Kelantan	– 9.7	–33.8	– 69.7	–102.9
Malacca	–54.7	–86.6	– 99.8	–205.2
Negri Sembilan	9.5	7.9	– 44.9	–107.9
Pahang	37.6	57.5	130.3	212.3
Penang	–58.3	–53.9	– 25.9	– 23.2
Perak	–15.8	–25.7	– 72.8	–144.8
Perlis	50.0	45.2	25.4	– 21.4
Selangor	13.5	54.2	122.4	203.4
Trengganu	1.2	9.6	14.7	– 14.5

portion of foreign-born population was reduced from 22 per cent in 1947 to 5 per cent in 1980. Secondly, the method covers only the final destination of the inter-state migrants as noted at the census date and does not take into account those intermediate moves to other states and those moves out of a state and back to it again.

According to the figures in Table 4.11, the magnitude and pattern of life-time in-migrants among the 11 states have altered over the years. During the first intercensal period 1947–57, lifetime in-migrants increased by nearly three-fold in three states and more than twofold in almost all the other states. But during the second period, as many as eight states recorded much less than a twofold increase in in-migrants and the number managed to increase by two times in Trengganu and two and a half times in Pahang and Selangor. The last two states again recorded the biggest increase, slightly more than twice, during the third intercensal period, with the other states having much lower increases. It is obvious that the distribution of lifetime in-migrants according to the 11 states would alter in these years, though Selangor has remained the top state for in-migrants throughout the whole period. The least popular state for lifetime in-migrants shifted from Kelantan in 1947 and 1957 to Perlis in 1970 and 1980. The second most popular state shifted from Kedah in 1947 to Perak in 1957, and finally to Pahang in the last two census years. In the long haul the distribution of lifetime in-migrants has become more lopsided, with Selangor emerging as the dominant state for inter-state migrants.

A close examination of the figures in respect of lifetime out-migrants in Table 4.11 will reveal the less pronounced variation in the magnitude of inter-censal increases among the 11 states. As a result there were less shifts in the relative position of the 11 states and also a much smaller movement towards a lopsided distribution. The lowest number of lifetime out-migrants continued to come from Perlis and the highest number from Perak throughout the whole period. The number of lifetime out-migrants for Perak in 1980 amounted to 388,700, which was far lower than the 617,300 lifetime in-migrants for the top state of Selangor. Again eight states had more than 120,000 lifetime out-migrants in 1980 as compared to only five states with more than this number of lifetime in-migrants in the same year.

Of greater significance are the figures for lifetime net migrants which reflect the relative attractiveness of the various states for internal migrants and the different levels of socio-economic development of these states. Furthermore, the figures in Table 4.12 are significant in the sense that they constitute an-other factor, in addition to fertility, mortality and international migration, that had determined the rate of population growth of the 11 states during the three intercensal periods. The bottom section of the table gives the net internal migration rate which may be defined as the number of lifetime net migrants per thousand population in the state. This rate can be employed to measure the differences in the extent of lifetime net migration among the 11 states.

The pattern of lifetime inter-state migration observed at the beginning of the period in 1947 has altered over the years. In 1947 the four states that suffered a net loss of lifetime net migrants were Kelantan, Malacca, Perak and Penang, in ascending order of magnitude. Among the other seven states, the greatest gainer was Kedah with a surplus of 17,584 lifetime net migrants, followed closely by Johore with 15,562. In 1957 the same four states suffered a loss and the same seven states a gain in lifetime net migrants, but the exact magnitude and its relative position have undergone some changes. The top two gainers were replaced by Selangor with 55,435 and Pahang with 17,979 while the greatest loser was now Perak instead of Penang. A more radical change in the pattern of inter-state migration is revealed by the 1970 figures. The number of states that suffered a loss of lifetime net migrants was enlarged from the original four to seven: the new ones being Johore, Kedah and Negri Sembilan. The pattern continued to evolve in recent years into a more lopsided one in 1980 when nine states now contributed lifetime net migrants to the two states of Selangor and Johore. Selangor emerged as the premier region for inter-state migration, with a massive gain of 477,100 lifetime net migrants in 1980. This was far ahead of the gain of 163,200 lifetime net migrants recorded in Pahang.

The above discussion of the absolute numbers does not reflect the extent to which the state population was subjected to lifetime net migration, which can only be measured by the rates given in the bottom half of Table 4.12. These rates, expressed in terms of the number of lifetime net migrants per thousand population, attempt to measure the volume of internal migration in each state by taking into consideration the size of the population which varies appreciably in the different states. Among the four net out-migrating states in 1947, Penang recorded the highest rate of lifetime net migration equivalent to 58.3 per thousand population, followed closely by Malacca with a rate of 54.7. This relative position was reversed ten years later in 1957 when Malacca recorded the highest rate of 69.7 and Penang the second highest of 53.9. Since then the rate for Malacca has not only remained as the highest but has taken a sharp upturn to reach 99.8 in 1970 and finally 205.2 in 1980. This was caused by a persistent decline in traffic handled by its port, the closure of the British military base at Trendak in the mid-1960s, the absence of any major industrial estates, and the lack of potential agricultural areas for huge land development schemes.

Perak, one of the original four states with a loss of lifetime net migrants in 1947, also experienced a steep upward trend in its rate from 15.8 per thousand population at the beginning of the period to the second highest rate in 1980 with 144.8. The two adverse factors operating in this state in the 1960s were the control of Ipoh Municipality and several neighbouring town councils by the opposition party, Peoples' Progressive Party, and the decline of the tin-mining industry as tin deposits were rapidly diminished.[20] During the opposition regime the flow of federal funds to the state was not forthcoming and the problem facing the tin industry deepened with the resulting stagnation occurring in tin-mining towns like Chemar, Pusing, Papan, Gopeng, Kampar, Temah, Tapah and Bidor. Another one of the original four that suffered the same fate was Kelantan where the rate rose sharply from 9.7 per thousand in 1947 to 102.9 in 1980. The state, under the opposition government of the Pan-Malayan Islamic Party, was starved of Federal Funds to an even greater extent, and little economic progress was made in the 1960s. Other contributory factors were the lack of a good sheltered deep-sea port, potential agricultural areas, and effective communications with the other states.

It is interesting to note that Penang is the only state that has reduced the lifetime net migration outwards that it experienced at the commencement of the period. The highest rate of 58.3 per thousand in 1947 was lowered to only 23.2 in 1980, the sixth highest among the nine states with negative rates. The loss of its free port status was more than compensated by the establishment of industrial estates and the expansion of the tourist industry. Pahang and Selangor, with gains of lifetime net migration in 1947, are the two other states that have seen improvement in their rate. Pahang's rate rose from 37.6 in 1947 to the top spot of 212.3 in 1980, and Selangor's rate from 13.5 to 203.4 during the same period. As mentioned earlier, Pahang benefited the most from land development projects and Selangor has within the states the national capital of Kuala Lumpur, the first and biggest new town of Petaling Jaya, the national airport and seaport, and the most extensive industrial development in the country.[21]

Having seen the evolution of the pattern of inter-state migration into one whereby movement was now essentially outwards from nine states into two states, we will proceed a step further by looking at the direction of migration streams. In Table 4.13 we have presented figures extracted from the general census report showing the state of origin of lifetime in-migrants to Selangor and Pahang and the destination state of lifetime out-migrants from five major states.[22] With regard to the most popular state of Selangor, the general inflow of population was from the more developed and urbanised states on

20. Gavin J. Jones and Manjit S. Sidhu, "Population Mobility in Peninsular Malaysia", *Development Forum*, Vol. 9, No. 2, December 1979.

21. For more details on land development projects, see C. MacAndrews, *Mobility and Modernization: A Study of the Malaysian Federal Land Development Authority and Its Role in Modernizing the Rural Malay*, Ph.D. Thesis, Massachusetts Institute of Technology, 1976.

22. Khoo Teik Huat, *Malaysia: General Report of the Population Census, 1980*, Vol. 1 (Kuala Lumpur: Department of Statistics, 1983).

TABLE 4.13
DIRECTION OF LIFETIME IN-MIGRANTS AND LIFETIME OUT-MIGRANTS BY STATE, 1980

State of Origin or Destination	Lifetime In-Migrants to ('000)				Lifetime Out-Migrants from ('000)		
	Selangor	Pahang	Perak	Kedah	N. Sembilan	Malacca	Kelantan
Johore	69.0	24.1	23.1	9.5	18.6	30.3	6.4
Kedah	42.2	26.8	25.5	—	2.0	1.6	3.6
Kelantan	27.8	37.7	5.7	3.3	1.9	1.5	—
Malacca	69.3	11.0	6.2	2.1	15.7	—	2.0
N. Sembilan	91.1	16.9	11.7	3.6	—	24.3	3.2
Pahang	35.9	—	45.6	26.8	16.9	11.0	37.7
Penang	48.3	9.5	47.9	51.9	2.5	2.3	2.5
Perak	208.7	45.6	—	37.7	6.4	4.6	5.0
Perlis	5.7	3.4	3.0	14.6	0.3	0.2	0.6
Selangor	—	33.2	208.7	42.2	91.1	69.3	27.9
Trengganu	12.0	27.5	3.9	1.7	1.5	1.3	29.5
Total	610.2	235.7	381.8	193.4	156.9	146.4	118.4

the west coast of the Peninsula. In addition to the incredibly huge number of 208,700 or 34 per cent of the total in-migrants from Perak by 1980, Selangor received substantial numbers from Negri Sembilan (91,100), Malacca (69,300), Johore (69,000) and Penang (48,300). On the other hand, Pahang succeeded in attracting in-migrants from the western state of Perak (45,600) and Selangor (33,200), apart from the predominantly agricultural states of Kelantan (37,700), Trengganu (27,500) and Kedah (26,800). The people who moved into Selangor went for the jobs in the manufacturing and the services sectors as well as the city life of the national capital, whilst those who chose to migrate to Pahang participated mainly in the land development projects backed by government direction and assistance.

The tremendous popularity of Selangor to the out-migrants from Perak exerted a conspicuous impact on the direction of population outflow from this state, the number that went to Selangor constituting as much as 55 per cent of the total out-migrants. The other out-migrants moved mainly to four other states, viz. Penang (47,900), Pahang (45,600), Kedah (25,500) and Johore (23,100). In Negri Sembilan an equally large member, 91,100 or 58 per cent, shifted to Selangor, with the remaining going primarily to Johore (18,600), Pahang (16,900) and Malacca (15,700). The outflow of lifetime migrants from Malacca was also concentrated towards Selangor (69,300) and Johore (30,300), and its immediate neighbour Negri Sembilan (24,300). A different direction of out-migration stream is revealed by the figures for the predominantly agricultural state of Kedah in the north, the most popular destination being Penang (51,900) instead of Selangor (42,200). Besides, some 14,600 moved across the boundary into Perlis, apart from the bigger numbers that went further afield to Perak (37,700) and Pahang (26,800). The out-migrants from the agricultural state of Kelantan in the east were more selective, resettling mainly in Pahang, Trengganu and Selangor.

Bearing in mind the geographical relationship of the above states that proved to be popular for lifetime out-migrants from a particular state, it would appear that distance is an important factor that determines the magnitude of inter-state migration. This is in accordance with one of the migration laws which states that the rate of migration between two points will be inversely related to the distance between these points.[23] Neighbouring states were more attractive to internal migrants, the best example being the sizeable number that moved from Kedah to the small state of Perlis as against the negligible numbers from the other states.

The other factor that has exerted considerable influences is the irresistible

---

23. E.G. Ravenstein, "The Laws of Migration", *Journal of the Royal Statistical Society*, June 1879.

pull of the big cities with better job opportunities and superior living conditions. This is the key reason for the popularity of Selangor with the premier
city of Kuala Lumpur and its surrounding industrial estates among out-
migrants from the other states. If this factor and the distance factor operate
simultaneously, we approach the enhanced positions in respect of the tremendous concentration of Perak's out-migrants towards Selangor across its
southern border and the biggest proportion of Kedah's out-migrants towards
the neighbouring state of Penang. The third pull-factor that emerged in Peninsular Malaysia refers to the land development projects as evidenced from
the fair number of out-migrants from the other states to the state with the
largest of such projects, Pahang.

Pattern of Intra-State Migration

It is necessary to proceed from the preceeding analysis of internal migration
across the boundaries of the 11 states to a discussion of movements of people
among and within smaller areas or districts in the various states. The importance of distance in influencing the volume of migration implies that internal
movements among small areas constitute the other vital part of overall
population movements within the country. Unlike inter-state migration, our
analysis of intra-state migration cannot be based on place-of-birth data because
such detailed data have never been compiled and published in the census
reports. Instead, intra-state movements will be examined in terms of a different
set of data, namely, the place of last previous residence as collected in the last
two population censuses.

An idea of the relative importance of inter-state, inter-district and intra-
district migration in Peninsular Malaysia is obtainable in the summary of the
figures for these three types of movements in Table 4.14. For the country as
a whole, a total of 2,630,480 persons participated in internal movements of
all kinds by the time of the 1970 Census, a figure equivalent to a rate of 298.6
per thousand population. A decade later in 1980 the number increased to
3,617,600 or a rate of 332.3 per thousand. What it means is that 3 out of 10
persons in the country have changed their place of residence in the past from
1970 to 1980.

The underlying importance of the figures in the light of our present discussion is that out of the total of 2,630,480 internal migrants in 1970 only 36
per cent moved across state boundaries and the other 64 per cent shifted
residence within the state. The latter percentage can be divided into 26 per
cent that moved among districts and 38 per cent within districts. By 1980 the
proportion of inter-state migrants had risen to 44 per cent, accompanied by
a reduction in the proportions of inter-district migrants and intra-district

TABLE 4.14
INTER-STATE, INTER-DISTRICT AND INTRA-DISTRICT
MIGRATION, 1970 AND 1980

Type of Migration	Number		Rate	
	1970	1980	1970	1980
Inter-state	953,680	1,603,400	108.3	147.3
Inter-district	674,100	865,800	76.5	79.5
Intra-district	1,002,700	1,148,400	113.8	105.5
Total	2,630,480	3,617,600	298.6	332.3

migrants to 24 per cent and 32 per cent respectively. But the relatively greater importance of the last two types combined together as compared with inter-state migration still prevailed in 1980. The increased incidence of overall population movements mentioned just now was brought about mainly by inter-state migration where the rate rose from 108.3 per thousand in 1970 to 147.3 in 1980. In contrast, the inter-district migration rate managed to rise only slightly from 76.5 to 79.5 and the intra-district migration rate even suffered a decline from 113.8 to 105.5 during the same period.

Before commenting in detail on the figures presented in Table 4.15, it would be useful to say something about the nature of the data. Central to the process of collecting the data is the use of the term 'locality' which refers to an area with a name, for example, a local authority area, a kampong, or an estate. For persons who had made multiple moves involving different localities by the census date, information was collected only on the locality from which the last move was made.[24] The information was collected from all inhabitants staying in the locality regardless of whether they were born in the country or not. The statistics used to study inter-district and intra-district movements have therefore a superior coverage as compared with that for place-of-birth data used in our inter-state migration study because those persons born outside the country were excluded.

First of all, let us look at the changes in the absolute figures that occurred during the intercensal period 1970–80. Except for intra-district migration in

24. Khoo Teik Huat, *Malaysia: General Report of the Population Census, 1980*, Vol. 2 (Kuala Lumpur: Department of Statistics, 1983).

TABLE 4.15
INTER-DISTRICT AND INTRA-DISTRICT MIGRANTS BY STATE, 1970 AND 1980

State	1970			1980		
	Inter-District	Intra-District	Total	Inter-District	Intra-District	Total
Number ('000)						
Johore	127.2	135.5	262.7	197.5	174.7	372.2
Kedah	86.9	125.4	212.3	100.9	151.4	252.3
Kelantan	70.6	53.4	124.0	84.6	57.9	142.5
Malacca	12.7	27.2	39.9	17.6	54.4	72.0
Negri Sembilan	35.0	46.6	81.6	52.2	63.6	115.8
Pahang	37.1	52.3	89.4	75.7	89.5	165.2
Penang	40.4	59.0	99.4	49.6	99.4	149.0
Perak	130.1	205.4	335.5	138.3	236.1	374.4
Perlis	—	23.5	23.5	—	30.7	30.7
Selangor	101.8	234.2	335.9	105.0	130.7	235.7
Trengganu	32.3	40.3	72.6	44.4	60.0	104.4
Total	674.1	1,002.7	1,676.8	865.8	1,148.4	2,014.2
Rate						
Johore	99.6	106.1	205.7	125.0	110.5	235.5
Kedah	91.0	131.3	222.4	93.6	140.5	234.1
Kelantan	102.9	77.8	180.7	98.5	67.4	165.8
Malacca	31.4	67.3	98.7	39.4	121.8	161.1
Negri Sembilan	72.7	96.8	169.5	94.7	115.3	210.0
Pahang	73.5	103.6	177.1	98.5	116.4	214.9
Penang	52.1	76.1	128.2	55.1	110.3	165.4
Perak	82.9	130.9	213.8	79.3	135.4	214.7
Perlis	—	194.2	194.2	—	212.0	212.0
Selangor	62.4	143.6	206.0	44.8	55.7	100.5
Trengganu	79.6	99.4	179.0	84.5	114.2	198.7
Total	76.5	113.8	190.3	79.5	105.5	185.0

Selangor, all the states recorded an increase in the number of inter-district migrants and also in the number of intra-district migrants. As expected these changes vary considerably from state to state, but it would be more fruitful to examine the changes in the intra-state migration rates given in the bottom half of Table 4.15. It should however be noted that the number of intra-district migrants in Selangor suffered a sharp decline from 234,100 in 1970 to 130,700 in 1980. This decline can be explained by the fact that while movements of residents within the present Federal Territory were included as intra-district migration for Selangor in 1970 such movements have not been classified as intra-district migration since the whole of the Federal Territory was considered as one locality in the 1980 census.[25]

The level of inter-district migration within a state as measured by the rate expressed in terms of the total population in the state seems to vary with the land size of the state and the number of districts into which the state is divided. The best example is the smallest state of Perlis which was regarded in the population census as one district for the purpose of collecting data on intra-state movement, and hence there is zero level of inter-district migration for this state. This may be an extreme example, but the next two smallest states of Penang and Malacca experienced the two lowest level of inter-district migration in 1970. The same position prevailed in 1980.

The decade 1970–80 witnessed considerable variation in the changes in the level of inter-district migration, generally a rise in eight states and a reduction in the other three states. Among the former group of states, a significant rise in the level of inter-district movement is noticeable in Johore, Malacca, Negri Sembilan and Pahang, and a minor rise in the other four states. The reduction in the incidence of inter-district movement was also minor in Kelantan and Perak, quite unlike the sharp downturn from 62.4 per thousand to 44.8 in Selangor. As noted earlier, this is due to the 1980 Census treating the whole Federal Territory as one district. The recent varying intensity of movement led to some important shifts in the rate of inter-district migration. In 1980 Johore with a rate of 125.0 emerged as the top state and Kelantan and Pahang jointly second with the identical rate of 98.5. This was very closely followed by Negri Sembilan (94.7) and Kedah (93.6).

No distinct pattern among the 11 states is discernible with regard to short distance moves as reflected by the intra-district figures given in Table 4.15. In 1970 the highest rate of intra-district migration was recorded in the smallest state of Perlis, 143.6 per thousand population. On the other hand,

25. Khoo Teik Huat, *Malaysia: General Report of the Population Census, 1980*, Vol. 1, op. cit., p. 74.

the medium-size states of Kedah and Selangor also recorded fairly high rates of 131.3 and 143.6 respectively, as did the second largest state of Perak with a rate of 130.9. A close scrutiny of the latest census figures again reveal no clear pattern of intra-district migration among the 11 states. The similar highest rate recorded by Perlis in 1980, strongly suggests that the peculiar situation has arisen from the fact that all residential movements within the state came under the category of inter-state migration.

Changes in the level of intra-district migration during the decade under consideration are again noticeable. Only two states experienced a decline in the rate, Kelantan from 77.8 per thousand population to 67.4 and Selangor from 143.6 to 55.7. The tumbling of the rate in Selangor is attributable directly to the reclassification of the Federal Territory as one single locality in the 1980 Census. Among the states that witnessed a rise in the level of intra-state migration, the biggest rise was recorded by Malacca where the rate increased from 67.3 in 1970 to 121.8 in 1980, and the smallest rise by Perak with an increase from 130.9 to only 135.4. In 1980 Perlis maintained its top position regarding the level of intra-district migration and due to the special reason noted, Selangor now experienced the lowest level. The other interesting feature is that Kelantan appeared to be recording a rather low rate of 67.4.

The diverse changes in the rates for inter-district and intra-district movements obviously affected the pattern of intra-state migration. In 1970 the three states with the highest level of intra-state migration were, in descending order, Kedah (222.4), Perak (213.8) and Selangor (206.0), but in 1980 the top three states were Johore (235.5), Kedah (234.1) and Pahang (214.9). At the lower end of the scale, the three states with the smallest rates changed from Malacca (98.7), Penang (128.2) and Negri Sembilan (169.5) to Selangor (100.5), Malacca (161.1) and Penang (165.4). By its very nature, intra-state migration involving short distance moves is essentially determined by a wide variety of reasons operating within the family unit and the local area, and is therefore less amenable to the general principles applicable at the national level.

Rural and Urban Migration

The availability of the relevant data in the recent census reports enables us to study the movements of the population between and within rural and urban areas, which occupy a central position in the study of internal migration in the country. The four specific types of movements that will be investigated into are rural to urban, rural to rural, urban to urban and urban to rural. In the 1980 Census the data on locality of last previous residence were also tabulated according to rural and urban areas based on the demarcation point of 10,000 persons, and hence the required statistics for the four types of population flows can be derived. The statistics have been made more useful with a further cross-tabulation by the duration of present residence in the urban or rural area at the time of the census. Attention should be drawn to the main defect of these statistics in that they capture only the last move prior to the census date and do not therefore tell us something about differences in the propensity of migration during a given time span.

The figures in Table 4.16 reveal that some 3,459,700 persons have participated in internal movements between and within rural and urban areas by the time of the 1980 Census. In Peninsular Malaysia the major form of internal migration was movement from rural to rural areas which involved 1,565,100 persons and accounted for 45.2 per cent of the total migration. This was due purely to the much larger pool of population in the rural areas and partly to the rural development and land development projects. However, there is a possibility that the figures for the rural areas are overestimated, while conversely those for the urban areas are underestimated. If rural migrants settled in the outer fringes of the boundaries of urban areas though working in towns, they would have been classified in the census as having moved from rural to rural

TABLE 4.16

RURAL AND URBAN MIGRANTS BY TYPE AND PERIOD, 1980

Type of Migration	Total	0–10 Years	11 & More Years
	Number		
Rural-Urban	523.6	390.0	133.6
Urban-Rural	601.0	446.1	154.9
Urban-Urban	770.0	559.4	210.6
Rural-Rural	1,565.1	1,081.2	483.9
Total	3,459.7	2,476.7	983.0
	Percentage		
Rural-Urban	15.1	15.7	13.6
Urban-Rural	17.4	18.0	15.8
Urban-Urban	22.3	22.6	21.4
Rural-Rural	45.2	43.7	49.0
Total	100.0	100.0	100.0

rather than rural to urban. Even if they did not work in the towns, these fringe areas would have the characteristics of the urban areas. Rural-urban movement, on the other hand, was the least preferred form of migration, constituting only 15.1 per cent of the total movement. Urban-rural migration accounted for a slightly larger proportion, 17.4 per cent, and an even larger proportion of 22.3 per cent was contributed by urban-urban migration. The comparatively small rural-urban drift is a common experience shown by some other Asian countries.[26]

The figures for 0–10 years refer to the ten years prior to the 1980 Census and can therefore be equated to the intercensal period 1970–80. For every type of internal migration, there was a much larger number of migrants during the last ten years than during the period more than ten years ago, with however some significant differences among the four types of migration. The number of migrants in the recent period compared with that in the older period was 2.9 times for rural-urban migration and also for urban-rural migration as against the 2.7 times for urban-urban migration and 2.2 times for rural-rural migration. It would appear that the 1970s has witnessed an acceleration in the speed of rural-urban migration and a marked slowdown in rural-rural migration. This is also reflected in the rise in the proportion of rural-urban migrants from 13.6 per cent in the older period to 15.7 per cent in the recent period, accompanied by a reduction in the proportion of rural-rural migrants from 49.0 per cent to 43.7 per cent. It should however be mentioned that the absolute figures refer to the survivors of internal migration at the census time and do not include those migrants who died before the census, and are therefore affected by mortality differential between the rural and urban areas. Chances of survival are generally greater among the urban-urban group than among the rural-rural group.

The figures in Table 4.17 for the three main races are also affected by the past differential mortality among these races. The volume of each of the four types of internal migration among these races is determined by, among other factors, the population size of each race in the urban or rural area. This explains the predominance of the rural-rural type among the Malay migrants, accounting for 54.7 per cent of the Malays who shifted residence within the country in the past. The other three types were of almost equal importance, 15.4 per cent rural-urban migrants, 15.6 per cent urban-rural migrants and 14.3 per cent urban-urban migrants. The figures for the two sub-periods reveal

26. See, for example, the following Economic and Social Commission for Asia and the Pacific publications: (a) *Migration, Urbanization and Development in the Republic of Korea*, 1980; (b) *Migration, Urbanization and Development in Indonesia*, 1981 and (c) *Migration, Urbanization and Development in Sri Lanka*, 1980.

TABLE 4.17
DISTRIBUTION OF RURAL AND URBAN MIGRANTS BY TYPE
AND PERIOD FOR THREE MAIN RACES, 1980

Type of Migration	Number ('000)			Percentage		
	Total	0–10 Years	11 & More Years	Total	0–10 Years	11 & More Years
Malays						
Rural-Urban	327.5	261.5	66.0	15.4	16.5	12.1
Urban-Rural	331.7	259.8	71.9	15.6	16.4	13.2
Urban-Urban	304.5	242.6	61.9	14.3	15.3	11.4
Rural-Rural	1,163.7	818.4	345.3	54.7	51.7	63.3
Total	2,127.4	1,582.3	545.1	100.0	100.0	100.0
Chinese						
Rural-Urban	146.2	93.7	52.5	15.7	15.4	16.3
Urban-Rural	187.3	125.7	61.6	20.1	20.6	19.1
Urban-Urban	362.8	245.3	117.5	38.9	40.2	36.4
Rural-Rural	236.1	145.0	91.1	25.3	23.8	28.2
Total	932.4	609.7	322.7	100.0	100.0	100.0
Indians						
Rural-Urban	48.2	33.6	14.6	12.5	12.2	13.2
Urban-Rural	79.8	58.7	21.1	20.7	21.4	19.1
Urban-Urban	97.0	67.6	29.4	25.2	24.6	26.6
Rural-Rural	159.9	114.4	45.5	41.5	41.7	41.1
Total	384.9	274.3	110.6	100.0	100.0	100.0

some interesting differences. The predominance of rural-rural migration was even more pronounced in the second period of longer than 10 years ago, but the last ten years saw a shift towards the other types, particularly rural-urban migration.

An entirely different pattern of internal migration was experienced by the

Chinese in that the most common type was urban-urban migration which accounted for 38.9 per cent of total recorded moves. The second most popular type was rural-rural migration accounting for 25.3 per cent, followed by urban-rural migration with 20.1 per cent and rural-urban migration with 15.7 per cent. In the older period where the considerable resettlement of rural Chinese during the Emergency occurred, the rural-rural migrants constituted 28.2 per cent of the total migrants but this proportion was reduced to 23.8 per cent in the recent period. The swing was mainly towards urban-urban migration which accounted for 40.2 per cent of the total during the more recent period. Unlike the Malays, there was a minor shift among the Chinese away from rural-urban migration in recent years, falling from 16.3 per cent in the older period to 15.4 per cent in the recent period. It is clear that notwithstanding the recent changes the Chinese pattern of preferences for the four types of internal migration is distinctly different from that of the Malays.

By comparison the Indians have experienced the least changes in the relative importance of these four types of internal migration. The most popular form of migration has always been rural-rural movement, accounting for slightly more than 40 per cent at all times. The second most preferred type was urban-urban migration accounting for about one-quarter, followed by urban-rural migration (about one-fifth) and rural-urban migration (about one-tenth). Indian internal migration was not subjected to any special factor that affected their preferences for the four types of internal migration.

Another way of looking at the process of internal migration among the races is to analyse the changing race composition of each of the four types presented in Table 4.18. The race composition of each type of internal migration has undergone significant changes over the years. With regard to rural-urban migration, the proportion of Malay migrants rose from 49.4 per cent during the older period to 67.1 per cent in the recent period, while the Chinese proportion moved in the opposite direction, falling from 39.3 per cent to 24.0 per cent. As can be noted in Table 4.18, the increase in the absolute figures over the two periods was from 66,000 to 261,500 for the Malay migrants and from 52,500 to 93,700 for the Chinese migrants. The enhanced participation of the Malays in rural-rural migration in recent years was due to the active encouragement of the government under the New Economic Policy, and contributed to the more rapid urbanisation of the Malays noted earlier. In fact, there was some increase in the participation of the Malays in the other three types of internal migration as well.

An innovation introduced in the 1980 Census was the collection of information on the reasons for internal migrants moving to their present place of residence. But the data suffer from certain shortcomings. First, in view of the various constraints in the actual enumeration of respondents in the census,

TABLE 4.18
PERCENTAGE DISTRIBUTION OF RURAL AND URBAN
MIGRANTS BY TYPE AND RACE, 1980

Type of Migration	Malays	Chinese	Indians	Others	Total
0–10 Years					
Rural-Urban	67.1	24.0	8.6	0.3	100.0
Urban-Rural	58.2	28.2	13.2	0.4	100.0
Urban-Urban	43.4	43.9	11.5	1.2	100.0
Rural-Rural	75.7	13.4	10.6	0.3	100.0
Total	63.9	21.1	11.0	10.1	100.0
11 & More Years					
Rural-Urban	49.4	39.3	10.9	0.4	100.0
Urban-Rural	46.4	39.8	13.6	0.2	100.0
Urban-Urban	29.4	55.8	14.0	0.8	100.0
Rural-Rural	71.4	18.8	9.4	0.4	100.0
Total	55.5	32.8	11.6	0.1	100.0

only the main reason for changing residence was obtained, and in many instances the migrants have moved because of a combination of reasons. Second, the answers were subject to errors arising out of the use of proxy respondents, recall biases and *post hoc* rationalisation. Finally, since the answers referred to the reasons for moving to the locality of enumeration, the information collected is only related to the pull-factor, and there is no corresponding information on the push-factor. The limitations should be borne in mind in interpreting the figures given in Table 4.19.

The reasons that influenced people to move to their present place of residence seemed to vary among the four types of internal migration. Some 32.2 per cent of the rural-urban migrants moved to the urban centres because of employment reasons as against the lower figure of 21.5 per cent for rural-rural migrants and 24.7 per cent for urban-rural migrants. The slightly higher proportion for urban-urban migrants, 27.1 per cent, serves to confirm the greater job opportunities in the urban centres. Again, the better educational facilities in

TABLE 4.19
PERCENTAGE DISTRIBUTION OF INTERNAL MIGRANTS BY TYPE
AND REASONS, 1980

Reasons	Rural-Urban	Urban-Rural	Urban-Urban	Rural-Rural
Employment	32.2	24.7	27.1	21.5
Rural Dev. Project	0.5	2.1	0.5	5.6
Education	9.5	1.9	4.1	2.9
Marriage	13.4	13.9	11.7	18.2
Followed Family	33.7	42.9	40.7	41.6
Others	10.7	14.5	15.9	10.2
Total	100.0	100.0	100.0	100.0

these centres as perceived by migrants are manifested in the higher proportion of migrants moving on account of education among the rural-urban migrants with 9.5 per cent and the urban-urban migrants with 4.1 per cent. Only 1.9 per cent of the urban-rural migrants and 2.9 per cent of the rural-rural migrants moved because of education. It is obvious that the biggest proportion for rural development project reason should be registered by the rural-rural migrants, 5.6 per cent, and the second biggest by the urban-rural migrants, 2.1 per cent. The relatively smaller proportion, 33.7 per cent, of rural-urban migrants who moved just to follow the family was obviously due to the fact that there were more single persons among this group. By and large, migrants moved to the urban centres on account of economic reasons, and those who moved to the rural areas were influenced more by social reasons.

5

Mortality Trends and Differentials

T he size and structure of the population of Peninsular Malaysia at any time are determined by the interactions of migration, mortality and fertility in the immediate past. While a previous chapter has dealt with migration, this chapter will be devoted to an account of mortality trends and differentials among the major races and the various regions of the country. In this task we are confronted with the problem of obtaining time series data for a period when there were varying dates for compulsory death registration in the different states. It was in the early 1930s that compulsory registration of deaths became effective in all the 11 states and death statistics for the whole Peninsula was made available from 1934 onwards. In the prewar years the collection and tabulation of death statistics were not handled by a central authority so that considerable effort has to be spent to collate the dispersed statistics from various sources. The position improved after the war when the statistics were published by the Registrar-General in a single report, and subsequently also by the Department of Statistics in a more comprehensive publication for the year 1963 onwards. Appendix E gives a more detailed account of the development of death statistics.

General Mortality Trends

The paucity of statistics compels us to examine the long-term trend in mortality way back to 1934 in terms of the crude death rate defined as the number of deaths occurring in a year per 1,000 mid-year population.[1] This rate is not a perfect measure of overall mortality level because it is distorted primarily by differences in the age composition of the population and to some

---

. 1. It should be pointed out that the death statistics used in this study are all according to date of registration since similar figures by date of occurrence have never been published. The difference between the two figures is negligible since almost all deaths are registered within a few days.

extent by differences in the sex composition. In view of the fluctuation in the annual figures, the number of deaths and the rates are presented in Table 5.1 in terms of three-year periods. The population denominator employed in the calculation of the crude death rate is the average of the three mid-year populations in each of the three-year periods.

Despite the inherent shortcoming of the rate as a measure of mortality, the data presented on Table 5.1 are of some use in indicating the broad trends in overall mortality over the years as well as the adverse mortality conditions prevailing during the Japanese Occupation. The gradual reduction in the crude death rate over the major part of the past fifty years since 1934 suggests that the secular swing in the general mortality level has been essentially downward. From a level of 22.0 per 1,000 population in the period 1934–36, the death rate eventually reached the low of 5.3 in the latest period 1982–84. By and large, this decline may be attributed to advances in medical knowledge,

TABLE 5.1

ANNUAL AVERAGE DEATHS AND CRUDE DEATH RATES, 1934–84

Period	Annual Average Deaths	Crude Death Rate	Percentage Decline	
			Deaths	CDR
1934–36	86,346	22.0	—	—
1937–39	88,079	19.8	+ 2.0	+10.0
1940–42	92,139	19.6	+ 4.6	1.0
1943–45	132,391	27.4	+43.7	+39.8
1946–48	93,786	19.0	29.5	30.7
1949–51	78,865	15.1	15.9	20.5
1952–54	72,559	12.7	8.0	15.9
1955–57	72,670	11.7	+ 0.2	7.9
1958–60	67,500	10.1	7.1	13.7
1961–63	67,811	9.2	+ 0.5	8.9
1964–66	63,358	7.9	6.6	14.1
1967–69	65,207	7.5	+ 2.9	5.1
1970–72	63,954	6.8	1.9	9.3
1973–75	64,545	6.4	+ 0.9	5.9
1976–78	64,402	6.0	0.2	6.3
1979–81	63,374	5.5	1.6	8.3
1982–84	65,830	5.3	+ 3.9	3.6

discovery of new drugs, better medical facilities, improved public hygiene and sanitation, and enhanced living conditions brought about by social and economic progress.[2] Many tropical diseases, particularly malaria, that used to take a heavy toll of human lives, were slowly but effectively brought under control. It should however be mentioned that the shift towards a more even sex ratio and younger age structure over time may be partly responsible for the decline in the crude death rate.

The death statistics for the years 1942–45 affected by the war were incomplete for the whole country due to the loss of records in certain states. The deaths for the affected years are obtained from independent estimates prepared by the author in a paper published earlier.[3] It is not surprising that the crude death rate shot up from 19.6 in 1940–42 to 27.4 in 1943–45, an increase of 39.8 per cent. A better picture is portrayed by the figures for the individual years shown below. The detailed figures show that mortality reached the peak of 30.3 in 1944,

Year	Deaths	Rates
1941	84,668	18.1
1942	99,257	20.9
1943	123,282	25.7
1944	146,476	30.3
1945	127,416	26.3
1946	105,040	21.1

and dropped in the following year when the war ended in Peninsular Malaysia on 9 September 1945. Mortality conditions must have improved appreciably in the immediate postwar period when medical facilities were quickly restored, public health measures improved, and food rationing increased.

The principal causes of death during the war years were malaria due to the neglect of anti-malarial works and shortage of quinine, beri-beri resulting from deficient diets over-loaded with tapioca and potato carbohydrates, and dysentery also due to deficient and improper diets.[4] In general, the exceptionally high death rate can be traced to the twin-effect of malnutrition and under-nutrition as well as the disruption and lack of preventive and curative medical facilities.

2. For more details, see "The Situation and Recent Trends of Mortality in the World", *Population Bulletin of the United Nations*, No. 6 (New York: Department of Economic and Social Affairs, 1962).

3. The method developed to prepare these estimates is described fully in Saw Swee-Hock, "A Problem of Estimating a Contingency Table Arising in Demographic Analysis", *Population Studies*, Vol. 19, No. 3, March 1966.

4. Malayan Union, *Report of the Medical Department, 1946* (Kuala Lumpur: Government Press).

Deaths from active combat among armed forces and civilians were not substantial, except during the first two or three months following the outbreak of war in December 1941. The fighting in the country was all over in a matter of about 70 days from 8 December 1941 to 15 February 1942 when the British armed forces surrendered to the Japanese. Furthermore, the Japanese Occupation came to a sudden end without any fighting when Japan surrendered unconditionally after the atomic bomb was dropped on Hiroshima and Nagasaki on 6 and 9 August 1945 respectively.

The first three-year period of peace-time conditions in 1946–48 recorded a death rate of 19.0 per 1,000 which represents a decline of 30.7 per cent as compared with the 27.4 in the previous period. During the first 20 years after the war, the death rate declined rapidly and reached 7.9 in 1964–66. The next 20 years witnessed a slower decline in the death rate which finally reached the low of 5.3 in 1982–84. There is no doubt that the crude death rate has stabilised at slightly above the level of five per 1,000 population. The shifts towards a normal sex composition and also towards a young population have now been completed, and the death rate might even commence to go upwards as the population starts to age in the near future. The annual average deaths, which have been falling after the war, seem to have stopped going downwards after 1963 and have instead fluctuated at slightly below the 65,000 level in general.

One of the most spectacular demographic changes that occurred in every part of the world after the Second World War was the rapid decline in mortality and its consequent effect on the rate of population growth. The progress made in reducing mortality has been particularly impressive in the developing countries, not excluding Peninsular Malaysia where better medical and public health facilities and improved living conditions produced a marked downward shift in the level of mortality for the total population and for most of its components. Though the postwar downtrend in overall mortality appeared to have been disclosed by the crude death rate, it is necessary to examine this mortality decline in terms of more reliable indices. Table 5.2 presents the infant mortality rate, neonatal mortality rate and maternal mortality rate for similar three-year periods from 1946 to 1984.

The infant mortality rate, defined as the number of deaths under one year of age per 1,000 live-births, is generally accepted as a good index of mortality conditions prevailing in the country. The past 40 years or so witnessed a continuous reduction in this rate which was brought down from 94.7 per 1,000 live-births in 1946–48 to 19.9 in 1982–84. It is however important to note that the speed of decline was not the same during the period. The early postwar years witnessed a sluggish decline in the infant mortality rate which was lowered from 94.7 in 1946–48 to 71.5 in 1958–60, a reduction of 24.5 per cent in the 15-year period. The reduction was almost doubled in the next 15-year

TABLE 5.2
INFANT MORTALITY RATES, NEONATAL MORTALITY RATES AND
MATERNAL MORTALITY RATES, 1946–84

Period	Infant Mortality Rate	Neonatal Mortality Rate	Maternal Mortality Rate	Percentage Decline		
				I.M.R.	N.M.R.	M.M.R.
1946–48	94.7	36.3	6.5	—	—	—
1949–51	93.2	33.1	5.4	1.6	8.8	16.9
1952–54	85.5	31.1	4.7	8.3	6.0	13.0
1955–57	76.3	28.9	3.6	8.5	7.1	23.4
1958–60	71.5	30.3	2.4	6.3	+4.8	41.7
1961–63	58.5	29.5	2.2	18.2	2.6	8.3
1964–66	48.8	25.5	2.0	16.6	13.6	9.1
1967–69	43.5	23.4	1.7	10.9	8.2	15.0
1970–72	39.1	22.7	1.3	10.1	3.0	23.5
1973–75	35.7	21.4	0.9	8.7	3.5	30.8
1976–78	30.2	18.5	0.8	15.4	15.5	11.1
1979–81	24.2	15.2	0.6	19.9	17.8	25.0
1982–84	19.9	12.3	0.4	17.8	19.1	33.3

period when the rate was lowered by 45.3 per cent, bringing it down from 71.5 in 1958–60 to 39.1 in 1970–72. In the more recent years the decline has even gathered momentum as evidenced by the reduction of 49.1 per cent in the 15-year period 1970–84. The faster decline recorded after the attainment of independence from the British is clearly indicative of the concern of the government for the high infant mortality particularly in the rural areas and the strong emphasis placed on medical and health measures to lower the infant mortality.[5]

The level of infant mortality can be further examined in terms of its two main components, viz. neonatal mortality and post-neonatal mortality. Neonatal mortality refers to deaths during the first four weeks and post-neonatal mortality to deaths during the remainder of the first year after birth. The latter is attributed to exogenous causes and is more amenable to environmental and medical controls, while the former is due to endogenous factors which respond to these controls up to a point only. This is disclosed by the figures

5. See, for example, Malaya, *Malaya: First Five-Year Plan, 1956–60* (Kuala Lumpur: Government Press, 1956).

in Table 5.2 where the reduction in the neonatal mortality rate has been usually smaller than that in the infant mortality rate during the whole period under review. Except for the period 1958–60, the trend in neonatal mortality was downwards all the way during the postwar years. The downtrend was apparently much steeper in the late 1970s and early 1980s.

It is to be noted that the maternal mortality rate is defined in this study as the number of female deaths due to puerperal causes per 1,000 live-births. This slight departure from the standard practice of including the still-births in the denominator in computing the rate is adopted in Peninsular Malaysia mainly because until as late as 1 August 1958 there was no compulsory registration of still-births throughout the country.[6] Prior to this date there was only registration of still-births in the two former Straits Settlement states of Penang and Malacca.

The improvement in mortality conditions during the postwar period was also reflected in the downward movement of the maternal mortality rate which was lowered from 6.5 per 1,000 live-births in 1946–48 to only 0.4 in 1982–84. According to the figures given in the last column of Table 5.2, the reduction in the maternal mortality rate from one three-year period to another was most irregular, ranging from a high of 17.8 per cent in 1979–81 to a low of 2.6 per cent in 1961–63, not forgetting the increase in one particular period. The only possible explanation is that this irregularity is due to the random fluctuations in the small number of maternal deaths from year to year.

An idea of the extent and nature of decline in mortality at the other ages may be observed in Table 5.3 showing the age-specific death rates for four three-year periods centred around the four census years. The figures also demonstrate the considerable variations in mortality over the whole age range. In comformity with observations made in other countries, mortality in Peninsular Malaysia is very high in the first few years of life and decreases rapidly to the lowest level in the teenage group of 10–14, and then begins to rise gradually until about the mid-40s after which it rises progressively faster until the last survivors of the generation are extinguished. Such a pattern of high mortality at the very young and at the very old and low mortality at the early teens prevails in the Peninsula irrespective of the general level of mortality at the four different time-periods.

The data given in Table 5.3 point to a fairly substantial, though expectedly not uniform, decrease in mortality at the various age groups. In the first period 1946–58 the mortality decline was most pronounced in the age groups from age 1 to 14 with reductions ranging from 62 to 67 per cent, followed by lesser

---

6. Ibrahim Bin Ali, *Malaya: Report of the Registrar-General on Population, Births, Deaths, Marriages and Adoptions, 1963* (Kuala Lumpur: Government Press, 1965).

TABLE 5.3
AGE-SPECIFIC DEATH RATES, 1946–81

Age Group	1946–48	1956–58	1969–71	1979–81
Rates				
0*	94.73	76.75	40.81	24.19
1– 4	24.65	8.89	4.56	2.16
5– 9	8.26	2.70	1.47	0.82
10–14	4.36	1.64	0.95	0.64
15–19	4.93	2.36	1.29	1.01
20–24	7.56	3.37	1.80	1.43
25–29	9.44	4.28	2.10	1.56
30–34	11.57	5.16	2.68	1.80
35–39	12.55	6.43	3.45	2.37
40–44	15.02	7.83	4.71	3.53
45–49	19.62	10.66	7.41	5.65
50–54	26.58	14.92	12.39	9.06
55 & Over	64.10	57.15	43.15	40.08
Percentage Decline				
0	—	19.0	46.8	40.7
1 4	—	63.9	48.7	52.6
5– 9	—	67.3	45.6	44.2
10–14	—	62.4	42.1	32.6
15–19	—	52.1	45.3	21.7
20–24	—	55.4	46.6	20.6
25–29	—	54.7	50.9	25.7
30–34	—	55.4	48.1	32.8
35–39	—	48.8	46.3	31.3
40–44	—	47.9	39.8	25.1
45–49	—	45.7	30.5	23.8
50–54	—	43.9	17.0	26.9
55 & Over	—	11.6	24.5	7.1

Note: * Per thousand live-births.

128 THE POPULATION OF PENINSULAR MALAYSIA

reductions of 52 to 55 per cent in the age groups from 15 to 34 and still lesser reductions towards the older age groups. The progressively slower speed of decline at the old ages can be seen to occur in the next two periods 1956–71 and 1969–81. The resistance to decline at the older ages may be attributed to what is commonly known as the generation factor, i.e. deaths at old ages are essentially caused by degenerative ailments which are not so readily amenable to medical science. In contrast, the greatest decline in mortality appears to have occurred in the young age groups as evidenced by the largest reduction of 67.3 per cent in the 5–9 age group in 1946–58, 48.7 per cent in the 1–4 age group in 1956–71, and 52.6 per cent in again the 1–4 age group in 1969–81.

So far we have not answered the important question as to the precise extent of reduction in the overall level of mortality that has taken place in the various periods. To do this satisfactorily, we must employ the age-specific death rates given in Table 5.3 to compute the age-standardised death rates for the four respective periods.[7] These rates, shown below, are not influenced by the differences in the age composition of the population in the four periods, and can therefore be used to measure changes in overall mortality.

Period	Standardised Rate	% Decline
1946–48	17.73	—
1956–58	11.01	37.9
1969–71	7.13	35.2
1979–81	5.63	21.0

The results of the standardisation reveal that a fall of 37.9 in overall mortality was recorded in the first 13-year period, 35.2 per cent in the 16-year period 1956–71, and 21.0 per cent in the latest 13-year period in 1969–81. This confirms what we have observed earlier in that there was an acceleration in overall mortality decline in the early postwar years. After the spectacular achievement in the early years, it should not surprised us to see the mortality decline slackening in recent years.

By far the most sophisticated technique of measuring overall mortality is by means of a life table based on a closed cohort of persons who are assumed to be subject throughout their life to the death rates of the period. Three sets of abridged life tables by sex and race have been constructed by the author. The first set for the period 1956–58 was published earlier in another paper,[8] while

7. In computing the age-standardised death rates for the four periods the population by age enumerated in the 1980 Census was used as the standard population.
8. Saw Swee-Hock, *Construction of Malayan Abridged Life Tables, 1956–58* (Hong Kong: Department of Statistics, University of Hong Kong, 1970).

the two sets for 1969–71 and 1979–81 are presented in Appendix A which also details the methodology developed to compute these tables. A summary of the results with regard to the average life expectancy at birth and at age 60 are given in Table 5.4.

The average life expectancy of a person at birth rose from 56.7 years in 1956–58 to 64.4 years in 1969–71, an increase of 7.7 years or 13.6 per cent. Thereafter, the upward movement slackened as the life expectancy improved further by only 4.3 years or 6.7 per cent to reach 68.7 years in 1979–81. This slower rise in recent years is consistent with what we have said about the overall mortality trend as measured by the standardised death rate. The advance in life expectancy was of course experienced by the women as well as by men, but the improvement was definitely faster for women during the whole period under review. As a result of these diverse movements, the gap between the life expectancy at birth between men and women has widened. In 1956–58 the male life expectancy was 55.7 years as against the female figure of 57.6 years, and by 1979–81 the gap was widened to 66.3 years and 71.2 years respectively.

Whilst the life expectancy at birth serves as a good indicator of the overall level of mortality and hence the general health conditions of a country, the life expectancy at age 60 is significant in that it may be taken to indicate the

TABLE 5.4
LIFE EXPECTANCY AT BIRTH AND AT AGE 60 BY SEX, 1956–81

| Sex | 1956–58 | 1969–71 | 1979–81 | Increase | | | |
| | | | | 1956–71 | | 1969–81 | |
				Year	%	Year	%
At Birth							
Both Sexes	56.7	64.4	68.7	7.7	13.6	4.3	6.7
Male	55.7	62.2	66.3	6.5	11.7	4.1	6.6
Female	57.6	66.7	71.2	9.1	15.8	4.5	6.7
At Age 60							
Both Sexes	14.2	15.8	16.9	1.6	11.3	1.1	7.0
Male	13.3	14.3	15.5	1.0	7.5	1.2	8.4
Female	15.0	17.2	18.2	2.2	14.7	1.0	5.8

number of years left after retirement. The figures show that Peninsula men have a life expectancy of 13.3 years at age 60 in 1956–58, and this improved over the years to reach 15.5 years in 1979–81. What it means is that, assuming that both the economically active and economically inactive population experience the same mortality level, a male worker at age 60 can expect to live for another 15.5 years or so. A female worker retiring at age 60 in 1979–81 can be expected to live much longer, that is 18.2 years. One should avoid making the common mistake of saying that since female life expectancy at birth is 71.2 years, a woman can live another 11.2 years when she retires at 60. An important implication of this is that the lengthening of life expectancy at this old age, coupled with the increasing number of old people in the future, require the channelling of more resources to the care of the aged.

Mortality Trends by Race

It would be interesting to see how the three main races have participated in the postwar mortality decline that was observed to have occurred in the Peninsula. In doing this, we have decided not to examine in detail the movement in the crude death rates for each of the three main races because of the distortions introduced by the variations in the sex-age composition of the three main races. Suffice it to say that the crude death rate of all the three races moved downwards over the years. The rate was reduced from 24.5 per thousand population in 1934–36 to 5.2 in 1982–83 for the Malays, from 20.1 to 5.2 for the Chinese, and 19.1 to 6.8 for the Indians during the same period. It is obvious that the downward movement was partly the result of the general decline in mortality experienced by each of these races, but the precise amount of mortality reduction cannot be measured by the changes in the crude death

TABLE 5.5
STANDARDISED DEATH RATES FOR THREE MAIN RACES,
1946–81

Period	Malays	Chinese	Indians	Percentage Decline		
				M	C	I
1946–48	22.09	13.10	16.52	—	—	—
1956–58	12.14	7.49	7.58	45.0	42.8	42.0
1969–71	7.47	5.83	8.54	38.5	22.2	10.9
1979–81	5.33	5.06	7.25	28.6	13.2	15.1

rate as these changes were most probably affected by shifts in the sex-age composition of the respective population.

For an accurate picture of mortality trends among the three races, it is necessary to compute the standardised death rates. Table 5.5 gives the standardised death rates for four three-year periods centred around the four postwar censuses. The rates were calculated according to the direct method using the age distribution of the Malay population in 1980 as the standard population. The standardised death rate for the Malays decreased from 22.09 in 1946–48 to 5.33 in 1979–81, representing a mortality reduction of 75.9 per cent during the 36-year period. The other figures in the table reveal that the mortality of the Chinese declined at a slower pace of 61.4 per cent and that of the Indians at a still lower speed of 56.1 per cent during the same period.

The amount of mortality decline recorded by each race in the various sub-periods is given in the second part of the table. The mortality of the Malays decreased by 45.0 per cent in the 13-year period 1946–58, 38.5 per cent in the 15-year period 1956–71, and 28.6 per cent in the 13-year period 1969–81. The same slackening in mortality decline over the years was experienced by the Chinese with decreases of 42.8 per cent, 22.2 per cent and 13.2 per cent in the three respective periods. The mortality trend of the Indians was quite different: from a similarly rapid pace in the first period, the decline slowed down in the second period and picked up speed slightly in the third period. Another interesting point is that in all the three periods the Malays registered a greater decline than the Chinese. As can be observed in the table, the Malay mortality was rather high at the beginning of the period, and because of this it could record a faster speed of decline than the Chinese mortality. Experience in many developing countries has shown that the speed at which mortality declines over a period depends in part on the level at the beginning: the higher the initial level the faster would be the decline.

We will now examine the mortality declines that occurred in the various age groups of the three main races. For this purpose, we have included the age-specific death rates for these races for the two periods 1946–48 and 1979–81. It is not possible to compare the rates for older age groups from 55 onwards because the death statistics for the earlier period terminate at 55 and over. However, this does not diminish the usefulness of these rates in uncovering the major features of the age pattern of mortality declines that existed among the three races. It is clear that in the 36 years from 1946 to 1981 there was a general reduction of mortality throughout the age range in every one of the three races. What is perhaps more noteworthy is the common experience of a progressively smaller reduction in mortality with the advance of old age. Even so, there is a difference in that this tendency is more marked among the Indians and Chinese than among the Malays. For instance, in the last age group 55

TABLE 5.6
AGE-SPECIFIC DEATH RATES FOR THREE MAIN RACES, 1946–48 AND 1979–81

Age Group	Malays			Chinese			Indians		
	1946–48	1979–81	% Decline	1946–48	1979–81	% Decline	1946–48	1979–81	% Decline
0	119.89	26.99	77.5	67.39	16.92	74.9	93.75	27.67	70.5
1– 4	31.66	2.69	91.5	16.77	1.03	93.9	17.61	2.61	85.2
5– 9	11.17	0.99	91.1	5.09	0.51	90.0	6.35	0.86	86.5
10–14	6.01	0.69	88.5	2.57	0.49	80.9	3.87	0.83	78.6
15–19	6.34	0.94	85.2	3.15	0.96	69.5	5.24	1.54	70.6
20–24	8.74	1.31	85.0	5.32	1.37	74.2	8.84	2.13	75.9
25–29	10.55	1.52	85.6	6.99	1.38	80.3	10.30	2.31	77.6
30–34	13.73	1.83	86.7	8.80	1.53	82.6	11.19	2.53	77.4
35–39	14.85	2.44	83.6	9.89	1.98	80.0	13.38	3.67	72.6
40–44	20.06	3.46	82.8	12.83	2.97	76.9	14.98	6.03	59.7
45–49	22.33	5.23	76.6	15.53	5.12	67.0	18.42	9.39	49.0
50–54	39.42	8.79	77.7	22.16	8.06	63.6	28.29	15.92	43.7
55 & Over	75.77	36.82	51.4	51.41	41.79	18.7	60.44	51.04	15.6

and over the mortality reduction amounted to 51.4 per cent for the Malays as compared with the 15.6 per cent for the Indians and 18.7 per cent for the Chinese.

For all the three races the largest amount of decline was recorded in the two child age groups 1–4 and 5–9. Among all the age groups, the greatest reduction was 91.5 per cent in the 1–4 age group for the Malays, 93.9 per cent in also the 1–4 age group for the Chinese, and 86.5 per cent in the 5–9 age group for the Indians. This steep reduction in childhood mortality within the universal decline over the age range was also experienced in many developing countries during the phase of rapid mortality decline.[9] One interesting difference is that the amount of decline from one age group to another seems to fluctuate more among the Chinese than among the Malays or the Indians. On the whole, the similarities in the age pattern of decline in the postwar period have been quite remarkable considering how diverse the three races are in their social, cultural, economic and environmental conditions.

Another useful way of investigating mortality trends among the three races is to examine the life expectancy at birth for the three periods for which life tables by race have been computed. The figures given in Table 5.7 indicate the continuous improvement in life expectancy at birth that was recorded by every one of the three races during the years from 1956 to 1981. Looking first at the Malays, we see that the greatest gain in life expectancy at birth was achieved during the early years from 1956 to 1971. In these years the life expectancy of the Malay men rose from 52.2 years in 1956–58 to 62.4 years in 1969–71 representing a gain of 10.2 years or 19.5 per cent. This compares with the smaller gain of 4.7 years or 7.5 per cent from 1969 to 1981. Malay women were also subjected to the slowdown in the rise in life expectancy at birth: the gain in this life expectancy shrank from 11.3 years or 12.3 per cent in the early years to 6.1 years or 9.5 per cent in the later years.

In the case of the Chinese, the slower rise in the life expectancy at birth over the years appeared to be more pronounced among Chinese women than among their male counterparts. The gain in the life expectancy of Chinese men hardly varied at all considering that a rise of 3.7 years or 6.1 per cent was recorded during the 16 years from 1956 to 1971 as compared with the 3.3 years or 5.1 per cent during the 13 years from 1969 to 1981. The gain in the life expectancy of Chinese women amounted to 5.6 years or 8.5 per cent in the first period, which was clearly larger than the 2.7 years or 3.8 per cent during the second period. The trend in life expectancy was again different for the Indians. Surprisingly, the years 1956–71 saw Indian men managing to register a gain of only 0.2 years as compared with 2.5 years during the period 1969–81. Indian

---

9. See W.H.O., *Mortality in South and East Asia: A Review of Changing Trends and Patterns, 1950–1975* (Geneva: World Health Organisation, 1982).

TABLE 5.7
LIFE EXPECTANCY AT BIRTH BY SEX FOR THREE MAIN RACES,
1956–81

Period	Male			Female		
	Life Expectancy	Increase		Life Expectancy	Increase	
		Year	%		Year	%
Malays						
1956–58	52.2	—	—	53.0	—	—
1969–71	62.4	10.2	19.5	64.3	11.3	21.3
1979–81	67.1	4.7	7.5	70.4	6.1	9.5
Chinese						
1956–58	60.6	—	—	65.6	—	—
1969–71	64.3	3.7	6.1	71.2	5.6	8.5
1979–81	67.6	3.3	5.1	73.9	2.7	3.8
Indians						
1956–58	58.3	—	—	57.7	—	—
1969–71	58.5	0.2	0.3	61.1	3.4	5.9
1979–81	61.0	2.5	4.3	66.6	5.5	9.0

women too were subjected to a slower upturn of 3.4 years in the early period but a faster rise of 5.5 years in the more recent period. In spite of these variations in the upward movement of life expectancy at birth, there was the common feature in which the women of every race have been experiencing a more rapid increase in life expectancy than the men.

Some interesting aspects of life expectancy at birth between the sexes of each race can be observed in Table 5.7. One of the universal characteristics of longevity is that women in all countries have a longer life expectancy at birth than their male counterparts.[10] This normal sex differential in life expectancy at birth was present at all times among the Malays and the Chinese. There

10. United Nations, *Age and Sex Patterns of Mortality: Model Life Tables for Under-Developed Countries*, ST/SOA/Series A, Population Studies No. 22 (New York: Department of Social Affairs, 1955).

is however one interesting exception in Peninsular Malaysia where the Indians apparently witnessed a higher life expectancy at birth for their men than women in 1956–58, 58.3 and 57.7 years respectively. From the period 1969–71 onwards the normal differential of a higher value for the females had emerged.

The unique feature exhibited by the Indian population in the Peninsula during a period of moderate or high mortality has also been observed to exist in Indian populations in other countries such as Singapore, Sri Lanka, Bangladesh, Pakistan and India.[11] The very fact that this feature is prevalent among Indian communities in countries with diverse economic and environmental backgrounds strongly suggests that the explanation lies in deep-rooted attitudes that tend to discriminate against girls with regard to matters affecting their health conditions. As social and economic progress advanced to a certain level, such discriminatory practices diminished and the normal differential in life expectancy between the sexes emerged.

Race Mortality Differentials

Our discussion of mortality trends among the three main races has given us some indication of the presence of variations in mortality levels among these races at various times of the postwar period. An evaluation of these mortality differentials has assumed great significance nowadays in the context of the New Economic Policy because such differentials are often regarded as pointers to the unbalanced social and economic progress that occurred among the major ethnic groups in the past. Indeed, the various five-year development plans implemented since the attainment of independence in 1957 have placed considerable emphasis on the improvement of medical and health programmes particularly in the rural areas. It is heartening to observe in this section that there has been a significant narrowing in the differences in mortality levels among the major races.

In Table 5.8 the differences in the levels of mortality among the three races are analysed in terms of the standardised death rate, the infant mortality rate and the neonatal mortality rate. Since the standardised death rates were all computed by using one standard population, i.e. the 1980 age distribution of the Malays, the rates can be employed to measure accurately mortality

---

11. Kingsley Davies, *The Population of India and Pakistan* (Princeton: Princeton University Press, 1951); ESCAP, *Population of Bangladesh*, Country Monograph No. 9 (Bangkok: Economic and Social Commission for Asia and the Pacific, 1981); N.K. Sarkar, *The Demography of Ceylon* (Ceylon: Government Press, 1957); Saw Swee-Hock, *Singapore Population in Transition* (Philadelphia: University of Pennsylvania Press, 1980) and Saw Swee-Hock, "Increasing Life Expectancy in Singapore during 1969–81", *Singapore Medical Journal*, Vol. 25, No. 3, June 1984.

TABLE 5.8
STANDARDISED DEATH RATES, INFANT MORTALITY RATES AND
NEONATAL MORTALITY RATES FOR THREE MAIN RACES, 1946–81

Period	Malays	Chinese	Indians	Malays = 100	
				C	I
Standardised Death Rate					
1946–48	22.1	13.1	16.5	59	75
1956–58	12.1	7.5	9.6	62	79
1969–71	7.5	5.8	8.5	77	113
1979–81	5.3	5.1	7.2	96	136
Infant Mortality Rate					
1946–48	119.8	67.5	93.8	56	78
1956–58	97.4	47.6	74.0	48	76
1969–71	47.3	28.1	47.9	59	101
1979–81	27.0	16.9	27.7	63	103
Neonatal Mortality Rate					
1946–48	40.6	28.9	46.5	71	115
1956–58	35.9	22.8	31.0	64	86
1969–71	24.5	19.0	27.6	78	113
1979–81	16.2	12.8	15.7	79	97

differentials among the races. It should be pointed out that the figures for the
two periods 1956–58 and 1969–71 in respect of infant mortality and neonatal
mortality are not for the same periods as those shown in Table 5.2. They have
been recalculated so that the two three-year periods coincide exactly with the
corresponding two periods for the standardised death rates.

According to the standardised death rates, the Malays were experiencing
the highest mortality in the early postwar years 1946–48 and the Chinese the
lowest, with the Indians occupying an intermediate position. To be more
precise, the Chinese mortality in those days was about 41 per cent lower than
the Malay mortality. This gap between these two principal races was however
reduced over the years as the Malays experienced the greatest improvement
in mortality conditions over time. The difference in mortality levels was

reduced to 38 per cent in 1956–58, 13 per cent in 1969–71, and finally to only 4 per cent in 1979–81. At the beginning the Indian mortality was 25 per cent lower than the Malay mortality and this was slightly narrowed to 21 per cent in 1956–58. But by 1969–71 there emerged a complete reversal of the position with the Indians now recording a mortality level that was 13 per cent higher. This was further widened to 36 per cent in 1979–81. During the whole period the Chinese were experiencing better mortality conditions than the Indians.

In the first period 1946–48 the infant mortality rate was 119.8 per thousand live-births for the Malays and 67.5 for the Chinese, the latter being 44 per cent lower than the former. This differential worsened to 52 per cent in 1956–58, but subsequently improved to 41 per cent in 1969–71 and 37 per cent in 1974–81. This differential in infant mortality did not improve as fast as the differential in overall mortality as measured by the standardised rates, which may be a reflection of the difficulty of improving infant mortality in the rural areas where proportionately more Malays are staying. The infant mortality rate of the Indians was also lower, by 22 per cent than that of the Malays, but by 1969–71 the differential has almost disappeared and the two races continued to record almost the same level of infant mortality until the most recent period.

Smaller differences in mortality for the first four weeks of life seem to exist among the three races. For instance, the neonatal mortality rate of the Chinese was only 29 per cent lower than that of the Malays in 1946–48 as compared to 44 per cent indicated by the infant mortality rate. In a way this may be taken to mean that the three races were subjected to greater differences in post-neonatal mortality than in neonatal mortality. What this amounts to is that the variations in infant mortality rates among the races are to a large extent engendered by exogenous factors, commonly equated to environmental and medical conditions. It is to be noted that the relative position between the neonatal mortality rate of the Malays and the Indians is not so clear-cut. In the first and third periods the Malays were experiencing a lower rate, but a higher rate in the other two periods.

The unfavourable mortality conditions that prevailed among the Malay community in the early postwar years can be explained in terms of a few inter-dependent factors. In the first place, the proportion of the population residing in the rural areas in those days was exceptionally high among the Malays. This is relevant in that in these places the medical and public health facilities were quite inadequate, and the environment was less satisfactory with regard to modern standards of personal hygiene and sanitation due to paucity of basic services such as pipe-water, proper drainage and a modern sewerage system. The second factor, which was particularly responsible for the much higher infant mortality, can be linked to nutritional deficiencies of the Malay diet due to poverty and food habits. These deficiencies tended to weaken the children and render them more susceptible to fatal diseases.[12] Finally, some authorities seem to attribute the high Malay mortality in those days to superstitious practices involving *pawangs* and *bomohs*, and hence not relying on modern medical facilities.[13] In this respect one must also take into consideration the fact that these facilities were not only inadequate but also not within easy access of the Malays, especially those who lived in the more remote areas. As mentioned earlier, the years after independence have seen considerable expansion in the medical and health programmes throughout the whole country. This, coupled with improved living conditions consequent on social and economic progress, has lead to a more rapid improvement in the mortality level of the Malays. Mortality differences among the races have narrowed over time, though their existence is still noticeable.

The variations in mortality levels among the three races at the various ages may be observed in Table 5.9 which depicts the age-specific death rates by sex for the latest period 1979–81. It is worth mentioning that these rates were employed to compute the six abridged life tables by sex for the three main races given in Appendix A.[14] We have decided to present the rates for each sex separately in order to secure a more meaningful and interesting analysis. A close scrutiny of the figures will reveal the presence of some kind of relationship between the age pattern of mortality between the males and the females. The usual pattern of women experiencing lower death rates than the men at ages from the youngest age group to the oldest group can be seen to exist in each of the three races. There was however one exception in that among the Indians the death rate in the childhood age group was higher for the girls than the boys. This is in fact an integral part of the unique feature of Indian mortality in many countries where at a low general mortality level the women tend to record higher death rates than the women at the lower or younger end of the age range.

Our main focus of attention in Table 5.9 is however the differences in age pattern of mortality between the three races. Confining ourselves to the male figures, we can see the existence of higher death rates for Malay men than for Chinese men in the young ages below 15 years and in the two groups between 35 and 44 years. In the other age groups the opposite position prevailed. As compared with Indian men, Malay men were experiencing higher death rates

---

12. Malaya, *Report of the Medical Department, 1957* (Kuala Lumpur: Government Printer, 1958).
13. See, for instance, T.E. Smith, *Population Growth in Malaya* (London: Oxford University Press, 1952), p. 21.
14. As a matter of convenience two minor modifications were introduced: the figures were provided for the 1–4 age group as a whole instead of single years and for 70 and over instead of 85 and over.

TABLE 5.9
AGE-SPECIFIC DEATH RATES BY SEX FOR THREE MAIN RACES, 1979-81

Age Group	Malays	Chinese	Indians	Malays = 100	
				C	I
Male					
0	30.80	18.84	29.52	61	96
1- 4	2.76	1.07	2.52	39	91
5- 9	1.09	0.58	0.93	53	85
10-14	0.76	0.63	1.01	83	133
15-19	1.19	1.36	1.63	114	137
20-24	1.78	2.04	2.58	115	145
25-29	1.88	1.95	3.06	104	163
30-34	1.90	1.93	3.19	102	168
35-39	2.53	2.49	4.78	98	189
40-44	3.84	3.76	7.75	98	202
45-49	6.05	6.72	12.53	111	207
50-54	10.15	10.88	20.25	104	193
55-59	16.73	17.17	27.72	103	166
60-64	26.16	27.89	43.60	107	167
65-69	42.66	45.68	67.70	107	159
70 & Over	82.92	94.48	111.97	114	135
Female					
0	23.69	14.77	26.21	62	111
1- 4	2.63	1.00	3.28	38	125
5- 9	0.88	0.43	0.78	49	89
10-14	0.61	0.35	0.64	57	105
15-19	0.70	0.56	1.45	80	207
20-24	0.90	0.75	1.70	83	189
25-29	1.18	0.84	1.60	71	136
30-34	1.76	1.13	1.86	64	106
35-39	2.36	1.43	2.51	61	106
40-44	3.09	2.11	4.32	68	140
45-49	4.46	3.58	5.98	80	134
50-54	7.24	5.47	10.06	76	139
55-59	12.76	8.59	16.52	67	129
60-64	21.32	15.00	30.74	70	144
65-69	35.65	25.10	48.41	70	136
70 & Over	74.74	70.44	90.00	94	120

in the childhood ages under 10 years and lower rates in the other age groups. A more distinctive picture emerges when we compare the figures for Chinese men and Indian men, the latter registering higher death rates at all ages. Another interesting feature is that the death rates for ages above 25 years were higher among Indian men than among men of the other two races.

The female figures shown in the lower section of Table 5.9 seem to bring out another type of pattern of mortality differentials between the races. It is clear that much lower death rates throughout the whole age range were recorded by Chinese women than Malay women. On the other hand, higher death rates were experienced by Indian women than Malay women in all ages, except in the age group 5–9. It may be observed that the death rates for Indian women were again consistently higher than those of Chinese women.

As mentioned earlier, the above age-specific death rates were employed to compute the abridged life tables for the period 1979–81 given in full in Appendix A. The average life expectation at selected ages for each sex of the three main races is laid out in Table 5.10. The most common measure of the comparative longevity of different populations is the average duration of life or the expectation of life at birth. There are significant variations in the life expectancy at birth among the three main races, 70.8 years for the Chinese, 68.8 years for the Malays and 63.8 years for the Indians.[15] This relative position is also noticeable for each sex of the three main races. The life expectancy at birth was 67.6 years for Chinese men, 67.1 years for Malay men and 61.0 years for Indian men. The three corresponding female figures are 73.9 years, 70.4 years and 66.6 years. It would appear that the Chinese are obviously the healthiest and are expected to live the longest of all the three races, followed by the Indians, then the Malays.

It is to be noted that moving from birth to age one, the value of the life expectancy increases slightly in all the six sex-race components. This is not an uncommon feature as it also exists in many countries and can be attributed to the exceptionally high mortality that infants under one year of age are exposed to. From this peak value at age one, the life expectancy decreases consistently with the advance of old age until it reaches less than nine years in general at age 85. Another common characteristic of the pattern of life expectancy refers to the longer life expectancy enjoyed by women at all ages among every one of the three ethnic groups. As the highest life expectancy at birth recorded in the world nowadays is very near 80 years, there is still considerable scope for the life expectancy in Peninsular Malaysia to improve further in the future.

---

15. The figures for both sexes are obtained by simply averaging the two figures for the two sexes of the respective populations.

TABLE 5.10
LIFE EXPECTANCY AT SELECTED AGES BY SEX FOR THREE MAIN
RACES, 1979–81

Age	Malays		Chinese		Indians	
	Male	Female	Male	Female	Male	Female
0	67.1	70.4	67.6	73.9	61.0	66.6
1	68.2	71.1	67.9	74.0	61.9	67.4
2	67.5	70.4	67.0	73.1	61.2	66.7
3	66.7	69.5	66.1	72.2	60.3	65.8
4	65.8	68.7	65.1	71.3	59.4	65.0
5	64.9	67.8	64.2	70.3	58.5	64.1
10	60.3	63.1	59.4	65.4	53.8	59.3
15	55.5	58.3	54.5	60.6	49.0	54.5
20	50.8	53.4	49.9	55.7	44.4	49.9
25	46.2	48.7	45.4	50.9	39.9	45.3
30	41.6	44.0	40.8	46.1	35.5	40.6
35	37.0	39.3	36.2	41.4	31.0	36.0
40	32.4	34.8	31.6	36.6	26.7	31.4
45	28.0	30.3	27.1	32.0	22.7	27.0
50	23.8	25.9	23.0	27.5	19.0	22.8
55	20.0	21.7	19.1	23.2	15.8	18.8
60	16.5	18.0	15.6	19.1	12.7	15.2
65	13.4	14.8	12.6	15.4	10.2	12.3
70	11.1	12.2	10.2	12.2	8.4	10.0
75	9.1	10.3	7.6	9.4	6.8	8.3
80	8.1	9.2	6.0	7.1	5.8	7.8
85	7.6	8.8	4.9	5.4	5.4	7.5

Regional Mortality Differentials

The uneven development of the Peninsula in the past naturally implies that
the various parts of the country are poised at markedly different stages of
social and economic development. Among the many adverse effects of unbalanced growth is one relating to variations in the level of mortality between
the urban and the rural areas as well as among the 11 states. Such variations
in mortality conditions have attracted the concern of the government which
has taken steps to improve the medical and health services in the rural area

as part of its overall strategy to uplift the living standards of the rural people. Commencing from the early 1960s, the government has placed strong emphasis on the expansion of rural health and medical facilities as evinced by the following statement from the 1961–65 five-year development plan.[16]

> Eventually, it is the goal of the Ministry of Health and Social Welfare to establish a network of health units serving the entire rural population. A long step forward towards this goal will be taken during 1961–65 with the establishment of 37 main rural health centres, 148 sub-centres and 652 mid-wives clinics. These facilities will provide additional medical and health services to more than 2 million of the rural population. These centres provide both preventive and curative services with special emphasis on maternity and child health care, environmental sanitation and hygiene, and health education with a view to improving the standard of health of the rural population and reducing further therefore the mortality rate, particularly that of the infant mortality, among the rural people.

Similar emphasis on the expansion of rural health and medical facilities is accorded priority in all subsequent five-year development plans.

An idea of the changes in the differences in the infant mortality rate between the urban and the rural areas over the years are presented in Table 5.11. The

TABLE 5.11
INFANT MORTALITY RATES FOR URBAN AND RURAL AREAS,
1965–84

Year	Urban	Rural	U = 100
1965	37.2	56.3	151
1970	35.1	43.3	123
1975	24.8	36.5	147
1980	17.2	27.0	157
1984	13.6	22.9	146

rates are based on infant deaths and live-births tabulated according to the place of residence of the deceased infants and the place of residence of the mother. There is always the possibility that some sick infants from rural areas may die in the urban centres where they were receiving better or the necessary medical attention. In 1965 the infant mortality rate in the rural area was 56.3

16. Malaya, *Malaya: Second Five-Year Plan, 1961–65* (Kuala Lumpur: Government Press, 1961), p. 47.

per 1,000 live-births, which was 51 per cent higher than the urban rate of 37.2. By 1983 the urban rate has fallen by 57 per cent to reach 16.0, while the rural rate was reduced by almost the same amount, 59 per cent. The infant mortality rate of 19.9 in the rural area in 1984 was about 46 per cent higher than that in the urban area. It would appear that the differential in infant mortality between the urban and the rural areas has not been radically reduced in the last two decades or so.

An attempt at evaluating variations in mortality conditions among the 11 states in the early years is made in Table 5.12.[17] To facilitate our analysis,

TABLE 5.12

INFANT MORTALITY RATES AND SOME CONTRIBUTORY
FACTORS FOR ELEVEN STATES, 1961–63

State	Infant Mortality Rate 1961–63	% of Rural Population (<5,000)	% Literate in any Language	Number of Persons per		
				Doctor	Nurse	Hospital Bed
	(1)	(2)	(3)	(4)	(5)	(6)
Penang	45.8	41.3	56.8	3,847	1,214	314
Selangor	46.1	50.1	54.4	3,495	2,391	697
N. Sembilan	52.3	80.4	56.4	6,761	2,157	349
Johore	52.3	71.6	49.1	9,232	3,427	552
Pahang	55.4	72.9	46.0	7,974	2,328	450
Perak	55.8	66.6	53.1	7,541	3,122	612
Malacca	56.0	73.0	49.5	6,336	1,563	455
Perlis	65.6	93.3	39.9	13,372	2,140	424
Kedah	72.5	85.9	38.7	14,314	3,674	780
Kelantan	83.4	83.6	22.3	23,255	6,233	980
Trengganu	90.6	77.9	23.6	21,048	4,551	836

Note: The figures in columns (2) and (3) are for 1957 and those in (4) to (6) are for 1962.

17. See also, Saw Swee-Hock, "State Differential Mortality in Malaya", *Population Review*, Vol. 10, No. 1, January 1966.

the states in this table are arranged in ascending order of the level of the infant mortality rate. It is clear that the lowest infant mortality was recorded in the states of Penang and Selangor in the early postwar years. The favourable mortality conditions in these two states may be attributed, firstly, to the greater degree of social and economic advancement particularly in terms of better food, housing and education and, secondly, to the greater availability of medical and public health facilities. In part this can be verified by some of the contributory factors set out in the other five columns of the table.

In contrast the worst mortality condition in those days existed in the states towards the east and north, viz. Trengganu, Kelantan, Kedah and Perlis. This is not surprising considering the large rural population, the low literacy rate, and the acute shortage of basic medical amenities expressed in terms of doctors, nurses and hospital beds. Additional factors were the relatively low per capita income with the resultant greater incidence of under-nutrition and malnutrition and the paucity of public health measures such as anti-malarial works and sanitation. It is to be noted that the infant mortality rate of 90.6 that was recorded in Trengganu in 1961–63 was nearly twice that of 45.8 recorded in Penang. One practical lesson can be drawn from Table 5.12 in that the data serve to pinpoint the states where mortality could and ought to be reduced significantly and hence provide some guidance for the allocation of medical and public health resources with a view to minimising the state differentials in mortality.

6

Nuptiality Trends and Patterns

In recent years nuptiality has come to be recognised as an integral part of the study of the demography of any country, largely because the formation and dissolution of marital unions have an important bearing on the level of fertility. We may regard marriage as an event that marks the beginning of the potential period of childbearing and marital dissolution as the end of this period. It is also recognised that age at marriage can affect the level of fertility and hence the rate of population growth. In this chapter an attempt is made to examine nuptiality trends and patterns in the Peninsula during the postwar period.

Our study of nuptiality will be based on marital status data collected in the population census and classified into single, married, widowed and divorced. The data reflect unions in which the partners have participated in some form of legal marriage solemnised according to the various marriage laws. We should always bear in mind that the modern form of consensus unions among persons who have never been married according to either legal or customary rites is rather rare in the Peninsula. We should also note that it is not possible to investigate nuptiality by means of comprehensive data derived from marriage registration records since such statistics have never been compiled and published annually.

Marriage Customs and Laws

The great diversity of religions that we have observed in an earlier chapter necessarily implies that it would be quite difficult to have a common legislation to govern all the various types of marriages taking place in the country. It was inevitable that over the years separate laws were introduced to regulate these marriages which are solemnised according to the various religious and customary rites. There are one set of laws governing the marriage of persons both of whom are Muslim and another group of laws meant to regulate all the other marriages contracted between non-Muslims. Almost all these marriage laws have their roots during the colonial period, introduced in different parts of the country at different times as determined by the extent or concern of British rule or influence at that time.

The most important marriages are those contracted by persons both of whom profess the Islamic faith. Such Muslim marriages must be solemnised and registered under the provisions of the respective laws enacted by the state governments and the Federal Territory.[1] Examples of these regional laws are the Trengganu *Administration of Islamic Law Enactment, 1955*, Kedah *Administration of Muslim Law Enactment, 1962*, Perak *Administration of Muslim Law Enactment, 1965*, and *The Islamic Family Law (Federal Territory) Act, 1984*. If both parties are Muslims, they must marry according to the rules stipulated in the ordinances regardless of their racial origin. However, most of the Muslim marriages are contracted between Malays and a few are contracted between Indonesians, Pakistanis, Bangladeshis and Indians who follow the Islamic faith. The groom must be at least 18 years of age and the bride at least 16. In exceptional circumstances the Syariah judge may grant his permission to a man or woman below the minimum age to marry. By law Muslim marriages may be polygamous and the husband can take up to four wives at any point of time provided they are all treated equally. Most Muslim marriages are, however, monogamous.

Dissolution of Muslim marriages is governed by Islamic law which by tradition has allowed divorces to be affected in four different ways.[2] An easy and starkly simple method is for the husband to unilaterally divorce his wife by merely pronouncing *talak* three times in front of her at any time and place without the need for any witness to be present. If he pronounces one or two *talaks* only, the wife is also regarded as divorced but may not remarry another person for another 100 days. During this 100-day period known as *eddah*, the husband is allowed to change his mind and be reconciled with his wife. If the husband pronounces the three *talaks*, the divorce is irrevocable and the couple cannot be reunited as husband and wife unless she marries another man and is subsequently divorced. In some cases the husband, after rashly invoking three *talaks*, arranges for his ex-wife to marry another man on the understanding that he will quickly divorce her so that she may marry the first husband.

The second method is known as *pasah* by which a divorce is granted to a

---

1. Ahmad bin Mohamad Ibrahim, "Developments in Marriage Laws in Malaysia and Singapore", *Malaya Law Review*, Vol. 2, No. 2, December 1970.
2. See, for instance, M.B. Hooker, *Islamic Law in South-East Asia* (Oxford University Press, 1984) and Mohamed Din Bin Ali, "Malay Customary Law and Family", *Intisari*, Vol. 2, No. 2, 1965.

wife by a religious judge in cases where the husband deserts and fails to maintain the wife or where the husband is impotent, or abjures Islam. The third method of divorce is known as *ta'alik* which refers to the special conditions attached by the bride's guardian in the marriage contract. A divorce may be granted to the wife if it can be established that the husband has contravened these special conditions. Finally, a divorce by *khula* or *tebus talak* may be executed in cases where the wife seeks a divorce from a reluctant husband by offering him a sum of money or some form of property in compensation.

The other religious form of marriage refers to Christian marriages which were solemnised under the *Christian Marriage Ordinance, 1956*, Federation of Malaya, No. 33 of 1956, which was in operation in the 11 states of the Peninsula from 1 August 1957 to 28 February 1982. Prior to the introduction of this act, Christian marriages were solemnised in the Straits Settlements under the *Christian Marriage Ordinance, 1898* and later the *Christian Marriage Ordinance, 1940*, in the Federated Malay States under the *Christian Marriage Enactment, 1915*, and in Johore, Kelantan and Kedah under similar enactments.[3] But there were no such enactment in Perlis and Trengganu allowing the solemnisation of Christian marriages prior to 1957.

Christian marriages may be contracted between Christians of all denominations. Such marriages may be contracted between Christians as well as between persons one of whom is a Christian. The minimum age for contracting Christian marriages is 21 for both the groom and bride, but grooms aged 16 to 20 and brides aged 14 to 20 can still marry with the written consent of the parents or guardians. Unlike Muslim marriages, Christian marriages are monogamous and take place among a wider range of ethnic groups. Christian marriages are solemnised by authorised person in churches or other religious institutions and are registered in the Registry of Marriages.

The third distinct type of marriage refers to those solemnised and registered according to the provisions of the *Civil Marriage Ordinance, 1952*, Federation of Malaya, No. 44 of 1952, which was in operation in the 11 states of the Peninsula from 1 January 1955 to 28 February 1982. The ordinance was intended to enable persons in the 11 states to contract, if they so desire, a monogamous civil marriage whatever might have been their religion, faith or custom.[4] Christians could choose to marry under the provisions of this ordinance, but Muslims were specifically prohibited from contracting civil marriages even if only one of the couple was a Muslim. Twenty-one was the

---

3. Federation of Malaya, *Report of the Registrar-General on Population, Births, Deaths, Marriages and Adoptions, 1956* (Kuala Lumpur: Government Press, 1956).
4. Federation of Malaya, *Report of the Registrar-General on Population, Births, Deaths, Marriages and Adoptions, 1955* (Kuala Lumpur: Government Press, 1956).

minimum age required for both men and women to contract civil marriages but men aged 16 to 20 and women aged 14 to 20 may still contract marriages with the written consent of their parents. Prior to January 1955, civil marriages could only be contracted in the states of Penang and Malacca under the more restricted *Civil Marriage Ordinance, 1940*, Straits Settlements, No. 9 of 1940.

Apart from the above types of marriages governed by the three separate marriage laws, there were other marriages which were contracted outside these laws according to religious or customary rites. Until February 1982 there were no laws compelling these miscellaneous marriages to be registered, but married couples could apply to the Registrar of Marriage for their marriages to be registered under the then *Registration of Marriage Ordinance, 1952*, Federation of Malaya, No. 53 of 1952, which came into force on 1 January 1955. Marriages could only be registered under this ordinance if neither one of the parties professed the Islamic or Christian religion and besides they must be effected within three months of the marriage date. Marriages registered under this ordinance could be polygamous if the Registrar was satisfied that the religion or custom governing these marriages permitted polygamy, and marriages not registered at all could be polygamous. What is important is that until February 1982 non-Muslim couples could choose to marry outside the ambit of any marriage laws, and could also decide not to have their marriages registered at all. This means that there is no complete registration of all marriages taking place in the country.

In an effort to accord greater rights and protection to non-Muslim women, the government streamlined the marriage laws by enacting the *Law Reform (Marriage and Divorce) Act, 1976,* Malaysia 1976, which came into force on 1 March 1982. This act was based on the recommendations of the Royal Commission on non-Muslim Marriage and Divorce Laws and was designed to eradicate the confusions, complications and injustices of the then domestic laws concerning the marriage and divorce of non-Muslims.[5] The act repealed all the previous laws, discussed earlier, governing non-Muslim marriages, but it does not affect the validity of marriages solemnised under any law, religion or custom prior to the appointed date of the act. The most outstanding feature of the act is that it abolishes polygamy among non-Muslims whose marriages were contracted from 1 March 1982.[6] Also it became compulsory for all non-Muslim marriages to be registered regardless of

---

5. *The Malay Mail*, 10 March 1970.
6. For a detailed discussion of this piece of new legislation, see Rafiah Salam, "The Legal Status of Women in a Multi-Racial Malaysian Society" in Hing Ai Yun *et al.* (eds.), *Women in Malaysia* (Kuala Lumpur: Pelanduk Publications, 1984).

whether they were solemnised by the Registrar of Marriage in the Registry or by an authorised person in an approved place. The significance of this new act from the statistical point of view is that, coupled with the compulsory registration of Muslim marriages, there is complete registration of all marriages that occurred in the country from 1 March 1982. However, statistics of marriages solemnised under this act have yet to be compiled and published on a comprehensive and regular basis. Our analysis of nuptiality trends and patterns must by necessity depend on the marital status data published in the population census reports.

Age at First Marriage

An analysis of the average age at first marriage of women and men can be considered as a central piece in the study of nuptiality trends and patterns in any country. The age at marriage marks the beginning of marital formation on a permanent basis for the majority of the population, even though some may end up in divorce or separation. The age at marriage of women is recognised as one of the important factors that determine the level of fertility and hence the rate of population growth. The experience of many developing countries has demonstrated that the very low age at marriage of women has been the major factor responsible for the high level of fertility, particularly in situations where contraceptive use is negligible. A shift upward in this low marriage age is usually followed by a decline in fertility. In fact, the raising of the minimum marriage age for women through legislation has been resorted to by some developing countries as part of their overall strategy in trying to bring down the level of fertility.

Since the registration of marriages has been incomplete up to February 1982 and statistics based on complete registration after this date have yet to be compiled and published, it is not possible to calculate the average age at first marriage on an annual basis from registration records. Instead, we will study age at marriage in terms of the singulate mean age at marriage calculated from the population census years.[7] This method determines the mean age at first marriage for males and females in a synthetic censal cohort who marry for the first time before the age of 50. The estimation of the mean age at marriage consists in finding the total number of years lived in the single state by a generation from birth to age 50 years, and dividing this total by the number who have been removed by marriage from the cohort. This gives the mean duration of single life which is equivalent to the average age at first

---

7. John Hajnal, "Age at Marriage and Proportion Marrying", *Population Studies*, Vol. 7, No. 2, November 1953.

marriage and described as the singulate mean age at marriage (SMAM). If s_x denotes the proportion single in the age group x to $x + 5$ and s the average

$(s_{45} + s_{50}) \div 2$, then SMAM $= \dfrac{(5 \times \sum\limits_{x=0}^{45} s_x - 50s)}{1 - s}$.

According to the above formula, the singulate mean age at marriage for the men and women for the four postwar censuses was calculated and the results are given in Table 6.1. The singulate mean age at marriage for women rose from 18.4 years in 1947 to 19.4 years in 1957, giving an increase of 1.0 year or 5.4 per cent in the first postwar intercensal period. Thereafter, the marriage age moved up very rapidly and reached 22.3 years in 1970, an increase of 2.9 years or 14.9 per cent during the 13-year period. In the latest intercensal period, the advance in average marriage age was slowed down to an increase of only

TABLE 6.1
SINGULATE MEAN AGE AT MARRIAGE BY SEX, 1947–80

Year	Male	Female	Difference	Increase	
				Male	Female
1947	24.5	18.4	6.1	—	—
1957	23.8	19.4	4.4	−0.7	1.0
1970	25.4	22.3	3.1	1.6	2.9
1980	26.9	23.8	3.1	1.5	1.5

1.5 years or 6.7 per cent. The continuous uptrend in the singulate mean age at marriage of women may be attributed to a combination of factors. Among the more important ones were the normalisation of the sex ratio at marriageable ages, the enhanced educational attainment of women, the greater female participation in the modern sectors of the economy, and the general process of modernisation and economic development. The increasing trend in the marriage age of women was also experienced in many developing countries during the postwar period when fundamental social and economic changes occurred.[8]

8. See, for example, Peter C. Smith, "Asian Marriage Patterns in Transition", *Journal of Family History*, Vol. 5, No. 1, 1980.

An entirely different trend in the singulate mean age at marriage was displayed by the men in Table 6.1. By comparison the men experienced a much slower advance in their average age at marriage during the same period under review. As a matter of fact, there was a dip in the singulate mean age of marriage of men, falling from 24.5 years in 1947 to 23.8 years in 1957. It may be recalled that the sex ratio at the marriageable ages was extremely uneven in the prewar days and was still uneven immediately after the war. This surplus of male mates engendered the marriage squeeze whereby the men were forced to marry at an older age and the women at a younger age.[9] What it means is that as the sex ratio moved rapidly towards a more balanced position in the early postwar years, the availability of prospective female mates improved greatly and men were able to marry at an earlier age. As the sex ratio became almost normal and ceased to exert any influence on the marriage age, the other factors assumed greater importance and an upturn in the average marriage age of men emerged. Thereafter, the singulate mean age of men rose to 25.4 years in 1970 and finally to 26.9 years in 1980.

The different trends in marriage age exhibited by the women and men over the years have a considerable impact on the age difference between the bride and groom. In 1947 the men were marrying women who were slightly more than 6 years younger than themselves. Over the years the age gap has narrowed to 4.4 years in 1957 and 3.1 years in 1970. Since then the age difference appeared to have stabilised as it has remained at 3.1 years in 1980. The big difference between the average marriage age of women and men that existed at the beginning in 1947 was due to the marriage squeeze which we have already discussed.

The above position in regard to the singulate mean age at marriage of the total population reflects the net outcome of similar sets of figures for the three ethnic groups presented in Table 6.2. It may be observed that these figures bring out not only some similarities but also interesting differences among these three races with respect to their average age at first marriage. First of all, in the early postwar year 1947 Chinese women were marrying at a fairly late age of 20.4 years, which exceeded the marriage age of Malay women by 3.2 years and Indian women by 3.0 years. In those days the Chinese view of the minimum age at which young people become fit for wedlock appeared to be high in comparison with Malay and Indian customs.[10] The figures for the men reveal a unique feature in that in 1947 Indian men were marrying at an extremely late age of 27.8 years as against the 25.5 years for Chinese men and 23.5

---

9. Ruth B. Dixon, "Explaining Cross-Cultural Variations in Age at Marriage and Proportion Never Marrying", *Population Studies*, Vol. 25, No. 1, July 1971.

10. See, for example, Maurice Freedman, *Chinese Family and Marriage in Singapore* (London: H.M.S.O., 1957).

TABLE 6.2
SINGULATE MEAN AGE AT MARRIAGE BY SEX FOR
THREE MAIN RACES, 1947–80

Year	Male	Female	Difference	Increase	
				Male	Female
Malays					
1947	23.5	17.2	6.3	—	—
1957	22.7	17.9	4.8	−0.8	0.7
1970	24.7	21.1	3.6	2.0	3.2
1980	26.2	23.2	3.0	1.5	2.1
Chinese					
1947	25.5	20.4	5.1	—	—
1957	25.4	22.1	3.3	−0.1	1.7
1970	27.3	24.2	3.1	1.9	2.1
1980	28.0	24.9	3.1	0.7	0.7
Indians					
1947	27.8	17.4	10.4	—	—
1957	24.0	17.9	6.1	−3.8	0.5
1970	25.4	21.8	3.6	1.4	3.9
1980	26.8	24.1	2.7	1.4	2.3

years for Malay men. The explanation for the high marriage age of Indian men lies in the greater uneven sex ratio of the Indians and hence the stronger influence of the marriage squeeze factor.

Having looked at the position at the beginning of the period, we will now see what changes took place over the years among the three races. Three broad similarities may be detected, the general uptrend in the average marriage age of women, the dip in the average marriage age of men from 1947 to 1957 and the upturn thereafter, and the continuous narrowing in the gap between the marriage age of the two sexes of these three races. However, some interesting differences may be noticed. For instance, the rise in the average marriage age of women in the first period 1947–57 was much greater among the Chinese (1.7 years) than among the Malays (0.7 years) or the Indians (0.5 years). Having advanced faster initially, the marriage age of Chinese women went up much slower by comparison after 1957.

In a way the other two races also displayed a slight difference in the nature of the upward movement in their average age at marriage. In comparison with that of Indian women, the marriage age of Malay women advanced at a more rapid rate. Indian women marrying at an average of 24.1 years occupied an intermediate position. The common experience of a dip in the average marriage age of men from 1947 to 1957 shared by the three main races contained some subtle differences. This phenomenon, as mentioned earlier, was caused by the marriage squeeze resulting from the abnormal sex ratio.[11] But then the sex composition of the Malay population has always been quite normal, even in the prewar days. In the case of the Malays, the marriage squeeze was most probably engendered by the high divorce incidence whereby the divorced men compete with the bachelors for marriage partners. The drop in divorce rate would have the same impact as the normalisation of the sex ratio on the marriage age of men. With the marriage squeeze running out its course, the gap between the marriage age of men and women was narrowed over the years. The gap was reduced from 10.4 years in 1947 to 2.7 years in 1980 for the Indians, from 6.3 years to 3.0 years for the Malays, and from 5.1 years to 3.1 years for the Chinese. The big gap recorded by the Indians in 1947 was due to the exceptionally high marriage age of the Indian men as noted earlier.

It is known that the average age at first marriage varies between the urban and the rural areas, with the town folk marrying at an older age than the rural inhabitants. This aspect of the marriage age can be examined in Peninsular Malaysia since the prerequisite data are obtainable from the 1980 Population Census. From the census data on marital status tabulated according to urban-rural classification, we can compute the singulate mean age at marriage for each of these two areas and the results are presented in Table 6.3. It may be observed that the average marriage age of men in 1980 was 27.7 years in the urban area, about 1.5 years higher than the average of 26.2 years in the rural area. In the case of the women, the two figures were 25.0 years in the urban area and 22.9 years in the rural area, giving a bigger differential of 2.1 years. Greater significance should be attached to the female differential in view of its impact on the differences in the level of fertility between the urban and the rural areas.

Another important feature underlined by the figures in Table 6.3 refers to the wider gap between the male and female marriage age in the rural area than in the urban area. In the latter, the average marriage age was 27.7 years for

---

11. J.C. Caldwell, "Fertility Decline and Female Chances of Marriage in Malaya", *Population Studies*, Vol. 17, No. 1, July 1963.

TABLE 6.3
SINGULATE MEAN AGE AT MARRIAGE BY SEX, RACE AND
URBAN-RURAL AREA, 1980

Race	Urban	Rural	Difference
Male			
All Races	27.7	26.2	1.5
Malays	27.0	25.8	1.2
Chinese	28.2	27.5	0.7
Indians	28.0	25.8	2.2
Female			
All Races	25.0	22.9	2.1
Malays	24.1	22.6	1.5
Chinese	25.6	23.8	1.8
Indians	25.1	23.3	1.8

men and 25.0 years for the women, but in the former, the two corresponding
figures were 26.2 years and 22.9 years. This is probably a manifestation of the
pervasive influence of modernisation on the age at which women marry in the
urban centres. It is also to be noted that the traditional practice of men marrying younger women prevailed in the urban area as well as in the rural area
among all the three races.

The usual urban-rural differential in the average age at first marriage was
experienced by the men and women of the three main races. As can be seen
in Table 6.3, the difference in the marriage age of men was 1.2 years for the
Malays, 0.7 years for the Chinese and 2.2 years for the Indians. As for the more
important differential recorded by the women, the figure came to 1.8 years
for both Chinese women and Indian women and 1.5 years for Malay women.
It is quite possible that urban Malay women, who had only moved to the
urban centres in recent years, would have retained their rural attitudes towards
marriage and would have married earlier than the women born and bred in
these centres. There were relatively fewer recent rural migrants in the Chinese
or Indian urban population.

An analysis of the variations in the singulate mean age at marriage for each
sex separately among the 11 states is presented in Table 6.4. It may be observed that the average marriage age of women varies from a low of 21.6
years in Kelantan to a high of 25.0 years in Malacca, giving a large difference

of 4.4 years. Comparatively late marriages by women were also to be found in Penang with 24.9 years and Selangor with 24.8 years. It may seem somewhat strange that the women in the most economically developed state of Selangor were not experiencing an average marriage age that would be the highest in the country. The most plausible explanation is that the state has received in recent years the most number of rural migrants who brought with them attitudes favouring early marriages or had married earlier prior to migrating to the state. The other states where the women were marrying at a relatively early age were Trengganu with 21.9 years, Pahang with 22.3 years and Perlis with 22.6 years.

A comparison of male and female figures given in Table 6.4 reveals that the average marriage age of men followed essentially the same regional pattern as that of the women. The general pattern can be described as one where early marriages were taking place in the less modernised states and late marriages in the more economically advanced states along the west coast. No doubt the urban-rural differential in average marriage age noted earlier played a part in shaping this regional pattern since great variations in the level of urbanisation existed among these states. But we must not forget the race factor in view of our previous discussion about the differences in marriage among the three main races. What it amounts to is that the ethnic composition in each of the 11 states certainly exerts a strong influence on the relative position of the singulate mean age at marriage shown in Table 6.4. Bearing in mind what we have ascertained about the ethnic composition in these states, there is, for

TABLE 6.4

SINGULATE MEAN AGE AT MARRIAGE BY SEX AND STATE, 1980

State	Male	Female	Difference
Johore	27.1	24.1	3.0
Kedah	25.7	23.0	2.7
Kelantan	25.4	21.6	3.8
Malacca	27.4	25.0	2.4
N. Sembilan	26.9	24.0	2.9
Pahang	26.3	22.3	4.0
Penang	27.5	24.9	2.6
Perak	27.0	24.0	3.0
Perlis	25.7	22.6	3.1
Selangor	27.5	24.8	2.7
Trengganu	25.6	21.9	3.7

example, a close association between the low average marriage age and the proportion of Malays in the state. Good examples are Kelantan and Trengganu.

Before proceeding to the next section, it would be worth examining the recent advance in the average age at first marriage in terms of a completely different set of statistics collected in the 1980 Census. Since data on age at first marriage and of course year of birth of respondents were collected, it is feasible to analyse the median age at marriage for different birth cohorts of males and females. We wish to point out that the date of year of marriage was not collected and hence the median age at marriage cannot be related to the year of marriage. In Table 6.5 we have presented the median age at marriage by race for six

TABLE 6.5

MEDIAN AGE AT FIRST MARRIAGE FOR SELECTED
BIRTH COHORTS BY SEX AND RACE, 1980

Year of Birth	All Races	Malays	Chinese	Indians
Males				
1921–25	23.1	22.0	23.6	25.0
1926–30	23.2	22.2	24.7	24.6
1931–35	23.6	22.3	25.0	24.5
1936–40	23.9	22.5	25.6	24.6
1941–45	24.9	23.6	26.1	25.2
1946–50	25.2	24.5	26.2	25.2
Females				
1921–25	18.3	17.2	20.2	18.3
1926–30	18.4	17.2	20.5	18.4
1931–35	18.7	17.4	20.9	18.3
1936–40	19.0	17.7	21.9	18.5
1941–45	19.7	18.1	22.7	18.8
1946–50	21.6	19.0	23.1	19.8

birth cohorts of males and females.[12] The data are confined to persons surviving until the 1980 Census who first married before the age of 30 because the youngest persons in the youngest cohort shown, i.e. those born during

12. The figures are obtained from Table 4.10 in Khoo Teik Huat, *Malaysia: General Report of the Population Census, 1980*, Vol. 1, op. cit., p. 45.

1946–50, would have reached only age 30 in 1980. To make comparison between this cohort and other cohorts, it is necessary to include in the computation for each cohort only those married below age 30.

The figures in Table 6.5 serve to confirm the general uptrend in the average age at first marriage of men and women that was observed earlier. For instance, women born during 1921–25 married at an average age of 18.3 years, and every subsequent birth cohort of women was marrying at a progressively older age so that those born in the most recent years 1946–50 married at 20.6 years. The same increasing trend in marriage age was also experienced by the women in each of the three main races. Another feature that is confirmed by the figures concerns the relative position of the three main races. Among every birth cohort Malay women have always experienced the lowest marriage age and Chinese women the highest marriage age, with Indian women occupying an intermediate position. The principal features of the average marriage age of the men that were highlighted earlier appeared to be confirmed by the male figures given in the upper section of the table. Indeed, the greater impact of the marriage squeeze on the marriage age of Indian men can be seen in the dip in the median age at first marriage of Indian men born in the late 1920s and early 1930s.

Changes in Proportion Single

The next aspect of nuptiality that we will examine is the proportion of the population remaining single. The proportion single or never married serves as an important index that determines the extent of marriage formation and childbearing. The proportion single is in part influenced by the average age at first marriage discussed in the preceding section. From the census data, we can compute the percentage of the population aged 15 and over who had remained single at the time of the census, and the results of the computation are laid out in Table 6.6. We have decided to exclude the 10–14 age group in our study of nuptiality because nearly everyone in this teenage group would be single. We should also bear in mind that the data presented in this table and almost all the other tables were the results of the old marriage laws since even the latest figures collected in 1980 would not be affected by the new law introduced in February 1982.

It is evident that the postwar years have witnessed a general upward movement in the proportion single among the women. The proportion of women aged 15 and over who remained single has risen steadily from 13.1 per cent in 1947 to 31.1 per cent in 1980. In the early days there was a decidedly strong belief that the prime function of women is to marry and raise a family, and spinsterhood finds little social acceptance among the public at large. But changing attitudes towards spinsterhood, improved education of women, and greater and more meaningful job opportunities for women inevitably lead to more women remaining single. This is particularly true in the case of Malay women who saw their proportion single rise sharply from the low of 8.5 per cent in 1947 to 29.4 per cent in 1980. The same trend was experienced by Indian women whose proportion single went up from 10.1 per cent to 34.4 per cent in the same period. In both instances, the uptrend was rather gentle in the early part of the period but quite steep in recent years. Chinese women, who already had a high proportion of 20.1 per cent single in 1947, displayed a regular upward movement during the whole period under review.

The position concerning the changes in the proportion of men remaining single is less clear-cut. The proportion of single men in fact shrank from 33.8 per cent in 1947 to 32.2 per cent in 1957, and went up after that to reach 40.2 per cent in 1980. We can attribute the dip in the early postwar years to the rapid improvement in the uneven sex ratio at marriageable ages which gave men a better chance of securing female mates. This was most clearly manifested by the figures for Indian men whose proportion single tumbled from 40.4 per cent to 30.6 per cent in the first intercensal period. In contrast, only a minor drop from 40.5 per cent to 39.9 per cent was indicated by Chinese men in the same period. Furthermore, no such dip was experienced by Malay men but the rise was still very gentle, moving up from 25.3 per cent to 25.7 per cent.

A universal feature of nuptiality noticeable in Table 6.6 refers to the greater tendency among men to remain single. This characteristic may be seen to exist at all the census years and among all ethnic groups. But there was the decisive development towards a narrower difference in the proportion single between the two sexes. For instance, in 1947 the proportion single was 33.8 per cent for the men and 13.1 per cent for the women, but by 1980 the difference was reduced to 40.2 per cent and 31.1 per cent. This may be taken as a reflection of the greater equality accorded to women in almost every sphere of their life in education, employment, etc.

For a better appreciation of the changes in the proportion remaining single, we will examine the percentages of single persons in the various quinary age groups. In Table 6.7 are given the figures for the age-specific proportion single by sex and race for the four postwar censuses. One minor point is that as a matter of convenience the figures are given up to age group 55–59 instead of 65 and over since the exclusion of the two groups will not affect our analysis. A distinctive pattern of variation with age is disclosed by these figures. For the men the proportion single commences at well above 90 per cent in the youngest age group 15–19 and decreases rapidly until the mid-30s and then more gently until the late 50s when only a small proportion still remains single. By and large, the women exhibit the same shape but the curve is always lower than

TABLE 6.6
PROPORTION OF SINGLE PERSONS AGED 15 AND OVER BY SEX
AND RACE, 1947–80

Race	1947	1957	1970	1980
Males				
All Races	33.8	32.2	37.4	40.2
Malays	25.3	25.7	33.6	38.6
Chinese	40.5	39.9	43.6	42.5
Indians	40.4	30.6	35.6	41.5
Females				
All Races	13.1	16.3	26.6	31.1
Malays	8.6	10.4	22.2	29.4
Chinese	20.1	25.6	32.7	33.0
Indians	10.1	10.7	27.7	34.4

that of the males throughout the age range.

Since the two sexes hardly experienced any major change in their relation-ship in respect of the general shape of the proportion single, it would be more fruitful to compare the changes that occurred among each sex of the three races. Among Malay men, the proportion single decreased in all the age groups in the first intercensal period 1947–57, and continued to decrease in the groups aged 40 and over but decreased below age 40 in the next period. In the latest period 1970–80 there was an increase in the proportion in all the age groups. In the case of Chinese men, they experienced an increase in their proportion single in the first two age groups and a decrease in the other groups in the first period. In the second period the increase occurred in the three groups between 20 and 34 and the decrease in the other groups. This was followed by an in-crease in almost all the age groups in the third period. Indian men experienced the same trend as that of Malay men in the first period with a universal decrease in the proportion single over the age range. In the second period the decrease continued in all the age groups, except in the two youngest ones. Unlike the other two races, Indian men still registered a decrease in the age groups from age 40 upwards in the third period.

The common experience of a fall in the proportion single shared by the men of all the three races can be explained in terms of a combination of factors.

The exceptionally high proportion single in the middle and older ages in 1947 clearly reflects the pervasive influence of the abnormal sex composition, and the subsequent normalisation of the sex ratio was no doubt the cause of the conspicuous reduction in the proportion single in 1957. The minor reduction noted in the same period in the case of Malay women can be traced to the decline in divorce and polygamy and the postponement of marriage during the difficult war years. Of course, the impact of the latter factor has been completely overwhelmed by the powerful influence of the uneven sex ratio in the case of Chinese and Indian men.

Changes in the proportion single that took place among women of the three races are less complicated. In general women of every race have witnessed a continuous upward movement in their proportion single in the first four age groups between 15 and 34. It is also to be noted that this uptrend has been more pronounced during the period 1957–70. However, it is possible to detect one difference in that the changes have been far greater among Malay women and Indian women. This is no doubt related to the relatively lower age at first marriage of these women and hence the lower proportion single in the four age groups in 1947. At the older ages the changes have been less dramatic among all the three races; the extremely low proportion single indicate the unpopularity of celibacy among the women at all times.

The above changes reflect an unusual feature of the nuptiality pattern resulting from a combination of modern and traditional attitudes towards marriage.[13] The increasing proportion single at the younger ages reflects the rising marriage age, whilst the still small proportion single in the oldest age group 55–59 indicates that marriage has been virtually universal. This contrast between delayed marriage among younger women and universality of marriage among older women probably reflects a transitional phase in the nuptiality pattern of women. The data given in Table 6.7 should not be interpreted to suggest that women in the Peninsula have responded to modernisation by postponing marriage but not foregoing marriage completely. It is more likely that the figures for the younger age groups represent a more recent and modern type of nuptiality, whereas those for the older age groups reflect the traditional pattern of the earlier years. One has to wait for a few more decades to ascertain whether the young women who are now delaying their marriage will ultimately marry to the same extent as their old counterparts.

The variations in the proportion of persons remaining single in 1980 in the 11 states for each of the two sexes are portrayed in Table 6.8. For men the lowest proportion single was to be found in Perlis with 32.8 per cent and the

---

13. For more details, about the modern and traditional patterns of marriage, see Ruth Dixon, op. cit.

TABLE 6.7
AGE-SPECIFIC PROPORTION SINGLE BY SEX AND RACE, 1947–80

Age Group	Male				Female			
	1947	1957	1970	1980	1947	1957	1970	1980
Malays								
15–19	93.1	92.1	96.3	99.0	40.8	45.8	77.2	89.5
20–24	53.7	47.2	67.7	80.4	6.8	9.4	32.4	48.6
25–29	18.1	13.4	23.0	34.5	2.1	2.3	8.7	17.2
30–34	7.2	4.8	6.8	10.0	1.3	1.1	3.2	7.9
35–39	4.1	2.9	3.3	4.6	0.9	0.7	1.8	3.8
40–44	2.6	2.3	2.0	3.0	1.1	0.6	1.0	2.2
45–49	2.5	1.9	1.5	2.4	1.4	0.5	0.6	1.7
50–54	2.1	1.7	1.1	1.9	1.8	0.5	0.6	1.2
55–59	1.7	1.7	1.0	1.7	1.5	0.6	0.6	0.9
Chinese								
15–19	97.6	98.6	98.3	99.5	82.4	89.7	94.0	95.4
20–24	77.0	79.0	86.3	87.8	26.1	43.1	59.7	63.2
25–29	44.0	37.8	44.9	51.4	7.9	11.4	21.4	28.3
30–34	26.8	16.5	18.9	21.6	4.2	3.8	9.5	13.2
35–39	22.4	10.7	9.9	10.5	3.3	2.7	5.7	7.6
40–44	20.8	8.9	6.5	7.3	3.6	2.6	3.4	5.8
45–49	19.7	10.5	5.5	6.1	3.7	2.5	2.4	4.6
50–54	20.6	11.4	5.0	5.3	3.9	2.6	4.3	3.4
55–59	20.9	12.9	5.7	4.8	4.2	2.5	2.7	2.6
Indians								
15–19	98.3	96.8	97.1	99.2	47.7	46.8	83.0	91.2
20–24	80.2	67.4	75.4	82.1	6.8	9.4	37.0	54.8
25–29	53.6	34.0	31.9	42.4	1.8	2.5	11.7	24.3
30–34	35.3	16.2	11.7	14.7	1.2	1.1	3.9	10.6
35–39	23.4	11.3	5.8	7.2	1.0	0.5	2.1	5.1
40–44	17.6	9.8	4.6	4.4	1.4	0.5	1.4	2.9
45–49	15.1	9.1	4.4	3.9	1.6	0.5	0.9	2.2
50–54	15.2	8.8	4.9	3.8	2.6	0.6	0.7	1.6
55–59	13.5	8.5	5.2	4.4	2.1	0.5	1.1	1.4

TABLE 6.8
PROPORTION OF SINGLE PERSONS AGED 15 AND OVER BY SEX
AND STATE, 1980

State	Male	Female
Johore	41.6	32.7
Kedah	34.6	26.9
Kelantan	33.4	23.2
Malacca	41.6	34.5
N. Sembilan	40.3	31.5
Pahang	39.4	26.6
Penang	42.0	34.6
Perak	38.6	30.3
Perlis	32.8	24.0
Selangor	45.4	36.1
Trengganu	36.0	24.3

highest in Selangor with 45.4 per cent. In the case of women the lowest was in Kelantan with 23.2 per cent and the highest in Selangor with 36.1 per cent. The more important feature concerns the fairly strong tendency for the urbanised and industrialised states to have a higher proportion of single persons than the predominantly agricultural states. Good examples are the relatively higher proportion of spinsters in Selangor (36.1 per cent), Penang (34.6 per cent) and Malacca (34.5 per cent) and the lower proportion in Kelantan (23.2 per cent), Perlis (24.0 per cent) and Trengganu (24.3 per cent). Moving on to the male figures, we can observe the same regional pattern in the proportion of men remaining single. This pattern which exists among both the sexes is a manifestation of the fact that people residing in the less developed areas tend to marry earlier than their counterparts living in the more developed areas where the modernisation influence is more pervasive.

Divorce Trends and Patterns

Among those who do not remain single, their marriage may be dissolved through death of one spouse leading to widowhood or incompatibility leading to divorce or separation. The proportion of the population aged 15 and over who were widowed or divorced is usually very low. For example, in 1980 the proportion of men who were widowed was only 2.0 per cent and those who were divorced was 0.6 per cent. Widowhood is nothing more than a function

of the mortality level, while the incidence of divorce is determined by a variety
of factors, including the laxity or otherwise of the laws concerning marital
dissolution. In Peninsular Malaysia greater emphasis is placed on divorce
which has considerable impact on the stability of marriage and hence fertility
level. The incidence of divorce is known to vary considerably among the different races as well as the 11 states, apart from the fact that there have been
significant changes in divorce in the postwar period.

Table 6.9 gives the figures for the proportion of divorced persons aged 15
and over by sex and race at the four postwar censuses. It should be pointed out
that these figures refer to persons who have been formally divorced as well as
those who have permanently separated from their spouses. A common feature
of the table refers to the lower proportion of divorced persons among men
than among women. This is in part due to the generally greater social stigma
attached to female divorcees and hence their chances of re-marrying are less
than that of the divorced men. With regard to changes over time, the proportion
of divorcees shows a downward trend for both men and women. The proportion of divorced among men declined continuously from 2.4 per cent in
1947 to 0.6 per cent in 1980, while that among women fell from 4.7 per cent
to 1.4 per cent in 1970 and then went up to 2.1 per cent in 1980.

Considering what we have discussed previously about the divorce procedures

TABLE 6.9

PROPORTION OF DIVORCED PERSONS AGED 15 AND OVER BY SEX
AND RACE, 1947–80

Race	1947	1957	1970	1980
Males				
All Races	2.4	1.5	1.0	0.6
Malays	4.5	2.5	1.1	0.8
Chinese	0.7	0.6	0.7	0.4
Indians	0.9	1.0	1.3	0.6
Females				
All Races	4.7	3.1	1.4	2.1
Malays	8.1	6.2	2.1	3.0
Chinese	0.6	0.4	0.5	0.8
Indians	0.7	1.0	0.9	1.1

under Muslim law, we should expect Malays to be exposed to a much higher incidence of divorce than the other two races. To a very limited extent, this is confirmed by the figures given in Table 6.9. In 1947, for instance, the proportion of divorced women in the Malay community was 8.1 per cent which was in sharp contrast to the 0.6 per cent for Chinese women and 0.7 per cent for Indian women. In fact, the most notable feature of the table is the extremely low proportion of divorced persons in both the Chinese and the Indian communities during the whole 33-year period under review. No definite trend is revealed by the figures for these two races, the Chinese proportion for both the males and females oscillating below 1 per cent and similarly the Indian proportion around 1 per cent. As for the Malays, the general downward movement in the proportion of divorced men has been from 4.5 per cent in 1947, to 0.6 per cent in 1980, while the proportion of divorced women went down from 8.1 per cent in 1947 to 2.1 per cent in 1970 and then went up to 3.0 per cent in 1980.

In Table 6.10 we examine the proportion of divorcees in the various quinary age groups for the Malays. As expected, similar figures for the Chinese and the Indians are extremely small and do not disclose anything of significance. It was therefore decided to exclude these figures. According to the table, there was a fall in the proportion of divorced Malay men in every age group from

TABLE 6.10

PROPORTION OF DIVORCED PERSONS IN THE MALAY
POPULATION BY SEX AND AGE GROUP, 1947–80

Age Group	Male				Female			
	1947	1957	1970	1980	1947	1957	1970	1980
15–19	1.1	0.6	0.1	0.0	7.5	3.7	0.4	0.3
20–24	5.7	2.6	0.5	0.2	9.5	5.2	1.1	1.0
25–29	6.7	2.7	1.0	0.5	7.6	4.7	1.5	1.7
30–34	5.4	2.5	1.1	0.7	7.1	5.0	1.5	2.3
35–39	4.3	2.3	1.1	0.7	6.7	5.7	1.7	2.8
40–44	4.1	2.3	1.1	0.9	8.2	7.0	2.2	3.5
45–49	3.7	2.5	1.2	1.1	8.7	8.2	2.8	4.2
50–54	4.1	2.9	1.6	1.4	9.7	10.3	3.6	5.7
55–59	3.9	3.3	1.9	1.6	9.3	10.5	4.4	7.3
60–64	4.9	3.8	2.5	2.3	10.7	11.7	5.6	9.7
65 & Over	5.7	5.0	3.7	3.9	9.6	10.7	6.8	12.5

15 to 65 and over during the whole period under review. In the case of Malay women, this continuous reduction in the proportion of divorcees is seen to have occurred during the years 1947 to 1970. From 1970 to 1980 the proportion decreased in the first two age groups below age 25 but increased in all the other age groups. The rise in the proportion of divorcees with the advance of old age that is particularly noticeable among Malay women does not necessarily mean that the incidence of divorce increases with age. It rather reflects the fact that with increasing age there are fewer chances for a divorced person, especially a woman, to find a suitable mate to remarry. However, this does not necessarily mean that the recent rise in the proportion of divorced women at ages above 24 reflects the greater difficulty for them to remarry. It could well be that during the period of expanding job opportunities in the 1970s Malay women who were divorced by their husband were able to find jobs which pay well enough for them to upkeep themselves and their children obviating the need to remarry quickly, if at all.

The census data on divorces provide a static position of divorced persons enumerated at various points of time in the postwar censuses and does not give any idea of the dynamic position of divorce over the years. Though divorce statistics have yet to be compiled and published by the government on an annual basis, some rudimentary figures on Muslim divorces that occurred in the 11 states for some years were collected and included in certain publications from time to time. These figures merely refer to the total number of divorces occurring in the year and are not classified by any characteristics of the divorced persons, not even by age or race. However, they are the only available data that can provide a good indication of the annual incidence of Muslim divorces in the 11 states in the years for which figures are available.

A summary of the statistics collected by Shirle Gordon and Judith Djamour is given in Table 6.11 where the figures for Muslim marriages have also been included in order to give an idea of the extent of Muslim divorces.[14] Though persons of any ethnic group may contract these marriages as long as they profess the Islamic faith, the figures may be taken to represent the Malay position in view of the fact that almost all Malays are Muslims and also relatively few non-Malays contract Muslim marriages. The second point to note is that for the first four years the figures are not complete for the whole of Peninsular Malaysia since the figures for Pahang are not available as indicated below the table. Notwithstanding these shortcomings, the data can provide a fairly good idea of the high frequency of divorce among the Malay community.

---

14. Shirle Gordon, "Malay Marriage/Divorce in the Eleven States of Malaya and Singapore", *Intisari*, Vol. 2, No. 2, n.d. and Judith Djamour, op. cit.

TABLE 6.11
MUSLIM MARRIAGES AND DIVORCES, 1948–57

Year	Muslim Marriages	Muslim Divorces	Divorce Rate
1948[a]	41,139	28,781	67.0
1949[a]	47,370	28,990	61.2
1950[a]	50,264	29,846	59.4
1951[a]	55,885	28,878	51.7
1952	46,929	21,776	46.4
1953	44,253	20,564	46.5
1954	41,427	19,489	47.0
1955	42,483	19,398	45.7
1956	46,560	18,458	39.6
1957	42,574	18,345	43.1

Note: [a] Excluding Pahang.
Source: Shirle Gordon and Judith Djamour.

It may be observed that in 1948 the combined figures for the 10 of the 11 states give a total of 28,281 Muslim divorces as against 41,139 Muslim marriages. In this early postwar period the divorce rate of the Malays was therefore extremely high, 67.0 divorces per 100 marriages. This was followed by a general downtrend in the incidence of divorce, and by the end of the decade the divorce rate has dropped to 43.1 divorces per 100 marriages. But this divorce rate that emerged in 1957 was still high since it implies that for every 100 marriages that were contracted in the year, there were at the same time 43 existing marriages dissolved by divorce. Another way of measuring the incidence of divorce is to calculate the crude divorce rate defined as the number of divorces per thousand mid-year population. Assuming that all the Muslim divorces occurred among the Malays the crude divorce rate for the Malays in 1957 is calculated as 5.87 per thousand mid-year population.[15]

The statistics classified by state shown in Table 6.12 bring out another interesting characteristics of Muslim divorce in Peninsular Malaysia, and this concerns the wide variations in the incidence of divorce among the 11 states. The highest incidence of Muslim divorce was found in the eastern state of

---

15. The Malay population used in computing the rate was the figure of 3,125,474 enumerated in the 1957 census.

TABLE 6.12
MUSLIM MARRIAGES AND DIVORCES BY STATE, 1948–57

State	Period	Muslim Marriages	Muslim Divorces	Divorce Rate
Johore	1948–57	49,543	14,825	29.9
Kedah	1948–57	70,935	43,609	61.5
Kelantan	1948–57	116,767	90,296	77.3
Malacca	1948–57	20,433	6,567	32.1
N. Sembilan	1948–57	23,737	11,624	49.0
Pahang	1952–57	11,543	6,640	57.5
Penang	1948–57	23,583	9,784	41.5
Perak	1948–57	55,533	25,315	45.6
Perlis	1948–57	9,382	6,678	71.2
Selangor	1948–57	28,719	10,422	36.3
Trengganu	1948–57	54,791	39,052	71.3

Source: Shirle Gordon and Judith Djamour.

Kelantan with a rate of 77.3 divorces per 100 marriages. The second highest occurred in another eastern state, Trengganu with a rate of 71.3. This was followed very closely by the northern state of Perlis with a rate of 71.2. Its southern neighbour, Kedah with a much lower rate of 61.5, was in fourth position. The extremely high divorce incidence seemed to occur in states where the Islamic influence was particularly strong and the social and economic conditions were rather underdeveloped. In the more advanced states of Selangor, Malacca and Johore the incidence of Muslim divorce was very much lower. One of the main reasons for this state differential divorce was the decentralised administration of Islamic marriage and divorce laws whereby each state, with the ruler as the religious head, has its own rules and procedures governing marriage, divorce and remarriage. Uniformity is lacking in these rules and procedures applicable throughout the whole of the Peninsula.

Frequent marital dissolution among Malays in the early postwar years may be attributed to a variety of causes. First of all, we have already observed earlier the relative ease with which a husband can divorce his wife under Islamic law, and in the early years the *syariah* court was not very strict with couples seeking divorce, nor did it provide adequate conciliatory services. The second reason is that in those early days there was an absence of any strong social sanctions against divorce and marital dissolution, and a divorced woman carries little stigma of any kind.[16] Divorce is culturally accepted and remarriage of divorced persons is expected and encouraged. Another reason is that the economic deterrents to divorce are not strong. A divorced woman could always depend on her close kin for financial support; her children could be taken care of by her relatives or easily given away for adoption; and remarriage would not be an expensive affair.[17]

The Malays, especially the politicians, religious heads and women leaders, have been aware and concerned about the high incidence of divorce within their community. The attainment of independence in 1957 injected a certain momentum to this concern as part of the overall desire to improve the economic and social environment of the family unit through greater stability in marriage. The question of frequent divorces and their adverse effects on the affected families was often debated in state legislative assemblies, seminars and the mass media. On their part Malay women, who were more often than not the worst affected victims of marital breakdowns, were increasingly becoming more vocal in such public debates.[18] In due course stricter procedures regulating Muslim divorces were imposed by the *syariah* court in many states, and some new laws were even introduced to discourage divorce and to safeguard the interest of divorced women and their children. For example, the Selangor State Legislative Assembly passed the *Married Women and Children (Amendment) Act, 1968* to give more powers to the *syariah* court in dealing with the maintenance of married women and their children in divorce proceedings.[19]

It is not surprising that the general downward movement in the divorce rate that was observed to have taken place in 1948–57 continued in the next two decades or so. Partial evidence of this is given in Table 6.13 which is based on figures collected by Yoshihiro Tsubouchi for Kelantan[20] and Narifumi Maeda for Malacca.[21] The divorce rate, though fluctuating from year to year, has continued to decline after 1957. In Kelantan the divorce rate was reduced from 79.5 per 100 marriages in 1958 to 53.5 in 1970, and in Malacca the rate was more dramatically lowered from 27.2 to 12.6 during the same period. Figures for the other states are not available, but there is no reason to believe

16. Azizah Kassim, "Women and Divorce among the Urban Malays", in Hing Ai Yun *et al.* (eds.), *Women in Malaysia* (Kuala Lumpur: Pelanduk Publications, 1984).
17. See, for example, Judith Djamour, op. cit.
18. Lenore Manderson, *Women, Politics and Change: The Kaum Ibu UMNO* (Kuala Lumpur: Oxford University Press, 1981).
19. *Eastern Sun,* 28 June 1968.
20. Yoshihiro Tsubouchi, "Marriage and Divorce among Malay Peasants in Kelantan", *Journal of Southeast Asian Studies,* Vol. 6, No. 2, September 1975.
21. Narifumi Maeda, *The Changing Peasant World in a Melaka Village — Islam and Democracy in the Malay Tradition,* Ph.D. Thesis, University of Chicago, 1974.

TABLE 6.13
MUSLIM MARRIAGES AND DIVORCES IN KELANTAN AND
MALACCA, 1948–70

Year	Kelantan			Malacca		
	Muslim Marriages	Muslim Divorces	Divorce Rate	Muslim Marriages	Muslim Divorces	Divorce Rate
1948	12,488	11,625	93.1	1,767	711	40.2
1952	11,391	9,298	81.6	2,235	633	28.3
1956	13,830	7,846	56.7	2,099	625	30.0
1957	7,611	4,747	62.4	1,939	560	28.9
1958	10,723	8,530	79.5	1,969	536	27.2
1959	10,054	6,856	68.2	1,977	582	29.4
1960	9,810	6,363	64.9	2,003	564	28.2
1961	7,176	5,068	70.6	1,865	544	29.2
1962	8,399	5,463	65.0	1,441	213	14.8
1963	7,987	5,278	66.1	1,687	315	18.7
1964	8,264	5,270	63.8	1,633	263	16.1
1965	8,275	5,052	61.1	1,773	260	14.7
1966	8,177	4,395	53.7	1,672	170	10.2
1967	6,933	4,489	64.7	1,813	225	12.4
1968	7,703	4,423	57.4	1,772	225	12.7
1969	8,668	4,518	52.1	1,860	204	11.1
1970	8,136	4,352	53.5	1,908	240	12.6

Sources: Yoshihiro Tsubouchi and Narifumi Maeda.

that the emerging norms favouring lower divorce rate did not exert their influence in these states. Gavin Jones has also shown that the divorce rate among the Muslims in Trengganu has fallen from 1958 to 1975, but this was achieved by means of the general divorce rate presented graphically. Neither the computed rate nor the raw data were published in his article.[22]

Multiple Marriages

In the last two population censuses information on the number of times ever-married persons have married by the time of the census date was collected. Ever-married persons enumerated as having married only once would be those

22. Gavin Jones, "Trends in Marriage and Divorce in Peninsular Malaysia", *Population Studies*, Vol. 34, No. 2, July 1980.

who were still married, widowed and not-remarried, and also divorced and not-remarried at the census time. Similarly, ever-married persons enumerated as having married more than once could belong to the married, widowed or divorce category at the census time, but have married more than once. There is however, a difference in that all ever-married women who have married more than once must have at least remarried once after their divorce or death of husbands, but some ever-married men could have married more than once without being first going through widowhood or divorce. This is because of the possibility of polygamy being practised by Muslim men in accordance with Islamic laws and non-Muslim men according to traditional customs prior to the ban imposed by the 1982 marriage laws.

In view of what we mentioned in the previous paragraph, we cannot therefore equate the figure for "married once" in Table 6.14 to marital stability and the figure for "more than once" to marital dissolution.[23] However, the latter figure may be taken to represent the minimum level of marital dissolution since the former figure also includes some where marriage has been dissolved. One striking feature of the table is that it was more common for the ever-married men than ever-married women to marry more than once at all times and among all ethnic groups. The reason is that there is a greater tendency for the men to remarry after obtaining a divorce, and indeed the main motive underlying their divorce in many instances is to marry another women. Besides, more men than women tend to remarry on becoming a widow or widower notwithstanding the fact that women are more likely to have their marriages terminated by widowhood on account of their lower mortality. One must also not forget the one-sided practice of polygamy, i.e. polygamy is allowed among the Muslim but polyandry is not.

It may be observed that some changes in the position with regard to multiple marriages occurred in the Peninsula during the decade 1970–80. The proportion of ever-married men aged 15 and over who had married more than once dropped from 16.7 per cent in 1970 to 12.3 per cent in 1980. A similar downtrend was experienced by the ever-married women who saw their proportion marrying more than once reduced from 13.6 per cent to 10.0 per cent in the same period. This apparent movement towards greater marital stability may be traced to a combination of factors, viz. a fall in widowhood resulting from mortality decline, a drop in divorce incidence, and a reduced level of polygamy among the ever-married men. The falling frequency of multiple

---

23. It is not possible to exclude the age group 10–14 in the table because the figures given in the census report are for age 10 and over and are not tabulated by quinary age group. See Table 3.2 in Khoo Teik Huat, *Malaysia: General Report of the Population Census*, Vol. 2, op. cit., p. 251.

marriages was also seen to have occurred among the ever-married men of all the three main races, but only among the ever-married women of the Malays and the Indians. Multiple marriages among the ever-married Chinese women seem to have stabilised at the already low point of 1.2 per cent.

TABLE 6.14
PERCENTAGE DISTRIBUTION OF EVER-MARRIED PERSONS AGED 10 AND OVER BY NUMBER OF TIMES MARRIED, SEX AND RACE, 1970 AND 1980

Race	1970		1980	
	Married Once	More Than Once	Married Once	More Than Once
Males				
All Races	83.3	16.7	87.7	12.3
Malays	73.1	26.9	80.5	19.5
Chinese	96.7	3.3	97.4	2.6
Indians	92.8	7.2	94.9	5.1
Females				
All Races	86.4	13.6	90.0	10.0
Malays	77.2	22.8	83.2	16.8
Chinese	98.8	1.2	98.8	1.2
Indians	97.0	3.0	97.8	2.2

The above changes do not appear to have altered the relative position regarding multiple marriages among the three main races. Multiple marriages have always been rather common in the Malay community, with 19.5 per cent of the ever-married men and 16.8 per cent of the ever-married women having married more than once at the time of the 1980 Census. On the other hand, it was an extremely rare phenomenon among the Chinese as the two corresponding figures in 1980 were only 2.6 per cent and 1.2 per cent. The Indians too appeared to have a low frequency of multiple marriages that was slightly higher than the Chinese, viz. 5.1 per cent and 2.2 per cent for the ever-married men and women respectively. The decidedly much greater frequency of multiple marriages experienced by the Malays provides further evidence of the higher incidence of divorce and remarriage consequent on the relative ease of obtaining a divorce under the Islamic laws.

7

Fertility Trends and Differentials

O ne of the developments that we have taken note of in the previous chapters is the emergence of government concern at various times on certain aspects of the demography of the country and the subsequent implementation of government measures that had a direct or indirect impact on the future course of population trends. In the field of fertility, government measures were first introduced in the mid-1960s to encourage the decline of fertility and hence the slowing down of the rate of population growth. A recent development that will certainly affect the future course of fertility was the adjustment to the antenatalist policy in the early 1980s when the government declared that the population was not big enough and adopted a new policy of working towards a population of seventy million for the whole of Malaysia. It is apparent that an increasing significance would be attached to a thorough analysis of fertility trends and differentials. We will however begin with a discussion of the evolution of the population control programme in view of its direct impact on fertility trends.

Population Control Programme

The provision of family planning services on an organised basis dates back to 21 October 1954 when the Family Planning Association of Selangor was officially established as a voluntary organisation.[1] With the support of individuals, firms and foundations the Association was able to open two clinics in Kuala Lumpur in January 1954. These clinics, the first two of its kind in the country, ran only weekly sessions after office hours with the assistance of volunteers. In the early days the clinics were fairly well attended by many women and, encouraged by this modest success, more clinics were established in Selangor. Between July 1954 and August 1959 similar associations were

---

1. Malaya, *Annual Report of the Family Planning Association of Selangor, 1958.*

formed in the states of Johore, Perak and Malacca, and family planning services were made available in clinics operated by these associations.

The need to establish a national organisation to coordinate and strengthen the family planning movement in the country became increasing evident in the mid-1950s. This aim was finally realised in May 1958 which saw the formation of the Federation of Family Planning Associations (FFPA), incorporating all the then existing state associations.[2] In the remaining states similar associations were set up between May 1961 and May 1962, and they automatically became members of the FFPA. The main source of finance for the FFPA is the annual grant from the International Planned Parenthood Federation (IPPF) and from the government. In 1981 the grant from the IPPF amounted to $842,000, while the government grant was $200,000. Many individuals and institutional well-wishers also contributed gifts in kind and cash.

The number of attendances at the various clinics operated by the state associations rose sharply over the years. For instance, the total number of attendances at all the clinics in the country increased from 19,654 in 1962 to 237,997 in 1967, the year when government family planning clinics were first introduced. Thereafter, attendances at FFPA clinics naturally suffered a small setback, and more so with progressively more services offered by the government. In 1981 the FFPA attendances totalled 223,250, and out of the total number of 56,869 patients who visited the clinics during the year, 10,324 were new acceptors and the remaining 46,545 were previous patients. Though there are no precise data, it would appear that the cumulative total of new acceptors since 1954 was in the order of 200,000.

The work of the private associations up to 1967 demonstrated that there was an increasing demand for family planning services among women of all educational groups in the country. In fact, the results of the first National Family Planning Survey conducted in 1966–67 confirmed that the associations could never have catered to the needs of all these women. It was estimated that some 201,700 women on the eve of the government programme in 1967 would like to practise birth control immediately or very soon.[3] Further, an additional 104,500 women were estimated to like to practise birth control after one or more births and 211,500 more after two or more births. In this respect the institution of a government programme in 1967 was quite timely.

The government adopted a positive population policy in its First Five-Year

2. Federation of Family Planning Associations, *History and Activities of the Federation of Family Planning Associations, Federation of Malaya, 1958-1965,* Ref. F.F.P.A. Gen. 24. Kuala Lumpur, 1965.
3. Saw Swee-Hock, "Birth Control Use at Eve of the National Action Programme in West Malaysia", *Journal of Family Welfare,* Vol. 16, March 1970.

Plan 1966–70 which specifically advocated the introduction of a national population control programme to reduce the rate of population growth.[4] It was acknowledged that a reduction in the national birth rate was an important goal closely associated with the overall economic objective of raising aggregate as well as per capita income levels. The principal objective of the policy was the reduction of the then existing population growth of 3 per cent per annum to 2 per cent over a 20-year period. It was felt that if the rate of population increase remained at the existing level, the rate of growth of national income would be adversely affected in the years ahead because a large share of the increased income derived from economic growth would have to be diverted towards consumption in supporting a rapidly growing population rather than productive investment. In early 1966 the Malaysian Parliament passed the *Family Planning Act, 1966* under which the National Family Planning Board (NFPB) was established as an inter-ministerial organisation having statutory powers and a considerable degree of autonomy.[5]

The National Family Planning Board was formed on 10 June 1966 in an official ceremony with the inaugural address delivered by the Chairman of the Board and the government policy on birth control proclaimed by the Deputy Prime Minister.[6] At the same time plans were immediately made to launch a Family Planning Survey to collect baseline data to plan an action programme and to evaluate the work from time to time. The main objectives of the Board as spelt out in the Act are as follows:

(a) the formulation of policies and methods for the promotion and spread of family planning knowledge;
(b) the programming, directing, administering and coordinating of family planning activities;
(c) the training of all persons involved in the family planning extension work;
(d) the conducting of research on medical and biological methods related to family planning;
(e) the promotion of studies and research into inter-relationships between social, cultural, economic and population changes as well as research concerning fertility and maternity patterns;
(f) the setting up of a system of evaluation in order to assess the effectiveness

---

4. Malaysia, "Chapter XII: Health and Family Planning" in *First Malaysia Plan 1966–1970* (Kuala Lumpur: Government Press, 1965).
5. Malaysia, *Family Planning Act 1966*, No. 42 of 1966, Warta Kerajaan: Seri Paduka Baginda, Kuala Lumpur, 12 May 1966.
6. See Mohamed Khir Johari, "National Family Planning Board: Chairman's Inaugural Address" and Abdul Razak bin Hussein, "Government Policy on Birth Control in Malaysia", both in *Kajian Ekonomi Malaysia*, Vol. 3, No. 1, June 1966.

of the programme and the progress towards the attainment of national objectives.

The Board was therefore conceived as part of an integrated movement to tackle the population problem but the population growth rate objective was given greater prominence in the early discussions of population policy.[7]

The members of the Board consists of a Chairman, a Director-General, 10 members representing government departments or ministries, and another 10 representing the non-government sector.[8] The Director-General serves as the Chief Executive of the NFPB. The day-to-day operation is shared among four major divisions, viz. Administration, Finance and Supply Division, Service and Training Division, Information, Education and Communication Division and Research, Evaluation and Management Information System Division. At the state level there is a State Officer in charge of family planning.

The national family planning programme was implemented in four main stages with Phase One in the metropolitan areas and extending gradually to the rural areas in Phase Four. Phase One was launched in May 1967 in the eight largest towns with a government maternity hospital each, and Phase Two was put into effect in the following year in the smaller towns with some 50 district hospitals. Phase Three was to cover the health centres and sub-centres in the rural areas, while Phase Four was meant to cover the other rural areas which have no health centres at all but which could be reached through a combination of mobile clinics and *Kampong bidans*. The static clinics under the national programme were established in General Hospitals, District Hospitals, Maternity Hospitals, Main Health Centres, Health Sub-Centres and FELDA Midwife Clinic-cum-Quarters. Some difficulties due mainly to the lack of resources were encountered in the last two phases, and in the early 1970s some adjustments were introduced whereby family planning services were functionally integrated into the rural health services of the Ministry of Health as part of the total package for family planning for the populace. This Integration Programme was subsequently strengthened by the Population and Family Health Project.[9]

The Board commenced to offer family planning services in May 1967 in its clinics established in the large towns, and distributed mainly oral contraceptive

7. Nor Laily Aziz, *Malaysia: Population and Development* (Kuala Lumpur: National Family Planning Board, 1981).
8. The author, who was then Senior Lecturer in Statistics at the University of Malaya in Kuala Lumpur, was one of the members from the non-government sector.
9. Nor Laily Aziz, Tan Boon Ann, Ramli Othman and Kuan Lin Chee, *Facts and Figures: Malaysia National Population and Family Development* (Kuala Lumpur: National Family Planning Board, 1982).

pills and intra-uterine contraceptive devices (IUDs). During the first month 393 acceptors were recruited and by the end of the year the total number stood at 8,247. With the opening of more clinics, the number of acceptors rose sharply to 43,058 in 1968 and then to 48,140 in 1969. Since the Board also compiled statistics of acceptors recruited by the state Family Planning Associations, estates, and government and private doctors, figures for the whole country were made available. The figures according to the main agencies are given in Table 7.1. The combined total number of acceptors recruited by all four agencies came to 20,726 in 1967. In 1968, the Board's first full year of clinic service, the grand total from all agencies was 74,935, and with saturation effect coming into play, the number dropped to the low of 54,767 in 1971. Thereafter, the number increased consistently to touch the peak of 87,260 in 1979, and then went down to reach 65,061 in 1983. As expected, some potential acceptors were diverted from other agencies to the Board's clinics. The more significant point is that without the Board's clinical services for a full year

TABLE 7.1
FAMILY PLANNING ACCEPTORS BY AGENCY, 1967–83

Year	NFPB	Integrated Programme	FPA	Others	Total
1967	8,247	—	10,132	2,347	20,726
1968	43,058	—	25,158	6,719	74,935
1969	48,140	—	16,695	5,740	70,575
1970	39,441	—	13,495	3,045	55,981
1971	36,159	2,962	13,205	2,441	54,767
1972	35,011	4,904	12,957	3,545	56,417
1973	35,458	4,627	12,059	5,168	57,312
1974	36,628	7,422	12,379	5,251	61,680
1975	37,673	14,809	11,839	5,027	69,348
1976	36,050	22,894	11,515	4,751	75,210
1977	36,472	25,222	10,619	8,063	80,376
1978	36,881	24,670	10,750	7,861	80,162
1979	34,509	32,246	14,070	6,435	87,260
1980	32,446	31,195	15,013	2,409	81,063
1981	30,137	28,010	13,717	2,864	74,728
1982	29,032	27,402	13,300	2,592	72,326
1983	25,580	25,696	11,929	1,856	65,061

prior to 1968, there were only some 27,000 acceptors for the whole country but this figure increased by about threefold in 1969.

The overall targets of the national programme were clearly stated in the various Five-Year Development Plans. The First Malaysia Plan 1966–70 targeted for a reduction in the crude birth rate from 37.3 per 1,000 population in 1966 to 35.0 in 1970. This implied a recruitment of some 343,000 acceptors during the five-year period from both programme and non-programme sources. By the end of the period about 274,000 acceptors or 80 per cent of the target were successfully recruited. The crude birth rate, however, fell below the target to reach 32.6 in 1970. The Second Malaysia Plan 1971–75 called for a reduction in the crude birth rate from 35.0 to 30.0 and a recruitment of 535,000 acceptors from programme and non-programme sources.[10] At the end of the period the achievement was some 433,000 acceptors or 81 per cent, and the crude birth rate fell to 30.5 in 1975. Under the Third Malaysia Plan 1976–80, the crude birth rate was targeted to be lowered from 31.0 to 28.2 and the number of acceptors was fixed at 550,000. The actual figures turned out to be some 450,000 acceptors or 80 per cent and a birth rate of 30.3 in 1980. The present Fourth Malaysia Plan 1981–85 calls for a reduction in the birth rate from 28.2 to 26.0 and a recruitment of 518,000 acceptors. The persistence of the birth rate above the targeted level in the last three plans is due to the increasing proportion of women in the reproductive ages to the total population.

Before the end of the Fourth Plan the government introduced a major shift in the national programme by adopting a new policy of achieving a population of 70 million by the year 2100. This target of 70 million was first mooted by the Prime Minister in his address to the United Malay National Organisation (UMNO) general assembly in September 1982 and officially announced by him in Parliament in April 1984 in his presentation of the mid-term review of the Fourth Plan. The new policy naturally led to a de-emphasis of family planning and a change in the name of NFPB to National Population and Family Development Board. The new policy, aimed at establishing a larger consumer base to generate and support industrial growth, does not affect the fertility trends and differentials up to 1983 that we will discuss in the following section. It will have an impact on the future course of fertility and hence the future trends in the population and labour force of the country which will be dealt with in considerable detail in the last chapter.

---

10. The crude birth rate mentioned for the beginning of every five-year plan may appear inconsistent as compared to the actual rate attained in the last year of the previous plan, and this is due to the fact that a new five-year plan is prepared in advance of the expiry of the old one and hence the actual rate for the last year of the previous plan would not be available yet at that stage.

178

THE POPULATION OF PENINSULAR MALAYSIA

General Fertility Trends

In examining the general trends in fertility in Peninsular Malaysia we can go as far back as 1934 only on account of the paucity of data for the period prior to this year as has been observed in the first chapter. Even so the births were not tabulated by age of mothers and hence the gross reproduction rate cannot be calculated. In using the available statistics, we have also decided to present the births and the computed crude birth rates in terms of three-year periods in order to remove the annual fluctuations and to enable us to concentrate on the long-term movements. The annual average births and the crude birth rates for three-year periods from 1934 are presented in Table 7.2. The population denominator adopted in the calculation of the rates refers to the average of the three mid-year populations in each given period. It should be noted that the birth statistics for all states for 1941, 1942 and 1945 were not

TABLE 7.2
ANNUAL AVERAGE BIRTHS AND CRUDE BIRTH RATE, 1934–83

Period	Annual Average Births	Crude Birth Rate	Percentage Change	
			Births	C.B.R.
1934–36	145,831	37.1	—	—
1937–39	176,673	39.8	+21.1	+ 7.3
1940–42	176,164	37.6	- 0.3	- 5.5
1943–45	154,266	32.0	-12.4	-14.9
1946–48	198,829	40.3	+28.9	+25.9
1949–51	225,063	43.2	+13.2	+ 7.2
1952–54	250,611	44.0	+11.4	+ 1.9
1955–57	278,448	44.9	+11.1	+ 2.0
1958–60	282,261	42.1	+ 1.4	- 6.2
1961–63	299,070	40.5	+ 6.0	- 3.8
1964–66	303,499	37.7	+ 1.5	- 6.9
1967–69	302,961	34.7	- 0.2	- 8.0
1970–72	304,694	32.4	+ 0.6	- 6.6
1973–75	309,783	30.7	+ 0.2	- 5.2
1976–78	323,667	30.1	+ 4.5	- 2.0
1979–81	348,817	30.4	+ 7.8	+ 1.0
1982–83	368,447	30.2	+ 5.6	- 0.7

available, and the births for these years were obtained from estimates prepared by the author in an earlier article.[11]

The movement in the annual average number of births was generally upwards during the 50-year period from 1934 to 1983, except on three occasions, and the numbers increased by more than twofold from 145,831 during 1934–36 to 368,447 during the latest period 1982–83. The crude birth rate, on the other hand, exhibited a different trend, moving up from 37.1 per thousand population during 1934–36 to the peak of 44.9 during 1952–54 and thereafter going down to 30.2 during 1982–83. The rise in the early years was caused partly by a normalisation of the uneven ratio with an excess of males and partly by an increase in fertility, whilst the downward movement from the late 1950s was due more to a decline in fertility. The low birth rate of 32.0 for the period 1943–45 may be attributed to the postponement of marriages and/or births in the extremely difficult conditions prevailing during the Japanese Occupation. The 1942 war year also affected the 1940–42 period when the birth rate was reduced by 5.5 per cent as compared with the previous three-year period.

The lack of good statistics for analysing fertility still existed in the early postwar years as annual births tabulated by age of mothers were only available for the year 1958 onwards.[12] In Tables 7.3 and 7.4 the gross reproduction

TABLE 7.3
FERTILITY INDICES, 1947 AND 1957

Indices	1947	1957	Percentage Increase
Child-Woman Ratio	644.4	852.3	32.3
Crude Birth Rate	43.2	46.1	6.7
General Fertility Rate	188.5	198.6	5.4
Gross Reproduction Rate	292.4	3.186	9.0

rate for 1947 and 1957 was calculated by the substitution method using the 1958 age-specific fertility rates. In Table 7.3 the general fertility rate was derived by relating the annual births to the female population aged 15–49 in the census years, while the census child population aged 5–9 and the same census female

11. The estimates and the methodology underlying these estimates are given in Saw Swee-Hock, "A Problem of Estimating a Contingency Table Arising in Demographic Analysis", *Population Studies*, Vol. 19, No. 3, November 1965.
12. These statistics are published in *States in Malaya: Vital Statistics 1964* (Kuala Lumpur: Department of Statistics).

population aged 15–45 were employed to compute the child-woman ratio. There is no hard and fast rule regarding the choice of the age group for the child population to be used; 5–9 group was adopted because of the greater degree of under-enumeration at the younger ages in the census.

All the four indices laid out in Table 7.3 clearly point to a rising trend in fertility over the early postwar years though not to the same extent of increase. The big increase of 32.2 per cent in the child-woman ratio was caused partly by the improvement in the census enumeration of children and partly by the fairly rapid decline in child mortality during the decade. The children aged 5–9 at the 1947 Census and the 1957 Census were born approximately during 1938–42 and 1948–52 respectively and the children of the former period were exposed to the higher mortality in the prewar years as well as to the abnormally high mortality during the Japanese Occupation. This seems to be the principal factor, though the improvement in the coverage in enumerating children at the later census did play a part in the big increase. The smaller rise indicated by the crude birth rate, 6.7 per cent, and the general fertility rate, 5.4 per cent, was due to a reduction in the proportion of women in the reproductive ages to the total population. This proportion has in fact dropped from 23.7 per cent in 1947 to 21.6 per cent in 1957. According to the gross reproduction rate, there was an increase of 9.0 per cent in fertility during the decade 1947–57 or slightly less than 1 per cent per annum on the average. This may be taken as the most accurate picture of the fertility trend in these years because the gross reproduction rate, defined as the average number of children produced by each woman during her whole reproductive period, is the best measure of fertility level.

The very high fertility that prevailed during the early postwar period was deeply embedded in the cultural and religious traditions of the people of all races. Firstly, as compared with regions of low fertility there was in the Peninsula the interaction of the lower mean age at marriage of women, the higher marriage rate, and the larger proportion ultimately married. Women were expected to marry early; marriage was universal and celibacy found little social acceptance among the people. Secondly, the average size of family was known to be large, a manifestation of the tradition of desiring large families among practically all the races in the country. Lastly, the masses in general did not practise family limitation to such a significant extent as to influence fertility level. The idea of reducing the mortality rate through medical and public health measures has long been accepted by the people, but the not unimportant notion of taking concrete steps to space as well as limit the number of children ultimately produced was still something new and revolutionary in the minds of the general public at that time. As we have noted earlier, the comparatively new family planning movement up to 1957 was in the hands of a small private voluntary organisation which lacked the vast government resources which could make its work widely felt among the masses. The British colonial government, which lasted until August 1957, had not adopted any population policy whatsoever in the area of population control.

The fertility trends after 1957 can be examined in much greater detail and accuracy because of the availability of superior statistics. The number of births, the crude birth rate and the gross reproduction rate for yearly periods from 1957 to 1983 are presented in Table 7.4. The crude birth rate and the gross reproduction rate for the years 1958 to 1969 have been calculated by using the revised intercensal population estimates,[13] while those for 1971 to 1979 are also based on revised intercensal population estimates but adjusted for under-enumeration in the 1980 Census.[14] In addition, the population figures used to calculate the rate for 1980–83 also refer to those adjusted for under-enumeration in the last census. In the years 1958–62 and 1967–68, the births tabulated by age of mothers were not classified into males and females, and the gross reproduction rate for these years was therefore derived by applying the sex ratio at birth to the computed total fertility rate.

Though the number of births is observed to increase from 289,905 in 1957 to 368,438 in 1983, the movement during the 27 years has not been upwards all the way as can be clearly seen in Figure 7.1. The births even fell during the first few years and picked up very slowly to pass the 300,000 mark in 1964. In the next 10 years no definite trend seems to have emerged, with the births fluctuating between 295,000 and 309,000. It was not until during the most recent decade that a clear uptrend in the births was discernible, going up progressively faster from 312,740 in 1974 to 368,438 in 1983. As will be elaborated upon shortly, the annual number of births is influenced to a certain extent by the changing proportion of women in the reproductive ages to the total population.

The movement in the crude birth rate during the same period was in the opposite direction, reducing from 46.1 per 1,000 population in 1957 to 29.8 in 1983. Within this general downtrend there occurred two important events in 1963 and 1978 when the rate dropped below that 40 level and the 30 level respectively. Further decline in the birth rate after 1978 seemed to have met considerable resistance on account of the increasing proportion of women in the reproductive ages to the total population. Instead of giving the computed percentage for every year, we present below the figures for selected years,

---

13. Malaysia, *Estimates of the Inter-Censal Population by Sex, Community and Age Group, Peninsular Malaysia, 1957–1970* (Kuala Lumpur: Department of Statistics, 1974).

14. Malaysia, *Peninsular Malaysia: Revised Intercensal Population Estimates, 1971–79* (Kuala Lumpur: Department of Statistics, 1985).

TABLE 7.4
BIRTHS, CRUDE BIRTH RATE AND GROSS REPRODUCTION RATE, 1947–83

Year	Number of Births	Crude Birth Rate	Gross Reproduction Rate	Percentage Change		
				Births	CBR	GRR
1947	210,815	43.2	2.924	—	—	—
1952	244,624	44.4	*	+16.0	+ 2.8	—
1957	289,905	46.1	3.186	+18.5	+ 3.8	+ 9.0
1958	281,594	43.3	3.076	− 2.9	− 6.1	− 3.5
1959	282,435	42.1	3.012	+ 0.3	− 2.8	− 2.1
1960	282,755	40.9	2.960	+ 0.1	− 2.8	− 1.7
1961	299,030	41.8	3.021	+ 5.8	+ 2.2	+ 2.1
1962	298,229	40.4	2.952	− 2.7	− 3.3	− 2.3
1963	299,952	39.4	2.914	+ 0.6	− 2.5	− 1.3
1964	305,679	39.1	2.924	+ 1.9	− 0.8	+ 0.3
1965	295,155	36.7	2.759	− 3.4	− 6.1	− 5.6
1966	309,662	37.3	2.787	+ 4.9	+ 1.6	+ 1.0
1967	301,419	35.4	2.644	− 2.7	− 5.1	− 5.1
1968	309,501	35.5	2.629	+ 2.7	+ 0.3	− 0.6
1969	297,963	33.4	2.475	− 3.7	− 5.9	− 5.9
1970	297,358	32.6	2.378	− 0.2	− 2.4	− 3.9
1971	309,378	32.8	2.391	+ 4.0	+ 0.6	+ 0.5
1972	308,347	32.0	2.293	− 0.3	− 2.4	− 4.1
1973	302,867	30.7	2.159	− 1.8	− 4.1	− 5.8
1974	312,740	31.1	2.128	+ 3.3	+ 1.3	− 1.4
1975	313,741	30.5	2.049	+ 0.3	− 1.9	− 3.7
1976	324,759	30.9	2.030	+ 3.5	+ 1.3	− 0.9
1977	322,916	30.0	1.954	− 0.6	− 2.9	− 3.7
1978	323,541	29.5	1.884	+ 0.2	− 1.7	− 3.6
1979	336,848	30.0	1.894	+ 4.1	+ 1.7	+ 0.5
1980	347,015	30.3	1.886	+ 3.0	+ 1.0	− 0.4
1981	362,587	30.9	1.901	+ 4.5	+ 1.7	+ 0.8
1982	368,456	30.9	1.861	+ 1.6	− 1.0	− 2.1
1983	369,240	29.9	1.809	+ 0.2	− 3.2	− 2.8

Note: * Not available.

including the critical year 1966 when the figure was the lowest, to illustrate the
long-term movement:

1947	23.7	1970	22.3
1957	21.6	1976	24.0
1966	21.4	1983	25.9

The reduction in the proportion during 1947–57 noted earlier continued until
it reached the bottom of 21.4 per cent in 1966, after which an upturn appeared
and prevailed right up to 1983. In the main this rising proportion of women
in the reproductive ages was responsible for the birth rate not declining further
below the 30 level in recent years, and also for the conspicuous uptrend in the
number of births.

For a good idea of fertility trends, we need to proceed to examine the figures
in respect of the gross reproduction rate given in Table 7.4 and graphically
presented in Figure 7.1. While the early postwar period up to 1957 was characterised by a very high fertility that even went up slightly, the period following
was dominated by a general downward movement in fertility. During the years
1957–83 the decline in fertility only faltered on six different occasions when
small increases in the gross reproduction rate of generally less than 2.1 per
cent were recorded. But then, in the other years of rising fertility, the annual
decline in the rate was also not substantial. The greatest decline was the single-
digit figure of 5.9 per cent in 1969, and in most years the percentage decline
was much lower. It would appear that unlike the rapid fertility decline in some
countries, the fertility decline in Peninsular Malaysia has taken place on a
moderate though steady pace. For instance, the extent of fertility decline was
43.2 per cent in Peninsular Malaysia as compared with 76.3 per cent in Singapore for the same period 1957–83.

A convenient and meaningful way of looking at the long-term fertility trend
is to examine the percentage decline in the following five short periods on the
basis of certain important events:

Period	Decline
1957–61	5.2
1961–66	7.7
1966–72	17.7
1972–78	17.7
1978–83	4.0

A moderate reduction of 5.2 per cent was recorded during the first period 1957–
61, and this was maintained in the next period 1961–66 which registered a
reduction of 7.7 per cent. Thereafter, there was an acceleration in fertility decline
which amounted to 17.7 per cent during the third period 1966–72; this was

undoubtedly a reflection of the effectiveness of the national family planning programme implemented in May 1967. The influence of the national programme continued to be felt in the fourth period 1972–78 when a decline of 17.8 per cent was recorded. By the time of the latest period covering 1978–83, the impact of the national programme seemed to have waned as evidenced by the pronounced slackening in the decline to only 4.0 per cent during this period.

It should be emphasised at the very outset that the failure of fertility decline to be sustained at the rapid pace in recent years cannot be attributed to the 70 million policy because that was officially adopted after 1983. The most plausible explanation lies in the fact that family planning services under the national programme were provided in the first two stages in the urban areas and in the rural areas in the next two stages which also encountered certain major constraints. The national programme was therefore able to speed up the fertility decline in the urban areas during the early years, but was not capable of securing the same effect in the rural areas where the inhabitants were usually less responsive to family planning campaigns. Another factor that contributed to the slackening of fertility decline in recent years was that after the rapid decline in the first 12 years or so the national programme was not strengthened by beyond family planning measures. Such measures usually include legalised induced abortion on demand, legalised voluntary sterilisation, and incentives and disincentives aimed at affecting fertility reduction. Finally, the slackening in fertility decline may be traced to the different speed of decline among the main races resulting in part to their varying responses to the national programme. This will be elaborated upon in the next section dealing with fertility trends among the main races.

In the meantime we will move on to investigate the changes in the level of fertility that have taken place at the various age groups. This is indicated in Table 7.5 showing the age-specific fertility rates at five-year intervals of time from 1958 to 1983 and in Figure 7.1 presenting graphically these rates for every year in this period.[15] Similar rates for years prior to 1958 are not available because birth statistics classified by age of mothers were first made available in this year. It has been established that among the countries of the world there are three basic types of age pattern of fertility: the early-peak type in which fertility is highest at ages 20–24 years, the late-peak type in which peak fertility occurs at ages 25–29, and the broad-peak type characterised by maximum and nearly uniform fertility levels in age groups 20–24 and 25–29.[16] Table 7.5 reveals

---

15. Since only a small number of births occur to women under 15 and above 49 years of age, the computation of all the age-specific fertility rates in this book has been performed by including those below 15 in the 15–19 age group and those above 49 in the 45–49 age group.

16. United Nations, *Conditions and Trends of Fertility in the World Population*, Bulletin No. 7 (New York: United Nations Department of Economic and Social Affairs, 1976).

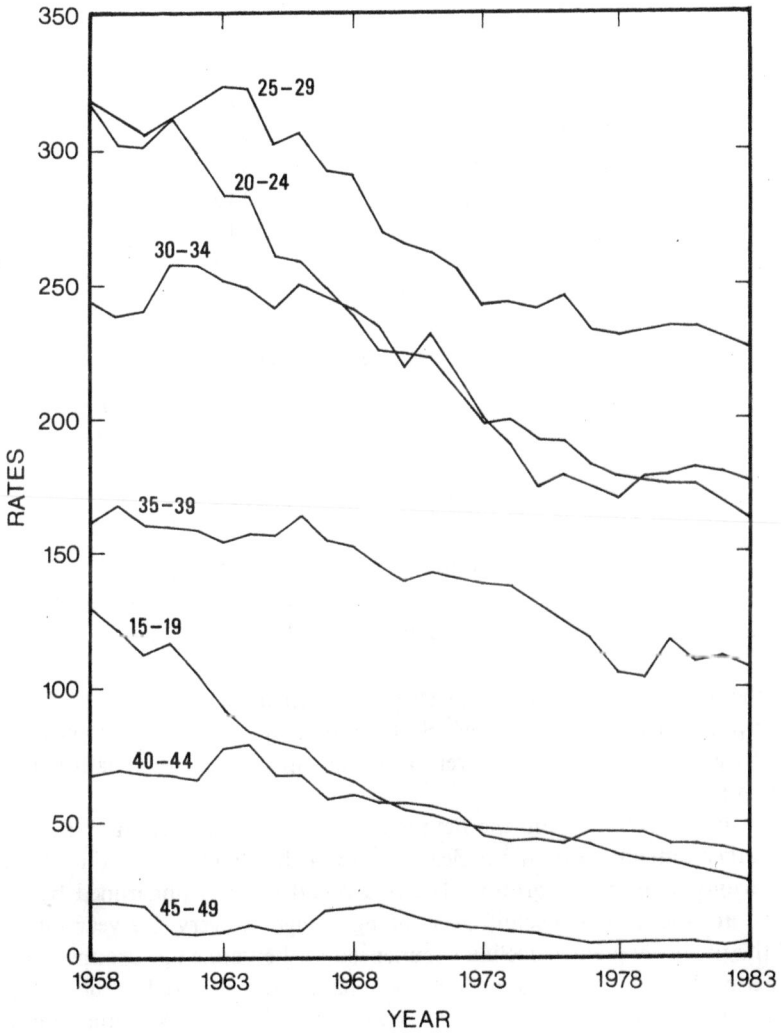

FIGURE 7.1
AGE-SPECIFIC FERTILITY RATES, 1958–83

TABLE 7.5
AGE-SPECIFIC FERTILITY RATES, 1958–83

Age Group	1958	1963	1968	1973	1978	1983
Rates						
15–19	128.4	91.0	65.3	47.1	38.8	28.2
20–24	318.4	283.2	240.6	199.6	178.2	162.5
25–29	317.6	323.5	291.4	243.9	231.3	225.9
30–34	242.9	251.5	250.2	200.3	169.6	177.3
35–39	161.8	153.5	152.3	139.1	105.5	107.8
40–44	67.5	72.1	61.0	45.4	45.1	38.7
45–49	19.5	18.7	18.5	10.3	5.4	5.1
Percentage Change						
15–19		−29.1	−28.2	−27.9	−17.6	−27.3
20–24		−11.1	−15.0	−17.0	−10.7	− 8.8
25–29		+ 1.9	− 9.9	−16.0	− 5.2	− 2.3
30–34		+ 3.5	− 0.5	−19.9	−15.3	+ 4.5
35–39		− 5.1	− 0.8	− 8.7	−24.2	+ 2.2
40–44		+ 6.8	−15.4	−25.6	− 0.7	−14.2
45–49		− 4.1	− 1.1	− 4.4	−47.6	− 5.6

that the age pattern of fertility in Peninsular Malaysia resembled that of the broad-peak type in 1958, after which it shifted gradually to the late-peak type in 1963 and has remained so ever since, notwithstanding the changes in the rates over time.

As can be observed from the figures given in the lower section of Table 7.5, it is rather difficult to obtain a clear picture of the changes in fertility level at the various quinary age groups. The two broad features underlined by these figures are the general decline over the age range at every five-year intervals and the relatively greater decline experienced at the young age groups. During the period 1958–63, the most pronounced change was observed in the youngest age group where the rate was brought down from 128.4 per 1,000 female population to 91.0, a reduction of about 29.1 per cent. In the second age group the reduction was 11.1 per cent and in the other older age groups the reduction was less than 7 per cent. As can also be verified in Figure 7.1, the relatively greater decline at the young ages appeared to have prevailed until 1983. There is no doubt that the major reason responsible for this tendency has been the consistent rise in the average age at marriage of women, noted earlier. It was also this rise in marriage age that triggered off the initial fertility decline in Peninsular Malaysia in the second half of the 1950s.

To obtain a broader overview of the changes, we provide below the percentage decline in the age-specific fertility for two sub-periods:

Age Group	1958–68	1968–83
15–19	49.1	56.8
20–24	24.4	32.5
25–29	8.2	22.5
30–34	+3.0	29.1
35–39	5.9	29.2
40–44	9.6	36.6
45–49	5.1	72.4

The above figures for the first 10-year period serve to confirm the much larger reductions recorded at the young ages during the early years. This pattern of decline over the age range differed from that observed in Western Europe[17] and Taiwan[18] where the decreases have concentrated among women at the older age groups. The slowdown in the rise of marriage age and the growing extensive use of birth control to limit family size since 1967 caused the pattern of fertility declines to take on a new direction whereby the older women were experiencing larger reductions. This was reinforced by the activity of the national family planning programme which was obviously aimed at the high parity women who were to be found at the older age groups.

The variation in the changes in fertility at the different age groups has an impact on the relative contribution of each group of women to gross total fertility. The greater reduction in fertility at the young ages during the initial phase of overall decline and the subsequent greater reduction at the older ages during the later phase resulted in the initial spread of the total fertility becoming more concentrated in essentially the three age groups between 20 and 34. Compared with the 67 per cent in 1958, these three groups contributed no less than 76 per cent of the total fertility in 1983. The concentration of fertility in an increasingly narrow portion of the reproductive period that was observed to have occurred in Peninsular Malaysia is one of the major characteristics of declining fertility in a country. This increasing concentration is expected to continue in the Peninsula until such time as fertility reached the replacement level.

17. United Nations, *Recent Trends in Fertility in Industrialised Countries,* ST/SOA Series A, No. 27 (New York: United Nations Department of Economic and Social Affairs, 1968).
18. *1973 Taiwan Demographic Fact Book.*

To obtain a better understanding of the nature of fertility decline we will examine the changes in fertility rates by birth order or parity as depicted in Table 7.6 for the year 1964 onwards.[19] The figures refer to the gross total fertility

TABLE 7.6
GROSS TOTAL FERTILITY RATES BY BIRTH ORDER, 1964–83

Birth Order	1964	1968	1973	1978	1983
Rates					
1	150.7	167.5	164.3	172.3	158.2
2	165.2	160.5	146.6	155.6	149.1
3	172.6	152.6	128.1	126.6	127.0
4	159.3	138.3	110.1	94.7	94.1
5	143.8	121.8	91.8	68.0	64.9
6	121.6	100.4	74.2	50.4	44.2
7	95.8	79.5	56.4	36.4	30.3
8	71.0	58.8	43.6	26.5	20.6
9	47.3	40.3	27.7	17.1	13.1
10 & Over	65.1	57.8	38.5	22.7	17.4
Percentage Decline					
1		+11.1	1.9	+ 4.9	8.2
2		2.8	8.9	+ 6.1	4.2
3		11.6	16.1	1.1	+ 0.3
4		13.2	20.4	14.0	0.6
5		15.3	24.6	25.9	4.6
6		17.4	26.1	32.1	12.3
7		17.0	29.1	35.5	16.8
8		17.2	25.9	39.2	22.3
9		14.8	31.3	38.3	23.4
10 & Over		11.2	33.4	41.6	23.3

rate of a given birth order obtained by adding the age-specific fertility rates for births of that order calculated for quinary age groups. This form of measure-

19. The earliest year in which the statistics for births by age of mothers are given according to birth order is 1964, and they are published in *States of Malaya: Vital Statistics 1964* (Kuala Lumpur: Department of Statistics, n.d.).

ment is superior to the general fertility rate by birth order because it isolates the influence of the changes in the age composition of women within the reproductive age range, and it thus serves our purpose better in view of the changes in the age structure of the female population that have taken place during the period under consideration.

During the years 1964 to 1968 there was a rise in the rate for the first order and a fall for the second order and above. The extent of decrease became progressively greater from the second order to the sixth order and then became progressively less towards the higher orders. A different pattern of change was registered during the period 1968–73. There was a decrease in the rate for every birth order, and the reduction became progressively larger from the first order to the higher birth orders. During the period 1973–78 there was a rise in the rates for the first and second orders and a decrease in the other higher orders with the same progression towards a greater reduction in the higher orders. This pattern of greater reduction in the higher orders occurred during the years when accelerated decline in the overall fertility of the population was experienced. During the latest period 1978–83 the changes in the rates assumed a completely different pattern. Though there was a decrease in the first and second orders, the decrease in the fourth and fifth orders appeared to have been rather negligible compared to previous periods. The sixth and higher orders also experienced a much smaller reduction in their rates. This period of smaller reductions from the fourth birth order upwards coincided with the slackening in the overall fertility decline in recent years.

Fertility Trends among Main Races

In order to obtain a greater insight into the nature and causes underlying the decline in overall fertility in the country, we will proceed a step further in our investigation by analysing the changes in the levels and patterns of fertility encountered by the three main races. In doing this, we will plunge immediately into the heart of the matter by examining the gross reproduction rate which is the best measure for comparing fertility trends among different population. The gross reproduction rates for the three main races are presented in Table 7.7; the problems encountered in computing these rates and the solution adopted are similar to those mentioned earlier with regard to the rate for the overall population. Briefly, the rates for 1947 and 1957 were computed by the substitution method using the 1958 age-specific fertility rates, the rates for 1958–62 and 1967–68 were based on total births (both sexes combined) and applying sex-ratio at birth to the total fertility rate, and the rates for the intercensal years were based on revised intercensal estimates. In analysing these rates it is important to bear in mind that, taking into consideration the race composition

TABLE 7.7
GROSS REPRODUCTION RATES FOR THREE MAIN RACES, 1947–83

Year	Malays	Chinese	Indians	Percentage Annual Change		
				M	C	I
1947	2.516	3.499	3.441	—	—	—
1957	2.961	3.486	3.765	+17.7	– 0.4	+ 9.4
1958	2.902	3.260	3.663	– 2.0	– 6.5	– 2.7
1959	2.844	3.174	3.689	– 2.0	– 2.6	+ 0.7
1960	2.830	3.066	3.581	– 0.5	– 3.4	– 2.9
1961	2.931	3.081	3.644	+ 3.6	+ 0.5	+ 1.8
1962	2.856	3.028	3.544	– 2.6	– 1.7	– 2.7
1963	2.869	2.899	3.458	+ 0.5	– 4.3	– 2.4
1964	2.930	2.827	3.417	+ 2.1	– 2.5	– 1.2
1965	2.713	2.737	3.320	– 7.4	– 3.2	– 2.8
1966	2.881	2.621	3.128	+ 6.2	– 4.2	– 5.8
1967	2.670	2.551	3.027	– 7.3	– 2.7	– 3.2
1968	2.753	2.421	2.829	+ 3.1	– 5.1	– 6.5
1969	2.625	2.270	2.616	– 4.6	– 6.2	– 7.5
1970	2.483	2.248	2.415	– 5.4	– 1.0	– 7.7
1971	2.520	2.263	2.284	+ 1.5	+ 0.7	– 5.4
1972	2.436	2.123	2.203	– 3.3	– 6.2	– 3.5
1973	2.306	1.983	2.040	– 5.3	– 6.6	– 7.4
1974	2.306	1.897	2.032	0.0	– 4.3	– 0.4
1975	2.272	1.754	1.919	– 1.5	– 7.5	– 5.6
1976	2.150	1.897	1.862	– 5.4	+ 8.2	– 3.0
1977	2.187	1.654	1.767	+ 1.7	–12.8	– 5.1
1978	2.015	1.635	1.704	– 7.9	– 1.1	– 3.6
1979	2.128	1.582	1.687	+ 5.6	– 3.2	– 1.5
1980	2.176	1.512	1.648	+ 2.3	– 4.4	– 1.8
1981	2.229	1.471	1.621	+ 2.4	– 2.7	– 1.6
1982	2.214	1.419	1.534	– 0.7	– 3.5	– 5.4
1983	2.201	1.313	1.464	– 0.6	– 7.5	– 4.6

of the total population, changes in the Malay rate would have a greater impact on the overall fertility trends as compared with changes in the Chinese rate. The influence of the Indian rate would be negligible.

The gross reproduction rates reveal that right from the early postwar years diverse fertility trends were experienced by the major races. During the period 1947–57 the fertility of the Malays rose appreciably by 17.7 per cent as against the very minor drop of 0.4 per cent in the fertility of the Chinese. The Indian fertility also went up but by a smaller amount of 9.4 per cent. The upward trend in the overall fertility in the country which was observed to have taken place during this period was therefore engendered primarily by the rise in the Malay fertility. The rates should however be treated with some caution since they are estimates based on the substitution method. It is also unfortunate that we do not have the relevant data to derive the rates for the intervening years in order to ascertain the peak point in the period and hence the exact year when the onset of fertility decline occurred. All we know for certain is that the figures for 1957 and 1958 show that every race experienced a fertility reduction in 1958. In the case of the Chinese, it would appear that fertility would have started falling prior to 1958.

We would be moving to firmer ground when we consider fertility trends from 1958 onwards because the gross reproduction rates are based on the prerequisite statistics by age of mothers and are available for every one of the 27 years. According to the rates given in Table 7.7, a general downtrend in fertility was experienced by every race though the nature of the downward path was by no means similar. Another common experience shared by the three races refers to the absence of violent fluctuations in fertility levels from year to year as evidenced by the figures in respect of percentage annual change. With regard to the fertility of the Malays, the trend was generally downward, with, however, a reversal in the decline in 10 years. The increase in fertility occurred at different years within the whole period, but there were three consecutive increases in recent years, 1979, 1980 and 1981. The fertility increase never surpassed 6.2 per cent, and the annual decline did not exceed 7.9 per cent.

As for the fertility of the Chinese, the downward path was steeper and smoother. Aside from the fertility increase happening in only three years spread widely apart, the annual increase in the other years was more often than not greater than that of the Malays. Except for the large reduction of 12.8 per cent in 1977, the Chinese experienced an annual fertility decline of not more than 7.5 per cent during the period. An even more straightforward downtrend in fertility was experienced by the main minority group, the Indians.

Apart from the minor rise in 1959 and 1961, the fertility of this community fell steadily and continuously well below the maximum of 7.7 per cent achieved in 1970. Taking the whole period 1957–83, the fertility of the Malays was brought down by only 25.7 per cent as against the decidedly larger reduction of 62.3 per cent and 61.1 per cent attained by the Chinese and the Indians respectively.

It is necessary to analyse the above general fertility trends in terms of six sub-periods that were employed earlier to study the overall fertility of the country. These sub-period figures, shown below, bring out clearly some addi-tional similarities and differences among the three main races.

Period	Malays	Chinese	Indians
1957–61	– 1.0	– 11.6	– 3.2
1961–66	– 1.7	– 14.9	– 14.2
1966–72	– 15.4	– 19.0	– 19.6
1972–78	– 17.3	– 23.0	– 22.7
1978–83	+ 9.2	– 19.7	– 14.3

First of all, the comparatively lower reduction of Malay fertility may be observed to prevail in the first four periods from 1957 to 1978, not forgetting the increase in the latest period 1978–83. The slower decline can be explained by the fact that the Malays are predominantly rural inhabitants whose repro-ductive behaviour is less amenable to influences that favour lower fertility. The most plausible reason for the rise of Malay fertility in recent years is that the Malay women, who had earlier responded very positively to the national family planning programme to space their children, were now beginning to produce the postponed births without really reducing their ultimate family size. Another contributory factor could be the reduction in the incidence of divorce among the Malays consequent on the introduction of new rules or even laws by many state governments to exercise a stricter control on Muslim divorces. This upturn in Malay fertility was responsible for the considerable slowing down in overall fertility decline in recent year.

A somewhat related phenomenon refers to the sharp rise in the reduction of Malay fertility from only 1.7 per cent in 1961–66 to 15.4 per cent in 1966–72, as compared to the corresponding rise of 14.9 per cent to 19.0 per cent for the Chinese and 14.2 per cent to 19.6 per cent for the Indians. The stark contrasting reduction in Malay fertility between the pre-national programme period and the national programme period may be attributed to the extremely low base level of contraceptive use. According to the 1966–67 baseline survey, only 4.1 per cent of Malay women aged 25–34 were currently using contraception as against the 26.5 per cent of Chinese women and 14.1 per cent of Indian women.[20] Whilst Malay women were not covered significantly by the private programme, they responded positively to the national programme under the encouragement, support and blessings of the government. This is reflected in the race composition of the acceptors in 1967–77, with 40 per cent Malay acceptors.[21] However, we should mention that there was also an acceleration in Chinese fertility decline and Indian fertility decline during the national programme period. It is only to be expected that the national programme should have a positive effect on the reproductive behaviour of the women of all races.

The earlier onset of fertility decline among the Chinese and the more rapid decline once it started even prior to the national programme appeared to be consistent with the experience of Chinese populations in Singapore, Hong Kong and Taiwan. In these countries there was early and substantial fertility decline among the Chinese even prior to or without a government family planning programme. As mentioned above, Chinese women in the Peninsula were already practising birth control to a relatively great extent in 1966–67 on the eve of the national programme. Another common experience of the Chinese population wherever they were is the sustained decline for many years until the replacement level is attained. In the Peninsula, Chinese fertility decline continued without any marked slackening well into the latest period 1978–83 as compared with the slight slackening of Indian fertility decline and, of course, the complete turnaround of Malay fertility decline. The annual figures in Table 7.7 show that the decline in Chinese fertility continued unabated in recent years to touch the low of 1.313 in 1983. The almost equally rapid decline in Indian fertility during the national programme period can be attributed to the special family planning services provided for Indian couples in rubber, oil palm and other estates by hospital assistants, estate social workers and other trained staff with the assistance of the National Family Planning Board and the state Family Planning Associations.[22] This means that the majority of the rural Indians were well catered for with regard to their family planning needs.

A further understanding of fertility trends among the main races can be obtained by analysing the changes in the age-pattern of fertility decline among these races. In Table 7.8 the age-specific fertility rates have been presented

20. Saw Swee-Hock, "Family Planning Knowledge, Attitude and Practice in Malaya, 1966–1967", *Demography*, Vol. 5, No. 2, 1968.
21. J.Y. Peng, Tan Boon Ann, Leslie Corsa and Shamsuddin bin Abdul Rahman (Compilers), *Family Planning Annual Statistical Report, 1967–1970* (Kuala Lumpur: National Family Planning Board, 1974).
22. Joan R. Labrooy, "Estates and Family Planning", *Proceedings of the First National Family Planning Seminar, 10–12 June 1968* (Kuala Lumpur: National Family Planning Board).

TABLE 7.8
AGE-SPECIFIC FERTILITY RATES FOR THREE MAIN RACES, 1957–83

Age Group	1957	1966	1978	1983	Percentage Change		
					1957–66	1966–78	1978–83
Malays							
15–19	179.2	106.8	44.5	34.1	−40.4	−58.3	−23.4
20–24	344.9	283.1	189.0	184.0	−17.9	−33.2	− 2.6
25–29	286.9	297.3	234.8	249.3	+ 3.6	−21.0	+ 6.2
30–34	209.0	244.2	185.4	214.8	+16.8	−24.1	+15.9
35–39	135.6	164.5	131.2	152.9	+21.3	−20.2	+16.5
40–44	44.6	65.4	62.7	63.1	+46.6	− 4.1	+ 0.9
45–49	16.3	19.5	6.6	7.7	+19.6	−66.2	+16.7
Chinese							
15–19	46.6	32.1	25.7	16.0	−31.1	−19.9	−37.7
20–24	287.6	211.8	152.4	123.2	−26.4	−28.0	−19.2
25–29	396.3	314.2	228.7	195.4	−20.7	−27.2	−14.6
30–34	335.5	263.6	157.1	136.0	−21.4	−40.4	−13.4
35–39	235.8	169.2	80.9	58.1	−28.2	−52.2	−28.2
40–44	115.4	75.9	25.3	12.6	−34.2	−66.7	−50.2
45–49	27.5	18.4	4.1	1.8	−33.1	−77.7	−56.1
Indians							
15–19	236.6	123.0	45.5	33.7	−48.0	−63.0	−25.9
20–24	422.5	325.8	200.4	164.6	−22.9	−38.5	−17.9
25–29	380.5	339.9	225.9	202.4	−10.7	−33.5	−10.4
30–34	273.2	252.3	135.3	131.8	− 7.7	−46.4	− 2.6
35–39	158.3	156.6	60.8	55.8	− 1.1	−61.2	− 8.2
40–44	47.1	56.3	19.4	9.7	+19.5	−65.5	−50.0
45–49	13.3	14.3	2.4	1.4	+ 7.5	−83.2	−41.7

in such a manner that we can look at the changes in three distinct stages representing the pre-national programme period 1957–66, the initial programme period 1966–78, and the late programme period 1978–83. The first period saw Malay fertility recording a decline in the first two youngest age groups below age 25 but an increase in the five older age groups. The minimum change occurred in the 25–29 age group, with progressively greater changes towards the oldest and the youngest age groups. Clearly, the rise in the average age at marriage of women caused the decline in fertility at the young ages and of course the onset of the decline. The fertility increases at the other ages may be attributed partly to the drop in divorces (resulting in greater exposure) of women to childbearing and the rescheduling of their childbearing to older ages in order to have almost the same number of children. In the first 12 years of the national programme, Malay women experienced substantial fertility reduction over the whole reproductive age range as they began to practise birth control to space their children under the national programme. Their overall fertility decline gathered momentum in these years. The recent period 1978–83 witnessed another shift in this pattern of fertility changes, a reduction in the first two age groups only and a rise in all the older age groups. The re-emergence of fertility uptrend at these ages was now engendered by the women producing the children which they postponed having immediately after becoming family planning acceptors.

The figures for the Chinese in Table 7.8 did not show any significant variation in the changes in the age pattern of fertility in the three different periods. In the first period 1957–76 there was a substantial reduction in fertility in all the seven age groups, with however slightly greater reduction at the younger and older ages. It would appear that the first phase of decline with significant reduction in the first age group engendered by a rising marriage age had taken place in the pre-1957 period when overall fertility was already falling. In the main, this also accounted for the smaller reduction, 31.1 per cent, in the age group 15–19 among the Chinese than among the Malays and the Indians. In the second period 1976–83 the Chinese experienced progressively greater reduction at the older age groups as the women, after delaying childbearing in the early years, also stopped having children earlier after achieving their smaller desired family size. There was a follow-through in this pattern of change into the latest period, resulting in the continuation of the sustained rapid fertility decline right up to 1983.

The position of the Indians in regard to the changes in their age pattern of fertility lies somewhere between the Malays and the Chinese. There was a rise in the two oldest age groups and a reduction in the other age groups in 1957–66, and a reduction in all age groups in 1966–78 and also in 1978–83. The rise in marriage age caused fertility to go down relatively faster at the young ages in the first period, while the desire for a smaller family size resulted in the reduction at the old ages, the reduction being slightly greater in the period 1966–68 but more markedly so in the latest period. The persistence of substantial reduction at all age groups in the last two periods has naturally led to the overall fertility decline of the Indians to be sustained right up to 1983.

Sufficient has been said to underline the singular role played by a rise in the average age at marriage of women in the initial phase of fertility decline in any population. We have also shown that the rise in marriage age may just imply a postponing of childbearing to older ages, and if it is not accompanied or followed by a reduction in the ultimate number of children produced, the fertility decline could not possibly be substantial or sustained in the later phases. It is necessary to investigate this aspect of reproductive behaviour in order to secure a better understanding of the diverse fertility trends and patterns displayed by the three main races. This task will be accomplished by means of the age-specific marital fertility rates laid out in Table 7.9. These rates relate the births in each quinary age group to the female married population in the same group as enumerated in the last three population censuses. In the case of the rates for 1957, the births by age of mothers were derived by applying the actual 1958 proportionate distribution of births among the seven age groups. It should be emphasised that these rates are absolutely useful and meaningful since fertility within marriage accounts for almost all the births in a country where illegitimate births are quite rare.

Confining ourselves to the Malays first, we can see a general rise in marital fertility rates in the first intercensal period 1957–70. In the two age groups where there was a fall in fertility, the percentage reduction was quite small, amounting to 0.2 per cent in the 25–29 age group and 1.9 per cent in the 20–24 group. On the other hand, the increase in the old age groups above 29 was substantial but rather small in the first age group. The second intercensal period also witnessed a decline in two, though not the same, age groups and a rise in the other five age groups. The combined effect of these changes can be conveniently considered in terms of the total marital fertility rate calculated from these age-specific rates. The total marital fertility rate of the Malays was reckoned to be 7.558 in 1970, 7.801 in 1970, and 8.036 in 1980. Relating this back to our earlier discussion of overall Malay fertility, it is now abundantly clear that the uptrend in marital fertility had dampened the fertility decline, triggered off by the rise in marriage age, in the four sub-periods from 1957 to 1978 and, more importantly, had pushed fertility upwards in recent years. It may also be recalled that the rise in the average age at marriage of Malay women has been levelling off in recent years. Unless marital fertility declines, and this depends on greater contraceptive practice within marriage to achieve a smaller family size, there would be little chance for Malay fertility to move

TABLE 7.9
AGE-SPECIFIC MARITAL FERTILITY RATES FOR THREE MAIN RACES, 1957–80

Age Group	1957	1970	1980	Percentage Change	
				1957–70	1970–80
Malays					
15–19	348.9	350.7	407.7	+ 0.5	+16.8
20–24	398.5	391.0	393.6	– 1.9	+ 0.7
25–29	307.9	307.3	321.6	– 0.2	+ 4.7
30–34	226.8	250.3	242.1	+10.4	– 3.3
35–39	154.0	167.7	163.0	+ 8.9	– 2.8
40–44	56.0	69.1	69.3	+23.4	+ 0.3
45–49	23.4	24.0	9.5	+ 2.6	–60.4
Chinese					
15–19	427.5	447.9	535.8	+ 4.8	+19.6
20–24	476.9	502.0	437.0	+ 5.3	–12.9
25–29	426.0	379.1	326.1	–11.0	–14.0
30–34	338.5	260.5	187.6	–23.0	–28.0
35–39	243.6	156.5	74.6	–35.8	–52.3
40–44	127.3	68.5	23.2	–46.2	–66.1
45–49	33.6	16.1	3.6	–52.1	–77.6
Indians					
15–19	444.2	432.2	531.6	– 2.7	+23.0
20–24	467.2	453.5	473.3	– 2.9	+ 4.4
25–29	393.1	309.0	326.0	–21.4	+ 5.5
30–34	285.8	221.8	173.7	–22.4	–21.7
35–39	173.5	130.0	63.5	–25.1	–51.2
40–44	57.9	51.8	18.5	–10.5	–64.3
45–49	19.5	13.1	4.2	–32.8	–67.9

downwards. In this respect, we should never forget that both the rural and urban Malays are strongly influenced by the pronatalist tendencies of Islam, apart from their concern about their numerical numbers *vis-à-vis* the other races.

A completely different pattern of change in marital fertility over the reproductive age range was seen to have taken place among the Chinese. In the first period the Chinese marital fertility increased slightly in the two youngest age groups, 4.5 and 5.3 per cent, but fell progressively from 11.0 per cent in the 25–29 age group to 52.1 per cent in the last age group. What is more significant is that in the shorter 10-year period of 1970–80, the reduction in marital fertility became more pronounced, with the same progressive reduction over the age range towards the old age. The other difference noticeable in this period was the rise in only the first age group. The total marital fertility of the Chinese was reduced from 10.367 in 1957 to 9.153 in 1970 and finally to 7.940 in 1980. The nature and extent of the decline in the marital fertility of the Chinese have in turn been manifested in the sustained rapid fertility decline experienced by the Chinese up to 1983.

By now we should not be surprised that the pattern of change in the marital fertility of the Indians mirrored very closely that experienced by the Chinese, with some minor differences in detail. The Indians recorded a reduction in marital fertility in all the age groups in the first period, with however a minor reduction in the first two age groups. In the second period they witnessed an increase in the first three age groups but a much greater reduction in the four old groups as compared with the first period. The net effect of all these changes is that total marital fertility rate was lowered from 9.206 in 1957 to 8.057 in 1970 and then to 7.954 in 1980.

Race Fertility Differentials

In Peninsular Malaysia the process of racial assimilation has taken place on such a minor scale that each of the main races still retain its own basic traits as determined by diverse religious and cultural backgrounds. The earliest racial integration was known to have occurred in the early nineteenth century when some of the Chinese men, faced with a shortage of women of their own race, had taken Malay women as their wives. These Straits-born Chinese or *Babas* adopted Malay customs, language, attire and food but very rarely the Islamic religion. Being mostly followers of Buddhism and Confucianism, their marriage and childbearing behaviour conforms closely to that of the Chinese population in general. In the course of time, however, most of their offsprings showed an increasing tendency to take spouses from among the Chinese community and this early racial intermingling soon vanished. A more enduring case refers to the Indian Muslims who have assimilated with the Malays through a common religion and/or inter-marriage. Such Indians do become fully integrated with the Malay community, but then the vast majority of the Indians have not assimilated under such conditions. With almost no racial integration, the three main races have always exhibited some interesting and significant differences in their fertility levels and patterns.

The differences in the fertility levels of the three races are analysed in Table 7.10 which reproduces the gross reproduction rates originally given in Table 7.6 but for only five selected years. It may be recalled that the gross reproduction rate is the best measure of fertility level, and is therefore the most suitable index for the purpose of studying fertility differentials. It may be observed that the estimated gross reproductive rates for 1947 derived from the substitution method show that the highest fertility registered in that early postwar year was that of the Chinese with a rate of 3.499. This is about 39 per cent higher than the rate of 2.516 recorded by the Malays. The Indian rate, very near that of the Chinese, was about 37 per cent higher than the Malay rate. By the time of the 1957 Census, the Malay fertility was still much lower than the Chinese fertility but the Indian fertility was now the highest. An attempt will be made in the following paragraphs to explain the fertility differentials in particular.

The first variable that may explain the fertility differentials among the three races is obviously the average age at marriage of women, which determines the span of reproductive life of married women. By and large, Chinese attitudes towards the minimum age at which persons become suitable for wedlock appears to be high in comparison with that of the Indians and the Malays. Among the Malays in those days, it was widely expected that a girl should marry within two to three years of her having reached puberty which usually occurred around her fourteenth birthday. According to the singulate mean

TABLE 7.10

GROSS REPRODUCTION RATES FOR THREE MAIN RACES, 1947–83

Year	Malays	Chinese	Indians	Malays = 100	
				Chinese	Indians
1947	2.516	3.499	3.441	139.1	136.8
1957	2.961	3.486	3.765	117.7	127.2
1966	2.881	2.621	3.128	91.0	108.6
1969	2.625	2.270	2.616	86.5	99.7
1983	2.201	1.313	1.464	59.7	66.5

age at marriage of women computed from census data, the average marriage age of Chinese women in 1957 was 22.05 years, which was nearly four years higher than that of Malay women (17.68 years) or Indian women (17.71 years).

A closely related variable that may affect fertility differentials among the races is the proportion of women ultimately married since almost all births in the country took place within marriage in the absence of illegitimate births at that time. The higher proportion of ultimately married tends to increase the number of women exposed to the risk of childbearing, particularly in a country where the unmarried women do not produce any children. According to the 1957 Census data, the standardised proportion of ever-married women aged 10 to 49 was calculated to be 56.9 per cent for Chinese women as compared with the 72.4 per cent for Malay women and 71.6 per cent for Indian women.

Fertility differentials among the races may be affected by infertility, viz. the inability of married women to produce children. An idea of the extent of infertility among ever-married women may be inferred from the census data in respect of the distribution of ever-married women according to the stated number of children ever born. However, the 1957 Census collected this type of information from all women regardless of marital status. The number of ever-married women aged 45–54 with no children was estimated by subtracting the number still single from the total number of childless women on the assumption that there were no illegitimate births in the Peninsula. Among this group of women who would have completed childbearing, the proportion of childless was reckoned to be 5.8 per cent for the Chinese women and 8.0 per cent for the Malay women, with the Indians (7.7 per cent) a shade lower than the latter.

By far the most important variable that had influenced fertility differentials among the three races in those days was the incidence of divorce. The religious and social customs of the Chinese and Indians are such that it is neither easy for a husband or wife to procure a divorce nor is divorce generally sanctioned by their society. In the case of the Malays, almost all of whom are Muslims, the operation of the Muslim law regarding marriage and divorce is such that it is easy for a man to divorce his wife, and divorce is generally not regarded with great displeasure, particularly in those early days. All that a husband has to do is to declare once, twice or thrice to his wife in the presence of a religious personage that she is divorced, and to register the divorce accordingly. Besides this lax nature of the law regarding divorce, it is possible to single out certain factors that were conducive to the high divorce rate among the Malays. The more important factors were that the economic deterrents to divorce are not strong, remarriage is easy and inexpensive, a female divorcee can always depend on her relatives for practical and moral supports, and there is freedom of access to children by both parents.

From the 1957 Census data on marital status, we can calculate the age-standardised proportion of divorced women age 10–49. The proportion was 4.3 per cent for Malay women as against the 0.8 per cent and 0.3 per cent for Indian women and Chinese women respectively. Supplementary materials on Muslim marriages and divorces taken from registration records confirm the high divorce rate among the Malays. In the period 1952–57 the number of registered Muslim marriages was 257,880 and the number of Muslim divorces in the same period amounted to 143,708.[23] Expressing the latter as a percentage of the former gives us a figure of 55.7 per cent which may be taken to mean that one out of every two marriages ended up in divorce. Whilst the census data represented a static view at the census data, the registration records provide an idea of the dynamic situation in which the somewhat unstable female married population was subjected to the continuous process of frequent divorcing and some remarrying as indicated earlier by the data on number of times married. The concomitant effect of this extremely unstable married life was a reduction in the period during which the women were exposed to the risk of childbearing. This is the key explanation for Malay women experiencing the lowest fertility in 1957.

Another special factor that could be responsible for the lower Malay fertility is the practice of polygamy as permitted by Muslim law on condition that all wives, maximum of four at any one time, are equally treated by the husband. It is generally known that in the 1950s polygamy existed among the Malays, but it is also accepted that polygamy among the Malays was the exception rather than the general rule. Statistics showing the number of women involved in polygamous marriages are not available, and besides there appears to be no consensus as to whether polygamy will increase or lower the fertility of the women involved.

We will now attempt to explain the factors responsible for the higher fertility experienced in 1957 by Indian women as compared with Chinese women, bearing in mind that this differential was not that pronounced. Going back to the gross reproduction rates given in Table 7.10 we see that in 1957 the fertility of the Indians was no more than 8 per cent higher than that of the Chinese. It may be recalled that the average age at marriage of Indian women was 17.71 years in 1957 as compared with the 22.05 years for Chinese women. Again, the age-standardised proportion of ever-married women in the 10–49 age group in 1957 was 71.6 per cent for Indian women as compared with 56.9 per cent for Chinese women. The other figures quoted before in respect of

---

23. For greater details, see Shirle Gordon, op. cit., pp. 23-32.

divorce and infertility are not of any use in explaining the relative fertility between these two races. Taking all factors into consideration, it would appear that the lower age at marriage and the higher proportion of married women were most probably the two most decisive factors responsible for the higher fertility of the Indians in 1957.

A comparison of the pattern of age-specific fertility rates among the three main races in 1957 is presented in Table 7.11. The derivation of these 1957 rates was explained previously when they were given in Table 7.8. The general picture conveyed by these figures is one where Malay women and Indian women displayed a somewhat similar pattern of childbearing behaviour that differed markedly from that of Chinese women. For the women of the first two races, fertility was highest in the early 20s and next highest in the late 20s. The position of Chinese women was quite different in the sense that fertility stood at its highest in the late 20s and second highest in the early 30s and not in the early 20s. Furthermore, Chinese women recorded comparatively higher fertility at the last three older age groups. The difference between the fertility pattern of the Malays and the Indians was quite clear-cut, the latter having higher fertility from the youngest age group to the 40–44 age group but lower fertility in the last age group.

If we examine the figures carefully, we would be struck by the exceptionally low rate of 46.6 recorded by Chinese women in the first age group, only about one-fourth that of Malay women and one-fifth that of Indian women. The explanation lies in the two somewhat interdependent factors of a higher average age at first marriage of women and the lower incidence of marriage below age 20 among the Chinese. The average age at marriage, as noted

TABLE 7.11

AGE-SPECIFIC FERTILITY RATES FOR THREE MAIN RACES, 1957

Age-Group	Malays	Chinese	Indians	Malay = 100	
				Chinese	Indians
15–19	179.2	46.6	236.6	26.0	132.0
20–24	344.9	287.6	422.5	83.4	122.5
25–29	286.9	396.3	380.5	138.1	132.6
30–34	209.0	335.5	273.2	160.5	130.7
35–39	135.6	235.8	158.3	173.9	116.7
40–44	44.6	115.4	47.1	258.7	105.6
45–49	16.3	27.5	13.3	168.7	81.6

previously, was 22.05 years in 1957 for Chinese women as against the 17.68 years for Malay women and 17.71 years for Indian women. In 1957 the proportion of ever-married women in the 15–19 age group was 10.3 per cent for the Chinese, contrasting sharply with the 54.1 per cent for the Malays and 53.2 per cent for the Indians. In the second age group the Chinese proportion was still conspicuously lower, 56.9 per cent as compared with the 90.6 per cent for Malay women and 90.6 per cent for Indian women. This was responsible for the lower Chinese fertility in this second age group. The late start in producing children has resulted in Chinese women shifting the termination of childbearing to later ages, and hence the higher fertility among the older age groups in comparison with the other two races.

An explanation of the minor variation in age pattern of fertility between the Malays and the Indians can perhaps be obtained in Table 7.12 showing the proportion of divorced women among the Chinese in quinary age groups. First of all, the proportion of divorced women among the Chinese was very small in all the age groups, an indication that divorce was not a major determinant of Chinese fertility over the reproductive age range. The really important point is that without any exception the proportion of divorced women among Malay women was considerably higher than among Indian women. For instance, in the very first age group the percentage divorced among Malay women was seven times higher than among Indian women, and in the second age group Malay women has a divorce rate which was five times higher. It would therefore be reasonable to attribute the variation in age pattern of fertility between the Malays and the Indians to essentially the differences in divorce rates over the age range.

TABLE 7.12

PERCENTAGE OF DIVORCED WOMEN IN AGE GROUPS FOR THREE MAIN RACES, 1957

Age-Group	Malays	Chinese	Indians
10–14	0.21	0.00	0.03
15–19	3.76	0.06	0.71
20–24	4.97	0.31	1.21
25–29	4.73	0.48	0.98
30–34	5.03	0.49	0.93
35–39	5.72	0.53	0.94
40–44	7.10	0.50	1.25
45–49	8.29	0.57	1.14

The varying speed in the decline of fertility among the three main races since 1957 naturally resulted in a shift in the relative position among these races. With regard to the Malays and the Chinese, we can observe from Tables 7.7 and 7.10 that the lower fertility experienced by the Malays in 1947 continued until 1966 when the relative position was completely reversed, and after that the higher Malay fertility has been maintained right up to 1983. A somewhat similar movement in the relative position between Malay fertility and Indian fertility can be seen to prevail, except that the former first became higher a few years later in 1969. As for the relative position between the Chinese and the Indian, the latter has always recorded a slightly higher fertility since 1957. By the latest year in 1983 the Malays, with a gross reproduction rate of 2.201, were experiencing a level of fertility that was 40 per cent higher than the Chinese with a rate of 1.313 and 33 per cent higher than the Indians with a rate of 1.464. It should also be noted that the fertility of Indians was about 12 per cent higher than that of the Chinese. These latest fertility differentials, being essentially the outcome of past variation in fertility trends among the three races, are best explained in terms of variables related to birth control practice and certain socio-economic indicators.

The fertility differentials among the three main races may be attributed in part to the differences in the level of birth control use among these races. The KAP Survey conducted during mid-1966 to mid-1967 revealed that only 7.8 per cent of Malay women aged 15 to 44 have ever used contraception or sterilisation as compared with 32.6 per cent of Chinese women and 14.3 per cent of the Indian women.[24] The fertility differentials can also be partly explained in terms of the extent of participation of women in economic activities which is known to be inversely related to the level of fertility. Indeed, the labour force participation rate of Malay women aged 10 and over was 29.6 per cent in 1980, lower than the 32.5 per cent for Chinese women and the 37.7 per cent for Indian women. We have already mentioned earlier the effect of the average age at marriage of women on the level of fertility. In this respect the average age at marriage computed from the 1980 Census was 23.15 years for Malay women which was lower than the corresponding figures of 24.89 years for Chinese women and 24.06 years for Indian women.[25] Finally, bearing in mind that the level of fertility tends to be higher among the rural than the urban inhabitants, one can associate the higher Malay fertility to the higher proportion of their population residing in the rural area. The 74.9 per cent of the Malay population staying in the rural area was certainly much higher than

24. Saw Swee-Hock, "Family Planning Knowledge, Attitudes, and Practice in Malaya", op. cit.
25. These figures refer to the singulate mean age at marriage of women computed according to John Hajnal's method.

the 43.9 per cent of the Chinese and the 59.1 per cent of the Indians.

It would be interesting to see what kind of race differences in the age pattern of fertility have emerged in recent times as a result of past changes. For this purpose, we will look at the 1983 age-specific fertility rates presented in Table 7.13. The figures seem to bring out certain similarities and differences among the three races. A general similarity refers to the common feature shared by the three races in experiencing a late-peak type of age pattern of fertility with the highest rate occurring in the 25–29 age group. This was no doubt due mainly to the fairly high average age at which the women of these races married, as noted in the preceeding paragraph.

Malays and Chinese displayed by far the most contrasting age pattern of fertility. In the youngest age group the Chinese rate was 16.0 per 1,000 female population, which was about 53 per cent lower than the Malay rate. This gap was narrowed towards the 25–29 age group when it stood at 22 per cent, but thereafter it widened again towards the last age group where the Chinese rate was about three-fourths lower. By comparison, Malay women therefore commenced producing children earlier and continued their child-bearing until much older ages, with the result that their overall fertility was some 40 per cent higher than that of the Chinese. The divergence between the age fertility pattern of the Malays and the Indians was not only less pronounced but also quite distinctive. The Indian rate commenced at 33.7 per 1,000 female population in the 15–19 age group, almost similar to the rate of 34.1 for the Malays. But this extremely small gap widened slowly until the early 20s and then very rapidly until the Indian rate was about 82 per cent lower than the Malay rate in the last age group. It would appear that both

TABLE 7.13

AGE-SPECIFIC FERTILITY RATES FOR THREE MAIN RACES, 1983

Age-Group	Malays	Chinese	Indians	Malays = 100	
				Chinese	Indians
15–19	34.1	16.0	33.7	46.9	98.8
20–24	184.0	123.2	164.6	67.0	89.5
25–29	249.3	195.4	202.4	78.4	81.2
30–34	214.8	136.0	131.8	63.3	61.4
35–39	152.9	58.1	55.8	38.0	36.5
40–44	63.1	12.6	9.7	20.0	15.4
45–49	7.7	1.8	1.4	23.4	18.2

Malay women and Indian women commenced to produce children at almost the same time but the latter stopped their childbearing sooner. Consequently, the overall fertility of the Malays was about 33 per cent higher than that of the Indians.

To throw more light on the recent fertility differentials among the three races, we will study the gross total fertility rates by birth order given in Table 7.14 in respect of the year 1983. It may be recalled that the gross total fertility rate of a given birth order is obtained by adding the age-specific fertility rates for births of that order computed for quinary age groups. This rate is superior to the general fertility by birth order because it eliminates the influence of differences in the age composition of women within the reproductive age range among the three races. The general overview underlined by these rates is that fertility among the three races differed in varying degrees from one birth order to another, though within a fairly regular manner.

In the first birth order the Chinese rate was only about 9 per cent lower than the Malay rate, but this divergence became progressively wider towards the higher birth orders. For instance, the Chinese rate was 26 per cent lower in the third birth order, 65 per cent lower in the fifth birth order, and 84 per cent lower in the seventh birth order. These tendencies may be interpreted to mean that the Malays ceased to produce children at a much larger family size than the Chinese, and hence their higher overall fertility. This also explains the

TABLE 7.14
GROSS TOTAL FERTILITY RATES BY BIRTH ORDER FOR THREE MAIN RACES, 1983

Birth Order	Malays	Chinese	Indians	Malays = 100	
				Chinese	Indians
1	169.3	154.0	149.4	91.0	88.2
2	162.0	145.4	135.6	89.8	83.7
3	148.5	109.7	113.5	73.9	76.4
4	121.1	55.8	77.2	46.1	63.7
5	91.9	32.4	49.8	35.3	54.2
6	68.2	15.5	27.3	22.7	40.0
7	48.8	7.8	16.2	16.0	33.2
8	34.9	4.1	8.3	11.7	23.8
9	22.5	1.9	4.7	8.4	20.9
10 & Over	29.9	2.9	7.0	9.7	23.4

higher fertility among the Malays than among the Indians. It is to be noted that the Indians too experienced a progressively lower rate than the Malays from the first birth order to the higher birth orders. With regard to the Chinese and the Indians, the latter recorded lower rates in the first and second birth orders but progressively higher rates from the third birth order upwards. The net outcome was the higher overall fertility for the Indians as noted earlier.

Regional Fertility Differentials

The different regions of the country differ quite sharply in the degree of urbanisation, the extent of educational attainment, the type of economic activity, the level of socio-economic development, and the racial composition of the population. It is to be expected that these diverse conditions would lead to the emergence of differences in fertility among the 11 states and between the urban and the rural areas. We will investigate these interesting fertility differentials not only within the total population but also within each of the principal races in so far as the availability of data would allow us to do so. Aside from internal migration, these fertility differentials constitute one of the important variables that determine the rate of population increase in the various regions of the country.

In studying regional fertility differentials, it is of vital importance to use reliable indices so as not to mistake the apparent for the genuine position. It is preferable to use the gross reproduction rate, as it is the best measure of fertility, to evaluate the differences in fertility among the 11 states. However, for the early postwar years we do not have the prerequisite birth statistics tabulated by the age of mother for us to compute the gross reproduction rates for the 11 states. We resorted to an alternative method of deriving these rates by using the data on the number of children ever born to women collected in the 1947 and 1957 Population Censuses. Briefly, if $_5C_x^t$ represents the average number of children ever born by one woman in a five-year age group at a census at time t, then $_5C_{x-10}^{t-10}$ would represent the corresponding number for the same cohort at a previous census at time $t-10$. The difference, $_5C_x^t - _5C_{x-10}^{t-10}$, is the average number of children born to a woman in this cohort during the ten-year intercensal period. Similar rates for all the cohorts exposed to the risk of childbearing during the period may be computed. Since the children were born over a period of 10 years and since the woman spend five calendar years in each of the cohorts, the rate should be multiplied by $5/10$ in order to arrive at the average number of children produced by one woman in a generation's passage through the cohort. By scaling down $5/10 \ (_5C_x^t - _5C_{x-10}^{t-10})$ into female births only, the total number of daughters produced by one woman during her whole reproduction period is obtained.[26]

The gross reproduction rates computed in the above manner may be taken to represent the fertility level for the whole intercensal period from about mid-1947 to mid-1957 rather than for any particular year. In one respect these rates have a special merit in that, unlike the customary rates for one year, they were not subjected to annual fluctuations which would have certainly distorted the fertility differences among the 11 states. The computed gross reproduction rates for 1947–57 are given in column (1) of Table 7.15, which also includes the figures for seven variables that may throw some light on the state differences in fertility.

According to the gross reproduction rates, the early postwar years experienced a fairly well-defined pattern of fertility differences among the 11 states. Fertility was on the high side in the southern states of Johore with 3.878 and Malacca with 3.744, and on the low side in the northern states of Penang (2.663), Kelantan (2.800), Perlis (2.917), Kedah (3.137) and Trengganu (3.159). Intermediate rates were to be found in Negri Sembilan (3.419), Selangor (3.345), Perak (3.337) and Penang (3.320). A closer inspection of the figures will reveal that in general a movement from the south towards the north will be accompanied by a gradual fall in the level of fertility. The data provided in the rest of the table might provide some answers to the pattern of fertility differences among the 11 states.

A comparison of columns (1) and (2) discloses very little connection between variation in average age at marriage of women and state differences in fertility. The figures given in columns (3) and (4) suggest that the completed size of family and the divorce rate of women were probably the two major factors influencing fertility differences among the states. Observations in many countries have shown that a low level of fertility tends to correspond to a high degree of urbanisation, a high literacy rate, and a low proportion in agricultural occupations. It is surprising to note that the figures included in columns (5) to (7) seem to cast considerable doubt on the tenability of this hypothesis in Peninsular Malaysia. Leaving aside the exceptional case of Penang, one could hardly fail to notice the somewhat low fertility among the predominantly rural, illiterate and agricultural population in the northern and north-eastern states of Perlis, Kedah, Kelantan and Trengganu.

The fairly strong correlation between the level of fertility and the proportion of Malays to the total population in each state given in column (8) provides a clue to the most plausible explanation for the anomalour situation. It may be recalled that because of the greater incidence of divorce and unstable marriage,

---

26. For a detailed discussion of the method, see Saw Swee-Hock, "Fertility Differentials in Early Postwar Malaya", *Demography*, Vol. 4, No. 2, 1967.

TABLE 7.15
GROSS REPRODUCTION RATES AND SOME CONTRIBUTORY FACTORS FOR ELEVEN STATES, 1947–57

State	GRR 1947–57 (1)	Average Age at Marriage of Women Under 50 (2)	Average No. of Children per Woman Age 45–54 (3)	Age Standardised % Divorced Women Aged 10–49 (4)	% Urban Population (>5,000) (5)	% Literate in any Language (15 & Over) (6)	% In Agricultural Occupation (10 & Over) (7)	% Malay Population (8)
Johore	3.878	19.42	5.35	1.64	28.4	49.1	59.2	35.6
Malacca	3.744	20.02	5.08	2.00	27.0	49.9	47.4	47.3
N. Sembilan	3.419	19.40	4.77	2.39	19.1	56.4	59.6	39.0
Selangor	3.345	20.05	4.90	1.11	49.9	54.5	38.3	19.2
Perak	3.337	20.18	4.94	1.65	33.4	53.1	50.8	34.5
Pahang	3.320	18.83	4.82	2.78	27.1	46.0	66.2	50.7
Trengganu	3.159	16.78	4.57	5.91	22.1	23.6	66.0	91.8
Kedah	3.137	18.17	4.74	2.98	14.1	38.7	72.2	67.0
Perlis	2.917	18.08	4.39	3.54	6.7	39.9	78.2	78.2
Kelantan	2.800	16.29	4.26	6.98	16.4	22.3	76.2	90.7
Penang	2.663	20.97	4.37	1.22	58.7	56.8	28.0	28.4

Note: The data presented in columns (2) & (8) are derived from the 1957 Census.

the Malays were recording the lowest fertility and as will be demonstrated, shortly, even within this racial grouping the Indonesian immigrant component did in fact experience higher fertility. It so happened that the indigenous Malays are by tradition mainly engaged in agricultural pursuits in the rural areas. Viewed from a wider angle, it is possible to state that, as a general rule, in area where an appreciable concentration of the immigrant races prevails, the fertility level could be expected to be on the higher side.

Similar sets of figures for the Malays and the Chinese are presented in Tables 7.16 and 7.17 respectively. It may be observed that the pattern of state differences in fertility was not quite similar for the two races, except that the state with the highest fertility was undoubtedly Johore in both instances. In addition, the two races displayed some contrasting features in the relationships between the differences in fertility and the differences in the variables depicted in the other columns.

Taking the Malays first, only a minor part is played by the average age at marriage of women in the state fertility differences as opposed to the more significant influence of the completed family size and the divorce rate. These two factors seemed to be equally important in certain instances. For example, if the low fertility in Perlis is compared with the high fertility in Trengganu, it may be noticed that, on the one hand, the divorce rate was higher and, on the other, the family size was also higher in the latter state. To supplement the evidence given in column (4) of Table 7.16, we should refer to the figures of Muslim marriages and divorces for the years 1945–58 given in Table 6.12. Though the Muslim marriages and divorces could encompass non-Malays, almost all these marriages and divorces were contracted by Malays. The strong correlation between the higher fertility in Johore, Selangor and Malacca and the lower percentage of divorces to marriages is indeed striking.

In view of what has been said earlier, it is not surprising to see the differences in fertility corresponding in most cases with the variation in the proportion of Indonesian immigrants in the total Malay population and rarely with the variation in percentage of urban population, literacy rate and proportion in agricultural occupations. It is probably true that the incidence of divorce and unstable marriage were more common among the less literate Malay farmers in the rural areas than among the more literate Malays in the towns. Though it would be extremely difficult to demonstrate, it could well be that the indigenous Malays who have inter-married or came into contact with the Indonesian immigrants were in actual fact experiencing higher fertility.

The more direct evidence, taken from the 1947 Census, of the higher fertility of the Indonesian immigrants shown below points to the lower age at marriage, the lower divorce rate, and the larger completed family size as being the principal deciding factors.

TABLE 7.16
MALAY GROSS REPRODUCTION RATES AND SOME CONTRIBUTORY FACTORS FOR ELEVEN STATES, 1947–57

State	GRR 1947–57 (1)	Average Age at Marriage of Women Under 50 (2)	Average No. of Children per Woman Age 45-54 (3)	Age Standardised % Divorced Women Aged 10–49 (4)	% Urban Population (>5,000) (5)	% Literate in any Language (15 & Over) (6)	% In Agricultural Occupation (10 & Over) (7)	% Indonesian To Total Malays (8)
Johore	3.966	18.45	6.02	2.88	16.0	45.7	69.9	25.5
Selangor	3.821	18.42	5.78	3.01	24.1	54.8	54.9	31.9
Malacca	3.535	19.05	5.04	3.41	6.5	47.7	58.8	3.5
Perak	3.313	18.39	5.33	3.43	11.2	57.2	71.2	10.2
N. Sembilan	3.162	17.80	4.88	4.85	6.2	57.5	68.2	4.6
Trengganu	3.126	16.55	4.52	6.24	18.1	20.6	70.4	0.2
Kedah	3.087	17.31	4.65	3.89	7.0	33.7	85.0	1.1
Pahang	3.047	17.64	4.96	4.30	11.3	42.1	76.3	2.4
Penang	2.844	18.63	4.32	3.18	26.6	60.9	56.4	1.7
Kelantan	2.804	16.02	4.26	7.31	14.4	20.1	79.1	0.1
Perlis	2.783	17.42	4.23	4.18	3.5	38.5	87.1	1.9

Note: The data presented in columns (2) & (8) are derived from the 1957 Census.

	Indigenous Malays	Indonesian Immigrants
Child-Woman Ratio	610.50	674.90
Average No. of Children per Woman aged 45–54	4.41	4.87
Singulate Mean Age at Marriage of Women under 50	17.07	16.70
Age-Standardised Per Cent Divorced Women aged 10–49	6.68	4.55

The amalgamation of the indigenous Malays and the Indonesian immigrants into one single group in almost all the tables in the 1957 Census Reports renders it impossible to derive a similar set of figures for the child-woman ratio, etc. for the year 1957. However, the 1947 figures are quite adequate for demonstrating the point under consideration.

So far only the state fertility differentials for groups of somewhat mixed races have been considered and it would be instructive to see what kind of differentials was displayed by the more homogenous group of Chinese. Table 7.17 shows that the average age at marriage of women appears to constitute a more significant factor than in the case of the Malays, and thus led to the slightly diminished influence of the family size in some states. However, concentrating on the two states with the lowest and the highest fertility, there is no doubt about the high average age at marriage and the smaller family size in Penang, and vice versa in Johore. Except for Kelantan and perhaps Trengganu, the difference in the generally low divorce incidence could only explain, if at all, to a very small extent the state fertility differences among the Chinese. The customary association between the level of fertility and degree of urbanisation, literacy rate, and proportion in agricultural occupations prevailed among the Chinese throughout the country. The most striking example was Penang where fertility in those days was the lowest and the population was most urban, most literate, and least dependent on agriculture for a living.

One rather interesting feature underlined by the figures in Tables 7.16 and 7.17 is that among the 11 states Kelantan and Trengganu recorded the highest incidence of divorce for the Chinese as well as for the Malays. This strongly suggests that either the divorce habits of the Chinese in a predominantly Malay area have been influenced by those of the Malays or a larger proportion of the Chinese women, perhaps through marrying Malay men, have embraced the Islamic faith in these two states.

It is possible to elaborate on our previous observation about the likely association between the level of fertility and the extent of urbanisation by resorting to a direct analysis of fertility differentials between the rural and the

TABLE 7.17
CHINESE GROSS REPRODUCTION RATES AND SOME CONTRIBUTORY FACTORS FOR ELEVEN STATES, 1947–57

State	GRR 1947–57 (1)	Average Age at Marriage of Women Under 50 (2)	Average No. of Children per Woman Age 45–54 (3)	Age Standardised % Divorced Women Aged 10–49 (4)	% Urban Population (>5,000) (5)	% Literate in any Language (15 & Over) (6)	% In Agricultural Occupation (10 & Over) (7)
Johore	4.232	21.05	5.13	0.25	41.6	49.1	53.7
Pahang	4.099	21.61	4.67	0.24	51.5	49.7	58.6
N. Sembilan	4.073	21.87	4.77	0.32	31.1	53.8	56.9
Malacca	4.030	21.41	5.22	0.38	44.0	49.9	35.6
Kedah	3.693	21.66	5.12	0.50	35.7	49.4	34.5
Perlis	3.669	21.48	4.87	0.63	18.5	47.8	38.4
Perak	3.663	22.73	4.77	0.19	52.5	49.0	35.2
Selangor	3.324	22.10	4.63	0.19	68.3	51.2	27.5
Trengganu	3.225	20.47	4.67	0.72	71.2	52.5	27.3
Kelantan	3.026	20.53	4.56	2.25	47.5	49.5	35.6
Penang	2.761	22.61	4.40	0.27	72.4	52.1	17.9

Note: The data presented in columns (2) & (8) are derived from the 1957 Census.

urban areas based on the child-woman ratio according to the residence of children and women at the time of the census. In interpreting the data for this index, it is important to remember that by comparison the rural figures were affected by greater under-enumeration of child population and by higher mortality among children. Any excess of the rural figures over the urban figures may thus be taken as a sure sign of the existence of the usual rural-urban differentials, though only the minimum amount of the actual differences would be revealed. However, a misleading conclusion might be reached if we use these figures to depict differences in rural (or urban) fertility among the three main races.

The urban figures given in Table 7.18 pertain to the municipal areas of nine state capitals, the only classification by age group published in the 1957 Census Reports. The rural figures refer to the other areas. These nine towns were by no means the nine largest centres of urban conglomeration in Peninsular Malaysia, the state capitals of Kelantan and Trengganu were only the thirteenth and sixteenth largest towns respectively. The inclusion of the other urban centres in the calculation of the rural ratios might tend to lower these ratios somewhats.

Table 7.18 shows that the child-woman ratio in 1957 was 695.1 in the rural area and 622.5 in the urban area, a clear indication of higher fertility in the rural than in the urban areas of the country. This higher rural fertility may also be seen to exist within each of the three main races. However, a more marked rural-urban fertility differential prevailed among the Chinese than among the Malays, and curiously enough the differential seemed to be almost insignificant in the case of the Indians. The only plausible explanation for the peculiar position of the Indians was that the majority of the Indians in the rural areas reside in modernised plantations with conditions that were not so rural in character as compared with those of the isolated villages or farms where the bulk of the rural Malays and rural Chinese resided. Another likely reason could be the practice of sending Indian children from the estates to stay and

TABLE 7.18

CHILD-WOMAN RATIOS BY RURAL-URBAN AREA AND RACE, 1957

Race	Rural	Urban	U = 100
All Races	695.1	622.5	111.7
Malays	641.2	588.0	109.0
Chinese	775.1	625.1	124.0
Indians	776.7	764.5	101.6

attend schools in towns where they were enumerated on census day in 1957.

The 1980 Census provides data that are more suitable for studying differences in fertility among rural-urban divisions by means of the child-woman ratio. In fact, the information is sufficiently detailed for us to derive the ratio for three distinct divisions, viz. metropolitan area with 75,000 or more persons, urban area with 10,000 to 74,999 persons, and rural area with less than 10,000 persons. As can be seen in Table 7.19, the child-woman ratio for the metropolitan area in 1980 was 114.1 children aged 5–9 per 1,000 population. This was lower than the ratio of 125.1 in the urban area, which was in turn lower than that in the rural area with 142.1.

TABLE 7.19

CHILD-WOMAN RATIOS BY RURAL-URBAN AREA AND RACE, 1980

Races	Metropolitan	Urban	Rural	Metropolitan = 100	
				U	R
All Races	114.1	125.1	142.1	109.6	124.5
Malays	119.3	124.2	143.3	104.1	119.4
Chinese	111.2	126.0	142.0	113.3	129.5
Indians	109.7	122.9	136.8	112.0	123.4

The child-woman ratio for the three main races, also shown in Table 7.19, brings out the existence of the normal variation in fertility among the three regions, lowest in the metropolitan area and highest in the rural area, with an intermediate level in the urban area. Even the Indians, who displayed the rather peculiar negligible difference between the twofold division of rural and urban areas in 1957, were now experiencing a bigger but normal difference among the three regions in 1980. Of greater significance is the extent of the gap among the three ratios within each of the three races. In the case of the Malays, the urban ratio and the rural ratio were 4.1 per cent and 19.4 per cent respectively higher than the metropolitan ratio. On the other hand, far greater differentials among the three regions may be seen to prevail among the Chinese, and only slightly less pronounced differentials were registered by the Indians. The relatively smaller differentials experienced by the Malays could be caused by the fact that a sizeable proportion of the Malays staying in the metropolitan and urban areas in 1980 were recent migrants from the rural area and had retained most of the norms favouring a large family size. It should also be remembered that the child-woman ratio does not in fact measure fertility level in 1980 but rather in a five-year period from about mid-1970 to mid-1975.

8

Labour Force

The amount of labour available for the production of goods and services in a country is determined by a variety of demographic, social and economic factors. The size of the total population and its composition with respect to sex and age determine the maximum limits of the number of persons who can participate in economic activities. Other factors such as the race composition, the degree of urbanisation and the proportion of married women play an important part in influencing the proportion of the population which will be represented in certain age groups in the working population. Among the more important economic and social factors are the industrial structure of the economy, the mode and organisation of production, the per capita income and the traditional attitudes towards working women and working children. By and large, demographic factors are the major determinants of the size of the male working population since by convention nearly all men are engaged in some form of gainful work from the time they reach adulthood until they approach the retirement age. On the other hand, socio-economic factors seem to exert a greater influence on the size of the female working population.

Concepts and Definitions

The labour force statistics of a country can be collected by means of the gainful worker approach or the labour force approach.[1] The older gainful worker concept was widely used before the Second World War and even during the early postwar years in some countries. In Peninsular Malaysia it was last used in September 1947 when the first postwar census of population was conducted.

---

1. For a discussion of these two concepts, see United Nations, *Handbook of Population Census Methods, Volume II: Economic Characteristics of Population*, Series F, No. 5, Rev. 1, Studies in Methods (New York, 1958).

According to this concept the respondents were requested to state their usual occupation or gainful work from which they earned their income without reference to any time period. Those who were ascertained to have engaged in gainful work were considered as in the labour force, while those without any such work were classified as outside the labour force. Apart from the absence of a reference period to which the data could refer to, this method of collecting statistics cannot provide figures for the employed and the unemployed separately.

According to the labour force approach all respondents aged 10 years and over were asked to state whether they were working during the reference period, and if not, whether they were actively looking for work. Working is defined as being engaged in the production of goods and services. All those who were identified as working or actively looking for work were considered as economically active and included in the labour force, while the others were included in the economically inactive population. Persons returned as working constitute the employed, while those identified as not working but actively looking for work comprise the unemployed. The former group includes persons who were actually working during the reference period as well as persons who had a job but were temporarily laid off on account of sickness, leave, strike, bad weather, etc., and would be returning to work in due course. The employed group consists of persons who had worked previously and were looking for jobs during the reference period as well as those who had never worked before and were looking for jobs for the first time. Actively looking for work is defined as registering at an employment exchange, inserting and answering job advertisements, applying directly to prospective employers, making enquiries from relatives and friends, or taking step to start one's own business.

The economically inactive population includes all persons who were not working and not actively looking for work during the reference period. Among the more important categories in the inactive population are those doing housework without pay, students, unpaid voluntary social workers, inmates of penal, mental or charitable institution, retired persons, persons permanently disabled, persons deriving their income from rent, dividend, interest, etc., and all others not engaged in economic activities. It should be pointed out that among the economically inactive persons are those who have worked before and may re-enter the labour force in the future. But a much larger number, such as young students, would not have worked before and would enter the labour force for the first time in subsequent years.

Persons who were identified as economically active during the reference period were classified by employment status. This refers to the status of an individual with respect to his employment, that is, whether he is an employer, own account worker, unpaid family worker or employee. Employers refer to persons who operate either on their own or jointly with other partners a business, trade or profession and hire one or more employees, whereas those who do not engage any employees at all are known as own account workers. Employees refer to persons who work for individuals, firms or organisations and receive regular wages or salaries from them. Unpaid family workers refer to persons who assist in the family business, trade or enterprise without receiving any fixed wage or salary.

There were some variations in the actual application of the labour force approach to the collection of statistics in the last three population censuses. The most important difference concerns the reference period. In the 1957 Census the reference period adopted to determine whether a person was working was taken as at least a total of four months during the 12-month period prior to the preliminary enumeration.[2] In the 1970 and 1980 Censuses the usual reference period of one week preceeding the enumeration of the respondents was used. At the same time, it was recognised that this short reference period might not take into consideration the seasonality of some economic activities, and hence supplementary information on usual activity based on the much larger time reference of 12 months was collected. However, almost all the basic tables in respect of the labour force published in the 1970 and the 1980 reports pertain to those collected on the one-week basis. These figures are analysed in this chapter. The extent to which changes in labour force measurement between 1957 on the one hand and 1970 and 1980 on the other affect the comparability of the figures is difficult to assess. Presumably the one-year reference period used in 1957 would result in the inclusion of marginal workers in the labour force. The same holds true in the case of the absence of a reference period in the gainful worker approach used in 1947 and before.

Growth of the Labour Force

The economically active population aged 10 years and over stood at 1,904,100 in 1947, and a decade later it had increased by 13.7 per cent to reach 2,164,900 in 1957. Table 8.1 shows that the next 13 years experienced a further rise of 32.6 per cent in the labour force which was enumerated as 2,870,900 in 1970. In the latest intercensal period the labour force grew by 41.8 per cent so that by 1980 it exceeded the four million mark to touch 4,069,700 in 1980. The acceleration in the rate of growth since 1947 is a reflection of rapid population growth immediately after the war, reinforced subsequently by the high economic growth since the late 1960s.

During the postwar period the female labour force has grown much faster

---

2. Saw Swee-Hock, "Sources and Methods of Labour Force Statistics in Malaya", *Ekonomi*, Vol. 3, No. 1, December 1966.

TABLE 8.1
GROWTH OF LABOUR FORCE BY SEX, 1947–80

Year	Number ('000)			Intercensal Increase (%)		
	Total	Males	Females	Total	Males	Females
1947	1,904.1	1,462.7	441.4	—	—	—
1957	2,164.9	1,635.1	529.8	13.7	11.8	20.5
1970	2,870.9	1,958.3	912.7	32.6	19.8	72.3
1980	4,069.7	2,707.4	1,362.3	41.8	38.3	49.3

than the male labour force. The former increased by a significantly higher rate of 20.0 per cent during 1947–57, 72.3 per cent during 1957–70, and 49.3 per cent during 1970–80. In contrast the male labour force grew by only 11.8 per cent, 19.8 per cent and 38.3 per cent respectively during the same three periods. As a result, the female labour force was multiplied rapidly from 441,400 in 1947 to 529,800 in 1957, 912,700 in 1970, and then 1,362,300 in 1980, a threefold increase for the whole period. On the other hand, the male labour force did not even double during the period, rising from 1,462,700 in 1947 to 2,707,400 in 1980. One outcome of this is that the proportion of women in the labour force increased during the last three decades or so. The more rapid growth of the female labour force may be attributed to the improvement in educational attainment of women, the more favourable attitudes towards female employment, the shrinking of male immigrant labour, and the better job opportunities for women in many rapidly growing sectors of the economy. Examples of such sectors are the electronics industry, the textile and garment manufacturing sector, and the services sector.

During the intercensal period 1970–80 the growth of the labour force varies appreciably among the main racial groups in Peninsular Malaysia. As can be observed in Table 8.2, by far the highest growth was recorded by the Malays with an increase of 47.8 per cent in their labour force as compared to the 34.1 per cent increase registered by the Chinese. The Indian labour force grew at an intermediate pace of 40.8 per cent. It should be remembered that among these three races a relatively larger population of Chinese were working in Singapore on a temporary basis, and the number has in fact been increasing over the years. This accounted partly for the slowest growth recorded by this racial group. The policy of according preference to *bumiputras* in employment, reinforced under the New Economic Policy introduced in the early 1970s,

TABLE 8.2
GROWTH OF LABOUR FORCE BY SEX FOR THREE MAIN RACES,
1970 AND 1980

Race	Number ('000)		Intercensal Increase (%)
	1970	1980	
Both Sexes			
Malays	1,502.1	2,220.1	47.8
Chinese	1,034.9	1,387.6	34.1
Indians	308.1	433.9	40.8
Males			
Malays	1,011.4	1,465.3	44.9
Chinese	709.2	938.4	32.4
Indians	219.8	285.2	29.7
Females			
Malays	490.7	754.8	53.8
Chinese	325.7	449.2	57.9
Indians	88.3	148.8	68.6

has contributed in no small measure to the Malay labour force registering the fastest rate of increase.

A greater insight into the differential growth rates among these three races may be obtained by examining the figures for the two sexes shown also in Table 8.2. The most interesting trend was displayed by the Indian labour force, with the men recording an increase of 29.7 per cent as against the 68.6 per cent by their female counterparts. Due to past migration the Indians had a relatively large number of immigrant male labourers, but with no fresh migration this number has been dwindling over the years. In a way this has also provided more job opportunities for the women within the Indian community. In fact, the proportion of women in the Indian labour force has increased from 28.7 per cent in 1970 to 34.4 per cent in 1980. The two major races recorded a much less pronounced difference in the growth rate between the sexes. Among the Malays the male labour force grew by 44.9 per cent and the female labour force by 53.8 per cent. The two corresponding figures for the Chinese were 32.2 per cent and 37.9 per cent.

Another interesting aspect of the labour force concerns the differences in the rate of increase between the urban area and the rural area. As in many developing countries, the economic growth of Peninsular Malaysia viewed in terms of job creation has been biased towards the urban area.[3] Table 8.3 reveals that during the decade 1970–80 the urban labour force grew by 95.3 per cent

TABLE 8.3

GROWTH OF LABOUR FORCE BY SEX, RACE AND URBAN-RURAL AREA, 1970 AND 1980

Sex	Number ('000)				Intercensal Increase (%)	
	Urban		Rural			
	1970	1980	1970	1980	Urban	Rural
All Races						
Total	803.5	1,569.0	2,067.4	2,500.8	95.3	21.0
Males	582.5	1,056.3	1,375.8	1,651.2	81.3	20.0
Females	221.0	512.7	691.5	849.6	132.0	22.8
Malays						
Total	199.0	568.7	1,303.1	1,651.4	185.8	26.7
Males	150.2	382.1	861.2	1,083.2	154.4	25.8
Females	48.8	186.6	441.9	565.2	282.4	27.9
Chinese						
Total	493.4	812.2	541.5	575.3	64.6	6.2
Males	340.8	540.1	368.4	398.3	58.5	8.1
Females	152.6	272.1	173.1	177.1	78.3	2.3
Indians						
Total	102.3	177.1	205.8	256.9	73.1	24.8
Males	84.8	126.2	135.1	159.0	48.8	17.7
Females	17.5	50.9	70.7	97.7	190.9	38.5

3. Malaysia, *Mid-Term Review of the Second Malaysia Plan, 1971–1975*, op. cit.

from 803,500 in 1970 to 1,056,300 in 1980. In sharp contrast, the rural labour force managed to edge up from 2,067,400 to 2,500,800, an increase of only 21.0 per cent during the same period. This is clearly a confirmation of the fact that there were very few job opportunities for people residing in areas with a population size of less than 10,000 and the rural folks have continued to move into the urban centres where jobs were more forthcoming.

The higher rate of growth of the labour force in the urban area was experienced by all the three main races, as can be seen in Table 8.3. The Malay labour force grew by 185.8 per cent in the urban area as against 26.7 per cent in the rural area. As for the Indians, the labour force grew by only 73.1 per cent in the urban area and by 24.8 per cent in the rural area. Even lower rates of growth were recorded by the Chinese labour force, 64.6 per cent in the urban area and 6.2 per cent in the rural area. The extremely slow expansion of the rural Chinese labour force could be caused partly by the greater movement of the rural Chinese to Singapore to work as guest workers.[4] The figures for the Malays demonstrate that relatively more of them were successful in securing jobs in the urban centres than in the rural area, which is in fact consonant with the policy of encouraging Malays to shift to these centres in order to be so placed as to benefit from the higher urban standard of living. Looking at the 1980 figures, we see that the labour force was larger in the rural area than in the urban area in the case of both the Malays and the Indians. On the other hand, the urban labour force was larger than the rural labour force among the Chinese. This pattern of urban-rural distribution among the three races was also indicated by the male and female figures given in Table 8.3.

In examining the growth of the labour force by employment status, we are fortunate that the data collected in the 1970 and 1980 Censuses were tabulated according to the usual four categories, viz., employer, employee, own account worker and unpaid family worker. In the 1957 Census there were only three categories, with employer and own account worker lumped together into one category known as self-employed.[5] In Table 8.4 we have therefore presented the figures for 1970 and 1980. It should be mentioned that these figures include those who were working during the reference week as well as those who were unemployed but had worked before. But the unemployed persons who had never worked before and hence had no previous employment status were excluded.

---

4. Saw Swee-Hock, *The Labour Force of Singapore* (Singapore: Department of Statistics, 1985) and Cheng Siok-Hwa, *Changing Labour Force of Singapore* (Manila: Council for Asian Manpower Studies, 1984).

5. H. Fell, *1957 Population Census of the Federation of Malaya*, Report No. 14 (Kuala Lumpur: Department of Statistics, 1960).

TABLE 8.4
GROWTH OF LABOUR FORCE BY SEX AND EMPLOYMENT STATUS,
1970 AND 1980

Employment Status	Number ('000)		Intercensal Change (%)
	1970	1980	
Both Sexes			
Employer	112.7	150.5	33.5
Employee	1,380.9	2,327.8	68.6
Own Account Worker	779.7	1,039.5	33.3
Unpaid Family Worker	462.9	275.2	–40.6
Total	2,736.2	3,793.0	38.6
Males			
Employer	89.2	113.6	27.3
Employee	996.6	1,584.8	59.0
Own Account Worker	605.0	740.2	22.3
Unpaid Family Worker	186.9	126.1	–32.5
Total	1,877.7	2,564.7	36.6
Females			
Employer	23.5	36.9	56.9
Employee	384.3	743.0	93.3
Own Account Worker	174.7	299.4	71.3
Unpaid Family Worker	276.1	149.1	–46.0
Total	858.6	1,228.4	43.1

The economic development of Peninsular Malaysia in recent years has lead to a more highly organised and modern economy with a larger proportion of the labour force centred in the wage sector and a lower proportion in the family enterprises. This was manifested in the pattern of change in the labour force during the latest intercensal period when employees recorded the highest growth but unpaid family workers experienced a negative growth. The number of employees increased by 68.6 per cent from 1,380,900 in 1970 to 2,327,800 in 1980, while unpaid family workers shrank from 462,900 to 275,200, a drop of 40.6 per cent. During the same period employers managed to grow by 33.5 per cent and own account workers by 33.3 per cent.

The above pattern of change was seen to have taken place among the two sexes, with however a decidedly more pronounced trend among the female workers. For instance, the female employees grew by 93.3 per cent as compared to the 59.0 per cent for the male employees. Again, the decline in unpaid family workers was 46.0 per cent for the females and 32.5 per cent for the males. More often than not, the development and modernisation of a country seem to exert a greater impact on the female component of the labour force. However, distinctive differences between the employment status of the males and females will continue to remain. By comparison, the women still have a larger proportion of 12.1 per cent working as unpaid family workers and a smaller proportion of 3.0 per cent as employers in 1980. The two respective male figures are 4.9 per cent and 4.4 per cent.

Labour Force Participation Rates

In the preceeding section we have observed the considerable increase in the labour force during the postwar period. To ascertain whether this increase was caused solely by population growth or also by a rise in the extent of participation of the people in economic activity, we will proceed to examine the labour force participation rate which may be defined as the percentage of economically active persons to the total population aged 10 years and over. This rate serves to give an idea of the proportion of the population aged 10 and over who supply the labour on which the economic life of the country depends. The participation rate will be examined in terms of sex, race, age and urban-rural area; it is not possible to cover other variables such as marital status, educational attainment and citizenship since the prerequisite data are not included in the census reports.[6]

The figures given in Table 8.5 reveal that the labour force participation rate in Peninsular Malaysia fell from 54.0 per cent in 1947 to 51.5 per cent in 1957 and then to 48.2 per cent in 1970. Thereafter, an upturn took place and the rate rose to 51.0 per cent in 1980. The downward trend up to 1970 was brought about by the decreasing proportion of people in the working-ages following the cessation of large-scale labour immigration and the normalisation of the

---

6. Data according to these variables are not even provided in the census report for the Population Census held in 1980. See Khoo Teik Huat, *1980 Population and Housing Census of Malaysia, General Report of the Population Census*, Vols. 1 and 2, op. cit.

TABLE 8.5

LABOUR FORCE PARTICIPATION RATES BY SEX AND RACE,
1947–80

Race	1947	1957	1970	1980
Both Sexes				
All Races	54.0	51.5	48.2	51.0
Malays	50.0	49.4	48.4	50.6
Chinese	52.1	48.8	47.7	50.8
Indians	74.3	68.0	48.5	53.5
Males				
All Races	77.4	74.8	65.8	68.9
Malays	76.5	75.2	66.2	68.4
Chinese	75.2	70.9	65.6	69.5
Indians	87.2	82.5	63.9	68.6
Females				
All Races	27.0	26.2	30.6	33.7
Malays	25.5	24.1	31.1	29.6
Chinese	22.7	24.9	29.9	32.5
Indians	53.2	45.6	30.3	37.7

sex ratio. It should be pointed out that the general downward movement did not in any way reflect a corresponding rise in the dependency burden borne by the working population. What happened was that an increasing proportion of the workers' dependents were residing in Peninsular Malaysia rather than in China or India. The rise in the participation rate in the last decade 1970–80 was a reflection of the rapid expansion recorded in many sectors of the economy during this period. The long downtrend followed by a short uptrend was experienced by all the principal races, with however an important difference in that the decline has been relatively faster for the Indians. The extremely high participation of 74.3 per cent recorded by this community in 1947 was due to the high proportion of immigrant labourers with a fair number of their families left behind in the Indian sub-continent.[7] Over the years this peculiar

7. Saw Swee-Hock, "The Structure of the Labour Force in Malaya", *International Labour Review*, Vol. 98, No. 1, July 1968.

characteristic began to diminish, and the Indian participation rate was correspondingly lowered to 53.5 per cent in 1980. This rate did not differ greatly from those of the Malays with 50.6 per cent and the Chinese with 53.5 per cent.

For a better understanding of the labour force, we will proceed to an examination of the differences in participation rates recorded between the two sexes. The data set out in Table 8.5 reveal that without a single exception the women in Peninsular Malaysia, like those in other countries, record a considerably lower participation rate than the men at all times. This worldwide sex differential is primarily conditioned by two deep-rooted traditional norms, viz., women are generally not expected to earn as a matter of course so as to support themselves and their families, and child-rearing, nurturing children and housekeeping tend to prevent them from engaging in gainful work outside their homes. In 1947 the women participated in the labour force to the extent of 27.0 per cent as compared with the high of 77.4 per cent registered by the men. Since then there has been a gradual narrowing of the gap as female participation increased on account of the normalising of the age pyramid. By 1980 the female rate had advanced to 33.7 per cent and the male rate fallen to 65.9 per cent, the former being about one-half of the latter as compared to the one-third position that prevailed in 1947.

There appears to be some slight variation in the traditional lower female participation among the three main races. Among the Malays and the Chinese, the female rate barely reached one-third that of the men in 1947, 25.5 per cent and 22.7 per cent as compared with 76.5 per cent and 75.2 per cent respectively. In contrast, the Indian position was quite unique, with the women managing to attain a rate of 53.2 per cent which was more than one-half that of the men with 87.2 per cent. Another interesting feature brought out by these figures is that the higher participation of the Indians noted earlier occurred among their men as well as women. Historical development and combined family contacts accounted for the large numbers of Indian women recruited to work as rubber tappers in the rubber estates without which some of the women might not have entered the labour force in Peninsular Malaysia. Over the years the Indian women saw their participation rate falling significantly to 45.6 per cent in 1957 and 30.3 per cent in 1970. On the other hand, the participation rate of the Chinese women climbed up continuously from 22.7 per cent in 1947 to finally 32.5 per cent in 1980. The Malay female rate followed a different path, moving down from 25.5 per cent in 1947 to 24.1 per cent in 1957, going up to 31.1 per cent in 1970 and then down again to 29.6 per cent in 1980.

It is known that the extent of participation in economic activity varies considerably among different age groups. To study this pattern of variation, we will use the age-specific labour force participation rate which may be defined as the percentage of economically active persons among the total population of a given age group. It is customary to calculate these rates for each sex separately in view of the traditional differences in the age pattern of participation rates between men and women at the various age groups. In Table 8.6 are presented the rate for quinary age groups from 10–14 years to 65 years and over; it is not possible to compute the rates for quinary age groups beyond 65 since 65 and over is the last age grouping used in the census reports to tabulate the economically active population.

A casual glance at the figures in Table 8.6 is sufficient to confirm the completely different pattern of age-specific rates displayed by each sex. Looking at the 1957 figures, we see that the male rate rises steeply at the young ages to a shade above the 90 per cent level at early twenties and remains around the neighbourhood of 97 per cent through ages 25 to 49, after which it falls consistently as disabilities gradually remove men from the labour force. This general shape, which continued to prevail in 1970 and 1980, merely reflects the traditional attitude that unless a man is sick or permanently disabled he should work even though he may be a person of some wealth. The female pattern differs in two important respects: the rates are appreciably lower at all ages and the progression of the curve follows quite a different path. From the young

TABLE 8.6

AGE-SPECIFIC LABOUR FORCE PARTICIPATION RATES BY SEX,
1957–80

Age Group	Males			Females		
	1957	1970	1980	1957	1970	1980
10–14	9.6	9.0	7.8	7.4	7.7	5.2
15–19	60.0	62.3	47.3	27.9	33.0	33.0
20–24	92.7	87.1	90.6	31.2	41.9	53.3
25–29	97.5	93.5	97.1	27.7	38.4	44.0
30–34	97.4	94.4	97.7	30.5	39.0	39.9
35–39	97.7	94.0	97.9	34.2	40.0	42.1
40–44	97.2	93.2	97.5	35.3	40.0	43.3
45–49	96.2	91.5	96.4	36.3	40.7	40.8
50–54	93.7	86.7	92.3	33.7	36.6	36.0
55–59	88.4	75.6	76.8	29.4	29.2	30.3
60–64	81.6	65.2	68.1	22.3	23.7	24.6
65 & Over	61.1	46.0	48.7	11.5	12.9	17.8

FIGURE 8.1
AGE-SPECIFIC LABOUR FORCE PARTICIPATION RATES BY SEX, 1957, 1970 AND 1980

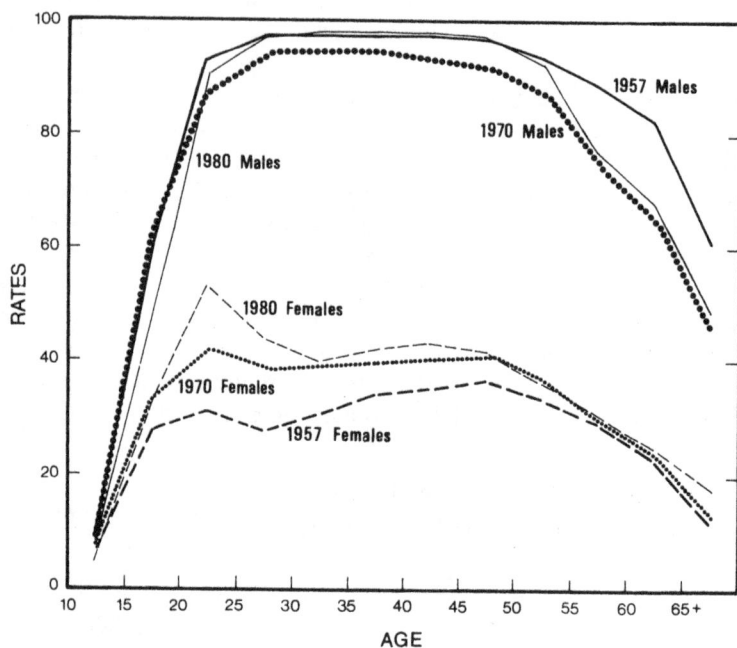

National University of Singapore

ages the rate rises to 31.2 per cent in the early 20s and immediately dips down a bit in the late 20s, then it raises very gradually until the peak of 36.3 per cent is attained in the late 40s after which it falls regularly until the last age group. Withdrawal of women from the labour force due to marriage or pregnancy is responsible for the dip, while subsequent re-entry after the birth of children or after the children are older causes the second rise from the early 30s onwards.

The broad shape of both the male rates and the female rates has remained the same during the last two decades or so, though some changes were noticeable at certain ages at the two ends of the span of potentially active life. During the period 1957 to 1980, the male rate was reduced from 9.6 per cent to 7.8 per cent in the age group 10–14 and from 60.0 per cent to 47.3 per cent in the group 15–19, while the last three old age groups 55–59, 60–64 and 65 and over saw their rates fall from 88.4 per cent to 76.8 per cent, 81.6 per cent to 68.1 per cent, and 61.1 to 48.7 per cent respectively. These trends reflect, on the one hand, a rise in the average age at which young males enter the labour force on account of the prolongation of education, and on the other hand, an increasing proportion of voluntary or involuntary retirement at the older ages. Either or both of these tendencies tend to compress men's working lives within a shorter age span have been observed in most countries in the neighbouring region which have witnessed the growth of facilities and demand for secondary and tertiary education, the contraction of opportunities for self-employment and unpaid family work, the development of public and private pension schemes, and the rising levels of income which have made possible both more education of the young and earlier retirement of the old.[8]

Unlike males, females have experienced changes in their participation rate at all ages during the same period under consideration. The youngest age group saw the rate increase from 7.4 per cent in 1957 to 7.7 per cent in 1970 and fall thereafter to 5.2 per cent in 1980. In all the other age groups there was a clear rise in the participation rate over the years from 1957 to 1970, and also from 1970 to 1980. By far the greatest improvement was recorded in the 20–24 age group where the rate rose from 31.2 per cent at the beginning to 41.9 per cent and finally to 53.3 per cent in 1980. As a result of differential changes the single peak of 36.3 per cent in the 45–49 age group in 1957 was replaced in 1970 by the twin-peak of 41.9 per cent in the 20–24 group and 40.7 per cent in the 45–49 group, and in 1980 back to the single peak of 53.3 per cent in the early 20s. This shifting of the peak participation rate may be attributed to the modernisation and industrialisation of the economy creating many new jobs for the young and better-educated women.

The data laid out in Table 8.7 illustrate the marked differences in the pattern of age-specific participation rates displayed by the three main races. In general, the differences are more pronounced and interesting for the females than for the males. Taking the latter first, both Chinese men and Indian men seem to commence work somewhat earlier in life than Malay men but this relative position persists up the late teens only and becomes almost negligible by the early 20s. Some significant differences appear again after the mid-fifties when a higher proportion of Malay men continues to work until the last age group. Even between the other two races there appears to be some differences, Indian men recording a slightly lower participation rate than Chinese men. Interestingly enough, the variation at these ages becomes more pronounced with the advance of old age. In the 55–59 age group the participation rate for

---

8. John D. Durand, *The Labour Force in Economic Development* (Princeton: Princeton University Press, 1975) and United Nations ECAFE, *Interrelation Between Population and Manpower Problems*, Asian Population Studies, No. 7, Bangkok, n.d.

TABLE 8.7
AGE-SPECIFIC LABOUR FORCE PARTICIPATION RATES BY SEX
FOR THREE MAIN RACES, 1980

Age Group	Males			Females		
	Malays	Chinese	Indians	Malays	Chinese	Indians
10–14	6.8	9.0	8.9	4.5	6.0	7.0
15–19	44.2	51.3	51.3	29.3	37.5	38.8
20–24	89.9	91.5	92.1	49.6	59.3	55.6
25–29	97.0	97.2	97.3	42.3	45.2	49.4
30–34	97.6	97.8	97.8	39.2	38.8	48.6
35–39	97.8	98.1	98.1	44.4	39.4	48.9
40–44	97.4	97.7	97.4	44.9	39.1	48.7
45–49	96.4	96.4	95.8	44.7	33.7	45.0
50–54	93.5	90.5	91.2	42.0	25.5	35.5
55–59	81.0	74.2	63.3	38.8	18.1	18.9
60–64	76.4	60.6	50.0	33.2	14.2	13.1
65 & Over	66.4	39.0	34.0	25.6	10.9	10.8

Malay men, Chinese men and Indian men in 1980 were 81.0 per cent, 74.2 per cent and 63.2 per cent respectively, but in the last age group of 65 and over the three corresponding rates were 60.4, 39.0 and 34.0 per cent.

With regard to the female rates that are also given in Table 8.7, it is possible to pinpoint more differences than similarities in the pattern of participation rates among the three races. One noticeable similarity concerns the peak rate which occurred in the 20–24 age group for women of all three races. In a way, this demonstrates that among all races, women in their early 20s were able to benefit most from the greater job opportunities created for women in recent years. The other common characteristic is that the traditional down-up trend still persisted, for women of all three races registered a dip in the 30–34 age group. However, there is one difference in that the rise in the rate after this dip was quite pronounced among Malay women, rising from 39.2 per cent in the early 30s to 44.9 per cent in the early 40s. This was not so in the case of Chinese and Indian women who recorded a short gentle rise after the dip, the Chinese rate edging up from 38.8 per cent in the early 30s to 39.4 per cent in the late 30s and the Indian rate from 48.0 per cent to 48.9 per cent. It is most likely that the twin-peak pattern will give way to the single-peak in the near future among the women of these two races.

FIGURE 8.2
FEMALE AGE-SPECIFIC LABOUR FORCE PARTICIPATION
RATES FOR THREE MAIN RACES, 1980

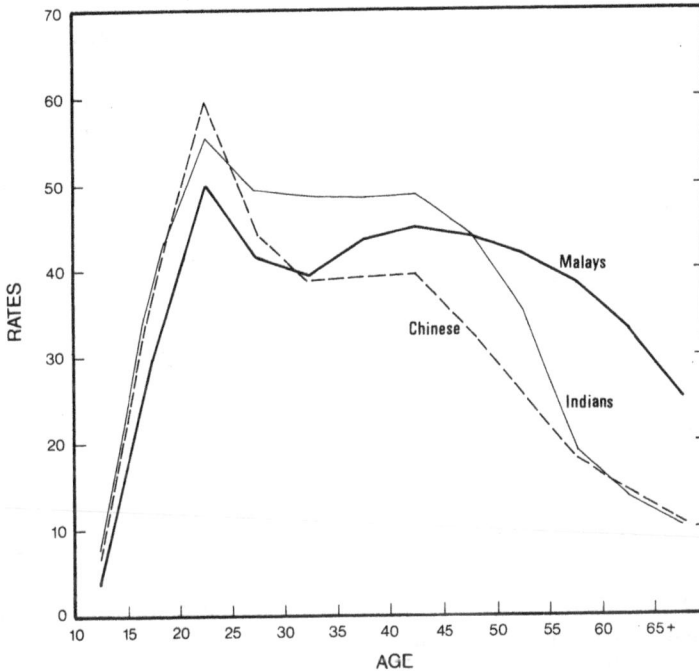

Apart from the above differences, there appears to be some clear-cut differences in the general shape of the age-specific participation rates. By and large,
the Malay women have experienced lower economic participation than the
Chinese women at the earliest working age to the late 40s, but progressively
much greater participation from the early 50s to the late 60s. In fact, from the
late 50s Malay women were engaged in economic activities to the extent of
more than twice that of Chinese women. As compared with Indian women,
Malay women were experiencing lower rates from the youngest age group
right up to the late 50s. Except for the last two age groups and the 20–24 group,
Indian women were recording a higher participation rate.

We will now proceed to examine the pattern of age-specific participation
rates by the important variable of urban-rural area as presented in Table 8.8.

TABLE 8.8

AGE-SPECIFIC LABOUR FORCE PARTICIPATION RATES BY SEX
AND URBAN-RURAL AREA, 1980

Age Group	Males		Females	
	Urban	Rural	Urban	Rural
10–14	7.2	8.0	5.1	5.3
15–19	44.6	49.1	34.7	31.9
20–24	88.7	92.2	59.3	48.7
25–29	97.0	97.2	47.2	41.7
30–34	97.7	97.7	38.2	41.2
35–39	98.0	97.9	35.8	46.2
40–44	97.5	97.5	32.4	49.6
45–49	96.3	96.4	28.1	47.9
50–54	90.9	93.1	22.7	43.0
55–59	67.7	81.5	17.4	37.2
60–64	56.5	74.0	14.6	30.1
65 & Over	37.5	54.4	11.9	21.4

Looking at the urban and rural rates for the males, we see that they conform
to the usual pattern of higher rural than urban rates at the first three age
groups between 10 and 24 and at the last four age groups from 50 to 65 and
over. At the four intermediate age groups between 25 and 49, the differences
between the rural and urban rates are almost negligible. Better opportunities
in the urban centres for education and jobs that require relatively high educational qualifications are factors making for the lower economic participation
of young males in the urban than in the rural sector. For older men, the
predominance of wage employment in the urban sector and of self-employment
in the rural sector is a factor conducive to higher retirement rates in the urban
sector.

A completely different pattern of urban-rural differences was underlined
by the female rates given in Table 8.8. Of greater significance is the presence
of the usual twin-peak shape of the participation rates in the rural area as
compared to the single-peak shape in the urban area. In the latter the peak
amounting to 59.3 per cent occurred in the 20–24 age group, while in the former
the first peak touched 48.7 per cent in the same age group and the second
peak managed to go higher to 49.6 per cent in the 40–44 group. What it means

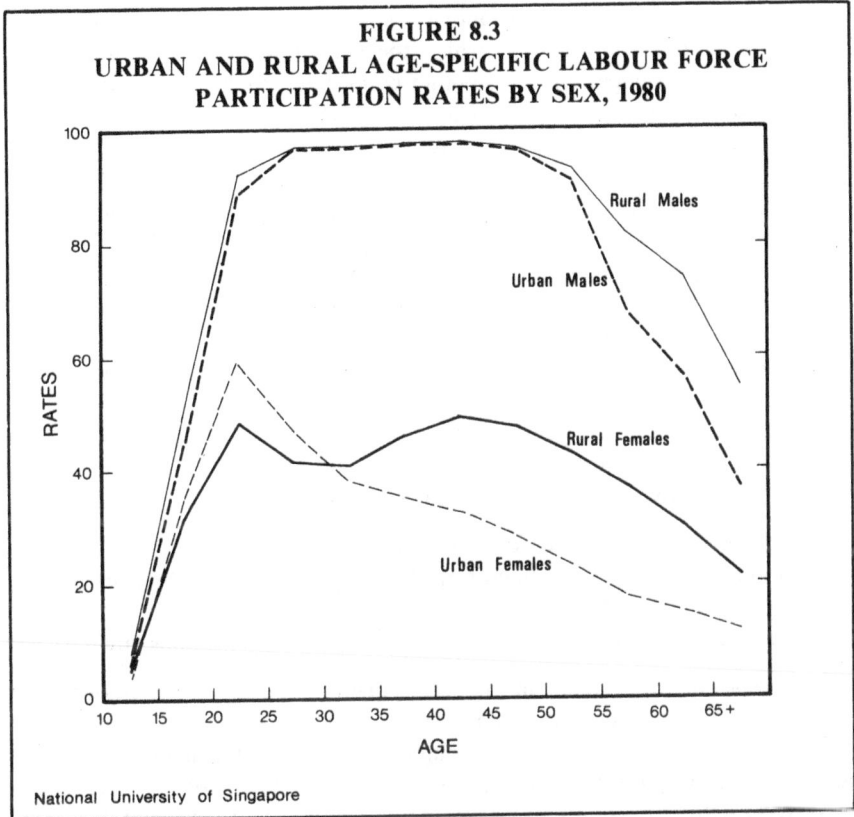

FIGURE 8.3
URBAN AND RURAL AGE-SPECIFIC LABOUR FORCE
PARTICIPATION RATES BY SEX, 1980

National University of Singapore

is that in Peninsular Malaysia the phenonenon of women withdrawing from the labour force and subsequent re-entry takes place only in the rural area where this tradition can be practised as they are in the main unpaid family workers in the family farms. It is difficult for the urban women to do this in the monetised urban economy where they work as employees with fairly rigid terms and conditions. From the early 30s onwards, the rural rates became progressively higher than the urban rates, and became even twice as high from the early 50s. In the predominantly agricultural rural economy the women could work in the family farms without being affected by legal retirement.

Industrial Structure of Labour Force

The labour force of a country identified by means of the labour force approach is always classified according to industry and occupation. Industry is used to refer to the economic activity or the nature of business of the firm, establishment or department in which the person was employed during the reference week. Occupation, on the other hand, refers to the trade or profession followed or the type of work performed during the reference week. The tabulation of the labour force by occupation serves to indicate the degree and nature in which division of labour is arranged, while the classification by industry serves to underline the integration of occupations and the type of units into which work is organised. By and large, an investigation into the industrial structure and occupational pattern of the labour force will show how the people in Peninsular Malaysia are organised to earn their livelihood in the production of goods and services.

The data on industry were processed and tabulated according to the Malaysian Industrial Classification which is based on the United Nations Standard Classification of All Economic Activities.[9] In analysing the long-term changes in the industrial structure of the labour force, we will look first at the data in terms of the following three broad sectors of economic activity:

1. Agriculture: agriculture, forestry, hunting and fishing
2. Industry: mining, manufacturing, building and construction, electricity, gas and water
3. Services: commerce, transport, storage and communications, and services

Broadly speaking, the trends in the percentage distribution of the labour force by the above three sectors would give us an idea of the past changes that have taken place in the economy. Though the figures for the first three censuses are based on the gainful worker concept, the labour force concept used in the next recent three censuses was deemed similar enough to warrant the comparison of the data shown in Table 8.9 particularly when we are dealing with extremely broad groupings over a long period of time.

During the last 60 years all the three broad sectors recorded a growth in the labour force, though at different rates. Looking at the prewar period 1921–47, we see that the agricultural sector increased by 13 per cent, the industry sector by 8 per cent, and the services sector by 42 per cent. More pronounced differences in the growth rate occurred during the postwar period 1947–80. This period saw the labour force grow by only 14 per cent in the agricultural sector as against the 342 per cent and 350 per cent for the industry and services sectors respectively. In fact, the rapid growth in the last two sectors took place primarily in the 1970s when greater emphasis was placed on the restructuring of the economy. The latest 10-year intercensal period 1970–80 registered an

---

9. The Industrial Classification used in the various population censuses is usually reproduced in the respective final census reports.

TABLE 8.9
DISTRIBUTION OF LABOUR FORCE BY THREE BROAD SECTORS
OF ECONOMIC ACTIVITY, 1921–80

Sector	1921	1931	1947	1957	1970	1980
	Number ('000)					
Agriculture	1,092.3	1,165.6	1,235.0	1,244.8	1,359.2	1,413.7
Industry	185.8	197.4	200.9	273.6	386.8	820.6
Services	326.3	381.0	462.0	589.7	847.2	1,468.3
Total	1,604.4	1,744.0	1,897.9	2,108.1	2,591.2	3,702.6
	Percentage					
Agriculture	68.1	68.8	65.1	59.0	52.4	38.2
Industry	11.6	11.3	10.6	12.1	14.9	22.2
Services	20.3	21.9	24.3	27.9	32.7	39.6
Total	100.0	100.0	100.0	100.0	100.0	100.0

increase of 112 per cent in the labour force in the industry sector as compared with 41 per cent during 1957–70 and 36 per cent during 1947–57. The three corresponding growth rates in the services sector were 350 per cent, 44 per cent and 28 per cent respectively.

As a result of the above changes a swing away from employment in the agricultural sector has taken place consistently over the last 60 years. The proportion for the agricultural sector fell from 68.1 per cent in 1921 to 65.1 per cent in 1947, and more steeply thereafter to 38.2 per cent in 1980. Accompanying this swing was the rise in the relative importance of the service sector, moving up from 20.3 per cent in 1921 to 39.6 per cent in 1980. Different trends were delineated by the industry sector; its relative importance was reduced slightly from 11.6 per cent in 1921 to 10.6 per cent in 1980. The shift in the relative position of the three broad sectors of the labour force should be viewed in terms of the emphasis on the production of primary products during the colonial period, the diversification programme based mainly on industrialisation during the early years of independence, and the New Economic Policy introduced in 1971.

A more detailed presentation of the changes in the industrial structure of the labour force is given in Table 8.10 showing the distribution by nine industrial

TABLE 8.10
DISTRIBUTION OF LABOUR FORCE BY MAJOR INDUSTRY, 1947–80

Industry	1947	1957	1970	1980
	Number ('000)			
1. Agriculture, forestry, hunting and fishing	680.5	572.8	611.3	591.8
2. Agricultural products requiring substantial processing	560.1	672.0	747.8	821.9
3. Mining and quarrying	47.7	58.5	55.3	44.7
4. Manufacturing	126.1	135.4	251.9	565.7
5. Construction	13.5	68.1	59.9	185.9
6. Electricity, gas, water and sanitary services	4.6	11.6	19.8	24.3
7. Commerce	173.1	195.2	274.6	465.0
8. Transport, storage and communication	65.9	74.8	98.0	144.8
9. Services	197.6	319.7	472.6	858.5
Total	1,869.7	2,108.1	2,291.3	3,702.6
	Percentage			
1. Agriculture, forestry, hunting and fishing	36.4	27.2	23.6	16.0
2. Agricultural products requiring substantial processing	30.0	31.9	28.9	21.7
3. Mining and quarrying	2.6	2.8	2.1	1.2
4. Manufacturing	6.7	6.4	9.2	14.9
5. Construction	0.7	3.2	2.3	4.9
6. Electricity, gas, water and sanitary services	0.2	0.6	0.8	0.7
7. Commerce	9.3	9.3	10.6	12.6
8. Transport, storage and communication	3.5	3.5	3.8	3.9
9. Services	10.6	15.2	18.2	23.2
Total	100.0	100.0	100.0	100.0

Note: Persons with industry not classifiable are excluded.

sectors for the four postwar censuses. It may be observed that three of these sectors, agriculture, forestry, hunting and fishing; mining and quarrying; and construction did not exhibit any common trend in the number of workers during the postwar period. They appeared to have registered positive as well as negative growth in a completely haphazard manner during the various inter- censal periods. On the other hand, the other six industrial sectors experienced a continuous increase in the number of workers over the period 1957–80. For the whole period, the highest growth of 428 per cent was registered by the electricity, gas, water and sanitary services sector and the lowest growth of 110 per cent was recorded by the transport, storage and communication sector. However, the greatest employment growth took place in the construction sector where the number of workers multiplied by some 14 times from 13,500 in 1947 to 185,900 in 1980.

While the above observations provide a useful broad survey of the changes, it should be interesting to examine more closely the changes during the latest intercensal period 1970–80. By and large, this period witnessed a drop in employment in the agriculture, forestry, hunting and fishing sector and the mining and quarrying sector and an increase in the other seven sectors. A spectacular growth of 210 per cent was generated in the construction sector where the number of workers shot up from 59,900 in 1970 to 185,900 in 1980. The second fastest growth occurred in the manufacturing sector which saw the number of workers rise from 251,900 to 565,700, an increase of 125 per cent during the 10-year period. Next comes the services sector which experi- enced a fair growth of 82 per cent, bringing the total employed from 472,600 to 858,500 during the same period. The growth in the commerce sector was also satisfactory, amounting to some 69 per cent. All the other three remain- ing sectors recorded relatively slower growth in employment. The changes that occurred during the latest intercensal period are reflective of the develop- ment strategies, with emphasis on the restructuring of the economy, imple- mented since the early 1970s.

One way of gauging the effect or success of the restructuring of the economy is to examine the shifts in the proportionate distribution of the labour force among the main industrial sectors as depicted in the bottom half of Table 8.10. Between 1947 and 1980 there was a sharp drop in the proportion of workers engaged in agriculture and its related activities, falling from 36.4 per cent to 16.0 per cent. The other primary sector encompassing mining and quarrying saw its small share of employment of 2.6 per cent falling further to 1.2 per cent by 1980. A fairly sizeable drop was also recorded by workers engaged in agri- cultural products requiring processing, the proportion there was reduced to 21.7 per cent in 1980 from 30.0 per cent in 1947. Consistent with the country's industrialisation programme, the share of employment in the manufacturing sector went up from 6.7 per cent to 14.9 per cent during the period. Another two-fold rise in the share of employment has occurred in the services sector where the percentage was raised from 10.6 per cent to 23.2 per cent. The three remaining sectors recorded only a moderate rise in their share of employment.

The fundamental changes in the share of employment noted during the postwar period have resulted in a radical shift in the pattern of employment according to the nine industrial sectors. In 1947 the sector covering agriculture and its related activities was the top sector providing jobs to 36.4 per cent of the labour force, followed very closely by agricultural products requiring processing with 30.0 per cent. The third position was occupied by the services sector with a much lower share of 10.6 per cent. By 1980 the services sector came up well on top with 23.2 per cent, and the agricultural products sector maintained its second position but with a much reduced share of employment of 21.7 per cent. The next three sectors in order of importance were agriculture and its related activities with 16.0 per cent, manufacturing with 14.9 per cent, and commerce with 12.6 per cent. In terms of employment, the economy of Peninsular Malaysia has clearly succeeded in moving away from one that was predominantly based on the agricultural sector to a more balanced economy with a good spread of employment among the various sectors.

The considerable attention accorded to the pattern of economic activities of the three major races in the country requires us to examine the industrial structure of the labour force among these races. In Table 8.11 separate figures for agricultural products requiring substantial processing are not available, and persons engaged in these activities have been included in the first group, viz., agriculture, forestry, hunting and fishing. According to the data laid out in the table, the Malay labour force had recorded a significant reduction in the proportion engaged in agriculture and related activities from 73.0 per cent in 1957 to 46.8 per cent in 1980. The swing was mainly towards the services and the manufacturing sectors, the former seeing its share of employment rising from 5.6 per cent to 26.0 per cent and the latter from 2.7 per cent to 11.8 per cent during the period 1957–80. Good progress was also attained in the commerce sector where the proportion was lifted to 8.8 per cent in 1980 from the original figure of 3.2 per cent. By and large, this rise in the relative importance of these three sectors may be attributed to the government-backed *bumiputra* policy which accorded job preferences in the civil service to *bumiputras* and required the reservation of a certain quota of jobs for *bumiputras* in the private sector, especially newly established companies. By 1980 the pattern of Malay employment has shown marked improvement with only 46.8 per cent in agriculture and related activities and significant proportions in services (26.0 per cent), manufacturing (11.8 per cent), and commerce (8.8 per cent). In 1957 the four respective proportions stood at 73.0 per cent, 5.6

TABLE 8.11

PERCENTAGE DISTRIBUTION OF LABOUR FORCE BY MAJOR INDUSTRY FOR
THREE MAIN RACES, 1957–80

Industry	Malays			Chinese			Indians		
	1957	1970	1980	1957	1970	1980	1957	1970	1980
1. Agriculture, forestry, hunting and fishing	73.0	67.8	46.8	41.4	31.4	22.0	57.2	48.6	38.3
2. Mining and quarrying	1.0	1.0	0.7	5.3	4.0	2.0	2.2	1.7	1.3
3. Manufacturing	2.7	5.4	11.8	13.0	17.6	19.6	3.3	4.9	15.9
4. Construction	2.2	1.0	2.8	4.3	4.6	8.6	4.0	1.3	3.4
5. Electricity, gas, water and sanitary services	0.4	0.7	0.2	0.4	0.4	0.1	1.4	2.3	0.4
6. Commerce	3.2	4.7	8.8	17.0	19.2	26.7	10.8	10.7	12.8
7. Transport, storage and communication	2.7	3.0	3.0	3.9	4.2	4.8	5.3	6.1	4.8
8. Services	5.6	16.4	26.0	14.7	18.6	16.2	15.8	24.4	23.2
Total	100.0	100.0	100.0	100.0	100.0	100.0	100.0	100.0	100.0

per cent, 2.7 per cent and 3.2 per cent.

The 23-year period also witnessed a decline in the relative importance of agriculture and its related activities as a source of employment for the Chinese: the proportion engaged in this sector was reduced from 41.4 per cent to 22.0 per cent. But unlike the Malays, the greatest improvement among the Chinese occurred in the commerce sector where the proportion went up from 17.0 per cent to 26.7 per cent. Significant progress was registered in the manufacturing sector with a rise of 13.0 per cent to 19.6 per cent. Without any job preference in the public sector, the Chinese labour force managed to make a small gain only in the services sector, edging up from 14.7 per cent to 16.2 per cent. Another difference is that the proportion of the Chinese labour force involved in mining and quarrying was more than halved from 5.3 per cent to 2.0 per cent. This contraction was largely due to the fall in the production of the tin-mining industry which has been adversely affected by rising costs resulting from a shortage of available tin-mining areas. By 1980 the commerce sector (26.7 per cent) has replaced the agricultural sector (22.0 per cent) as the top sector; the second and third positions have also changed with manufacturing assuming third position instead of services.

As for the Indians, there was also a swing in employment away from agriculture and its related activities, falling from 57.2 per cent in 1957 to 38.3 per cent in 1980. But unlike the other two races, the most spectacular improvement among the Indians occurred in the manufacturing sector where the proportion shot up from 3.3 per cent to 15.9 per cent. Furthermore, the Indians did not show any marked improvement in the commerce sector, the proportion moving from 10.8 per cent to 10.7 per cent in 1970 and then to 12.8 per cent in 1980. In the services sector, however, a moderate rise in the proportion from 15.8 per cent to 23.2 per cent was recorded. In 1980 the services sector still retained its second position, and so did the agricultural sector its top position. Notwithstanding the somewhat different shifts in the pattern of employment among the eight industry groups experienced by the three races, there is no doubt that the last two decades have witnessed a common widening in the spread of employment among the various sectors of the economy. This is clearly a result of the economic diversification policy introduced during the post-independence period to bring about rectification of the lopsided economy dominated by the production of primary products.

We will now proceed to examine the variation in the industrial structure of the labour force between the two sexes. According to the figures given in Table 8.12, the greatest concentration of female workers in 1980 was to be found in the agricultural sector with 44.3 per cent. A poor second was taken up by the services sector which absorbed 20.6 per cent of the female labour force, followed closely by manufacturing with 19.0 per cent. The fourth position

TABLE 8.12
PERCENTAGE DISTRIBUTION OF LABOUR FORCE BY SEX AND
URBAN-RURAL AREA, 1980

Industry	Sex		Area	
	Males	Females	Urban	Rural
1. Agriculture, forestry, hunting and fishing	34.0	44.3	8.1	55.9
2. Mining and quarrying	1.6	0.4	0.6	1.6
3. Manufacturing	12.9	19.0	21.2	10.9
4. Construction	6.7	1.1	6.9	3.9
5. Electricity, gas, water and sanitary services	0.2	0.0	0.2	0.1
6. Commerce	16.2	13.8	25.2	9.2
7. Transport, storage and communication	5.3	0.7	5.3	2.8
8. Services	23.1	20.6	32.4	15.9
Total	100.0	100.0	100.0	100.0

Note: Persons with industry not classifiable are excluded.

was occupied by commerce with 13.8 per cent. An extremely negligible proportion of the female workers was engaged in the other four sectors, ranging from 1.1 per cent to only 0.4 per cent. As for the male workers, the largest group was also located in the agricultural sector but with a much lower proportion of 34.0 per cent. The next three major sectors for the male workers in descending order of importance were services (23.1 per cent), commerce (16.2 per cent) and manufacturing (12.9 per cent). Moreover, the transport, storage and communication and construction sectors absorbed a sizeable share of the male workers, 5.3 per cent and 6.7 per cent respectively. It would appear that, as compared to their male counterpart, the female workers still have a tendency to cluster in a few industrial groups.

Another noteworthy aspect of the labour force is the one concerning the industrial distribution in the urban and the rural areas as portrayed in Table 8.12. In the urban area the services sector provided jobs to the largest group of workers, 32.4 per cent; the commerce and the manufacturing sectors absorbed 25.2 per cent and 21.2 per cent respectively. The other five sectors took in much lower proportions, not exceeding 8.1 per cent in general. Not surprisingly, some 55.9 per cent of the labour force in the rural area was engaged in agricultural and its related activities, in sharp contrast with the corresponding figure of only 8.1 per cent in the urban area. Some 15.9 per cent of the workforce were involved in services, 10.9 per cent in manufacturing, and 9.2 per cent in commerce.

Occupational Pattern

Having examined in some detail the industrial structure of the labour force in the preceeding section, we will proceed to study the equally important aspect of the labour force in terms of the occupational classification. The occupation of a person refers to the trade or profession followed or the type of work performed during the reference week. Tabulation of the labour force by occupation presents both an inventory of skills possessed by a country at any point in time and useful information on the rate of development of a country. Changes in occupational pattern provide some indication of the social mobility of the people consequent on enhanced educational attainment and increased economic opportunities. In some respects the occupation of a person also serves as a crude measure of his social status in society and is reflective of his earning capacity.

The data on occupation collected in the population censuses were processed and tabulated according to the Malaysian Occupational Classification which was revised from time to time and based essentially on the International Standard Occupational Classification of 1968 prepared by the International Labour Organisation.[10] The classification has been designed to present information on occupation in descending order of detail according to the one-digit, two-digit or three-digit levels. However, we will use mostly data at the one-digit level. The data on occupation refer to persons who were working during the reference week as well as those who were unemployed but had worked previously. These two categories are referred to as the experienced labour force in the Malaysian census report. Of course, the unemployed persons who have never worked before cannot be included in the classification since they did not have a previous occupation.

The distribution of the labour force according to major occupations at the one-digit level for the last three population censuses is laid out in Table 8.13. During the period 1957–70 all the major occupational groups registered an increase in the number of workers with the exception of administrative and

---

10. The Occupational Classification used in the various population censuses is usually reproduced in the respective final census reports.

TABLE 8.13
DISTRIBUTION OF LABOUR FORCE BY MAJOR OCCUPATION,
1957–80

Occupation	1957	1970	1980
	Number ('000)		
1. Professional and technical	67.7	129.4	261.9
2. Administrative and managerial	24.5	20.3	38.2
3. Clerical	114.2	133.3	304.5
4. Sales	182.3	236.7	357.3
5. Services	181.3	255.4	331.2
6. Agricultural and related workers	1,205.1	1,322.1	1,256.3
7. Production and related workers	342.8	542.8	993.4
Total	2,117.9	2,610.0	3,542.9
	Percentage		
1. Professional and technical	5.2	5.0	7.4
2. Administrative and managerial	1.2	0.8	1.1
3. Clerical	5.4	5.1	8.6
4. Sales	8.6	9.1	10.1
5. Services	8.6	8.6	9.3
6. Agricultural and related workers	56.9	50.7	35.5
7. Production and related workers	16.2	20.8	28.0
Total	100.0	100.0	100.0

managerial workers. Even in the case of this group, the decrease may be due to the exceptionally large number, amounting to some 13,900 classified as proprietors, owners and contractors not elsewhere classified in 1957, and some of whom might not really belong to the administrative and managerial group.[11] The 24,500 in this group in 1957 might be an overestimate as compared to the 20,300 in 1970. The other six groups, which showed increases in their number of workers, grew at rates ranging from a mere 9.7 per cent to 91.1 per cent. The highest rate of 91.1 per cent was recorded by the professional and technical group where the number of workers shot up from 67,700 in 1957 to 129,400

11. H. Fell, op. cit., Table 14, p. 129.

in 1970. Considering what we have said in the previous section, it is not surprising that the lowest growth of 9.7 per cent was experienced by the agricultural and related occupations.

The differences in the rate of growth among the seven major occupational groups continued to persist, and more conspicuously, during the latest intercensal period 1970–80. The only group to witness a decline was the one covering the agricultural and related workers, decreasing by 5.0 per cent from 1,322,100 to 1,256,300 in these years. This trend is not surprising as it is consistent with the drop in the number of workers engaged in agricultural and related activities that occurred during the same period. The most spectacular achievement was chalked up by the clerical group which recorded a hefty jump of 128.4 per cent, with the number of workers raised from 133,300 to 304,500. Another group that saw a doubling of its numbers was the professional and technical workers which increased by 102.4 per cent from 129,400 in 1970 to 261,900 in 1980. The other four occupational groups grew at a relatively slower rate, ranging from 88.2 per cent by the administrative and managerial workers to 46.9 per cent by the service workers.

The considerable differences in the rate of growth among the major occupational groups in the past two intercensal periods have obviously resulted in a shift in the proportion of workers engaged in these groups. In 1957 agricultural and related workers accounted for more than half, 56.9 per cent, of the total workforce, way ahead of the second position of 16.2 per cent occupied by the production and related workers. The third spot was held jointly by the sales and the services workers, with 8.6 per cent each. Some 23 years later the agricultural and related workers managed to maintain their number one position, but with a much lower proportion of 35.5 per cent. This reduced proportion has benefited the other occupational groups, except the administrative and managerial workers whose proportion stayed slightly above one per cent. A significant improvement was registered by the production and related workers with the proportion advancing sharply from 16.2 per cent in 1957 to 28.0 per cent in 1980, a reflection of accelerated industrialisation programme. Better progress was in fact portrayed by the professional and technical group which saw its proportion moving up from a low of 3.2 per cent in 1957 to 7.4 per cent at the end of the period. Over the years the occupational pattern of the labour force has clearly shifted to a more balanced one as a result of the diversification programme with an emphasis on industrialisation.

The shifts in the occupational pattern among the male and the female workers that took place during the intercensal period 1970–80 are shown in Table 8.14. Among the males, the agricultural and related workers were the largest group in 1970 with 45.2 per cent, and production and related workers ranked second with only 24.6 per cent. Further down were sales workers with 10.7 per cent

TABLE 8.14
PERCENTAGE DISTRIBUTION OF LABOUR FORCE BY MAJOR
OCCUPATION AND SEX, 1970 AND 1980

Occupation	1970		1980	
	Males	Females	Males	Females
1. Professional and technical	4.7	5.7	6.6	9.1
2. Administrative and managerial	1.1	0.1	1.4	0.3
3. Clerical	5.5	4.3	7.1	11.8
4. Sales	10.7	5.4	11.2	7.7
5. Services	8.3	9.4	9.3	9.4
6. Agricultural and related workers	45.2	63.2	32.7	41.4
7. Production and related workers	24.6	12.0	31.7	20.3
Total	100.0	100.0	100.0	100.0

and services workers with 8.3 per cent. This relative position of these four groups among the males did not alter at all by the time of the 1980 Census when four respective percentages were 32.7 per cent, 31.7 per cent, 11.2 per cent and 9.3 per cent. What is perhaps significant is that there was a shift towards the last three occupational groups at the expense of the predominantly agricultural group.

It is not surprising that the greater participation of women in economic activities in recent years would be accompanied by more drastic shifts in the proportional distribution of the female workforce among the major occupational groups.[12] In 1970, the occupational group that provided jobs to the largest number of females was agricultural and related workers, accounting for a huge 63.2 per cent out of the female workforce. The next three positions were taken up by production and related workers with 12.0 per cent, services workers with 9.4 per cent, and professional and technical workers with 5.7 per cent. By 1980, the agricultural and related workers still retained their top spot, but with a much reduced proportion of 41.4 per cent. Production and related workers continued to occupy second position, with however, a greatly enhanced proportion of 20.3 per cent. Clerical workers moved up from sixth

---

12. For more details about the role of women in the Malaysian economy, see Hing Ai Yun, Nik Safiah Karim and Rokiah Talib, *Women in Malaysia* (Kuala Lumpur: Pelanduk Publications, 1984).

to third position after experiencing a sharp rise in their proportion from 4.3 per cent to 11.8 per cent. Services workers shifted one step from third to fourth position as their proportion stayed at slightly above 9 per cent.

In a multiracial society like that of Peninsular Malaysia it would be necessary to analyse the differences in the occupational pattern of the three main ethnic groups since there has always been some specialisation along ethnic lines. This is attempted in Table 8.15 which presents the data for the distribution of the labour force by major occupational groups for the last two censuses. We will first examine the changes that have taken place during the decade 1970–80 within each of these races. Among the Malays, an extremely high proportion of 66.8 per cent of the workers engaged in agricultural and related occupations in 1970. By 1980 this group still maintained its top position, but its relative importance has been greatly diminished as it absorbed only 46.2 per cent of the Malay workforce. Production and related workers not only remained in second position but increased their relative importance from 13.5 per cent to 21.8 per cent. The same can be said about the third position occupied by services workers with the proportion improving from 7.6 per cent to 10.7 per cent. Clerical workers recorded a marked rise in their proportion from 3.5 per cent in 1970 to 8.1 per cent in 1980, and as a result even replaced professional and technical workers as the fourth largest group. The occupational pattern of the Malay labour force has therefore undergone significant changes during the latest intercensal period.

In the case of the Chinese labour force, there was also a marked reduction in the proportion engaged in agricultural and related occupations, lowering to 18.6 per cent from the 29.3 per cent prevailing 10 years earlier. Another occupational group which experienced a diminished relative importance was services, moving down from 9.3 per cent to 7.8 per cent. The proportion in the other five groups was enlarged during the period. The Indian labour force, on the other hand, was subjected to a more complex change in the occupational pattern. Three occupational groups, viz., agricultural and related workers, services workers and sales workers, suffered a reduction in the proportion of workers. But the extent of decline in the proportion engaged in agricultural and related occupations was not as pronounced as that experienced by the Malays and the Chinese. Another difference was that the Indians were able to register a more pronounced rise in the proportion engaged in production and related occupations, going up from 26.1 per cent to 30.8 per cent. The relative importance of Indian workers in the administrative and managerial group remained unaltered at 0.6 per cent, while those employed in the clerical and professional and technical groups had their proportion increased slightly.

Considering the nature of the changes outlined above, we should not be surprised to find that there were still considerable differences in the occupational

TABLE 8.15
PERCENTAGE DISTRIBUTION OF LABOUR FORCE BY MAJOR OCCUPATION FOR THREE MAIN RACES, 1970 AND 1980

Occupation	1970			1980		
	Malays	Chinese	Indians	Malays	Chinese	Indians
1. Professional and technical	4.3	5.3	6.0	7.6	7.1	6.8
2. Administrative and managerial	0.3	1.4	0.6	0.5	2.0	0.6
3. Clerical	3.5	6.8	7.2	8.1	9.6	8.0
4. Sales	3.9	16.6	9.1	5.5	18.0	7.5
5. Services	7.6	9.3	10.7	10.3	7.8	10.1
6. Agricultural and related workers	66.8	29.3	44.8	46.2	18.6	36.1
7. Production and related workers	13.5	31.4	21.6	21.8	37.0	30.8
Total	100.0	100.0	100.0	100.0	100.0	100.0

patterns of the three major races in 1980. The general impression conveyed by the 1980 figures shown in Table 8.15 is that the occupational pattern of the Chinese differed markedly from the other two races in not concentrating heavily in agricultural occupations. Thus, the largest number of Chinese workers were engaged in production and related occupations with 37.0 per cent, while the agricultural and related occupations accounted for only 18.6 per cent of the workforce. The relative position of these two occupational groups was completely reversed among the Malays and the Indians. Another important difference is that an extremely large proportion of the Chinese workforce was involved in sales occupations, 18.0 per cent as against the 5.5 per cent for the Malays and 7.5 per cent for the Indians. In general, the occupational pattern of the Chinese appears to be more evenly spread than those of the other two races.

In studying the differences in the occupational pattern among the three main races, it would be instructive to proceed a step further by looking at the figures for each sex separately given in Table 8.16. Though there is some awareness about the specialisation of labour by race, it is not so often fully appreciated that the specialisation is even more pronounced if we consider each sex in turn. It may be observed that the males exhibit a common feature in that slightly more than 63 per cent of the workforce were to be found in two major occupational groups, though not necessary the same two or in the same order of importance. These two predominant groups were agricultural and related occupations (44.1 per cent) and production and related occupations (23.9 per cent) for the Malays, production and related occupations (42.8 per cent) and sales workers (20.5 per cent) for the Chinese, and production and related occupations (35.2 per cent) and agricultural and related occupations (27.7 per cent) for the Indians. The one-fifth of Chinese men clustered in sales occupations presented a sharp contrast to the corresponding figure of 5.4 per cent for Malay men and 9.9 per cent for Indian men.

Further evidence of the economic specialisation of the three main races is provided by the female figures. Some 53.1 per cent of Indian women were engaged in agricultural and related occupations; in fact the majority of the 64,527 Indian women workers in this group were engaged as employees in rubber and oil palm plantations. Malay women too had an equally large proportion, 50.8 per cent, working in agricultural and related occupations, but most of them were unpaid family workers or own account workers in padi farms. The second most popular profession for Malay and Indian women was the production and related occupational group, and again Indian women had a higher proportion of 22.0 per cent as compared with the 17.5 per cent for Malay women. Furthermore, the figures for Indian women show services as their third occupational group (9.0 per cent), while Malay women indicated

TABLE 8.16

PERCENTAGE DISTRIBUTION OF LABOUR FORCE BY MAJOR OCCUPATION AND SEX FOR THREE MAIN RACES, 1980

Occupation	Malays		Chinese		Indians	
	Males	Females	Males	Females	Males	Females
1. Professional and technical	6.9	9.1	6.1	9.4	6.4	7.2
2. Administrative and managerial	0.7	0.2	2.6	0.5	0.9	0.1
3. Clerical	7.4	9.6	6.0	17.2	9.0	6.0
4. Sales	5.4	5.7	20.5	12.6	9.9	2.6
5. Services	11.7	7.2	5.3	13.0	10.7	9.0
6. Agricultural and related workers	44.1	50.8	16.6	22.8	27.7	53.1
7. Production and related workers	23.9	17.5	42.8	24.4	35.2	22.0
Total	100.0	100.0	100.0	100.0	100.0	100.0

the clerical group as their third most popular profession (9.6 per cent). A completely different occupational pattern was displayed by the figures for Chinese women. Their three most popular occupational groups were production and related workers (24.4 per cent), agricultural and related workers (22.8 per cent), and clerical workers (17.2 per cent). Besides, fairly substantial proportions of Chinese women gather in the services group (13.0 per cent) and the sales group (12.6 per cent).

The greater dispersion of Chinese women among the major occupational groups assumes significance if we compare their distribution with that of Chinese men. Indeed, the Chinese present a rather unusual feature in that the female workforce seems to exhibit a wider occupational spread than the male workforce. This is contrary to what one would expect in most populations. Both the Malays and the Indians show a greater occupational spread among their male workforce.

Sufficient has been said to shed some light on the occupational specialisation of the sex-race components of the population in Peninsular Malaysia where this aspect of the manpower of the country has featured prominently in the development plans of recent years. In a way the different needs and skills required in the major sectors such as padi, cash crop plantations, commerce, trade and manufacturing have been well provided by the different sex-race components with their own skills, resourcefulness, inclination and traditional preferences.

Table 8.17 shows the occupational distribution of the labour force by sex in the urban and the rural areas. As to be expected, the proportion of workers engaged in agricultural and related occupations in the urban area in 1980 was extremely low, only 5.6 per cent in sharp contrast to the 54.5 per cent in the rural area. It follows that a higher proportion in the urban area (36.8 per cent) than in the rural area (22.4 per cent) is being employed in production and related occupations, to which the bulk of the workers in the predominantly urban manufacturing establishments belong. The distinctive distribution of workers in these two major occupational groups in the urban and rural sectors serves to underline the relative levels of economic development, and hence poverty, productivity and living standards in these two sectors.

It would be interesting to see what kind of variation in the occupational pattern between the two sexes existed in the urban and rural areas. In the urban area the majority of male workers, 40.5 per cent, were engaged in production and related occupations, and so were female workers but with a lower proportion of 28.7 per cent. The second largest group of male workers were in sales occupations with 17.0 per cent, but female workers had the second largest group in clerical occupations with a high proportion of 22.8 per cent. Both male and female workers had very low proportions in agricultural and

TABLE 8.17
PERCENTAGE DISTRIBUTION OF LABOUR FORCE BY MAJOR OCCUPATION, SEX AND URBAN-RURAL AREA, 1980

Occupation	Urban			Rural		
	Total	Males	Females	Total	Males	Females
1. Professional and technical	11.2	9.8	14.4	4.6	4.9	5.7
2. Administrative and managerial	2.2	2.9	0.7	0.5	0.4	0.1
3. Clerical	15.0	11.4	22.8	4.3	4.5	4.9
4. Sales	15.1	17.0	11.1	7.5	6.9	5.6
5. Services	14.0	13.0	16.3	7.0	6.4	5.1
6. Agricultural and related workers	5.6	5.4	6.0	50.3	54.4	63.6
7. Production and related workers	36.8	40.5	28.7	25.9	22.4	15.0
Total	100.0	100.0	100.0	100.0	100.0	100.0

related occupations. The relatively higher proportion of female workers in professional and technical occupations may be attributed to the large number of teachers: some 33,500 or 54 per cent of female workers in this group were teachers as compared with the corresponding figure of 33 per cent for male workers.

In the rural area there was a greater concentration of female than male workers in agricultural and related occupations, 63.6 per cent and 50.3 per cent respectively. The second most popular occupational group was production and related workers for both male and female workers, except that the 25.9 per cent for male workers was much higher than the 15.0 per cent for their female counterparts. The relatively high third position occupied by professional and technical workers among female workers was again due to the predominance of teachers who accounted for some 67 per cent of the total in this occupational group. The data seem to suggest that in the rural area the male labour force was distributed more widely among the major occupational groups than the female labour force, but this position was reversed in the urban area.

Pattern of Male Working Life

Of the total number of males born during a particular period a fair number will die before they attain the age of 10 years, and among those who survive to this age the majority will postpone entering the working population in order to acquire education and training. By the age of 20 years almost all the boys will have entered the working population, leaving an extremely small proportion who will never enter the working population on account of chronic ill health, physical disability, insanity, etc., originating at birth or during childhood. In their course of working life a small number will leave the working population because of death, serious illness, industrial accidents and other reasons, while the majority will continue to work until their retirement age is reached. These and other aspects of the male labour force dynamics can be systematically studied with the aid of tables of working life. Such tables are less useful in the study of the female labour force in view of their inherent limitations on account of the serious and unpredictable fluctuations of the female participation rates over the age range caused by both economic and social factors which are more related to family and household considerations than to purely employment conditions.

The table of working life is essentially an extension of the ordinary life table based on the mortality experience of a past period, but it is different in that it also reflects the losses through causes other than death of a past period. It therefore shows what will happen to the working population in the future if these rates of losses remain unchanged. The table is constructed in such a manner as to provide information on the expected average number of years of working life remaining to those in a given age, on the chances that a man aged 30 years will be in the working population at age 60, on the pattern of withdrawals from the working population due to death and other causes, and on many other facets of working life. Among the main applications of the working life table are the computation of annual losses from the actual working population, the estimation of future replacement needs in any particular occupation or industry, and the reckoning — for social security purposes — of the man-years lost by persons of known age incurring industrial accidents.

Abridged tables of male working life for Peninsular Malaysia and for its three major racial components for 1970 and 1980 are given in full in Appendix B, which also incorporates a discussion of the methodology used. A third set of male abridged life tables for 1957 prepared by the author have already been published earlier.[13] The ordinary abridged life tables will be utilised to study the pattern of male working life.

The abridged life table for all races of males for 1979–80 reveals that 9,599 men out of the initial cohort of 10,000 born alive can expect to survive to their tenth birthday. Among these survivors, some 9,401 or 97.94 per cent will enter the labour force at some time or other during the remainder of their lives. The 1980 working life table also shows that these 9,401 men at exactly age 10 can expect to live collectively 491,514 man-years in the labour force. A division of the latter figure by the former will give the average expectation of working life of 52.3 years for a boy at age 10 in the labour force. The expectation of male working life undergoes a definite diminution from this maximum level with the advance of old age, falling for example to 33.5 years at age 30, 16.0 years at age 50 and 10.4 years at age 65.

The above expectation of working life refers to the expectation at each age of men who are in the working population at that age. It is also possible to derive the working life expectancy for all men living at a given age, particularly at birth, regardless of whether they are working or not. As mentioned earlier, the 10,000 males born alive can expect to spend a total of 491,514 man-years in the labour force, and therefore the average expectation of working life at birth will be 49.2 years. This is about 3.1 years less than the working life expectancy of 52.3 at age 10, which can be attributed to the substantial number of deaths that would take place among the boys before they attain their tenth birthday.

Since the sources of depletion from the labour force originate not only from

13. Saw Swee-Hock, "Malaya: Tables of Male Working Life, 1957", *Journal of the Royal Statistical Society*, Series A, Vol. 128, Part 3, 1965.

death but other causes as well, the working life expectancy $\overset{ow}{e}_x$ at a given age must necessarily be lower than the ordinary life expectancy $\overset{o}{e}_x$ at the corresponding age. Thus a boy at age 10 has a life expectancy of 59.0 years as compared with his working life expectancy of only 52.3 years in the working population. The difference of 6.7 years may be taken to represent the number of years that he can expect to live in retirement between the cessation of work and death; this is known as the expectation of retirement life which is denoted by $\overset{ow}{R}_x$. The relationship among these three types of expectancy at birth and at age 10 for the years 1957, 1970 and 1980 is examined in Table 8.18.

Of the total expectation of life at birth of 55.7 years in 1957, some 42.9 years would be spent in the working population and the remaining 12.8 years outside the labour force in retirement. What it means is that under the mortality conditions of 1956–58 and the labour force participation rates of 1957, an average male can be expected to devote 77.0 per cent of his life to the production of goods and services. Over the years the male life expectancy at birth improved from 55.7 years in 1957 to 62.2 years in 1970 and 66.3 years in 1980, while the male working life expectancy was raised from 42.9 years in 1957 to 44.3 years in 1970 and 49.2 years in 1980. As a result the retirement life expectancy for a man went up to 17.9 years in 1970 and then descended slightly to 17.1 years in 1980. A different trend was portrayed by the proportion of his life at birth

TABLE 8.18

MALE LIFE EXPECTANCIES AT BIRTH AND AGE TEN, 1957, 1970 AND 1980

Year	Life Expectancy $\overset{o}{e}_x$	Working Life Expectancy $\overset{o}{e}_x$	Retirement Life Expectancy $\overset{ow}{R}_x$	Percentage of $\overset{ow}{e}_x$ to $\overset{ow}{e}_x$
At Birth				
1957	55.7	42.9	12.8	77.0
1970	62.2	44.3	17.9	71.2
1980	66.3	49.2	17.1	74.2
At Age Ten				
1957	53.9	50.4	3.5	93.5
1970	56.8	50.7	6.1	89.3
1980	59.0	52.3	6.7	88.6

devoted to economic activity, moving down from 77.0 per cent to 71.2 per cent in 1970 and then up to 73.2 per cent in 1980.

At age 10 a male in 1957 has a life expectancy of 53.9 years, a working life expectancy of 50.4 years, and hence a retirement life expectancy of 3.5 years only. At that time he was then expected to spend as much as 93.5 per cent of his total expectation of life at age 10 in economic activity. Over the years both his life expectancy and working life expectancy improved, but the upward movement of the former was faster than the latter. Consequently, there was a continuous rise in his retirement life expectancy from 3.5 years in 1957 to 6.1 years in 1970 and finally to 6.7 years in 1980, accompanied by a sustained reduction in the proportion of his life devoted to economic activity from 93.5 in 1957 to 88.6 per cent in 1980. This decline in the proportion of male life devoted to economic activity is a common experience shown by most countries undergoing modernisation of the economy. Essentially, the process of economic development and modernisation tends to diminish the opportunities and willingness of the young and the elderly to work for income on account of increased schooling and earlier retirement following a rise in earnings and levels of living.

Having looked at the changes in recent years in the three types of life expectancy, we will now examine the pattern of these life expectancies over the age range as portrayed by the 1980 figures included in Table 8.19. Both the male life expectancy and the male working life expectancy undergo a sure and steady fall with the advance of old age, the former from 59.0 years at age 10 to 12.5 years at age 65, and the latter from 52.3 years at age 10 to 10.4 years at age 65. The decrease in life expectancy can be attributed entirely to mortality, but the decrease in working life expectancy may be pin-pointed to deaths as well as withdrawal from the labour force due to other causes. A completely different path over the age range is shown by the male retirement life expectancy. It climbs up very gently from 6.7 years at age 10 to 7.0 years at 35 and stays at this level up to 45, after which it descends gradually to age 55 and then more rapidly to touch the low of 2.1 years at age 65.

It may be observed that at age 10 a boy can expect to live another 59.0 years, and he is expected to spend 52.3 years or 88.6 per cent in the labour force and only 6.7 years or 11.4 per cent in retirement. In fact, the relatively small 'retirement' does not reflect withdrawal from the working population into the non-working population but rather attrition due almost entirely to death. As mortality becomes heavier from age 10 onwards and as withdrawal due to other causes become more conspicuous after age 35 or so, the proportion of the life expectancy that a man can anticipate to spend in retirement increases slowly at first and faster subsequently, from the low of 11.4 per cent at age 10 to 29.5 per cent at 50 and 29.1 per cent at 55 when most employees are subjected to mandatory retirement. After this the percentage takes a downturn and

TABLE 8.19
MALE LIFE EXPECTANCIES AT SELECTED AGES, 1980

Age	Life Expectancy $\overset{o}{e}_x$	Working Life Expectancy $\overset{ow}{e}_x$	Retirement Life Expectancy $\overset{ow}{R}_x$	Percentage of $\overset{ow}{R}_x$ to $\overset{o}{e}_x$
10	59.0	52.3	6.7	11.4
15	54.2	47.5	6.7	12.4
20	49.5	42.8	6.7	13.5
25	45.0	38.2	6.8	15.1
30	39.8	33.5	6.3	15.8
35	35.8	28.8	7.0	19.6
40	31.3	24.3	7.0	22.4
45	26.9	19.9	7.0	26.0
50	22.7	16.0	6.7	29.5
55	18.9	13.5	5.4	25.8
60	15.5	11.5	4.0	25.8
65	12.5	10.4	2.1	16.8

touches 16.8 per cent at age 65; at these old ages the elderly men who are not compulsorily retired tend to stay in the labour force until they are removed by death. What we have discussed here is undoubtedly related to the slight rise in the male retirement life expectancy up to age 40 and the progressive decline at the old ages.

Apart from measuring the expectancies of working life and hence retirement life, the working life table is extremely valuable in studying the characteristics of losses from the labour force. More specifically, this pattern of loss rates can be analysed in terms of the total loss rate, $_5m_x^s$ which has been conveniently subdivided into the actual death rate, $_5m_x^d$ and the actual retirement rate, $_5m_x^r$. As can be observed in Table 8.19, the total loss rate in 1980 stays at a fairly low level, below 5 per 1,000 working population below age 45. Thereafter, it shoots up to 12.4 in the 45–49 age group and continues to advance rapidly until it reaches 96.0 in the last age group 65 and over. The more interesting aspect of the pattern of losses concerns the age variation in each of the sub-component loss rate.

As for the death rate, we can see a gradual rise over the age range from 0.7 per 1,000 in the 10–14 age group up to the late 40s when it reaches 7.0, and thereafter a progressively faster rise to touch the high of 73.4 in the last age group 65 and over. On the other hand, the retirement rate remains small up to the late 40s, after which it jumps to 21.8 per 1,000 in the 50–54 age group and continues to move up to the peak of 42.5 in the early 60s. In the last age group the rate falls to 22.6. It should be pointed out that the absence of any figures in the retirement column in Table 8.20 for ages 10 to 34 is the outcome of adopting the constant proportion of working population equivalent to the maximum ever attained (see Appendix B). In any case, the actual retirement at these young ages could not be significant. It is important to remember that the term 'retirement' refers to persons leaving the labour force on account of illness, physical disablement, mental derangement and other factors incurred in the course of their working life.

What is even more significant is the impact of the contrasting pattern of death and retirement rates on the variation in their relative importance as factors determining withdrawals from the labour force at the different age groups. From the mid-50s onwards, the retirement rate begins to exert an increasingly greater influence relative to the death rate until the mid-60s. The difference between the two rates stands at its widest in the 50–54 age group where the retirement rate 21.8 per 1,000 is about twice that of the death rate

TABLE 8.20

LOSS RATES FROM MALE WORKING POPULATION BY AGE, 1980

Age Group	Total Loss Rates 1000 $_5m_x^s$	Loss Rates due to Death 1000 $_5m_x^d$	Loss Rates due to Causes other than Death 1000 $_5m_x^r$
10–14	0.7	0.7	—
15–20	1.3	1.3	—
20–24	2.0	2.0	—
25–29	2.1	2.1	—
30–34	2.0	2.0	—
35–39	3.2	2.7	0.5
40–44	5.8	4.2	1.6
45–49	12.4	7.0	5.4
50–54	33.1	11.3	21.8
55–59	48.9	18.3	30.6
60–64	71.4	28.9	42.5
65 & over	96.0	73.4	22.6

of 11.3 per 1,000. In Peninsular Malaysia many workers retire at the age of
55. The turnaround of the relative importance from the mid-60s should not
come as a surprise in view of the extremely heavy mortality prevailing at this
older age range.

A comparison of the male life expectancies among the three main races at
selected ages in 1980 is presented in Table 8.21. The highest life expectancy

TABLE 8.21

MALE LIFE EXPECTANCIES AT SELECTED AGES FOR THREE MAIN RACES, 1980

Race	Life Expectancy $\overset{o}{e}_x$	Working Life Expectancy $\overset{ow}{e}_x$	Retirement Life Expectancy $\overset{ow}{R}_x$	Percentage of $\overset{ow}{e}_x$ to $\overset{o}{e}_x$
At Birth				
Malays	67.1	51.1	16.0	76.2
Chinese	67.6	48.9	18.7	72.3
Indians	66.6	44.1	22.5	66.2
At Age 10				
Malays	60.3	54.8	5.5	90.9
Chinese	59.4	51.2	8.2	86.2
Indians	59.3	47.0	12.3	79.3
At Age 55				
Malays	20.0	15.7	4.3	78.5
Chinese	19.1	12.2	6.9	63.9
Indians	18.8	9.8	9.0	52.1

at birth of 51.1 years was recorded by Malay men as compared with the lowest
of 44.1 years by Indian men, with Chinese men occupying an intermediate
position of 48.9 years. On the other hand, Indian men enjoyed the highest retirement life expectancy at birth of 22.5 years and Malay men the lowest of 16.0
years. The retirement life expectancy of Chinese men was again situated somewhere between these two figures at 16.7 years. This relative race differential

position was maintained for working life expectancy as well as for retirement life expectancy at age 10 and also at age 55. One noticeable difference is that at these ages the differentials with respect to the retirement life expectancy were more pronounced, for example, at age 10 the 12.3 years for Indian men was more than twice the 5.5 years for Malay men. At birth the two respective figures were 22.5 years and 16.0 years.

It follows from the above observations that there would be a definite relationship among the men of the three races in the proportion of their life devoted to economic activity. The figures laid out in the last column of Table 8.21 reveals that Malay men is expected to spend 76.2 per cent of their life at birth to economic activity. The corresponding figures for Chinese men was maintained at age 10 and also at age 55. At the latter age when most workers tend to retire the disparity in the proportion of life at age 55 devoted to economic activity has in fact widened. The relative race differential in regard to working life expectancy, retirement life expectancy, and proportion devoted to economic activity can be explained in terms of the differences in employment status. Out of a total Indian male labour force of 273,278 in 1980, an extremely high proportion of 81.0 per cent were working as employees as against 61.4 per cent for Chinese men and 46.0 per cent for Malay men.[14] Employees are generally subjected to stricter terms of working conditions, especially in relation to retirement in the 50s.

14. Khoo Teik Huat, op. cit.

9

Future Population Trends

I n this final chapter we will make an attempt to examine the most plausible course of future trends in the population and labour force of Peninsular Malaysia. This can be accomplished by projecting the population and labour force into the future on the basis of certain assumptions concerning the future path of migration, mortality, fertility and labour force participation rates. The population projections that we have prepared are presented in full in Appendix C. Before analysing the salient features of these projected figures, we will discuss the newly-adopted pronatalist policy that is bound to exert some influence on the course of population dynamics in the country.

The 70 Million Policy

Many of the past demographic trends and patterns discussed earlier were influenced by government attitudes and policies, some of which are translated into administrative procedures or even enshrined in the laws of the country. In general, the future population trends will depend partly on what had already happened to the growth factors of fertility, mortality and migration in the immediate past and partly on government policies that are likely to affect the future path of population growth. In this respect, Malaysia stands out as one of the very few countries that are now advocating for a larger population than what was previously thought to be desirable and have even pin-pointed a particular population size to be achieved ultimately in the future.

The genesis of the new policy can be traced to September 1982 when the Prime Minister, Datuk Seri Dr. Mahathir Mohamad, first mooted the idea of an ultimate population size of 70 million in his presidential address to a general assembly of the United Malay National Organisation (UMNO). His rationale was that Malaysia needs a big population to provide a large domestic market to support its future industries in the face of an increasingly protectionist world market. The concept of a large population was in sharp contradiction to the existing population policy under which the government family planning programme has been functioning for many years since 1966. It is not surprising that this sudden pronouncement sparked off considerable controversies and discussions about the implications of 70 million people in the fields of housing, education, health, employment, food production, water requirements and energy consumption.[1] Some of the ensuing debates were rather confusing in the face of a failure to provide reasons for selecting 70 million and to specify the year in which this target is to be attained.

It was no surprise that the government established in January 1983 an *ad hoc* Committee on Population Issues to study the strategy and programme required to achieve the 70 million target. The terms of reference of the Committee were (a) to review the present population growth trends and prospects, (b) to prepare population projections based on several assumptions leading towards achieving 70 million population, (c) to study some social and economic implications of 70 million, and (d) to make recommendations.[2] By the second quarter of 1984 the Prime Minister was able to use information supplied by this Committee to provide more details about the new population policy in his presentation of the mid-term review of the Fourth Five-Year Plan, 1981–85 in Parliament in April 1984. He announced that the aim of the policy is to achieve a population of 70 million in the year 2100.[3]

The report of the Committee was completed in mid-1984 and was approved by the Cabinet on 1 August 1984. It recommended that the present rate of decline in fertility should be decelerated in order to delay the attainment of replacement fertility level to the year 2070. In this manner the target of 70 million would be reached during the year 2100, and the population is expected to grow slightly to stabilise at about 73 million by the year 2150. The report assured that the social and economic implications of the 70 million population should not be alarming since this size would only be attained in approximately 115 years' time. To slow down the downward movement in fertility, the report recommended the introduction of measures that would encourage a large family size.

The first pronatalist measure introduced by the government was connected to the question of paid maternity leave for female workers. The *Employment (Amendment) Act, 1984* was passed by Parliament to extend the eligibility for paid maternity leave for women working in the public service from the

---

1. See, for example, "Target: 70 Million", *Malaysian Business,* May 1984, and "Malaysia Moves on Major Boost to Population", *Asian Wall Street Journal,* 10 April 1984.

2. Abdullah bin Ayob (Chairman), *Towards a Population of Seventy Million* (Kuala Lumpur: National Population and Family Development Board, 1984).

3. *Asiaweek,* 20 April 1984.

first three to the first five births with effect from 1 June 1984.[4] Many female
workers in the private sector have also benefited from this new maternity leave
scheme since the working conditions in the private sector tend to fall in line
with those provided by the government.

The second pronatalist measure involved changes in the amount of child
relief allowed in the annual income tax assessment. In presenting the 1985
budget to Parliament on 19 October 1984, the Finance Minister announced
that the total amount of child relief in the income tax returns for the first five
children would be raised from $3,000 to $3,800.[5] The amount for each of these
children was modified as follows:

Birth Order	Old	New
First	$800	$650
Second	$700	$750
Third	$600	$800
Fourth	$500	$800
Fifth	$400	$800

By comparison, the new scheme penalises parents with only one child, and
even those with only two since the combined allowance is reduced from $1,500
to $1,400. But they will be able to enjoy an increasingly larger allowance when
they produce their third, fourth and fifth child.[6]

In March 1985 the government introduced another pronatalist measure
whereby female employees in the public service are now given maternity allowances up to the fifth birth instead of for the first three only.[7] In the private
sector employers are required by government regulations to pay maternity
allowance for the first four rather than the first two births only.

The pronatalist policy created problems for the National Family Planning
Board which has been spearheading the country's population control programme since 1966. It became apparently clear that the whole philosophy,
function and operational programme of the Board had to be modified. For
one thing, the name of the Board was no longer consistent with the new policy
and was accordingly changed to National Population and Family Development Board. This was accompanied by a shift in the Board's original objective.
Family planning is no longer meant to limit the ultimate size of the family but
to space the birth of children in the interest of the health of the mother and

4. *Malaysian Business Times*, 3 August 1984.
5. *Population Headliners*, ESCAP, No. 124, July 1985.
6. *New Straits Times*, 20 October 1984.
7. *The Straits Times*, 7 August 1985.

the general welfare of the family. In fact, parents are now urged to produce more children instead of stopping at two.

Future Population Growth

The above pronatalist policy was taken into consideration in preparing the population projections for the 40-year period from 1980 to the year 2020. As mentioned in Appendix C, the fertility of each of the three races is expected to decline in the future but at a moderate pace. More specifically, the Malay fertility is assumed to decline every five years by 2 per cent from 1980 to the year 2000 and thereafter by 1 per cent until the year 2020. The Chinese and the Indians have been assumed to experience a faster fertility decline, both recording a reduction of 3 per cent during 1980–2000 and 2 per cent during 2000–2020. The results of the projection based on these assumptions are summarised in Tables 9.1 to 9.4.

TABLE 9.1
PROJECTED POPULATION GROWTH, 1980–2020

| Year | Population | Population Increase | | |
| | | Number | Percentage | |
			5-year	Annual
1980	10,944,794	—	—	—
1985	12,439,953	1,495,159	13.7	2.59
1990	14,110,562	1,670,609	13.4	2.55
1995	15,962,291	1,851,729	13.1	2.50
2000	17,921,910	1,959,619	12.3	2.34
2005	19,986,668	2,064,758	11.5	2.20
2010	22,189,760	2,203,092	11.0	2.11
2015	24,571,945	2,382,185	10.7	2.06
2020	27,136,070	2,564,125	10.4	2.01

The figures given in Table 9.1 reveal that the population of Peninsular Malaysia is expected to grow by about 64 per cent from about 10.9 million in 1980 to 17.9 million by the end of this century. In the next 20 years the population will increase by about 51 per cent to reach 27.1 million in the year 2020. It is to be noted that, commencing from the beginning of the whole period, the time taken for the population to double itself is approximately 30 years.

The amount of increase for every five-year period is expected to indicate a rising trend throughout the whole period. The increase during the years 1980–85 amounted to about 1.5 million, and this will be enlarged progressively to peak at 2.6 million during the last period 2015–20. But the increase expressed in percentage terms will exhibit a falling trend, being reduced from 13.7 per cent during 1980–85 to 10.4 per cent during 2015–20. The implied annual rate of population growth is expected to slow down slightly, being reduced from about 2.6 per cent per annum during 1980–85 to 2.0 per cent during the last five-year period.

It would be interesting to proceed a step further by examining the differences in the future growth rate of the three main races. The figures given in Table 9.2 reveal that these three races share the common experience of a slowing down in the rate of population growth. There are, however, some important differences in the rate of population increase among these races. The deceleration in the growth rate is expected to be the slowest among the Malays, with the rate falling from about 3.0 per cent during 1980–85 to 2.4 per cent towards the end of the projected period in 2015–20. In contrast, the Chinese will experience the fastest deceleration in their growth rate which is projected to fall from about 2.1 per cent during 1980–85 to 1.3 per cent during the last five-year period. As for the Indians, the deceleration in their growth rate is just slightly less fast than the Chinese; their rate falling from 2.4 per cent at the beginning to 1.6 per cent at the end of the period.

TABLE 9.2

PROJECTED ANNUAL RATE OF POPULATION GROWTH BY RACE,
1980–2020

Period	Malays	Chinese	Indians
1980–85	2.95	2.05	2.40
1985–90	2.91	1.99	2.27
1990–95	2.86	1.94	2.12
1995–2000	2.70	1.78	1.91
2000–2005	2.56	1.61	1.80
2005–2010	2.47	1.45	1.77
2010–15	2.42	1.35	1.72
2015–20	2.37	1.25	1.63

Another important feature of Table 9.2 that deserves mention concerns the differences in growth rate among the three main races. At the beginning of the period during 1980–85, the Malays were registering the highest rate of 3.0 per cent and the Chinese the lowest rate of 2.1 per cent. The Indians occupied an intermediate position, with 2.4 per cent. This relative position is expected to be maintained throughout the whole 40-year period up to 2015–20. The maintenance of this relative position seems justified as the factors influencing the fertility level of these races are not expected to alter radically across ethnic lines.

Future Population Structure

In a country like Peninsular Malaysia where racial integration has hardly taken place at all, considerable significance is attached to the possible changes in the racial composition of the population. This is because such changes will certainly lead to shifts in the relative political strength among these races, which in turn will have serious ramifications in the field of social and economic development of these communities. It is now obvious as to why we have prepared separate population projections for these three races in Appendix C. Another equally important reason is that the projection for the total population in the country based on these three separate projections would be more reliable since it takes into account the variation in mortality and fertility among these three ethnic groups.

The figures for the projected population by race are given in Table 9.3. The differences in the rate of growth among the major races noted earlier will obviously be reflected in the increase in their population. Owing to the more rapid growth rate, the Malay population is expected to double in 25 years, from 6.1 million in 1980 to 12.2 million in 2005. On the other hand, a doubling of the Chinese population does not even quite materialise during the whole 40-year period, increasing from 3.7 million at the beginning to 7.1 million towards the end of the period. As for the Indians, their population will manage to double during the period, with the initial figure of 1.1 million reaching 2.2 million by 2015.

In looking at the future changes in the racial composition of the population, it should be noted that the proportion of the other races encompassing the Eurasians, Europeans, Japanese, etc. remains at 0.6 per cent in Table 9.3. This is because the total population for the whole country was derived by boosting up the combined figure for the three main races by the constant proportion of 0.6 per cent, representing the percentage for the other races as determined in the 1980 Census. The population of the other races is by comparison too small to justify a separate projection to be calculated.

TABLE 9.3
PROJECTED POPULATION BY RACE, 1980–2020

Year	Malays	Chinese	Indians	Others	Total
	Number				
1980	6,131,625	3,651,196	1,093,112	68,861	10,944,794
1985	7,089,322	4,041,357	1,230,961	78,313	12,439,953
1990	8,184,368	4,459,971	1,377,387	88,836	14,110,562
1995	9,422,250	4,910,183	1,529,358	100,500	15,962,291
2000	10,764,574	5,363,139	1,681,348	112,849	17,921,910
2005	12,212,238	5,810,258	1,838,258	125,914	19,986,668
2010	13,797,455	6,245,361	2,006,613	140,331	22,189,760
2015	15,553,208	6,679,128	2,184,860	154,749	24,571,945
2020	17,488,105	7,108,146	2,368,914	170,905	27,136,070
	Percentage				
1980	56.0	33.4	10.0	0.6	100.0
1985	57.0	32.5	9.9	0.6	100.0
1990	58.0	31.6	9.8	0.6	100.0
1995	59.0	30.8	9.6	0.6	100.0
2000	60.1	29.9	9.4	0.6	100.0
2005	61.1	29.1	9.2	0.6	100.0
2010	62.2	28.1	9.0	0.6	100.0
2015	63.3	27.2	8.9	0.6	100.0
2020	64.4	26.2	8.7	0.6	100.0

The percentage figures given in the lower section of Table 9.3 show that significant changes in the ethnic composition of the population will take place in the next 40 years. The proportion of Malays, which has been rising in the past, will continue to move upwards from 56.0 per cent in 1980 to 60.1 per cent in the year 2000 and finally to 64.4 per cent in the year 2020. On the other hand, the Chinese and Indians will experience a continuous reduction in their proportion during the same period. The Chinese accounted for about one-third (33.4 per cent) of the total population in 1980, but 40 years later their proportion will drop to one-quarter (26.2 per cent). The Indian proportion is expected to fall from 10.0 in 1980 to 8.7 per cent towards the end of the period.

We now come to the next important aspect of the results of the projections and this relates to the probable changes in the age structure of the future population briefly summarised in terms of five broad age groups in Table 9.4. One major development is apparent; the long-term movement in the proportions in the first three age groups is generally downward over the whole period. The clearest downturn will be recorded in the first age group 0–4 where the proportion can be expected to rise from 13.3 per cent in 1980 to 14.4 per cent in 1985, after which it will fall continuously to reach 11.8 per cent in 2020. In the second age group 5–14 the proportion moves down from 25.7 per cent in 1980 to 22.8 per cent in 1990 and then up to 23.5 per cent in 1995; after that it falls continuously to touch 20.6 per cent in 2020. The trend in the proportion in

TABLE 9.4

PROJECTED POPULATION BY BROAD AGE GROUP, 1980–2020

Year	Age Group					
	0–4	5–14	15–29	30–59	60 & Over	Total
Number						
1980	1,459,712	2,812,655	3,188,748	2,843,467	640,212	10,944,794
1985	1,785,659	2,898,587	3,649,325	3,382,485	723,897	12,439,953
1990	1,991,793	3,219,860	4,032,680	4,020,534	845,695	14,110,562
1995	2,194,712	3,752,051	4,222,679	4,821,304	971,545	15,962,291
2000	2,334,937	4,165,197	4,637,358	5,601,252	1,183,166	17,921,910
2005	2,476,010	4,511,363	5,171,512	6,447,428	1,380,355	19,986,668
2010	2,675,991	4,793,449	5,908,092	7,121,501	1,690,727	22,189,760
2015	2,930,648	5,133,320	6,461,440	7,980,910	2,065,627	24,571,945
2020	3,198,381	5,589,958	6,946,143	8,882,864	2,518,724	27,136,070
Percentage						
1980	13.3	25.7	29.1	26.0	5.8	100.0
1985	14.4	23.3	29.3	27.2	5.8	100.0
1990	14.1	22.8	28.6	28.5	6.0	100.0
1995	13.7	23.5	26.5	30.2	6.1	100.0
2000	13.0	23.2	25.9	31.3	6.6	100.0
2005	12.4	22.6	25.9	32.3	6.9	100.0
2010	12.1	21.6	26.6	32.1	7.6	100.0
2015	11.9	20.9	26.3	32.5	8.4	100.0
2020	11.8	20.6	25.6	32.7	9.3	100.0

the third age group 15–29 is less clear-cut, but over the long haul it is expected to drop from the peak of 29.3 per cent to the low of 25.6 towards the end of the period. The tendency towards a smaller proportion of children at the young ages is the direct result of assuming that every one of the three main races will register a continuous fall in fertility.

The other development underlined by the figures in Table 9.4 is that the two old age groups can certainly expect to experience a rise in their proportion over the years. The proportion in the age group 30–59 will rise consistently from 26.0 per cent in 1980 to 32.7 per cent in 2020. The same period will also witness a rise in the proportion in the last age group 60 and over, moving up from 5.8 per cent at the beginning to 9.3 per cent at the end of the period. This suggests that during the 40-year period under consideration the population of Peninsular Malaysia is not expected to undergo a process of ageing. The ageing process takes place only when the proportion aged 60 and over moves to about 20 per cent. The shifts in the age structure described earlier imply that the population is expected to move towards a middle-age one.

Some important implications may be drawn from the estimated changes in the age structure of the population in the next four decades. The pronounced fall in the combined proportion for the first two groups from 39 per cent to 32 per cent may be taken to mean that there will be a lessening of the young dependency burden. A smaller portion of the country's resources would be required to meet the problem of providing educational amenities and of creating employment opportunities for the younger members of the working population. On the other hand, the problem of the old dependency burden can be expected to worsen somewhat, though not reaching such a magnitude as that currently experienced by some European countries. On balance, the overall dependency burden is expected to be lighter for the members in the working-age group between 15 and 59 where the proportion is projected to rise from about 55 per cent to 58 per cent during the period.

Future Labour Force

The growth and structure of the labour force in the future can be examined with the aid of labour force projections. Given the detailed population projections by sex and age group in Appendix C, it would not be a difficult task to proceed a stage further to compute the projections of labour force. This can be accomplished by applying the 1980 age-specific labour force participation rates by sex to the population projections by sex for the relevant age groups from age 10 upwards. The results of the calculation are summarised in Table 9.5. Apart from the assumptions used in the population projections, the projected labour force is based on the additional assumption that the labour force participation rates prevailing in 1980 will remain unchanged throughout the period up to 2020.

Table 9.5 shows that the labour force will increase from 4.1 million in 1980 to almost double the size in 2005 with 8.1 million. After that it will still continue to increase until it reaches 11.3 million in 2020. During the first five-year period 1980–85, the labour force is expected to grow by about 724,000 or 145,000 per year on the average. This annual addition to the labour force will continue to rise progressively until it reaches about 219,000 per year during the last period 2015–20. The annual addition serves to underline the number of jobs that have to be created in order to absorb the new members of the labour force and to keep the volume of unemployment at its normal level.

Though the absolute number is expected to increase, the percentage increase in the labour force for every five-year period will be decreasing over the years. In the first five-year period 1980–85 the percentage increase will amount to 17.8 per cent, and this is expected to be lowered to 10.8 per cent at the beginning to 2.1 per cent towards the end of the period.

TABLE 9.5

PROJECTED LABOUR FORCE GROWTH, 1980–2020

Year	Labour Force	Labour Force Increase		
		Number	Percentage	
			5-year	Annual
1980	4,069,717	—	—	—
1985	4,793,686	723,969	17.8	3.33
1990	5,517,150	723,464	15.1	2.85
1995	6,257,203	740,053	13.4	2.55
2000	7,084,338	827,135	13.2	2.51
2005	8,048,005	963,667	13.6	2.58
2010	9,091,966	1,043,961	13.0	2.47
2015	10,167,772	1,075,806	11.8	2.26
2020	11,261,268	1,093,496	10.8	2.06

If we compare the annual rate of increase in the labour force with the annual rate of population growth shown in Table 9.1, we shall see that the labour force is expected to grow faster than the population itself. This development is the inevitable outcome of the decreasing proportion of children in the total population consequent on the assumed continuous fall in fertility. From the economic point of view, it is advantageous to have a smaller proportion of young and old dependents to be supported by a larger proportion of working persons. However, this will require the creation of sufficient jobs for the expected increase in working persons.

An examination of the projections by age reveals that some changes in the age structure of the labour force can be expected to take place. The proportion of young workers aged 10–29 will fall from about 47 per cent in 1980 to 39 per cent in 2020. In the middle age group 30–49, the proportion will rise slightly from 38 per cent to 40 per cent during the same period. For greater changes can occur in the old age group 50 and over; here the proportion will rise from 15 per cent to 21 per cent during the whole period. These relative shifts in the three proportions indicate that the labour force will be moving from a young labour force to a relatively older and mature workforce in the future.

Conclusion

The results of the population and labour force projections discussed above have been derived by taking cognizance of the present policy of working towards a final population of about 70 million for the whole of Malaysia by the end of the twenty-first century. The modifications introduced in the population control programme to promote a larger family size are not that radical and comprehensive as those pronatalist measures adopted by some European countries faced with an imminent decline in their population. Besides, the usual socio-economic variables favouring a smaller family norm will continue to operate in the future as the country undergoes further modernisation and economic development. The salient features of the future population trends highlighted in this concluding chapter are the outcome of assuming a continuation of fertility decline but at a slower speed.

APPENDIX A
ABRIDGED LIFE TABLES

Introduction

One of the most sophisticated techniques of measuring the mortality level of a population is by means of the period life table which shows, among other things, the expectation of life at different ages.[1] A period life table is constructed on the assumption that the population is a closed one not affected by migration and that the death rates for a chosen period of usually three years will prevail indefinitely. We normally commence with a radix of 10,000 at birth and trace this cohort over the age range as it is depleted by deaths in accordance with the selected schedule of mortality rates. The life table may take the form of a complete table with values for single years of age or an abridged table with figures for five-year age groups.

In this appendix we will discuss the methodology used in constructing the two sets of abridged life tables for the periods 1969–71 and 1979–81. For each period, a set of eight abridged life tables for the male and female segments of the three races and all races combined have been prepared. The techniques outlined here are applicable to all the tables estimated.

Data Used

The statistical data employed to construct the period abridged life tables are the annual average deaths for the years 1969 to 1971 obtained from the vital registration system and the population enumerated in the June 1970 Census. Data used in the calculation of the second set of abridged life tables are the annual average deaths for the years 1979 to 1981 and the population obtained in the June 1980 Census.

The statistics for deaths classified by age contained some deaths where ages have not been stated, and instead of ignoring these unspecified figures it was decided to pro-rate them to the various age groups from 0 to 85 and over so as to obtain a truer picture of overally mortality level. Similar adjustment for the census population figures tabulated by age was not necessary since they do not contain persons with unspecified ages.

---

1. A period life table is different from a cohort life table in that the latter records the mortality experience of a birth cohort throughout the history of a generation, while the former observes the state of mortality of a population in a period of say three years. Period life tables enables us to study mortality changes at different periods of times.

The adjusted death statistics for 1969–71 and 1979–81 and the population figures for 1970 and 1980 were used to compute the age-specific or central death rates for single years 1 to 4 and for quinary age groups from 5–9 to 85 and over for the two periods. These central death rates are known as the $_nm_x$ values and constitute the starting point for deriving the first function of the life table known as the life-table death rates, $_nq_x$. The central death rate for age 0 is not calculated because the $_nq_x$ value for this age has been derived separately from infant deaths and births.

Derivation of Life-Table Functions

The 1,000 $_nq_x$ column of the life table refers to the probability of dying per 1,000 alive at the beginning of the age interval. Except for age below one year, these life table death rates are derived from the central death rates by means of the formula $_nq_x = \dfrac{2n \cdot _nm_x}{2 + n \cdot _nm_x}$. The heavy mortality in the first year of life necessitates the calculation of q_0 directly from infant death and birth records in four separate computations according to the following formulae, where for instance β^{78}, β_4^{78} and β_D^{78} denote births in the year 1978, births in the fourth quarter of 1978, and births in December of 1978 respectively.

$$q_0 \ (0\text{--}1 \ \text{mth.}) = \frac{\text{Deaths in 1979--81 aged 0--1 mth.}}{\tfrac{1}{2}\beta_D^{78} + \beta^{79} + \beta^{80} + \beta^{81} - \tfrac{1}{2}\beta_D^{81}}$$

$$q_0 \ (1\text{--}3 \ \text{mth.}) = \frac{\text{Deaths in 1979--81 aged 1--3 mth.}}{\tfrac{1}{2}\,(\beta_0^{78} + \beta_N^{78}) + \beta_D^{78} + \beta^{79} + \beta^{80} + \beta^{81} - \tfrac{1}{2}\,(\beta_0^{81} + \beta_N^{81}) - \beta_D^{81}}$$

$$q_0 \ (3\text{--}6 \ \text{mth.}) = \frac{\text{Deaths in 1979--81 aged 3--6 mth.}}{\tfrac{1}{2}\,\beta_3^{78} + \beta_4^{78} + \beta^{79} + \beta^{80} + \beta^{81} - \tfrac{1}{2}\,\beta_3^{81} - \beta_4^{81}}$$

$$q_0 \ (6\text{--}12 \ \text{mth.}) = \frac{\text{Deaths in 1979--81 aged 6--12 mth.}}{\tfrac{1}{2}(\beta_1^{78} + \beta_2^{78}) + \beta_3^{78} + \beta_4^{78} + \beta^{79} + \beta^{80} + \beta^{81} - \tfrac{1}{2}(\beta_1^{81} + \beta_2^{81}) - \beta_3^{81} - \beta_4^{81}}$$

The sum of the above four probabilities of death will give the required mortality rate for q_0 for age under one year.

The ℓ_x column refers to the number of survivors at the beginning of age interval, and is obtained by a direct mathematical procedure on the bases of the life-table death rates according to the formula $\ell_x = \ell_{x-n} - (\ell_{x-n} \times {}_nq_{x-n})$.

The ${}_nd_x$ column refers to the number of deaths occurring within an age interval and can be easily obtained by a subtraction of successive values of ℓ_x. Thus, ${}_nd_x = \ell_x - \ell_{x-n}$.

The ${}_nL_x$ column represents the number of years that will be lived collectively within any one age interval by a cohort numbering 10,000 at birth and subject to the given mortality conditions. Owing to the very uneven distribution of deaths in the first year of life, it is necessary to derive L_0 in four separate stages by summing the results of the following four calculations.

$$L_{(0-1 \text{ mth.})} = \tfrac{1}{2}(\ell_{0 \text{ mth.}} + \ell_{1 \text{ mth.}}) \times 1/12$$

$$L_{(1-3 \text{ mth.})} = \tfrac{1}{2}(\ell_{1 \text{ mth.}} + \ell_{3 \text{ mth.}}) \times 2/12$$

$$L_{(3-6 \text{ mth.})} = \tfrac{1}{2}(\ell_{3 \text{ mth.}} + \ell_{6 \text{ mth.}}) \times 3/12$$

$$L_{(6-12 \text{ mth.})} = \tfrac{1}{2}(\ell_{6 \text{ mth.}} + \ell_{12 \text{ mth.}}) \times 6/12$$

It is known that the distribution of deaths in the second year of life is still uneven, and it has been ascertained that by equating L_1 to $0.45\,\ell_1 + 0.55\,\ell_2$ fairly satisfactory results can be attained.[2] For ages two to four, L_x is taken as the average of ℓ_x and ℓ_{x+1}, and for quinary age groups ${}_5L_x$ is equated to

$$\frac{5(\ell_x + \ell_{x+5})}{2}.$$

The T_x column indicates the number of years that will be lived collectively, from the given age upwards, by the survivors to that age from the original cohort of 10,000 births. The values of T_x may be obtained by cumulative addi-

---

2. For a derivation of the formula, see Appendix: Ascertaining Value of B in Formula $L_1 = \beta\ell_1 + (1-\beta)\ell_2$ in Saw Swee-Hock, "Malaya: Tables of Male Working Life, 1957", *Journal of the Royal Statistical Society*, Series A (General), Vol. 128, Part 3, 1965.

tions of the $_nL_x$ column from the bottom upwards, with first of all T_{85} (or L_{85}) taken as $\dfrac{\ell_{85}}{\overline{m_{85}}}$ in the case of the last age group.[3]

The last column $\overset{o}{e}_x$ represents the individual expectation of life at the beginning of the age interval, and is derived by dividing T_x by the corresponding ℓ_x. Thus $\overset{o}{e}_x = \dfrac{T_x}{\ell_x}$.

By means of the techniques outlined above, the 16 abridged life tables for the period 1969–71 and 1979–81 for each sex separately for the three principal races and for all races combined are computed and shown in full in Tables 1 to 16.

---

3. There is no explanation regarding the derivation of the value for T_{85} or L_{85} in the construction of the census report life tables, but a few recalculations of the figures show that in these tables L_{85} was obtained by multiplying ℓ_{85} by its own logarithm as suggested in *Manual III: Methods for Population Projections by Sex and Age*, ST/SOA Series A, No. 25 (New York: United Nations, Department of Economic and Social Affairs, 1956). This procedure is not quite tenable because there is no evidence of m_{85}, and in fact it implies equating ℓ_{85} to log ℓ_{85} but the former depends only on mortality *after* 85 and latter only on mortality *before* 85.

TABLE A.1
ABRIDGED LIFE TABLE FOR ALL RACES MALES, 1969–71

Year of Age	Mortality Rate	Of 10,000 Born Alive		Stationery Population		Average Remaining Life Time
	Number Dying per 1,000 Alive at Beginning of Age Interval	Number Alive at Beginning of Age Interval	Number Dying during Age Interval	In the Age Interval	In this and all Subsequent Age Intervals	Average Number of Years of Life Remaining at Beginning of Age Interval
x to $x+4$	$1{,}000\,{}_nq_x$	ℓ_x	${}_nd_x$	${}_nL_x$	T_x	$\overset{o}{e}_x$
0	45.98	10,000	460	9,637	621,980	62.2
1	7.76	9,540	74	9,499	612,343	64.2
2	4.63	9,466	44	9,444	602,844	63.7
3	3.54	9,422	33	9,406	593,400	63.0
4	2.59	9,389	24	9,377	583,994	62.2
5– 9	7.57	9,365	71	46,648	574,617	61.4
10–14	5.24	9,294	49	46,348	527,969	56.8
15–19	7.27	9,245	67	46,058	481,621	52.1
20–24	10.00	9,178	92	45,660	435,563	47.5
25–29	11.09	9,086	101	45,178	389,903	42.9
30–34	13.66	8,985	123	44,618	344,725	38.4
35–39	17.99	8,862	159	43,913	300,107	33.9
40–44	24.98	8,703	217	42,973	256,194	29.4
45–49	41.86	8,486	355	41,543	213,221	25.1
50–54	69.78	8,131	567	39,238	171,678	21.1
55–59	104.67	7,564	792	35,840	132,440	17.5
60–64	165.10	6,772	1,118	31,065	96,600	14.3
65–69	237.46	5,654	1,343	24,913	65,535	11.6
70–74	329.30	4,311	1,420	18,005	40,622	9.4
75–79	437.68	2,891	1,265	11,293	22,617	7.8
80–84	506.07	1,626	823	6,073	11,324	7.0
85 & Over	1,000.00	803	803	5,251	5,251	6.5

TABLE A.2
ABRIDGED LIFE TABLE FOR ALL RACES FEMALES, 1969-71

Year of Age	Mortality Rate Number Dying per 1,000 Alive at Beginning of Age Interval	Of 10,000 Born Alive Number Alive at Beginning of Age Interval	Number Dying during Age Interval	Stationery Population In the Age Interval	Stationery Population In this and all Subsequent Age Intervals	Average Remaining Life Time Average Number of Years of Life Remaining at Beginning of Age Interval
x to x + 4	$1,000_nq_x$	ℓ_x	$_nd_x$	$_nL_x$	T_x	$\overset{o}{e}_x$
0	33.30	10,000	333	9,731	666,896	66.7
1	7.38	9,667	71	9,628	657,165	68.0
2	4.71	9,596	45	9,574	647,537	67.5
3	3.54	9,551	34	9,534	637,963	66.8
4	2.57	9,517	24	9,505	628,429	66.0
5- 9	7.07	9,493	67	47,298	618,924	65.2
10-14	4.24	9,426	40	47,030	571,626	60.6
15-19	5.63	9,386	53	46,798	524,596	55.9
20-24	7.97	9,333	74	46,480	477,798	51.2
25-29	9.80	9,259	91	46,068	431,318	46.6
30-34	12.92	9,168	118	45,545	385,250	42.0
35-39	16.27	9,050	147	44,883	339,705	37.5
40-44	21.56	8,903	192	44,035	294,822	33.1
45-49	31.11	8,711	271	42,878	250,787	28.8
50-54	50.11	8,440	423	41,143	207,909	24.6
55-59	72.43	8,017	581	38,633	166,766	20.8
60-64	120.21	7,436	894	34,945	128,133	17.2
65-69	167.87	6,542	1,098	29,965	93,188	14.2
70-74	249.76	5,444	1,360	23,820	63,223	11.6
75-79	323.55	4,084	1,321	17,120	39,403	9.6
80-84	417.00	2,764	1,152	10,940	22,283	8.1
85 & Over	1,000.00	1,612	1,612	11,343	11,343	7.0

TABLE A.3
ABRIDGED LIFE TABLE FOR MALAY MALES, 1969–71

Year of Age	Mortality Rate — Number Dying per 1,000 Alive at Beginning of Age Interval	Of 10,000 Born Alive — Number Alive at Beginning of Age Interval	Number Dying during Age Interval	Stationary Population — In the Age Interval	In this and all Subsequent Age Intervals	Average Remaining Life Time — Average Number of Years of Life Remaining at Beginning of Age Interval
x to x + 4	$1,000\,{}_n q_x$	ℓ_x	${}_n d_x$	${}_n L_x$	T_x	${}^o e_x$
0	53.03	10,000	530	9,592	623,707	62.4
1	9.67	9,470	92	9,419	614,115	64.8
2	5.96	9,378	56	9,350	604,696	64.5
3	4.71	9,322	44	9,300	595,346	63.9
4	3.37	9,278	31	9,263	586,046	63.2
5– 9	9.65	9,247	89	46,013	576,783	62.4
10–14	5.93	9,158	54	45,655	530,770	58.0
15–19	7.62	9,104	69	45,348	485,115	53.3
20–24	9.06	9,035	82	44,970	439,767	48.7
25–29	10.59	8,953	95	44,528	394,797	44.1
30–34	13.56	8,858	120	43,990	350,269	39.5
35–39	17.35	8,738	152	43,310	306,279	35.1
40–44	25.57	8,586	220	42,380	262,969	30.6
45–49	39.41	8,366	330	41,005	220,589	26.4
50–54	63.56	8,036	511	38,903	179,584	22.3
55–59	96.28	7,525	725	35,813	140,681	18.7
60–64	154.30	6,800	1,049	31,378	104,868	15.4
65–69	223.68	5,751	1,286	25,540	73,490	12.8
70–74	290.67	4,465	1,298	19,080	47,950	10.7
75–79	389.82	3,167	1,235	12,748	28,870	9.1
80–84	432.85	1,932	836	7,570	16,122	8.3
85 & Over	1,000.00	1,096	1,096	8,552	8,552	7.8

TABLE A.4
ABRIDGED LIFE TABLE FOR MALAY FEMALES, 1969–71

Year of Age	Mortality Rate Number Dying per 1,000 Alive at Beginning of Age Interval	Of 10,000 Born Alive Number Alive at Beginning of Age Interval	Number Dying during Age Interval	Stationery Population In the Age Interval	In this and all Subsequent Age Intervals	Average Remaining Life Time Average Number of Years of Life Remaining at Beginning of Age Interval
x to $x+4$	$1{,}000 \, _n q_x$	l_x	$_n d_x$	$_n L_x$	T_x	$\overset{o}{e}_x$
0	41.13	10,000	411	9,688	642,763	64.3
1	9.13	9,589	88	9,541	633,075	66.0
2	6.03	9,501	57	9,473	623,534	65.6
3	4.69	9,444	44	9,422	614,061	65.0
4	3.37	9,400	32	9,384	604,639	64.3
5– 9	9.01	9,368	84	46,630	595,255	63.5
10–14	5.19	9,284	48	46,300	548,625	59.1
15–19	6.63	9,236	61	46,028	502,325	54.4
20–24	9.60	9,175	88	45,655	456,297	49.7
25–29	12.82	9,087	116	45,145	410,642	41.2
30–34	15.77	8,971	141	44,503	365,497	40.7
35–39	19.90	8,830	176	43,710	320,994	36.4
40–44	24.30	8,654	210	42,745	277,284	32.0
45–49	33.91	8,444	286	41,505	234,539	27.8
50–54	57.69	8,158	471	39,613	193,034	23.7
55–59	81.76	7,687	628	36,865	153,421	20.0
60–64	142.00	7,059	1,002	32,790	116,556	16.5
65–69	200.71	6,057	1,216	27,245	83,766	13.8
70–74	272.96	4,841	1,321	20,903	56,521	11.7
75–79	340.80	3,520	1,200	14,600	35,618	10.1
80–84	391.02	2,320	907	9,333	21,018	9.1
85 & Over	1,000.00	1,413	1,413	11,685	11,685	8.3

TABLE A.5
ABRIDGED LIFE TABLE FOR CHINESE MALES, 1969–71

Year of Age	Mortality Rate	Of 10,000 Born Alive		Stationery Population		Average Remaining Life Time
	Number Dying per 1,000 Alive at Beginning of Age Interval	Number Alive at Beginning of Age Interval	Number Dying during Age Interval	In the Age Interval	In this and all Subsequent Age Intervals	Average Number of Years of Life Remaining at Beginning of Age Interval
x to x + 4	$1,000{}_nq_x$	ℓ_x	$_nd_x$	$_nL_x$	T_x	$\overset{o}{e}_x$
0	31.67	10,000	317	9,736	642,626	64.3
1	4.15	9,683	40	9,661	632,890	65.4
2	2.40	9,643	23	9,632	623,229	64.6
3	1.85	9,620	18	9,611	613,597	63.8
4	1.28	9,602	12	9,596	603,986	62.9
5– 9	4.29	9,590	41	48,053	594,390	62.0
10–14	4.09	9,631	39	48,058	546,337	56.7
15–19	6.53	9,592	63	47,803	498,279	51.9
20–24	10.84	9,529	103	47,388	450,476	47.3
25–29	10.84	9,426	102	46,875	403,088	42.8
30–34	12.27	9,324	114	46,335	356,213	38.2
35–39	16.07	9,210	148	45,680	309,878	33.6
40–44	23.96	9,062	217	44,768	264,198	29.2
45–49	37.15	8,845	329	43,403	219,430	24.8
50–54	67.87	8,516	578	41,135	176,027	20.7
55–59	105.52	7,938	838	37,595	134,892	17.0
60–64	163.20	7,100	1,159	32,603	97,297	13.7
65–69	234.23	5,941	1,392	26,225	64,694	10.9
70–74	352.93	4,549	1,605	18,733	38,469	8.5
75–79	467.64	2,944	1,377	11,278	19,736	6.7
80–84	600.69	1,567	941	5,483	8,458	5.4
85 & Over	1,000.00	626	626	2,975	2,975	4.8

TABLE A.6
ABRIDGED LIFE TABLE FOR CHINESE FEMALES, 1969–71

Year of Age	Mortality Rate	Of 10,000 Born Alive		Stationery Population		Average Remaining Life Time
	Number Dying per 1,000 Alive at Beginning of Age Interval	Number Alive at Beginning of Age Interval	Number Dying during Age Interval	In the Age Interval	In this and all Subsequent Age Intervals	Average Number of Years of Life Remaining at Beginning of Age Interval
x to $x + 4$	$1,000{}_nq_x$	ℓ_x	${}_nd_x$	${}_nL_x$	T_x	$\overset{\circ}{e}_x$
0	24.42	10,000	244	9,804	712,040	71.2
1	3.68	9,756	36	9,736	702,236	72.0
2	2.32	9,720	23	9,709	692,500	71.2
3	1.67	9,697	16	9,689	682,791	70.4
4	1.11	9,681	11	9,676	673,102	69.5
5– 9	3.69	9,670	36	48,260	663,426	68.6
10–14	2.65	9,634	26	48,105	615,166	63.9
15–19	3.44	9,608	33	47,958	567,061	59.0
20–24	4.79	9,575	46	47,760	519,103	54.2
25–29	5.09	9,529	49	47,523	471,343	49.5
30–34	7.77	9,480	74	47,215	423,820	44.7
35–39	9.80	9,406	92	46,800	376,605	40.0
40–44	15.13	9,314	141	46,218	329,805	35.4
45–49	22.74	9,173	209	45,343	283,587	30.9
50–54	33.24	8,964	298	44,075	238,244	26.6
55–59	52.39	8,666	454	42,195	194,169	22.4
60–64	81.95	8,212	673	39,378	151,974	18.5
65–69	125.23	7,539	944	35,335	112,596	14.9
70–74	208.37	6,595	1,374	29,540	77,261	11.7
75–79	304.65	5,221	1,591	22,128	47,721	9.1
80–84	443.28	3,630	1,609	14,128	25,593	7.1
85 & Over	1,000.00	2,021	2,021	11,465	11,465	5.7

TABLE A.7
ABRIDGED LIFE TABLE FOR INDIAN MALES, 1969–71

Year of Age	Mortality Rate — Number Dying per 1,000 Alive at Beginning of Age Interval	Of 10,000 Born Alive — Number Alive at Beginning of Age Interval	Number Dying during Age Interval	Stationery Population — In the Age Interval	Stationery Population — In this and all Subsequent Age Intervals	Average Remaining Life Time — Average Number of Years of Life Remaining at Beginning of Age Interval
x to $x+4$	$1,000 {}_{n}q_{x}$	ℓ_{x}	${}_{n}d_{x}$	${}_{n}L_{x}$	T_{x}	$\overset{o}{e}_{x}$
0	53.48	10,000	535	9,582	584,519	58.5
1	8.98	9,465	85	9,418	574,937	60.7
2	4.54	9,380	43	9,359	565,519	60.3
3	3.13	9,337	29	9,323	556,160	59.6
4	2.56	9,308	24	9,296	546,837	58.7
5– 9	7.52	9,284	70	46,245	537,541	57.9
10–14	5.68	9,214	52	45,940	491,296	53.3
15–19	8.32	9,162	76	45,620	445,356	48.6
20–24	11.09	9,086	101	45,178	399,736	44.0
25–29	14.49	8,985	131	44,598	354,558	39.5
30–34	18.87	8,854	167	43,853	309,960	35.0
35–39	26.10	8,687	227	42,868	266,107	30.6
40–44	37.77	8,460	320	41,500	223,239	26.4
45–49	59.15	8,140	481	39,498	181,739	22.3
50–54	93.69	7,659	718	36,500	142,241	18.6
55–59	138.41	6,941	961	32,303	105,741	15.2
60–64	207.93	5,980	1,243	26,793	73,438	12.3
65–69	293.95	4,737	1,392	20,205	46,645	9.8
70–74	408.69	3,345	1,367	13,308	26,440	7.9
75–79	514.54	1,978	1,018	7,345	13,132	6.6
80–84	583.80	960	560	3,400	5,787	6.0
85 & Over	1,000.00	400	400	2,387	2,387	6.0

TABLE A.8
ABRIDGED LIFE TABLE FOR INDIAN FEMALES, 1969–71

Year of Age	Mortality Rate	Of 10,000 Born Alive		Stationery Population		Average Remaining Life Time
	Number Dying per 1,000 Alive at Beginning of Age Interval	Number Alive at Beginning of Age Interval	Number Dying during Age Interval	In the Age Interval	In this and all Subsequent Age Intervals	Average Number of Years of Life Remaining at Beginning of Age Interval
x to x + 4	$1,000_nq_x$	l_x	$_nd_x$	$_nL_x$	T_x	$\overset{o}{e}_x$
0	42.09	10,000	421	9,679	611,247	61.1
1	9.55	9,579	91	9,529	601,568	62.8
2	5.04	9,488	48	9,464	592,039	62.4
3	3.46	9,440	33	9,424	582,575	61.7
4	2.68	9,407	25	9,395	573,151	60.9
5– 9	8.07	9,382	76	46,720	563,756	60.1
10–14	4.79	9,306	45	46,413	517,036	55.6
15–19	7.97	9,259	74	46,110	470,623	50.8
20–24	11.34	9,185	104	45,665	424,513	46.2
25–29	11.88	9,081	108	45,135	378,848	41.7
30–34	16.17	8,973	145	44,503	333,713	37.2
35–39	19.56	8,828	173	43,708	289,210	32.8
40–44	28.15	8,655	244	42,665	245,502	28.4
45–49	42.77	8,411	360	41,155	202,837	24.1
50–54	70.76	8,051	570	38,830	161,682	20.1
55–59	118.58	7,481	887	35,188	122,852	16.4
60–64	179.71	6,594	1,185	30,008	87,664	13.3
65–69	280.61	5,409	1,518	23,250	57,656	10.7
70–74	379.88	3,891	1,478	15,760	34,406	8.8
75–79	470.77	2,413	1,136	9,225	18,646	7.7
80–84	498.30	1,277	636	4,795	9,421	7.4
85 & Over	1,000.00	641	641	4,626	4,626	7.2

TABLE A.9
ABRIDGED LIFE TABLE FOR ALL RACES MALES, 1979–81

Year of Age	Mortality Rate — Number Dying per 1,000 Alive at Beginning of Age Interval	Of 10,000 Born Alive — Number Alive at Beginning of Age Interval	Of 10,000 Born Alive — Number Dying during Age Interval	Stationery Population — In the Age Interval	Stationery Population — In this and all Subsequent Age Intervals	Average Remaining Life Time — Average Number of Years of Life Remaining at Beginning of Age Interval
x to $x+4$	$1,000 \cdot {}_nq_x$	ℓ_x	${}_nd_x$	${}_nL_x$	T_x	$\overset{o}{e}_x$
0	27.17	10,000	272	9,784	662,575	66.3
1	3.77	9,728	37	9,708	652,791	67.1
2	2.12	9,691	21	9,681	643,083	66.4
3	1.51	9,670	15	9,663	633,402	65.5
4	1.27	9,655	12	9,649	623,739	64.6
5– 9	4.54	9,643	44	48,105	614,090	63.7
10–14	3.69	9,599	35	47,825	565,985	59.0
15–19	6.43	9,564	61	47,668	518,160	54.2
20–24	9.80	9,503	93	47,283	470,492	49.5
25–29	10.20	9,410	96	46,810	423,209	45.0
30–34	10.25	9,314	95	46,333	370,399	39.8
35–39	13.46	9,219	124	45,785	330,066	35.8
40–44	20.68	9,095	188	45,005	284,281	31.3
45–49	34.59	8,907	308	43,765	239,276	26.9
50–54	55.00	8,599	473	41,813	195,511	22.7
55–59	87.31	8,126	709	38,858	153,698	18.9
60–64	134.72	7,417	999	34,588	114,840	15.5
65–69	209.41	6,418	1,344	28,730	80,252	12.5
70–74	285.47	5,074	1,448	21,750	51,522	10.2
75–79	395.99	3,626	1,436	14,540	29,772	8.2
80–84	494.12	2,190	1,082	8,245	15,232	7.0
85 & Over	1,000.00	1,108	1,108	6,987	6,987	6.3

TABLE A.10
ABRIDGED LIFE TABLE FOR ALL RACES FEMALES, 1979–81

Year of Age	Mortality Rate	Of 10,000 Born Alive		Stationery Population		Average Remaining Life Time
	Number Dying per 1,000 Alive at Beginning of Age Interval	Number Alive at Beginning of Age Interval	Number Dying during Age Interval	In the Age Interval	In this and all Subsequent Age Intervals	Average Number of Years of Life Remaining at Beginning of Age Interval
x to x + 4	$1,000_nq_x$	ℓ_x	$_nd_x$	$_nI_x$	T_x	$\overset{o}{e}_x$
0	21.38	10,000	214	9,833	711,515	71.2
1	3.51	9,786	34	9,767	701,682	71.7
2	2.21	9,752	22	9,741	691,915	71.0
3	1.60	9,730	16	9,722	682,174	70.1
4	1.24	9,714	12	9,708	672,452	69.2
5– 9	3.64	9,702	35	48,448	662,744	68.3
10–14	2.65	9,667	26	48,270	614,296	63.5
15–19	3.69	9,641	36	48,115	566,026	58.7
20–24	4.74	9,605	46	47,910	517,911	53.9
25–29	5.53	9,559	53	47,663	470,001	49.2
30–34	7.67	9,506	73	47,348	422,338	44.4
35–39	10.09	9,433	95	46,928	374,990	39.8
40–44	14.29	9,338	133	46,358	328,062	35.1
45–49	21.32	9,205	196	45,535	281,704	30.6
50–54	33.72	9,009	304	44,285	236,169	26.2
55–59	57.26	8,705	498	42,280	191,884	22.0
60–64	93.92	8,207	771	39,108	149,604	18.2
65–69	146.99	7,436	1,093	34,448	110,496	14.9
70–74	222.93	6,343	1,414	28,180	76,048	12.0
75–79	309.13	4,929	1,524	20,835	47,868	9.7
80–84	417.00	3,405	1,420	13,475	27,033	7.9
85 & Over	1,000.00	1,985	1,985	13,558	13,558	6.8

TABLE A.11
ABRIDGED LIFE TABLE FOR MALAY MALES, 1979–81

Year of Age	Mortality Rate	Of 10,000 Born Alive		Stationery Population		Average Remaining Life Time
	Number Dying per 1,000 Alive at Beginning of Age Interval	Number Alive at Beginning of Age Interval	Number Dying during Age Interval	In the Age Interval	In this and all Subsequent Age Intervals	Average Number of Years of Life Remaining at Beginning of Age Interval
x to x + 4	$1,000{}_nq_x$	ℓ_x	${}_nd_x$	${}_nL_x$	T_x	$\overset{o}{e}_x$
0	30.80	10,000	308	9,758	670,537	67.1
1	4.59	9,692	44	9,668	660,779	68.2
2	2.88	9,648	28	9,634	651,111	67.5
3	1.83	9,620	18	9,611	641,477	66.7
4	1.62	9,602	16	9,594	631,866	65.8
5– 9	5.44	9,586	52	47,800	622,272	64.9
10–14	3.79	9,534	36	47,580	574,472	60.3
15–19	5.93	9,498	56	47,350	526,892	55.5
20–24	8.86	9,442	84	47,000	479,542	50.8
25–29	9.36	9,358	88	46,570	432,542	46.2
30–34	9.46	9,270	88	46,130	385,972	41.6
35–39	12.57	9,182	115	45,623	339,842	37.0
40–44	19.02	9,067	172	44,905	294,219	32.4
45–49	29.80	8,895	265	43,813	249,314	28.0
50–54	51.20	8,630	442	42,045	205,501	23.8
55–59	80.29	8,188	657	39,298	163,456	20.0
60–64	122.77	7,531	925	35,343	124,158	16.5
65–69	192.74	6,606	1,273	29,848	88,815	13.4
70–74	264.27	5,333	1,409	23,143	58,967	11.1
75–79	374.71	3,924	1,470	15,945	35,824	9.1
80–84	446.36	2,454	1,095	9,533	19,879	8.1
85 & Over	1,000.00	1,359	1,359	10,346	10,346	7.6

TABLE A.12
ABRIDGED LIFE TABLE FOR MALAY FEMALES, 1979–81

Year of Age	Mortality Rate	Of 10,000 Born Alive		Stationery Population		Average Remaining Life Time
	Number Dying per 1,000 Alive at Beginning of Age Interval	Number Alive at Beginning of Age Interval	Number Dying during Age Interval	In the Age Interval	In this and all Subsequent Age Intervals	Average Number of Years of Life Remaining at Beginning of Age Interval
x to x + 4	$1,000{}_n q_x$	ℓ_x	$_n d_x$	$_n L_x$	T_x	$\overset{\circ}{e}_x$
0	23.69	10,000	237	9,819	703,590	70.4
1	4.18	9,763	41	9,740	693,771	71.1
2	2.71	9,722	26	9,709	684,031	70.4
3	1.97	9,696	19	9,687	674,322	69.5
4	1.56	9,677	15	9,670	664,635	68.7
5– 9	4.39	9,662	42	48,205	654,965	67.8
10–14	3.05	9,620	29	48,028	606,760	63.1
15–19	3.49	9,591	33	47,873	558,732	58.3
20–24	4.49	9,558	43	47,683	510,859	53.4
25–29	5.88	9,515	56	47,435	463,176	48.7
30–34	8.76	9,459	83	47,088	415,741	44.0
35–39	11.73	9,376	110	46,605	368,653	39.3
40–44	15.33	9,266	142	45,975	322,048	34.8
45–49	22.05	9,124	201	45,118	276,073	30.3
50–54	35.56	8,923	317	43,823	230,955	25.9
55–59	61.83	8,606	532	41,700	187,132	21.7
60–64	101.21	8,074	817	38,328	145,432	18.0
65–69	163.66	7,257	1,188	33,315	107,104	14.8
70–74	247.73	6,069	1,503	26,588	73,789	12.2
75–79	330.34	4,566	1,508	19,065	47,201	10.3
80–84	409.54	3,060	1,253	12,168	28,136	9.2
85 & Over	1,000.00	1,807	1,807	15,969	15,969	8.8

TABLE A.13
ABRIDGED LIFE TABLE FOR CHINESE MALES, 1979–81

Year of Age	Mortality Rate	Of 10,000 Born Alive		Stationery Population		Average Remaining Life Time
	Number Dying per 1,000 Alive at Beginning of Age Interval	Number Alive at Beginning of Age Interval	Number Dying during Age Interval	In the Age Interval	In this and all Subsequent Age Intervals	Average Number of Years of Life Remaining at Beginning of Age Interval
x to x + 4	$1,000_nq_x$	l_x	$_nd_x$	$_nL_x$	T_x	$\overset{o}{e}_x$
0	18.84	10,000	188	9,839	675,967	67.6
1	1.55	9,812	15	9,804	666,128	67.9
2	1.23	9,797	12	9,791	656,324	67.0
3	0.89	9,785	9	9,781	646,533	66.1
4	0.59	9,776	6	9,773	636,752	65.1
5– 9	2.90	9,770	28	48,780	626,979	64.2
10–14	3.15	9,742	31	48,633	578,199	59.4
15–19	6.78	9,711	66	48,390	529,566	54.5
20–24	10.15	9,645	98	47,980	481,176	49.9
25–29	9.70	9,547	93	47,503	433,196	45.4
30–34	9.60	9,454	91	47,043	385,693	40.8
35–39	12.37	9,363	116	46,510	338,650	36.2
40–44	18.62	9,247	172	45,805	292,140	31.6
45–49	33.04	9,075	300	44,625	246,335	27.1
50–54	52.96	8,775	465	42,713	201,710	23.0
55–59	82.32	8,310	684	39,840	158,997	19.1
60–64	130.36	7,626	994	35,645	119,157	15.6
65–69	204.99	6,632	1,359	29,763	83,512	12.6
70–74	239.75	5,273	1,264	23,205	53,749	10.2
75–79	396.28	4,009	1,589	16,073	30,544	7.6
80–84	531.49	2,420	1,286	8,885	14,471	6.0
85 & Over	1,000.00	1,134	1,134	5,586	5,586	4.9

TABLE A.14
ABRIDGED LIFE TABLE FOR CHINESE FEMALES, 1979–81

Year of Age	Mortality Rate	Of 10,000 Born Alive		Stationery Population		Average Remaining Life Time
	Number Dying per 1,000 Alive at Beginning of Age Interval	Number Alive at Beginning of Age Interval	Number Dying during Age Interval	In the Age Interval	In this and all Subsequent Age Intervals	Average Number of Years of Life Remaining at Beginning of Age Interval
x to x + 4	$1{,}000_nq_x$	l_x	$_nd_x$	$_nL_x$	T_x	$\overset{o}{e}_x$
0	14.77	10,000	148	9,876	739,075	73.9
1	1.76	9,852	17	9,843	729,199	74.0
2	1.04	9,835	10	9,830	719,356	73.1
3	0.71	9,825	7	9,822	709,526	72.2
4	0.54	9,818	5	9,816	699,704	71.3
5– 9	2.15	9,813	21	49,013	689,888	70.3
10–14	1.75	9,792	17	48,918	640,875	65.4
15–19	2.80	9,775	27	48,808	591,957	60.6
20–24	3.74	9,748	36	48,650	543,149	55.7
25–29	4.19	9,712	41	48,458	494,499	50.9
30–34	5.63	9,671	54	48,220	446,041	46.1
35–39	7.12	9,617	68	47,915	397,821	41.4
40–44	10.49	9,549	100	47,495	349,906	36.6
45–49	17.74	9,449	168	46,825	302,411	32.0
50–54	26.98	9,281	250	45,780	255,586	27.5
55–59	42.05	9,031	380	44,205	209,806	23.2
60–64	72.29	8,651	625	41,693	165,601	19.1
65–69	118.09	8,026	948	37,760	123,908	15.4
70–74	185.20	7,078	1,311	32,113	86,148	12.2
75–79	281.23	5,767	1,622	24,780	54,035	9.4
80–84	419.53	4,145	1,739	16,378	29,255	7.1
85 & Over	1,000.00	2,406	2,406	12,877	12,877	5.4

TABLE A.15
ABRIDGED LIFE TABLE FOR INDIAN MALES, 1979-81

Year of Age	Mortality Rate	Of 10,000 Born Alive		Stationery Population		Average Remaining Life Time
	Number Dying per 1,000 Alive at Beginning of Age Interval	Number Alive at Beginning of Age Interval	Number Dying during Age Interval	In the Age Interval	In this and all Subsequent Age Intervals	Average Number of Years of Life Remaining at Beginning of Age Interval
x to x + 4	$1,000_nq_x$	l_x	$_nd_x$	$_nL_x$	T_x	$\overset{o}{e}_x$
0	29.52	10,000	295	9,772	610,338	61.0
1	4.60	9,705	45	9,680	600,566	61.9
2	2.42	9,660	23	9,649	590,886	61.2
3	1.58	9,637	15	9,630	581,237	60.3
4	1.42	9,622	14	9,615	571,607	59.4
5- 9	4.64	9,608	45	47,928	561,992	58.5
10-14	5.04	9,563	48	47,695	514,064	53.8
15-19	8.12	9,515	77	47,383	466,369	49.0
20-24	12.82	9,438	121	46,888	418,986	44.4
25-29	15.18	9,317	141	46,233	372,098	39.9
30-34	15.82	9,176	145	45,518	325,865	35.5
35-39	23.62	9,031	213	44,623	280,347	31.0
40-44	38.01	8,818	335	43,253	235,724	26.7
45-49	60.75	8,483	515	41,128	192,471	22.7
50-54	96.37	7,968	768	37,920	151,343	19.0
55-59	129.62	7,200	933	33,668	113,423	15.8
60-64	196.57	6,267	1,232	28,255	79,755	12.7
65-69	289.50	5,035	1,458	21,530	51,500	10.2
70-74	366.38	3,577	1,311	14,608	29,970	8.4
75-79	485.25	2,266	1,100	8,580	15,362	6.8
80-84	582.36	1,166	679	4,133	6,782	5.8
85 & Over	1,000.00	487	487	2,649	2,649	5.4

TABLE A.16
ABRIDGED LIFE TABLE FOR INDIAN FEMALES, 1979–81

Year of Age	Mortality Rate	Of 10,000 Born Alive		Stationery Population		Average Remaining Life Time
	Number Dying per 1,000 Alive at Beginning of Age Interval	Number Alive at Beginning of Age Interval	Number Dying during Age Interval	In the Age Interval	In this and all Subsequent Age Intervals	Average Number of Years of Life Remaining at Beginning of Age Interval
x to x + 4	$1,000 \, {}_n q_x$	l_x	${}_n d_x$	${}_n L_x$	T_x	$\overset{o}{e}_x$
0	26.21	10,000	262	9,801	665,706	66.6
1	4.37	9,738	43	9,714	655,905	67.4
2	2.73	9,695	26	9,682	646,191	66.7
3	2.04	9,669	20	9,659	636,509	65.8
4	1.60	9,649	15	9,642	626,850	65.0
5– 9	3.89	9,634	37	48,078	617,208	64.1
10–14	3.19	9,597	31	47,908	569,130	59.3
15–19	7.22	9,566	69	47,658	521,222	54.5
20–24	8.46	9,497	80	47,285	473,564	49.9
25–29	7.97	9,417	75	46,898	426,279	45.3
30–34	9.26	9,342	87	46,493	379,381	40.6
35–39	12.47	9,255	115	45,988	332,888	36.0
40–44	21.37	9,140	196	45,210	286,900	31.4
45–49	29.46	8,944	263	44,063	241,690	27.0
50–54	49.07	8,681	426	42,340	197,627	22.8
55–59	79.32	8,255	655	39,638	155,287	18.8
60–64	142.73	7,600	1,085	35,288	115,649	15.2
65–69	215.92	6,515	1,407	29,058	80,361	12.3
70–74	300.01	5,108	1,532	21,710	51,303	10.0
75–79	437.03	3,576	1,563	13,973	29,593	8.3
80–84	472.44	2,013	951	7,688	15,620	7.8
85 & Over	1,000.00	1,062	1,062	7,932	7,932	7.5

APPENDIX B
ABRIDGED MALE WORKING LIFE TABLES

Introduction

The table of working life is essentially an elaboration of the ordinary life table based on the mortality experience of a past period, but it is different in that it also reflects the losses through causes other than death of a past period. It therefore shows what will happen to the working population in the future if these rates of losses remained unchanged. The table is built in such a manner as to provide information on the expected average number of years of working life remaining to those in a given age, on the chances that a man aged thirty will still be in the working population at age 60, on the pattern of withdrawals from the working population due to death and other causes, and on many other facets of working life. Among the principal uses of the working life table are the computation of annual losses from the actual working population, the estimation of future replacement needs in any particular occupation or industry, and the reckoning for social security purposes of the man-years lost by persons of known age incurring industrial accidents.

In this appendix we will discuss the methodology used in the computation of two sets of male working life tables for the years 1970 and 1980. For each set, four separate male working life tables are proposed for all races combined and for each of the three main races, the Malays, the Chinese and the Indians. The techniques described here are applicable to the construction of all the tables.

Data Used

The construction of the working life tables is essentially patterned on the ordinary life tables but it requires additional data on the working population. The first set of data used in the preparation of the tables refers to the ordinary male life tables for the two periods 1969–71 and 1979–81 which have been prepared in the previous appendix. More specifically, what we require from these life tables are the l_x values for ages at five-year intervals from age 10 to 75, the T_x value for age 75 and over, the d_x values for age groups 10–14 and 75 and over, and the L_x values, for age groups 10–14 and 75 and over. The second set of information required refers to the male working population enumerated in the 1970 and the 1980 Population Census. The term "working population" is used to refer to the economically active population identified in the population census by means of the labour force approached. The definition and method of obtaining the economically active population have been discussed in Chapter 7.

From the census data, we compute the percentage of male working population to the total male population in the various quinary age groups from age 10 to 65 and over for 1970 and 1980. The computed percentages designated as $_5W_x$, for the all races males and for males of the three main races are laid-out in the first column of Tables B.1 and B.2. A problem that has to be resolved concerns the fact that not all entrants to the labour force enter at the same age. If the working population at each age group is based on the actual proportion working at that age group (first column in Tables B.1 and B.2), the mean years of work per generation is correctly calculated, and, for some purposes, this is required. However, for purpose of estimating the expected years of working life and of retirement at each age group, this actual proportion cannot be used because at ages below that at which the last entrant enters, the total working life of the generation includes work of those yet to enter. If this was shared between the smaller numbers who have already entered the working population, false answers would be given. This may be overcome by using at age groups when all entrants have not yet entered, not the actual proportion working but the maximum value of this proportion in any quinary age group. This hypothetical proportion denoted as $_5W'_x$ is given in the second column in Tables B.1 and B.2, and may be interpreted as the proportion who have entered or are in training for employment. In other words, it represents the ratio of the actual and potential entrants into the labour force at a given age x or at some future point in their life time.

Derivation of Various Functions

The W_x function of the working life table refers to the proportion of persons in the working population at the beginning of the age interval. The values are calculated according to the formula $W_x = \frac{1}{2}(_5W'_x + _5W'_{x-5})$ where $_5W'_x$ is the proportion of working persons who have reached the xth birthday but have not reached their $(x + 5)^{th}$ birthday.

The ℓ_x^W function represents the number of persons in the working population at the beginning of the age interval out of the original cohort of 10,000 at birth. The figures are obtained by multiplying W_x by the corresponding ℓ_x given in the ordinary life table. Thus, $\ell_x^W = W_x \cdot_x$.

The $_5L_x^W$ function shows the number of man-years that will be lived collectively in the working population within any one age interval by a cohort numbering 10,000 at birth. On the assumption that withdrawals from the working population are uniformly distributed over the age interval, the values can be obtained by taking the product of the average number of persons in the working population within any age interval and the length of the interval. Thus, $_5L_x^W = \frac{5}{2}(\ell_x^W + \ell_{x+5}^W)$.

TABLE B.1
PROPORTION OF MALE WORKING POPULATION TO TOTAL MALE POPULATION OF AGE GROUP AND RACE, 1980

Age Group x to x+4 l.b.d.	Actual Proportion Working in Age Group from Exact Age x to x+5	Hypothetical Proportion Working in Age Group from Exact Age x to x+5	Actual Proportion Working in Age Group from Exact Age x to x+5	Hypothetical Proportion Working in Age Group from Exact Age x to x+5
	$_5W_x$	$_5W'_x$	$_5W_x$	$_5W'_x$
	All Races Males		**Malay Males**	
10–14	8.46	94.25	8.51	93.22
15–19	52.25	94.25	52.58	93.22
20–24	86.90	94.25	85.77	93.22
25–29	93.37	94.25	92.26	93.22
30–34	94.25	94.25	93.14	93.22
35–39	94.13	94.19	93.22	93.22
40–44	93.09	93.61	92.37	92.80
45–49	91.38	92.24	90.89	91.63
50–54	86.57	88.98	87.29	89.09
55–59	75.39	80.98	78.94	83.12
60–64	64.98	70.19	71.49	75.22
65 & Over	45.69	55.34	53.94	62.72
	Chinese Males		**Indian Males**	
10–14	8.81	95.38	7.01	95.70
15–19	53.18	95.38	47.45	95.70
20–24	88.64	95.38	86.48	95.70
25–29	94.65	95.38	93.96	95.70
30–34	95.38	95.38	95.70	95.70
35–39	94.90	95.14	95.40	95.55
40–44	93.86	94.38	94.13	94.77
45–49	91.80	92.83	92.29	93.21
50–54	85.50	88.65	85.92	89.11
55–59	75.54	80.52	64.04	74.99
60–64	63.10	69.32	47.14	55.59
65 & Over	40.52	51.81	29.91	38.53

TABLE B.2
PROPORTION OF MALE WORKING POPULATION TO TOTAL MALE POPULATION OF AGE GROUP AND RACE, 1980

Age Group x to x+4 1.b.d.	Actual Proportion Working in Age Group from Exact Age x to x+5 $_5W_x$	Hypothetical Proportion Working in Age Group from Exact Age x to x+5 $_5W'_x$	Actual Proportion Working in Age Group from Exact Age x to x+4 $_5W_x$	Hypothetical Proportion Working in Age Group from Exact Age x to x+4 $_5W'_x$
	All Races Males		**Malay Males**	
10–14	7.75	97.94	6.78	97.82
15–19	47.33	97.94	44.24	97.82
20–24	90.63	97.94	89.88	97.82
25–29	97.09	97.94	97.00	97.82
30–34	97.71	97.94	97.59	97.82
35–39	97.94	97.74	97.82	97.82
40–44	97.48	97.71	97.37	97.60
45–49	96.36	96.92	96.44	96.91
50–54	92.31	94.34	93.54	94.99
55–59	76.78	84.55	81.05	87.30
60–64	68.11	72.45	76.38	78.72
65 & Over	48.66	58.39	60.41	68.40
	Chinese Males		**Indian Males**	
10–14	9.02	98.09	8.93	98.08
15–19	51.31	98.09	51.26	98.08
20–24	91.50	98.09	92.05	92.05
25–29	97.25	98.09	97.26	98.08
30–34	97.85	98.09	97.83	98.08
35–39	98.09	98.09	98.08	98.08
40–44	97.65	97.85	97.45	97.77
45–49	96.42	97.04	95.81	96.63
50–54	90.46	93.44	91.24	93.53
55–59	74.19	82.33	63.30	77.27
60–64	60.62	67.41	50.04	56.67
65 & Over	39.00	49.81	33.48	42.01

The T_x^W function indicates the number of man-years that will be lived collectively in the working population, from the given age upwards, by the survivors to that age from the original cohort of 10,000 at birth. The values of T_x^W may be obtained by cumulative additions of the $_5L_x^W$ column from the bottom up. For the last age group, we may equate T_{65}^W to $W_{65}.T_{65}$, where W_{65} is the proportion of working population aged 65 and over and T_{65} the total number of man-years lived collectively from age 65 upwards by the survivors to this age from the original cohort of 10,000 births obtained from the ordinary male life tables.

The $\overset{ow}{e}_x$ function represents the average expectation of working life for the working population at the beginning of the age interval. The values are computed by dividing T_x^W by the corresponding ℓ_x^w. Thus, $\overset{ow}{e}_x = \dfrac{T_x^W}{\ell_x^w}$.

The $_5s_x^W$ function refers to the total number of persons lost from the working population within the age interval resulting from death and other causes. The values are derived by differencing of successive figures in the ℓ_x^w column. Thus, $_5s_x^W = \ell_x^w - \ell_{x+5}^w$.

The $_5d_x^W$ function shows the number of death occurring in the working population within an age interval, and is based on the assumption that the central death rate in the working population of any age interval is the same as that in the overall population of the corresponding age interval.[1] The latter death rate is equal to $_5d_x/_5L_x$, and this multiplied by the average number of persons in the working population $_5L_x^W$, will give the number of deaths from the working population. Thus, $_5d_x^W = {}_5L_x^W \left(\dfrac{_5d_x}{L_x} \right) = {}_5L_x^W._5m_x$.

The $_5r_x^W$ function represents the loss from the working population due to causes other than death, for instance illness, infirmity, old age and retirement. The values can be derived by subtracting each figure for $_5d_x^W$ from the corresponding figure for $_5s_x^W$. Thus, $_5r_x^W = {}_5s_x^W - {}_5d_x^W$.

---

1. For all quinary age groups up to 60 the margin of error involved in this assumption is perhaps very small as the working population forms a very large proportion of the total population. At the older age groups where the proportion becomes progressively smaller, the error would be somewhat greater. It is probably true that persons in the working population are healthier than those not in the working population, but they are affected by certain additional risks such as industrial accidents and other occupational hazards. See, for example, Saw Swee-Hock, "Occupational Mortality Variations in Singapore, 1970", *Journal of the Royal Statistical Society*, Series A (General), Vol. 139, Pt. 2, 1976.

The $_5m_x^s$, $_5m_x^d$ and $_5m_x^r$ functions refer to the central loss rates from the working population expressed in terms of per 1,000 of the working population as follows:

$$_5m_x^s = \frac{_5s_x^w}{_5L_x^w}, \quad _5m_x^d = \frac{_5s_x^d}{_5L_x^w} \quad \text{and} \quad _5m_x^r = \frac{_5r_x^d}{_5L_x^w}$$

It should be emphasized that

$$_5m_x^s = \ _5m_x^d + \ _5m_x^r \quad \text{and} \quad _5m_x^d = \ _5m_x = \frac{_5d_x}{_5L_x},$$

since the working population and the overall population have been assumed to experience the same mortality.

According to the techniques outlined above, the two sets of male working life tables for 1970 and 1980 for all races combined and for each of the three main races are compiled. The results of the computation are presented in full in Tables B.3 to B.10.

Working Life Table Probabilities

Apart from the information on the average expectation of working life and the central loss rates from the working population, the constructed tables of male working life provided data for deriving various probabilities of remaining in the working population or of leaving it owing to death or retirement. The general formulae for the principal probabilities are set out below.

1. The probability that a man in the working population aged x will leave the working population in n years' time because of death is

$$\frac{d_x^w + d_{x+5}^w + \ldots + d_{x+n-5}^w}{\ell_x^w}$$

2. The probability that a man in the working population aged x will leave the working population in n years' time from a cause other than death is

$$\frac{r_x^w + r_{x+5}^w + \ldots + r_{x+n-5}^w}{\ell_x^w}$$

3. The probability that a man in the working population aged x will leave the working population in n years' time is

$$\frac{\ell_x^w - \ell_{x+n}^w}{\ell_x^w}$$

4. The probability that a man in the working population aged x will still be in the working population in n years' time is

$$\frac{\ell^w_{x+n}}{\ell^w_x}.$$

TABLE B.3
ABRIDGED WORKING LIFE TABLE FOR ALL RACES MALES, 1970

Age Group x to x + 4 l.b.d.	Percentage of Population or Working Population at Exact Age x	Number of Working Population of 10,000 Born Alive			Expectation of Working Life at Exact Age x	Losses from the Working Population					
		At Exact Age x	From Exact Age x to x + 5	At Exact Age x and Above		Total		Due to Death		Due to Causes other than Death	
						Number	Per 1,000 in Working Population	Number	Per 1,000 in Working Population	Number	Per 1,000 in Working Population
x to x + 4	W_x	ℓ^w_x	$_5L^w_x$	T^w_x	e^{ow}_x	$_5d^w_x$	$1{,}000\,_5m^d_x$	$_5d_x$	$1{,}000\,_5m^d_x$	$_5r^w_x$	$1{,}000\,_5m^r_x$
10–14	94.25	8,760	43,683	443,812	50.7	47	1.1	47	1.1	—	—
15–19	94.25	8,713	43,408	400,129	45.9	63	1.5	63	1.5	—	—
20–24	94.25	8,650	43,035	356,721	41.2	86	2.0	86	2.0	—	—
25–29	94.25	8,564	42,580	313,686	36.6	96	2.3	96	2.3	—	—
30–34	94.25	8,468	42,038	271,106	32.0	121	2.9	121	2.9	—	—
35–39	94.19	8,347	41,235	229,068	27.4	200	4.9	148	3.6	52	1.3
40–44	93.61	8,147	39,935	187,833	23.1	320	8.0	204	5.1	116	2.9
45–49	92.24	7,827	37,655	147,898	18.9	592	15.7	320	8.5	272	7.2
50–54	88.98	7,235	33,400	110,243	15.2	1,110	33.2	484	14.5	626	18.7
55–59	80.98	6,125	27,195	76,843	12.5	1,372	50.5	601	22.1	771	28.4
60–64	70.19	4,753	19,705	49,648	10.4	1,624	82.4	709	36.0	915	46.4
65 & Over	55.34	3,129	29,943	29,943	9.6	3,129	104.5	2,377	79.4	752	25.1

TABLE B.4
ABRIDGED WORKING LIFE TABLE FOR MALAY MALES, 1970

Age Group x to x + 4 l.b.d.	Percentage of Population or Working Population at Exact Age x W_x	Number of Working Population of 10,000 Born Alive — At Exact Age x l^w_x	Number of Working Population of 10,000 Born Alive — From Exact Age x to x + 5 $5L^w_x$	Number of Working Population of 10,000 Born Alive — At Exact Age x and Above T^w_x	Expectation of Working Life at Exact Age x e^{ow}_x	Losses from the Working Population — Total — Number $5s^w_x$	Losses from the Working Population — Total — Per 1,000 in Working Population $1{,}000\,5m^d_x$	Losses from the Working Population — Due to Death — Number $5d_x$	Losses from the Working Population — Due to Death — Per 1,000 in Working Population $1{,}000\,5m^d_x$	Losses from the Working Population — Due to Causes other than Death — Number $5s^w_x$	Losses from the Working Population — Due to Causes other than Death — Per 1,000 in Working Population $1{,}000\,5m^r_x$
10–14	93.22	8,537	42,560	449,108	52.6	50	1.2	50	1.2	—	—
15–19	93.22	8,487	42,273	406,548	47.9	65	1.5	65	1.5	—	—
20–24	93.22	8,422	41,920	364,275	43.3	76	1.8	76	1.8	—	—
25–29	93.22	8,346	41,508	322,355	38.6	89	2.1	89	2.1	—	—
30–34	93.22	8,257	41,008	280,847	34.0	111	2.7	111	2.7	—	—
35–39	93.22	8,146	40,285	239,839	29.4	178	4.4	178	4.4	99	2.5
40–44	92.80	7,968	39,085	199,554	25.0	302	7.7	203	5.2	210	5.7
45–49	91.63	7,666	37,063	160,469	20.9	507	13.7	297	8.0	465	13.9
50–54	89.09	7,159	33,535	123,406	17.2	904	27.0	439	13.1	566	19.9
55–59	83.12	6,255	28,425	89,871	14.4	1,140	40.1	574	20.2	780	35.8
60–64	75.22	5,115	21,805	61,446	12.0	1,508	69.2	728	33.4	761	19.2
65 & Over	62.72	3,607	39,641	39,641	11.0	3,607	91.0	2,846	71.8		

TABLE B.5
ABRIDGED WORKING LIFE TABLE FOR CHINESE MALES, 1970

Age Group x to x+4 l.b.d.	Percentage of Population or Working Population at Exact Age x W_x	Number of Working Population of 10,000 Born Alive			Expectation of Working Life at Exact Age x e_x^{ow}	Losses from the Working Population					
		At Exact Age x ℓ_x^w	From Exact Age x to x+5 $_5L_x^w$	At Exact Age x and Above T_x^w		Total		Due to Death		Due to Causes other than Death	
						Number $_5s_x^w$	Per 1,000 in Working Population $1,000_5m_x^d$	Number $_5d_x$	Per 1,000 in Working Population $1,000_5m_x^d$	Number $_5s_x^w$	Per 1,000 in Working Population $1,000_5m_x^r$
10–14	95.38	9,186	45,838	459,431	50.0	37	0.8	37	0.8	—	—
15–19	95.38	9,149	45,595	413,593	45.2	60	1.3	60	1.3	—	—
20–24	95.38	9,089	45,200	367,998	40.5	98	2.2	98	2.2	—	—
25–29	95.38	8,991	44,710	322,798	35.9	98	2.2	98	2.2	—	—
30–34	95.38	8,893	44,138	278,088	31.3	131	3.0	131	3.0	—	—
35–39	95.14	8,762	43,288	233,950	26.7	209	4.8	139	3.2	70	1.6
40–44	94.38	8,553	41,910	190,662	22.3	342	8.2	205	4.9	137	3.3
45–49	92.83	8,211	39,400	148,752	18.1	662	16.8	299	7.6	363	9.2
50–54	88.65	7,549	34,853	109,352	14.5	1,157	33.2	488	14.0	669	19.2
55–59	80.52	6,392	28,285	74,499	11.7	1,470	52.0	631	22.3	839	29.7
60–64	69.32	4,922	20,000	46,214	9.4	1,844	92.2	710	35.5	1,134	56.7
65 & Over	51.81	3,078	26,214	26,214	8.5	3,078	117.4	2,197	83.8	881	33.6

TABLE B.6
ABRIDGED WORKING LIFE TABLE FOR INDIAN MALES, 1970

Age Group x to x+4 l.b.d.	Percentage of Population or Working Population at Exact Age x W_x	Number of Working Population of 10,000 Born Alive			Expectation of Working Life at Exact Age x e_x^{ow}	Losses from the Working Population					
						Total		Due to Death		Due to Causes other than Death	
		At Exact Age x l_x^w	From Exact Age x to x+5 $_5L_x^w$	At Exact Age x and Above T_x^w		Number $_5s_x^w$	Per 1,000 in Working Population $1,000\,_5m_x^d$	Number $_5d_x$	Per 1,000 in Working Population $1,000\,_5m_x^d$	Number $_5r_x^w$	Per 1,000 in Working Population $1,000\,_5m_x^r$
10–14	95.70	8,818	43,965	409,532	46.4	50	1.1	50	1.1	—	—
15–19	95.70	8,768	43,658	365,567	41.7	73	1.7	73	1.7	—	—
20–24	95.70	8,695	43,235	321,909	37.0	96	2.2	96	2.2	—	—
25–29	95.70	8,599	42,680	278,674	32.4	126	3.0	126	3.0	—	—
30–34	95.70	8,473	41,933	235,994	27.9	173	4.1	173	4.1	—	—
35–39	95.55	8,300	40,795	194,061	23.4	282	6.9	216	5.3	66	1.6
40–44	94.77	8,018	39,013	153,266	19.1	431	11.0	300	7.7	131	3.3
45–49	93.21	7,587	36,030	114,253	15.1	762	21.1	440	12.2	322	8.9
50–54	89.11	6,825	30,075	78,223	11.5	1,620	53.9	592	19.7	1,028	34.2
55–59	74.99	5,205	21,323	48,148	9.3	1,881	88.2	633	29.7	1,248	58.5
60–64	55.59	3,324	12,873	26,825	8.1	1,499	116.4	597	46.4	902	70.1
65 & Over	38.53	1,825	13,952	13,952	7.6	1,825	130.8	1,299	93.1	526	37.7

TABLE B.7
ABRIDGED WORKING LIFE TABLE FOR ALL RACES MALES, 1980

Age Group x to x+4 l.b.d.	Percentage of Population or Working Population at Exact Age x W_x	Number of Working Population of 10,000 Born Alive			Expectation of Working Life at Exact Age x e^{ow}_x	Losses from the Working Population					
		At Exact Age x ℓ^w_x	From Exact Age x to x+5 $5L^w_x$	At Exact Age x and Above T^w_x		Total		Due to Death		Due to Causes other than Death	
						Number $5S^w_x$	Per 1,000 in Working Population $1{,}000\,5m^d_x$	Number $5d_x$	Per 1,000 in Working Population $1{,}000\,5m^d_x$	Number $5S^w_x$	Per 1,000 in Working Population $1{,}000\,5m^r_x$
10–14	97.94	9,401	46,920	491,514	52.3	34	0.7	34	0.7	—	—
15–19	97.94	9,367	46,685	444,594	47.5	60	1.3	60	1.3	—	—
20–24	97.94	9,307	46,308	397,909	42.8	91	2.0	91	2.0	—	—
25–29	97.94	9,216	45,845	351,601	38.2	94	2.1	94	2.1	—	—
30–34	97.94	9,122	45,378	305,756	33.5	93	2.0	93	2.0	—	—
35–39	97.94	9,029	44,790	260,378	28.8	142	3.2	121	2.7	21	0.5
40–44	97.71	8,887	43,800	215,588	24.3	254	5.8	184	4.2	70	1.6
45–49	96.92	8,633	41,863	171,788	19.9	521	12.4	293	7.0	228	5.4
50–54	94.34	8,112	37,458	129,925	16.0	1,241	33.1	423	11.3	818	21.8
55–59	84.55	6,871	30,613	92,467	13.5	1,497	48.9	560	18.3	937	30.6
60–64	72.45	5,374	22,803	61,854	11.5	1,627	71.4	659	28.9	968	42.5
65 & Over	58.39	3,747	39,051	39,051	10.4	3,747	96.0	2,866	73.4	881	22.6

TABLE B.8

ABRIDGED WORKING LIFE TABLE FOR MALAY MALES, 1980

Age Group x to x+4 l.b.d.	Percentage of Population or Working Population at Exact Age x W_x	Number of Working Population of 10,000 Born Alive — At Exact Age x ℓ^w_x	Number of Working Population of 10,000 Born Alive — From Exact Age x to x+5 $5L^w_x$	Number of Working Population of 10,000 Born Alive — At Exact Age x and Above T^w_x	Expectation of Working Life at Exact Age x $\overset{o}{e}^w_x$	Losses — Total — Number $5S^w_x$	Losses — Total — Per 1,000 in Working Population $1{,}000\,5m^d_x$	Losses — Due to Death — Number $5d_x$	Losses — Due to Death — Per 1,000 in Working Population $1{,}000\,5m^d_x$	Losses — Due to Causes other than Death — Number $5r^w_x$	Losses — Due to Causes other than Death — Per 1,000 in Working Population $1{,}000\,5m^r_x$
10–14	97.82	9,326	46.543	510,638	54.8	35	0.8	35	0.8	—	—
15–19	97.82	9,291	46.318	464,095	50.0	55	1.2	55	1.2	—	—
20–24	97.82	9,236	45.975	417,777	45.2	82	1.8	82	1.8	—	—
25–29	97.82	9,154	45.555	371,802	40.6	86	1.9	86	1.9	—	—
30–34	97.82	9,068	45.125	326,247	36.0	86	1.9	86	1.9	—	—
35–39	97.82	8,982	44.578	281,122	31.3	133	3.0	111	2.5	22	0.5
40–44	97.60	8,849	43.673	236,544	26.7	229	5.2	166	3.8	63	1.4
45–49	96.91	8,620	42.045	192,871	22.4	422	10.0	252	6.0	170	4.0
50–54	94.99	8,198	38.365	150,826	18.4	1,050	27.4	403	10.5	647	16.9
55–59	87.30	7,148	32.690	112,461	15.7	1,220	37.3	546	16.7	674	20.6
60–64	78.72	5,928	26.118	79,771	13.5	1,409	53.9	692	26.5	717	27.5
65 & Over	68.40	4,519	53.653	53,653	11.9	4,519	84.2	3,589	66.9	930	17.3

TABLE B.9
ABRIDGED WORKING LIFE TABLE FOR CHINESE MALES, 1980

Age Group x to x+4 l.b.d.	Percentage of Population or Working Population at Exact Age x W_x	Number of Working Population of 10,000 Born Alive — At Exact Age x l_x^w	From Exact Age x to x+5 $_5L_x^w$	At Exact Age x and Above T_x^w	Expectation of Working Life at Exact Age x e_x^{ow}	Losses from the Working Population — Total Number $_5S_x^w$	Total Per 1,000 in Working Population $1,000\,_5m_x^d$	Due to Death Number $_5d_x$	Due to Death Per 1,000 in Working Population $1,000\,_5m_x^d$	Due to Causes other than Death Number $_5r_x^w$	Due to Causes other than Death Per 1,000 in Working Population $1,000\,_5m_x^r$
10–14	98.09	9,556	47,705	448,945	51.2	30	0.6	30	0.6	—	—
15–19	98.09	9,526	47,468	441,240	46.3	65	1.4	65	1.4	—	—
20–24	98.09	9,461	47,065	393,772	41.6	96	2.0	96	2.0	—	—
25–29	98.09	9,365	46,595	346,707	37.0	92	2.0	92	2.0	—	—
30–34	98.09	9,273	46,143	300,112	32.4	89	1.9	89	1.9	—	—
35–39	98.09	9,184	45,580	253,969	27.7	136	3.0	114	2.5	22	0.5
40–44	97.85	9,048	44,635	208,389	23.0	242	5.4	170	3.8	72	1.6
45–49	97.04	8,806	42,513	163,754	18.6	607	14.3	285	6.7	322	7.6
50–54	93.44	8,199	37,603	121,241	14.8	1,357	36.1	410	10.9	947	25.2
55–59	82.33	6,842	29,958	83,638	12.2	1,701	56.8	515	17.2	1,186	39.6
60–64	67.41	5,141	21,110	53,680	10.4	1,838	87.1	589	27.9	1,249	59.2
65 & Over	49.81	3,303	32,570	32,570	9.9	3,303	101.4	2,472	75.9	831	25.5

TABLE B.10
ABRIDGED WORKING LIFE TABLE FOR INDIAN MALES, 1980

Age Group x to x+4 l.b.d.	Percentage of Population or Working Population at Exact Age x	Number of Working Population of 10,000 Born Alive			Expectation of Working Life at Exact Age x	Losses from the Working Population					
		At Exact Age x	From Exact Age x to x+5	At Exact Age x and Above		Total		Due to Death		Due to Causes other than Death	
						Number	Per 1,000 in Working Population	Number	Per 1,000 in Working Population	Number	Per 1,000 in Working Population
x to x+4	W_x	ℓ_x^w	$_5L_x^w$	T_x^w	$\overset{o}{e}{}_x^w$	$_5s_x^w$	$1{,}000\,_5m_x^d$	$_5d_x$	$1{,}000\,_5m_x^d$	$_5s_x^w$	$1{,}000\,_5m_x^r$
10–14	98.08	9,379	46,778	441,164	47.0	47	1.0	47	1.0	—	—
15–19	98.08	9,332	46,473	394,386	42.3	75	1.6	75	1.6	—	—
20–24	98.08	9,257	46,025	347,913	37.6	104	2.3	104	2.3	—	—
25–29	98.08	9,153	45,383	301,888	33.0	153	3.4	153	3.4	—	—
30–34	98.08	9,000	44,645	256,505	28.5	142	3.2	142	3.2	—	—
35–39	98.08	8,858	43,698	211,860	23.9	237	5.4	210	4.8	27	0.6
40–44	97.77	8,621	42,045	168,162	19.5	424	10.1	324	7.7	100	2.4
45–49	96.63	8,197	39,123	126,117	15.4	745	19.0	489	12.5	256	6.5
50–54	93.53	7,452	32,538	86,994	11.7	1,889	58.1	657	20.2	1,232	37.9
55–59	77.27	5,563	22,788	54,456	9.8	2,011	88.2	631	27.7	1,380	60.5
60–64	56.67	3,552	14,168	31,668	8.9	1,437	101.4	618	43.6	819	57.8
65 & Over	42.01	2,115	17,500	17,500	8.3	2,115	120.9	1,626	92.9	489	27.9

APPENDIX C
POPULATION PROJECTIONS, 1980–2020

Introduction

In this appendix we will present a brief description of the methodology employed to prepare the population projections and the detailed results of the projections up to 2020 by sex-age groups for the Chinese, Malays and Indians separately and for All Races combined. The future growth and structure of the population as reflected by these projected figures have already been discussed at some length in the last chapter.

Method

The projections for each of the three main races were prepared by the component method which involves the separate projections of the number of males and females in each age group of the population. We usually project the population by time-intervals equal to the age-intervals into which it has been divided. Since the 1980 base population has been divided into quinary age groups, the projections are most easily made for five-year intervals of time. This implies that at the end of a five-year period all the survivors of one age group would have moved into the next higher age group.

Each cohort of the sex-age group is diminished to account for mortality with the passage of time. This step requires a set of five-year survival ratios which are deemed to represent mortality in each cohort during specific periods of time subsequent to 1980. A multiplication of the original number in each sex-age group by the relevant ratios will yield the estimated number of persons five years older at a date five years later in 1985. A repetition of the procedure will furnish the estimated population aged ten years older than those at the base date and for a date ten years later.

In the second step we are concerned with the estimation of the future number of children born in each five-year time interval subsequent to the base date in order to fill in the vacuum in the age group 0–4 at periods of time every five years later. To begin with, we need to formulate the most plausible assumption regarding the future course of fertility in terms of the age-specific fertility rates. These rates are then utilised in conjunction with the female population in the relevant reproductive age groups to derive the estimated number of births for the various five-year periods. The number of births surviving to the end of a given five-year period can be estimated by multiplying the number of births during the period with the appropriate survival ratio.

Another step would be required if international migration is taken into consideration in the computation. However, since we shall be assuming that no immigration and emigration will occur during the whole period of the projection, the procedure normally used to take migration into account need not be discussed here.

Assumptions

The results of any population projection depends primarily on the assumptions adopted in regard to migration, mortality and fertility. It may be recalled that immigration from overseas countries is now under very rigid control, while emigration to these countries will probably continue to be negligible in the future. It was therefore decided to assume that migration will not exact a significant influence on future population trends. We have observed that, though falling continuously in the past, mortality has not touched the bottom point and can continue to fall further in the future. In our computation we have therefore assumed that mortality will continue to decline. Fertility, which has been declining in the past, is also assumed to decline in the future. But the fertility decline in each of the three major races has been assumed to decline rather slowly in view of the 70 million policy.

The assumptions used to calculate the projections for each of the three main races may be summarized as follows:-

Migration

For every race, it is assumed that the population is a closed one not subject to international migration.

Mortality

For the Malays, it is assumed that the 1979 81 mortality level with a life expectancy at birth of 67.1 years for the males and 70.4 years for the females will improve respectively to 72.5 years and 75.4 years by 2020.

For the Chinese, it is assumed that the 1979–81 mortality level with a life expectancy at birth of 67.6 years for the males and 73.9 years for the females will improve respectively to 72.6 years by 2020 and 75.7 years by 2005.

For the Indians, it is assumed that the 1979–81 mortality level with a life expectancy at birth of 61.0 years for the males and 66.6 years for the females will improve respectively to 67.2 years and 72.4 years by 2020.

Fertility

For the Malays, it is assumed that their fertility will decline every five years from 2.176 in 1980 by 2 per cent up to 2000 and thereafter by 1 per cent up to 2020.

For the Chinese, it is assumed that their fertility will decline every five years from 1.512 in 1980 by 3 per cent up to 2000 and thereafter by 2 per cent up to 2020.

For the Indians, it is also assumed that their fertility will decline every five years from 1.648 in 1980 by 3 per cent up to 2000 and thereafter by 2 per cent up to 2020.

In deriving the population projections for All Races combined, it was further assumed that the proportion of the other races existing in 1980 will remain constant throughout the forty-year period.

Data

The 1980 base population classified by sex, race and quinary age group up to 85 and over is obtained from the Census of Population conducted in 1980. The survival ratios are obtained from the 1978–81 Abridged Life Tables given in Appendix A. The values of the survival ratios, P_x, for the various quinary age groups for each of the two sexes of the three main races are computed from the values of the L_x column of the relevant life tables.

TABLE C.1
POPULATION PROJECTIONS FOR ALL RACES, 1980–2020

Age	1980	1985	1990	1995	2000	2005	2010	2015	2020
0– 4	1,459,712	1,785,659	1,991,793	2,194,712	2,334,937	2,476,010	2,675,991	2,930,648	3,198,381
5– 9	1,452,691	1,450,255	1,773,796	1,981,844	2,186,324	2,327,792	2,468,463	2,667,832	2,921,713
10–14	1,359,964	1,448,332	1,446,064	1,770,207	1,978,873	2,183,571	2,324,986	2,465,488	2,668,245
15–19	1,254,148	1,355,950	1,443,207	1,442,335	1,766,823	1,975,526	2,180,171	2,321,367	2,461,650
20–24	1,052,387	1,248,328	1,348,989	1,437,770	1,438,160	1,762,427	1,970,965	2,175,139	2,316,007
25–29	882,213	1,045,047	1,240,484	1,342,574	1,432,375	1,433,559	1,756,956	1,964,934	2,168,486
30–34	741,545	874,160	1,037,155	1,233,124	1,336,060	1,426,420	1,427,686	1,749,826	1,956,956
35–39	557,473	732,462	865,860	1,029,040	1,224,879	1,328,184	1,418,200	1,419,543	1,739,920
40–44	530,381	548,277	722,428	855,631	1,018,339	1,213,434	1,316,359	1,405,808	1,407,274
45–49	394,001	517,977	556,717	708,718	838,048	1,002,652	1,195,942	1,297,717	1,386,184
50–54	351,429	379,134	500,459	520,229	688,513	819,122	978,442	1,167,943	1,267,711
55–59	268,638	330,475	357,915	474,562	495,413	657,616	784,872	940,073	1,124,819
60–64	227,339	243,375	301,618	328,725	438,293	460,041	612,958	734,533	882,844
65–69	161,510	194,235	209,533	262,195	288,158	387,004	408,907	547,523	659,643
70–74	128,111	127,808	154,853	168,842	213,811	237,175	321,142	341,973	460,501
75–79	66,605	90,802	91,335	112,056	123,396	158,158	177,216	242,136	259,841
80–84	34,626	40,247	55,812	56,911	71,026	78,952	101,546	114,065	156,392
85 & Over	22,021	27,430	32,544	42,816	48,482	59,025	68,958	85,397	99,503
Total	10,944,794	12,439,953	14,110,562	15,962,291	17,921,910	19,986,668	22,189,760	24,571,945	27,136,070

TABLE C.2

POPULATION PROJECTIONS FOR ALL RACES MALES, 1980–2020

Age	1980	1985	1990	1995	2000	2005	2010	2015	2020
0– 4	748,101	916,906	1,025,015	1,127,149	1,199,445	1,271,958	1,374,570	1,505,278	1,642,724
5– 9	741,805	743,006	910,411	1,019,452	1,122,436	1,195,366	1,267,633	1,369,896	1,500,161
10–14	691,372	739,240	740,503	908,248	1,017,727	1,120,747	1,193,692	1,265,859	1,371,607
15–19	620,664	688,782	735,815	738,041	906,078	1,015,630	1,118,729	1,191,544	1,263,580
20–24	503,664	616,690	684,155	732,229	735,374	903,456	1,012,988	1,115,819	1,188,446
25–29	427,630	498,915	611,665	680,016	728,854	732,720	900,305	1,009,544	1,112,026
30–34	372,211	422,892	494,435	607,402	676,267	725,502	729,440	896,343	1,005,102
35–39	282,625	367,047	418,187	489,944	602,788	671,866	720,926	724,928	890,875
40–44	268,587	277,282	361,343	412,594	484,235	596,550	665,145	713,903	718,007
45–49	193,909	260,965	270,036	352,834	400,949	475,273	586,691	654,451	702,651
50–54	174,609	184,701	250,055	259,784	340,499	391,189	461,599	570,710	637,012
55–59	130,858	161,785	172,007	234,280	244,588	321,864	371,360	439,930	546,164
60–64	110,667	116,202	145,034	155,216	212,959	223,661	295,859	343,203	408,626
65–69	80,354	91,812	97,337	122,849	132,591	183,681	194,430	258,952	302,554
70–74	63,205	61,449	70,760	75,960	97,144	106,011	148,632	158,952	213,287
75–79	33,784	42,986	42,078	49,118	53,469	69,438	76,822	109,245	117,717
80–84	16,021	19,088	24,719	24,665	29,558	32,479	42,473	47,222	67,767
85 & Over	9,268	11,583	13,948	17,710	19,513	23,006	26,289	32,569	37,486
Total	5,469,334	6,221,331	7,067,503	8,007,491	9,004,474	10,060,397	11,187,583	12,408,348	13,725,792

TABLE C.3

POPULATION PROJECTIONS FOR ALL RACES FEMALES, 1980–2020

Age	1980	1985	1990	1995	2000	2005	2010	2015	2020
0– 4	711,611	868,753	966,778	1,067,563	1,135,492	1,204,052	1,301,421	1,425,370	1,555,657
5– 9	710,886	707,249	863,385	962,392	1,063,888	1,132,426	1,200,830	1,297,936	1,421,552
10–14	668,592	709,092	705,561	861,959	961,146	1,062,824	1,131,294	1,199,629	1,296,638
15–19	633,484	667,168	707,392	704,294	860,745	959,896	1,061,442	1,129,823	1,198,070
20–24	548,723	631,638	664,834	705,541	702,786	858,971	957,977	1,059,320	1,127,561
25–29	454,583	546,132	628,819	662,558	703,521	700,839	856,651	955,390	1,056,460
30–34	369,334	451,268	542,720	625,722	659,793	700,918	698,246	853,483	951,854
35–39	274,848	365,415	447,673	539,096	622,091	656,318	697,274	694,615	849,045
40–44	261,794	270,995	361,085	443,037	534,104	616,884	651,214	691,905	689,267
45–49	200,092	257,012	266,681	355,884	437,099	527,379	609,251	643,266	683,533
50–54	176,820	194,433	250,404	260,445	348,014	427,933	516,843	597,233	630,699
55–59	137,780	168,690	185,908	240,282	250,825	335,752	413,512	500,143	578,655
60–64	116,672	127,175	156,584	173,509	225,334	236,380	317,099	391,330	474,218
65–69	81,156	102,423	112,196	139,346	155,567	203,323	214,477	288,571	357,089
70–74	64,906	66,359	84,093	92,882	116,667	131,164	172,510	183,021	247,214
75–79	32,821	47,816	49,257	62,938	69,927	88,720	100,394	132,891	142,124
80–84	18,605	21,159	31,093	32,246	41,468	46,473	59,073	66,843	88,625
85 & Over	12,753	15,847	18,596	25,106	28,969	36,019	42,669	52,828	62,017
Total	5,475,460	6,218,622	7,043,059	7,954,800	8,917,436	9,926,271	11,002,177	12,163,597	13,410,278

TABLE C.4
POPULATION PROJECTIONS FOR MALAY MALES, 1980–2020

Age	1980	1985	1990	1995	2000	2005	2010	2015	2020
0– 4	449,124	567,406	650,224	728,625	791,144	857,402	944,970	1,053,840	1,171,050
5– 9	427,096	444,812	562,186	646,063	725,273	788,454	854,487	941,757	1,050,257
10–14	390,883	425,131	443,166	560,724	644,900	724,258	787,350	853,291	940,439
15–19	349,785	389,007	423,218	441,748	559,434	643,739	722,954	785,933	851,755
20–24	279,791	347,197	386,478	421,229	440,202	557,979	642,065	721,074	783,890
25–29	230,890	277,245	344,558	384,314	419,418	438,705	556,082	639,882	718,622
30–34	193,548	228,720	274,916	342,318	382,316	417,573	436,775	553,635	637,067
35–39	146,219	191,419	226,364	272,634	339,922	379,984	415,026	434,111	550,258
40–44	143,334	143,923	188,739	223,670	269,826	336,761	376,450	411,166	430,074
45–49	100,739	139,851	140,454	184,700	219,465	265,374	331,743	370,841	405,040
50–54	98,737	96,669	134,704	135,735	179,085	213,474	258,793	323,516	361,644
55–59	75,527	92,289	90,444	126,622	128,147	169,790	203,249	247,354	310,381
60–64	61,596	67,929	83,466	82,286	115,834	117,870	157,039	188,940	231,053
65–69	37,935	52,018	57,753	71,555	71,087	100,799	103,313	138,665	167,968
70–74	29,670	29,415	40,543	45,515	56,979	57,168	81,839	84,686	114,662
75–79	14,229	20,443	20,346	28,429	32,325	40,979	41,635	60,332	63,125
80–84	7,982	8,508	12,413	12,566	17,853	20,300	25,735	26,147	37,888
85 & Over	5,486	7,009	8,075	10,662	12,088	15,581	18,672	23,109	25,633
Total	3,042,571	3,528,991	4,088,047	4,719,395	5,405,298	6,146,190	6,958,177	7,858,279	8,850,806

TABLE C.5
POPULATION PROJECTIONS FOR MALAY FEMALES, 1980–2020

Age	1980	1985	1990	1995	2000	2005	2010	2015	2020
0– 4	430,675	540,022	614,447	692,352	751,208	813,863	896,983	1,000,321	1,111,577
5– 9	412,762	426,971	535,972	611,252	689,790	749,180	811,665	894,561	997,620
10–14	383,297	411,235	425,775	534,954	610,396	689,100	748,431	810,853	893,666
15–19	361,896	382,070	410,248	425,009	534,259	609,602	688,204	747,458	809,799
20–24	312,056	360,448	380,733	409,181	424,159	533,190	608,383	686,828	745,963
25–29	250,419	310,433	358,862	379,439	408,076	423,014	531,750	606,740	684,974
30–34	194,251	248,591	308,229	356,888	377,769	406,566	421,449	529,783	604,495
35–39	148,334	192,250	246,428	306,041	354,782	375,805	404,452	419,257	527,028
40–44	145,655	146,331	189,674	243,619	303,072	351,766	372,911	401,338	416,029
45–49	106,965	142,946	143,917	186,886	240,403	299,405	347,510	368,399	396,482
50–54	101,958	103,895	139,101	140,377	182,681	235,403	293,597	340,768	361,252
55–59	79,773	97,023	99,002	133,120	134,888	176,050	227,423	284,202	330,375
60–64	63,705	73,319	89,630	92,052	124,481	126,822	166,138	215,279	269,736
65–69	37,297	55,372	64,103	79,098	81,954	111,672	114,596	150,903	196,378
70–74	31,216	29,767	44,624	52,321	65,327	68,391	94,128	97,292	129,007
75–79	13,174	22,385	21,423	32,647	38,833	49,159	51,991	72,262	75,538
80–84	8,896	8,408	14,349	13,910	21,521	26,006	32,922	34,818	48,394
85 & Over	6,725	8,865	9,804	13,709	15,677	21,114	26,745	33,867	38,986
Total	3,089,054	3,560,331	4,096,321	4,702,855	5,359,276	6,066,108	6,839,278	7,694,929	8,637,299

TABLE C.6
POPULATION PROJECTIONS FOR CHINESE MALES, 1980–2020

Age	1980	1985	1990	1995	2000	2005	2010	2015	2020
0– 4	223,864	254,001	272,991	292,648	300,876	302,540	308,635	321,242	335,231
5– 9	240,214	222,924	253,341	272,063	291,653	299,853	301,511	307,586	320,150
10–14	229,267	239,493	222,344	252,885	271,682	291,128	299,433	301,089	307,155
15–19	201,472	228,121	238,415	221,632	252,303	270,976	290,604	298,894	300,547
20–24	162,645	199,759	226,638	237,294	220,856	251,445	270,271	289,848	298,117
25–29	146,684	161,035	198,241	225,369	236,274	220,105	250,590	269,352	288,863
30–34	137,165	145,261	159,682	196,952	224,197	235,234	219,137	249,487	268,167
35–39	109,542	135,615	143,765	158,357	195,573	222,829	233,799	217,800	247,965
40–44	98,525	107,877	133,716	142,054	156,726	193,754	220,757	231,625	215,774
45–49	69,483	95,983	105,277	130,854	136,383	154,140	190,867	217,468	228,174
50–54	54,579	66,509	92,105	101,403	126,457	135,146	149,932	186,133	212,075
55–59	37,413	50,906	62,226	86,579	95,735	119,894	128,673	143,305	178,576
60–64	34,146	33,473	45,739	56,277	78,770	87,578	110,279	119,010	133,216
65–69	32,267	28,512	28,194	38,887	48,246	68,049	76,210	96,660	105,086
70–74	26,744	25,159	22,470	22,451	31,273	39,171	55,780	63,018	80,566
75–79	16,133	18,526	17,641	15,958	16,147	22,776	28,877	41,578	46,974
80–84	6,627	8,918	10,312	10,011	9,222	9,491	13,611	17,534	25,679
85 & Over	3,078	3,746	4,888	5,867	6,129	5,925	5,951	7,551	9,683
Total	1,829,848	2,025,818	2,237,985	2,467,541	2,698,502	2,930,034	3,154,917	3,379,180	3,601,998

TABLE C.7
POPULATION PROJECTIONS FOR CHINESE FEMALES, 1980–2020

Age	1980	1985	1990	1995	2000	2005	2010	2015	2020
0– 4	208,954	237,539	254,829	273,899	281,602	283,161	288,860	300,660	313,754
5– 9	226,580	208,223	236,898	254,141	273,159	280,842	282,425	288,109	299,878
10–14	216,947	226,149	207,931	236,661	253,887	272,886	280,561	282,143	287,821
15–19	201,493	216,470	225,742	207,661	236,353	253,557	272,531	280,196	281,776
20–24	172,033	200,848	215,907	225,291	207,246	235,880	253,050	271,986	279,634
25–29	152,598	171,362	200,165	215,324	224,683	206,686	235,243	252,367	271,252
30–34	134,519	151,850	170,608	199,424	214,527	223,852	205,921	234,373	251,433
35–39	101,025	133,672	150,954	169,721	198,387	213,411	222,688	204,850	233,154
40–44	89,936	100,136	132,536	149,792	168,414	196,859	211,768	220,973	203,273
45–49	71,548	88,668	98,814	130,932	147,980	166,376	194,477	209,206	218,299
50–54	59,098	69,952	86,824	96,897	128,392	145,109	163,148	190,704	205,147
55–59	44,696	57,065	67,581	84,046	93,942	124,476	140,683	158,172	184,888
60–64	42,917	42,157	53,852	63,972	79,768	89,339	118,377	133,790	150,422
65–69	37,266	38,870	38,291	49,124	58,605	73,355	82,156	108,859	123,033
70–74	29,469	31,695	33,230	32,965	42,581	50,799	63,584	71,213	94,359
75–79	17,841	22,741	24,608	26,092	25,884	33,435	39,887	49,926	55,916
80–84	8,875	11,791	15,230	16,480	17,474	17,335	22,391	26,712	33,435
85 & Over	5,553	6,351	7,986	10,220	11,753	12,866	13,294	15,709	18,674
Total	1,821,348	2,015,539	2,221,986	2,442,642	2,664,637	2,880,224	3,091,044	3,299,948	3,506,148

TABLE C.8
POPULATION PROJECTIONS FOR INDIAN MALES, 1980–2020

Age	1980	1985	1990	1995	2000	2005	2010	2015	2020
0– 4	71,061	89,552	95,152	98,565	99,645	103,766	112,049	120,433	125,788
5– 9	70,164	70,450	88,979	94,714	98,230	99,306	103,413	111,668	120,024
10–14	67,625	69,820	70,189	88,748	94,544	98,092	99,167	103,268	115,117
15–19	66,424	67,185	69,408	69,873	88,464	94,327	97,915	98,988	103,082
20–24	58,213	65,733	66,600	68,957	69,545	88,172	94,082	97,660	98,731
25–29	46,894	57,398	64,898	65,921	68,433	69,156	87,793	93,762	97,328
30–34	38,388	46,167	56,629	64,191	65,367	67,988	68,796	87,407	93,349
35–39	24,433	37,632	45,345	55,774	63,382	64,694	67,424	68,314	86,874
40–44	24,648	23,683	36,544	44,193	54,541	62,165	63,627	66,480	67,501
45–49	22,044	23,438	22,553	34,991	42,500	52,676	60,275	61,896	64,878
50–54	19,754	20,325	21,624	20,961	32,748	40,031	49,879	57,358	59,160
55–59	16,737	17,540	18,221	19,559	19,119	30,092	37,029	46,417	53,664
60–64	14,024	14,046	14,888	15,646	16,973	16,762	26,622	33,026	41,706
65–69	9,545	10,686	10,759	11,610	12,398	13,641	13,646	21,947	27,537
70–74	6,364	6,476	7,288	7,501	8,262	8,984	10,049	10,217	16,675
75–79	3,192	3,738	3,818	4,412	4,650	5,233	5,812	6,626	6,854
80–84	1,294	1,538	1,834	1,928	2,291	2,477	2,851	3,235	3,760
85 & Over	635	753	895	1,066	1,169	1,351	1,495	1,698	1,927
Total	561,439	626,160	695,624	768,610	842,261	918,913	1,001,924	1,090,400	1,183,955

TABLE C.9
POPULATION PROJECTIONS FOR INDIAN FEMALES, 1980–2020

Age	1980	1985	1990	1995	2000	2005	2010	2015	2020
0– 4	68,333	85,887	91,598	94,793	95,748	99,676	107,631	115,685	120,827
5– 9	67,618	67,739	85,243	91,122	94,442	95,489	99,407	107,340	115,373
10–14	64,894	67,381	67,549	85,081	90,994	94,348	95,394	99,308	107,233
15–19	67,010	64,557	67,085	67,326	84,877	90,876	94,225	95,270	99,179
20–24	61,508	66,487	64,137	66,763	67,090	84,656	90,694	94,037	95,079
25–29	48,490	61,004	65,955	63,752	66,469	66,862	84,427	90,449	93,783
30–34	37,674	48,073	60,571	65,592	63,471	66,223	66,615	84,115	90,114
35–39	23,267	37,263	47,559	60,044	65,126	63,097	65,879	66,269	83,678
40–44	24,451	22,874	36,671	46,922	59,359	64,494	62,561	65,372	65,759
45–49	20,188	23,830	22,323	35,894	46,049	58,380	63,546	61,735	64,581
50–54	14,498	19,399	22,951	21,582	34,817	44,810	56,944	62,116	60,451
55–59	12,267	13,575	18,190	21,650	20,464	33,177	42,883	54,717	59,861
60–64	9,175	10,921	12,146	16,426	19,710	18,776	30,649	39,873	51,166
65–69	6,012	7,556	9,117	10,274	14,059	17,055	16,416	27,048	35,499
70–74	3,726	4,492	5,726	7,029	8,047	11,174	13,745	13,399	22,339
75–79	1,510	2,398	2,925	3,815	4,783	5,585	7,903	9,892	9,803
80–84	683	831	1,324	1,659	2,220	2,848	3,400	4,905	6,255
85 & Over	369	534	693	1,024	1,362	1,819	2,370	2,930	3,979
Total	531,673	604,801	681,763	760,748	839,087	919,345	1,004,689	1,094,460	1,184,959

APPENDIX D
SOURCES OF DEMOGRAPHIC STATISTICS

In this appendix we will present an account of the demographic statistics which provide the basic information for us to study the population of Peninsular Malaysia. The demographic statistics that will be discussed here refer to those obtained from periodic censuses of population, registration of births, deaths, marriages and divorces, and administrative records regarding migration.

Population

The taking of a population census had its origin in the beginning of the nineteenth century when the inhabitants of the newly established British Settlements of Penang, Malacca and Singapore were first counted in 1801, 1826 and 1824 respectively. Other than the results quoted subsequently by various writers, nothing is known about these counts. Immediately following the first exercise, similar counts were made almost every year and later at longer intervals. By 1836 eight counts were taken in Penang, seven in Malacca and eleven in Singapore. The results of these counts were reproduced in *Political and Statistical Account of the British Settlements in the Straits of Malacca* by T.J. Newbold.[1] The statistics are not only very narrow in scope, being limited to sex and race, but are also seriously in error. After 1836 three population counts were conducted in 1840, 1849 and 1860 in Penang and Malacca as part of the Straits Settlements. The results of these head counts classified by sex and race only were reproduced by Thomas Braddell in *Statistics of the British Possessions in the Straits of Malacca*.[2] Apart from being not very reliable and not comprehensive, the statistics obtainable from these early head counts are for only two of the 11 states in Peninsular Malaysia.

The first proper census as understood today was taken in Penang and Malacca as part of the Straits Settlements in 1871 which coincided with the decennial census undertaken in Great Britain and her colonial territories. In each state a committee of government officials was in charge of the census and each committee submitted a report consisting of a brief administrative account and about 20 pages of tables to the Colonial Secretary, Straits Settlements. These reports were published in the *1871 Blue Book of the Straits Settlements*.[3] In

1. T.J. Newbold, *Political and Statistical Account of British Settlements in the Straits of Malacca*, Vol. I (London: John Murray, 1839).
2. T. Braddell, *Statistics of the British Possessions in the Straits of Malacca* (Penang: Penang Gazette Printing Office, 1961).
3. Straits Settlements, *1871 Blue Book of the Straits Settlements* (Singapore: Government Printer, 1872).

addition to the basic information on sex, age and race, the tables contain data on houses, occupation and geographical areas by simple town-country division. The next decennial census was conducted in 1881 in the Straits Settlements on the same lines as the first census, and the reports prepared by the respective Committees were published in the *1881 Blue Book of the Straits Settlements.*[4] Apart from the usual account on the census procedures and administration there was for the first time an attempt at analysing the population statistics in the reports. The items of information covered were similar to those of the previous census.

In 1891 the Federated Malay States, comprising Selangor, Perak, Negri Sembilan and Pahang, inaugurated the first proper census. Meanwhile the Straits Settlements had the third one under, not a committee but a superintendent responsible for the entire census operation. The results were published in a single report entitled *Report on the Census of the Straits Settlements, Taken on 5th April 1891.*[5] In this report the first section presents an analysis of the results and a description of the census administration in the Straits Settlements as a whole, followed by three similar sections dealing with each of the three settlements of Penang, Malacca and Singapore. It would appear that a report of the census executed for the first time in the Federated Malay States was never published, but the main results were incorporated in the Straits Settlements report. In 1901 the Straits Settlements and the Federated Malay States were again covered separately by one census each, and the results are to be found in the *Report on the Census of the Straits Settlements, Taken on 1st March 1901*[6] and the *Report on the Census of the Federated Malay States.*[7] In the former report the general pattern of the previous report was preserved in presenting the written text and tables.

The year 1911 is very significant in that it witnessed not only the continuation of the decennial censuses in the Straits Settlements and the Federated Malay States but the inauguration of census taking in the Unfederated Malay States of Perlis, Kedah, Kelantan, Trengganu and Johore. This means that 1911 is the earliest year in which population statistics for the whole of Peninsular Malaysia are made available. Furthermore, the census held in the Straits Settlements was a more ambitious one with many new items and some improvement

4. Straits Settlements, *1881 Blue Book of the Straits Settlements* (Singapore: Government Printer, 1882).
5. E.M. Merewether, *Report on the Census of the Straits Settlements Taken on the 5th April 1891* (Singapore: Government Printing Office, 1892).
6. J.R. Innes, *Report on the Census of the Straits Settlements Taken on the 1st March 1901* (Singapore: Government Printing Office, 1901).
7. G.T. Hare, *Report on the Census of the Federated Malay States, 1901* (Singapore: Government Printing Office, 1901).

in the written text of the report entitled *Census Report of the Straits Settlements, 1911.*[8] The scope was enlarged to include for the first time information on birth-place, religion and industry, as well as the re-introduction of occupation omitted since 1891. The results of the census held in the Federated Malay States were published in the *Review of the Census Operations and Results*, giving tables on sex, age, race, birth-place and occupation.[9] Instead of a single report on the whole of the Unfederated Malay States, short individual reports were issued for each of the states, and most of them are not available in libraries.

Another major improvement was introduced in 1921 when the whole of Peninsular Malaysia, together with Singapore, was enumerated under the supervision of a single superintendent who was also responsible for bringing out *The Census of British Malaya, 1921.*[10] In this census there was complete uniformity for all the states in the concepts and definitions used, the procedures for enumeration, and the items of information covered. This census covered all the items included in the 1911 Census of the Straits Settlements as well as two new items on literacy (ability to read and write) and language (ability to speak), thus increasing the coverage for the Federated and Unfederated Malay States. A point to note is that the census results are readily available in a single report which facilitates preservation and use of the figures. The second pan-Peninsula census was conducted in 1931, on the same basis as that of 1921, with no change in the list of items. The results were published in *British Malaya: A Report on the 1931 Census and on Certain Problems of Vital Statistics.*[11] The section on vital statistics is a new feature.

A census was planned for April 1941 but the increasing difficulties arising from the imminence of war led to the abandonment of the project at the eleventh hour resulting in a break in the series of decennial censuses started in 1871. After the war a census of Peninsular Malaysia and Singapore was completed in 1947 and the results appeared in *Malaya: A Report on the 1947 Census of Population.*[12] The two items on religion and language were excluded, but there were three new items, namely, household, year of first arrival for foreign-born persons, and number of children ever borne. It is of some interest to note that as opposed to the manual method employed in all the previous censuses, the

---

8. Hayes Marriot, *Census Report of the Straits Settlements, 1911* (Singapore: Government Printing Press, 1911).
9. A.M. Pountney, *Federated Malay States: Review of the Census Operations and Results, 1911* (London: Darling & Son, 1911).
10. J.E. Nathan, *The Census of the British Malaya, 1921* (London: Waterlow & Sons, 1922).
11. C.A. Vlieland, *British Malaya: A Report on the 1931 Census and Certain Problems of Vital Statistics* (London: Crown Agents, 1932).
12. M.V. Del Tufo, *Malaya: A Report on the 1947 Census of Population* (London: Crown Agents, 1949).

mechanical method using punched cards was utilised to process the 1947 census returns.

The next postwar census taken in 1957 marks a permanent departure from previous ones in that the census covered only Peninsular Malaysia, with a completely separate census conducted in Singapore. The newer labour force approach was adopted to identify and collect the data on the labour force. Another important development was the new method of collecting Chinese age statistics based on the animal-year system. Good age statistics were obtained in spite of the defective method used.[13] A third innovation was the publication of the census results in fourteen volumes rather than in a single report. The 14 volumes bear the general title of *1957 Population Census of the Federation of Malaya*, with Number 1 giving preliminary figures by race and geographical area, Numbers 2 to 12 the complete set of figures for the 11 states, Number 13 the administrative report, and Number 14 the national figures and some analysis.[14]

The next census was held more than 10 years later in 1970 and covered not only Peninsular Malaysia but Sabah and Sarawak which had become part of the larger political unit of Malaysia in September 1963. The year 1970 was chosen so as to have the census coincide with the United Nations census programme centred around that year. Aside from the reinstatement of religion, the new items introduced were period of residence in present locality, previous place of residence, reason for leaving previous residence, number of times married, and number of years married. A complete set of the census tables for each of the thirteen states appeared in 13 separate reports. The combined figures for Peninsular Malaysia and for the whole of Malaysia were published in a single report, while the analysis of the census results appeared in a final report entitled *Malaysia: General Report of the Population Census, 1970*.[15]

The latest census held in 1980 was executed on the same basis as that of the previous one, with however some changes in the items. A list of the items included in the census is given below:

1. Sex
2. Age
3. Race
4. Marital Status

---

13. Saw Swee-Hock, "Errors in Chinese Age Statistics", *Demography*, Vol. 4, No. 2, 1967.
14. H. Fell, *1957 Population Census of the Federation of Malaya*, No. 14, Final Report (Kuala Lumpur: Department of Statistics).
15. R. Chander, *Malaysia: General Report of the Population Census, 1970*, Vols. 1 and 2 (Kuala Lumpur: Department of Statistics, 1977).

5. Religion
6. Citizenship
7. Year of Birth
8. Place of Birth
9. Period of residence in Malaysia
10. Period of residence in permanent locality
11. Previous place of residence
12. Reason for leaving previous residence (new)
13. School attendance
14. Highest level of schooling
15. Vocational training (new)
16. Literacy
17. Language
18. Industry
19. Occupation
20. Employment status
21. Age at first marriage (new)
22. Number of times married
23. Number of children born alive

Besides the three new items indicated above, one item on the number of years married was omitted. The release of the census results was patterned on the same publication programme as that adopted in the previous census, with 13 separate reports containing the figures for the 13 states. The combined figures for Peninsular Malaysia and Malaysia are published in Volume 2 of *Malaysia: General Report of the Population Census, 1980*, and the analysis of the figures are given in Volume 1 of this publication.[16] One problem confronting the use of the census results refers to the delay in the release of the census reports, for example, the report for the last state was made available more than five years later in late 1985.

Births and Deaths

As in the case of a population census, the development of birth and death registration in Peninsular Malaysia was closely associated with the history of British influence in the country. It is therefore not surprising that compulsory registration of births and deaths was first introduced in January 1872 in the two states of Penang and Malacca as part of the overall system that came into effect in the Straits Settlements under the *Registration of Births and Deaths*

---

16. Khoo Teik Huat, *Malaysia: General Report of the Population Census*, Vols. 1 and 2 (Kuala Lumpur: Department of Statistics, 1983).

Ordinance. Under this ordinance the Chief Health Officer was made the Registrar-General of Births and Deaths, and he was required to compile a summary of births and deaths for inclusion in his annual report. This ordinance was subsequently repealed and re-enacted with considerable changes by the *Registration of Births and Deaths Ordinance, 1937.*[17] Among the important changes was the introduction of compulsory registration of still-births, which was not present in the old ordinance. The other important development was the establishment of a permanent Registry of Births and Deaths under the charge of a full-time Registrar.

In the Federated Malay States of Selangor, Perak, Negri Sembilan and Pahang the compulsory registration of births and deaths was introduced in the early 1920s under the *Births and Deaths Registration Enactment, 1920.*[18] This was followed by similar enactments effected at different times in Johore, Kedah, Kelantan, Perlis and Trengganu in the Unfederated Malay States. By the early 1930s there was therefore compulsory registration of births and deaths throughout the whole of Peninsular Malaysia. The various ordinances continued to govern the registration of births and deaths in the different states until the late 1950s. Soon after the formation of the Federation of Malaya in August 1957, the different laws concerning civil registration were repealed and consolidated under the *Births and Deaths Registration Ordinance, 1957* which came into operation on 1 August 1958.[19] This uniform ordinance made it compulsory for still-births to be registered throughout the whole country; prior to this it was only compulsory in Penang and. Malacca.

The present registration system is under the overall charge of the Registrar-General in the National Registration Department located in Petaling Jaya, and in each state there is a Registrar in charge of the State Registration Department. In each state there are also registration centres situated in hospitals, police stations, city halls in urban areas, while in the rural areas registration of vital events can be made with authorised persons such as village headsmen, headmasters and estate managers. According to the ordinance the time allowed for registration is 14 days for births and still-births and 12 hours for deaths; delayed registration can be effected but is subject to penalties.

The availability of birth and death statistics in the early years depended not only on the expansion of the registration system into the various parts of the

---

17. Straits Settlements, *Registration of Births and Deaths Ordinance, 1937,* No. 34 of 1937 (Singapore: Government Printer).

18. See "The Births and Deaths Registration Enactment, 1920" in A.B. Voules (compiler), *Laws of the Federated Malay States, 1877–1920* (London: Hayall, Watson & Viney, 1921).

19. Malaya, *Births and Deaths Registration Ordinance, 1957,* No. 61 of 1957 (Kuala Lumpur: Government Press, 1957).

country as determined by the introduction of the relevant legislation, but also on the establishment of a framework for generating statistics from the particulars contained in the reports. It is therefore to be noted that although the registration system was introduced in 1872 in Penang and Malacca, the first year for which statistics were made available was 1886 as published in the *Annual Report on the Registration of Births and Deaths for the Year 1886*.[20] In those early years the data on births were merely tabulated according to month, sex, race and registration area, while those for deaths were classified by month, sex, race, registration area, broad causes of death, and broad age groups. In the other states the statistics also became available some years after compulsory registration was introduced. For the whole of Peninsular Malaysia, 1934 was the year for which complete birth and death statistics were first made available.

Marriages and Divorces

Muslim marriages are solemnised and registered under the provisions of the respective state and Federal Territory laws. According to these laws Muslim marriages are required to be registered with the Department of Religious Affairs in these states and Territory. But comprehensive statistics have never been generated from this registration system. Even the annual number of Muslim marriages occurring during the year is not published regularly in official reports. What we have are the annual figures collected and published by various writers such as Judith Djamour, Shirle Gordon and Yoshihiro Tsubouchi. The same position applies to Muslim divorces which are performed according to Islamic laws and registered with the Department of Religious Affairs.

Until 28 February 1982, some of the non-Muslim marriages were registered under the *Registration of Marriage Ordinance, 1952*, the *Civil Marriage Ordinance, 1952*, and the *Christian Marriage Ordinance, 1952*. The very basic statistics in respect of marriages registered under the provisions of these three ordinances have been published in the annual report of the Registrar-General.[21] The characteristics included in the tables are month of marriage and age group of groom and bride with regard to civil marriages and Christian marriages. Other marriages registered under the first ordinance are tabulated by month of marriage only. It should be emphasised that the combined total for these three types of marriages registered on a voluntary basis represents only part of the total number of non-Muslim marriages contracted in any particular

---

20. See the various reports entitled *Report of the Registrar-General on Population, Births, Deaths, Marriages and Adoptions, 1955* (Kuala Lumpur: Government Press).
21. Ibid.

year. There is no way of ascertaining the total number of non-Muslim marriages that were not registered in any year.

With effect from 1 March 1982, all non-Muslim marriages are required to be registered under the provisions of the *Law Reform (Marriage and Divorce) Act, 1976*, which repealed all the previous laws governing these marriages. This means that it is now possible to compile statistics on non-Muslim marriages solemnised in the Peninsula. But to date no statistical system has been introduced to generate comprehensive statistics from this marriage registration system for publication on an annual basis. The annual number of such marriages can obviously be compiled from the marriage records kept in the Registrar-General's Office, but these annual figures are yet to be compiled and published on a regular basis. Divorce statistics relating to these marriages are also not available.

Migration

The situation regarding migration laws governing the entry of foreigners into Peninsular Malaysia and hence the compilation of migration statistics differ widely among the main ethnic groups. The entry of Chinese into the country was first placed under the provisions of the *Chinese Immigration Ordinance, 1877*, which established the Chinese Protectorate Office in the Straits Settlements. The main function of this office was to improve the terms and conditions of Chinese immigrants entering the country. The first attempt at controlling the number of Chinese immigrants was made in 1928 when the *Immigration Restriction Ordinance, 1928* was enacted. This was followed by more rigid controls as in the provisions of the *Aliens Ordinance, 1933*. One major administrative change introduced by the ordinance was the closure of the Chinese Protectorate Office and the transfer of its major functions to the new Immigration Department set up in 1933.

After the Second World War the old ordinance was no longer adequate and was replaced by the *Immigration Ordinance, 1953* which took into account the rapidly changing political and economic circumstances affecting and resulting from the immigration of Chinese and other races. The final step was taken after independence was attained on 1 August 1957 with the enactment of the new *Immigration Ordinance, 1959*. This ordinance, which came into force on 1 May 1959, was designed to safeguard the interest of the citizens of a newly independent country and to allow entry to only those who are deemed to be able to contribute to the social and economic development of the country. The ordinance, together with its subsequent amendments, is now used to regulate the entry of people of all races into the country.

The statistics on Chinese migration in the early days were compiled from the records of sea passengers embarking and disembarking at the ports of Peninsular Malaysia and Singapore, both treated as one single geographical unit in respect of migration matters. The figures tabulated according to sex and adults and children below age 12 were published by the Chinese Protector in his annual *Report of the Chinese Protector of Chinese* for the years 1881 to 1932.[22] With the closure of the Chinese Protectorate in 1933, the figures for 1933 to 1938 were published in the annual *Report of the Immigration Department.*[23] The figures for 1939 to 1941 are not available because the publication of the annual report was interrupted by the Second World War, and after the war the figures ceased to be compiled. For the postwar period the Department of Statistics publishes statistics on arrivals and departures of Chinese by air, sea and land, but these figures are defective in that they cover all categories of Chinese entering and leaving the country and may not even reflect the broad trends in Chinese migration.

Indian migration in the early days was different in that India and Peninsular Malaysia belonged to one political unit under the control of the India Office prior to 1867, and even after that year both were still British colonies under the purview of the Colonial Office. Indian migration was often considered as merely a movement of people from one colonial territory to another, and was subjected to rules and procedures established by the colonial government in India. Furthermore, Indian migration was closely associated with the import- ation of labourers to overcome the shortage of labour in certain sectors of the Peninsula economy. For many decades the entry of Indians, especially in- dentured immigrants, was regulated by laws enacted in India. The first local legislation affecting Indian migration was the *Indian Immigration Ordinance, 1884*, by which the Straits Settlements assumed direct control over Indian migration into the Peninsula. This law was subsequently supplemented by the *Tamil Immigration Fund Ordinance, 1907*, which established the Indian Immi- gration Fund under the supervision of the Indian Immigration Committee to promote the import of Indian labourers. In June 1938 the administration of the Fund was transferred to the Labour Department. Throughout the prewar period Indian migration was not covered by the various laws governing Chinese migration, and after the war it came under the control of the common *Immi- gration Ordinance, 1953* and later the newer *Immigration Ordinance, 1959*.

The statistics on Indian migration for the early years 1881 to 1911 were

22. Straits Settlements, *Report of the Protector of Chinese, 1881–1932* (Singapore: Government Press).
23. Straits Settlements, *Report on the Immigration Department, 1933–1938* (Singapore: Govern- ment Press).

published in the annual *Report on Indian Immigration*.[24] These figures were classified by sex, adult-children, and type of immigrants such as indentured, *kangany*-recruited, etc. The figures for 1912 to 1938 were published in the annual *Report of the Labour Department*.[25] The figures for 1939 onwards were never published because of the war. For the postwar period, the only statistics are those pertaining to arrivals and departures by air, sea and land, but they provide only a very crude picture of trends in Indian migration.

Until the early twentieth century the migration of Malays between the Peninsula and Indonesia under the then Netherlands East Indian Government was not controlled by any legislature at all. It was in 1909 that the *Netherlands Indian Labourers Protection Enactment, 1909* was passed by the Straits Settlements Government to regulate the movement and employment of Indonesian indentured immigrants. However, regarding Malay migration in the prewar days, there are no statistics similar to those for the Chinese and the Indians. The only statistics that can provide a rough idea of Malay migration are the figures on arrivals and departures by sea, land and air.

---

24. Straits Settlements, *Report on Indian Immigration, 1880–1911* (Singapore: Government Printer).
25. Straits Settlements, *Report of the Labour Department, 1912–1938* (Singapore: Government Printer).

BIBLIOGRAPHY

Census Reports

Census Committee, *Report of the Census Officers for the Settlement of Malacca, 1871* in 1871 Blue Book of the Straits Settlements (Singapore: Government Printing Office, 1872).

Census Committee, *Report of the Census Officers for the Settlement of Penang, 1871* in 1871 Blue Book of the Straits Settlements (Singapore: Government Printing Office, 1872).

Census Committee, *Report of the Census Officers for the Settlement of Malacca, 1881* in 1881 Blue Book of the Straits Settlements (Singapore: Government Printing Office, 1882).

Chander, R., *1970 Population and Housing Census of Malaysia* (Kuala Lumpur: Department of Statistics).

  (1) Volume 1 Basic Population Tables

      Part I   Perlis

      Part II   Penang and Province Wellesley

      Part III   Malacca

      Part IV   Negri Sembilan

      Part V   Selangor

      Part VI   Pahang

      Part VII   Trengganu

      Part VIII Kelantan

      Part IX   Kedah

      Part X   Perak

      Part XI   Johore

      Part XII   Sabah

      Part XIII Sarawak

  (2) General Report of the Population Census of Malaysia

      Volume 1 Administrative Report

      Volume 2 Tables

Fell, H., *1957 Population Census of the Federation of Malaya* (Kuala Lumpur: Department of Statistics).

  Report No. 1 Summary Tables

  Report No. 2 Selangor

  Report No. 3 Penang

Report No. 4 Kedah
Report No. 5 Malacca
Report No. 6 Johore
Report No. 7 Negri Sembilan
Report No. 8 Perak
Report No. 9 Pahang
Report No. 10 Kelantan
Report No. 11 Trengganu
Report No. 12 Perlis
Report No. 13 Administrative Report
Report No. 14 Final Report

Hare, G.T., *Report on the Census of the Federated Malay States, 1901* (Singapore: Government Printing Office, 1901).

Innes, J.R., *Report on the Census of the Straits Settlements Taken on the 1st March 1901* (Singapore: Government Printing Office, 1901).

Khoo Teik Huat, *1980 Population and Housing Census of Malaysia.*

(1) State Population Report
   Johore
   Kedah
   Kelantan
   Malacca
   Negri Sembilan
   Pahang
   Penang
   Perak
   Perlis
   Selangor
   Trengganu
   Welayah Persekutan
   Sabah
   Sarawak
(2) General Report of the Population Census of Malaysia
   Volume 1 Administrative Report
   Volume 2 Tables

Marriot, Hayes, *Census Report of the Straits Settlements, 1911* (Singapore: Government Printing Office, 1911).

Merewether, E.M., *Report on the Census of the Straits Settlements Taken on the 5th April 1891* (Singapore: Government Printing Office, 1892).

Nathan, J.E., *The Census of the British Malaya, 1921* (London: Waterlow & Sons, 1922).

Pountney, A.M., *Federated Malay States: Review of the Census Operations and Results, 1911* (London: Darling & Son, 1911).

Tufo, M.V. Del, *Malaya: A Report on the 1947 Census of Population* (London: Crown Agents, 1949).

Vlieland, C.A., *British Malaya: A Report on the 1931 Census and Certain Problems of Vital Statistics* (London: Crown Agents, 1932).

Other Government Publications

Malaya, *Federation of Malaya Annual Report, 1948–1965* (Kuala Lumpur: Government Press).

Malaya, *Malaya: First Five-Year Plan, 1956–1960* (Kuala Lumpur: Government Press, 1956).

Malaya, *Malaya: Second Five-Year Plan, 1961–1965* (Kuala Lumpur: Government Press, 1961).

Malaya, *Births and Deaths Registration Ordinance, 1957*, No. 61 of 1957 (Kuala Lumpur: Government Press, 1957).

Malaya, *Report on the Registration of Births and Deaths, 1948–1954* (Kuala Lumpur: Government Press).

Malaya, *Report of the Registrar-General on Population, Births, Deaths, Marriages and Adoptions, 1955–1965* (Kuala Lumpur: Government Press).

Malaya, *Vital Statistics, 1963–1964* (Kuala Lumpur: Department of Statistics).

Malaya, *Report of the Medical Department, 1957* (Kuala Lumpur: Government Printer, 1958).

Malaya, *Immigration Ordinance, 1959*, No. 12 of 1959 (Kuala Lumpur: Government Printer, 1959).

Malayan Union, *Report on the Registration of Births and Deaths, 1941–1947* (Kuala Lumpur: Government Press).

Malayan Union, *Report of the Medical Department, 1946* (Kuala Lumpur: Government Press).

Malaysia, *Report of the Registrar-General on Population, Births, Deaths, Marriages and Adoptions, 1966–1985* (Kuala Lumpur: Government Press).

Malaysia, *Annual Report of the National Family Planning Board, 1966–1983* (Kuala Lumpur).

Malaysia, *Family Planning Act 1966*, No. 42 of 1966 (Kuala Lumpur: Government Press, 1966).

Malaysia, *Second Malaysia Plan, 1971–1975* (Kuala Lumpur: Government Press).

Malaysia, *Mid-Term Review of the Second Malaysia Plan, 1971–1975* (Kuala Lumpur: Government Press, 1973).

Malaysia, *Third Malaysia Plan, 1976–1980* (Kuala Lumpur: Government Press, 1976).

Malaysia, *Mid-Term Review of the Third Malaysia Plan, 1976–1980* (Kuala Lumpur: Government Press, 1979).

Malaysia, *Estimates of the Inter-Censal Population by Sex, Community and Age Group for Peninsular Malaysia, 1957–1970* (Kuala Lumpur: Department of Statistics, 1974).

Malaysia, *Revised Intercensal Population Estimates for Peninsular Malaysia, 1971–1979* (Kuala Lumpur: Department of Statistics, 1985).

Malaysia, *Current Population Estimates for Peninsular Malaysia, 1984* (Kuala Lumpur: Department of Statistics, 1984).

Peninsular Malaysia, *Vital Statistics, 1965–1983* (Kuala Lumpur: Department of Statistics).

Singapore, *Malayan Statistics Monthly Digest, 1939–1958* (Singapore: Department of Statistics).

Straits Settlements, *Annual Report on the Administration of the Straits Settlements, 1960–1961* (Singapore).

Straits Settlements, *Blue Book of the Straits Settlements, 1871–1881* (Singapore: Government Printer).

Straits Settlements, *Report of the Protector of Chinese, 1881–1932* (Singapore: Government Press).

Straits Settlements, *Annual Report on the Registration of Births and Deaths, 1886–1939* (Singapore: Government Printer).

Straits Settlements, *Registration of Births and Deaths Ordinance, 1937*, No. 34 of 1937 (Singapore: Government Printer, 1937).

Straits Settlements and Federated Malay States, *Report on Indian Immigration, 1880–1911* (Singapore: Government Printer).

Straits Settlements and Federated Malay States, *Report of the Labour Department, 1912–1938* (Singapore: Government Printer).

Straits Settlements and Federated Malay States, *Report of the Immigration Department, 1933–1938* (Singapore: Government Press).

Books

Abdullah bin Ayob, *Towards a Population of Seventy Million* (Kuala Lumpur: National Population and Family Development Board, 1984).

Braddell, T., *Statistics of the British Possessions in the Straits of Malacca* (Penang: Penang Gazette Printing Office, 1961).

Cambell, P.C., *Chinese Coolie Emigration to Countries within the British Empire* (London: P.S. King and Son, 1923).

Cheng Siok-Hwa, *Changing Labour Force of Singapore* (Manila: Council for Asian Manpower Studies, 1984).

Corry, W.C.S., *A General Survey of New Villages* (Kuala Lumpur: Government Press, 1954).

Cowan, C.D. (ed.), *The Economic Development of South East Asia* (London: Allen and Unwin, 1964).

Davis, Kingsley, *The Population of India and Pakistan* (Princeton: Princeton University Press, 1951).

Dobby, E.H.G., *Southeast Asia* (London: London University Press, 1956).

Durand, John D., *The Labour Force in Economic Development* (Princeton: Princeton University Press, 1975).

E.C.A.F.E., *Interrelation Between Population and Manpower Problems*, Asian Population Studies No. 7 (Bangkok).

E.S.C.A.P., *Population of the Philippines*, Country Monograph Series No. 5 (Bangkok, 1978).

E.S.C.A.P., *Migration, Urbanization and Development in Sri Lanka* (Bangkok, 1980).

E.S.C.A.P., *Migration, Urbanization and Development in the Republic of Korea* (Bangkok, 1980).

E.S.C.A.P., *Migration, Urbanization and Development in Indonesia* (Bangkok, 1981).

E.S.C.A.P., *Migration, Urbanization and Development in Malaysia* (Bangkok, 1982).

Fernandez, Dorothy; Amos H. Hawley and Silvia Predaza, *The Population of Malaysia*, C.I.C.R.E.D. Series (1975).

Freedman, Maurice, *Chinese Family and Marriage in Singapore* (London: H.M.S.O., 1957).

Geoghegan, J., *Note on Emigration from India* (Calcutta: Government Press, 1873).

Gullick, J.M., *Malaya* (London: Ernest Benn, 1963).

Hall, D.G.E., *A History of South-East Asia* (London: MacMillan, 1958).

Hooker, M.B., *Islamic Law in South-East Asia* (London: Oxford University Press, 1984).

International Labour Office, *Proceedings of the 24th Session of the National Labour Conference* (Geneva, 1937).

Jackson, James C., *Planters and Speculators: Chinese and European Agricultural Enterprise in Malaya, 1786–1921* (Kuala Lumpur: University of Malaya Press, 1968).

Jackson, R.N., *Immigrant Labour and Development of Malaya* (Kuala Lumpur: Government Press, n.d.).

Kennedy, J., *A History of Malaya, A.D. 1400–1959* (London: MacMillan, 1962).

Kernial Singh Sandhu, *Indians in Malaya: Immigration and Settlement, 1886–1957* (London: Cambridge University Press, 1969).

Manderson, Lenore, *Women, Politics and Change: The Kaum Ibu UMNO* (Kuala Lumpur: Oxford University Press, 1981).

Manjit S. Sidhu and Gavin W. Jones (eds.), *Population Dynamics in a Plural Society: Peninsular Malaysia* (Kuala Lumpur: University of Malaya Co-operative Bookstore Publications, 1981).

Marjoribanks, N.E. and A.K.G. Ahmad Tambi Marakkaya, *Report on Indian Labour Emmigration to Ceylon and Malaya* (Madras: Government Press, 1917).

Nanjudan, S., *Indians in Malayan Economy* (New Delhi: Indian Government Press, 1950).

Newbold, T.J., *Political and Statistical Account of British Settlements in the Straits of Malacca* (London: John Murray, 1839).

Nor Laily Aziz, *Malaysia: Population and Development* (Kuala Lumpur: National Family Planning Board, 1981).

Nor Laily Aziz, Tan Boon Ann, Ramli Othman and Kuan Lin Chee, *Facts and Figure: Malaysia National Population and Family Development* (Kuala Lumpur: National Family Planning Board, 1982).

Ooi Jin Bee, *Peninsular Malaysia* (London: Longman, 1976).

Parmer, Norman, *Colonial Labour Policy and Administration* (New York: Monograph of the Association for Asian Studies, No. IX, 1960).

Parr, C.W.C., *Report of Commission Appointed to Enquire into the Conditions of Indentured Labour in the Federated Malay States* (Kuala Lumpur, 1910).

Peng J.Y.; Tan Boon Ann; Leslie Corsa and Shamsuddin bin Abdul Rahman (compilers), *Family Planning Annual Statistical Report, 1967–70* (Kuala Lumpur: National Family Planning Board, 1974).

Purcell, Victor, *The Chinese in Malaya* (London: Oxford University Press, 1948).

Purcell, Victor, *The Chinese in Southeast Asia* (London: Oxford University Press, 1951).

Sarkar, N.K., *The Demography of Ceylon* (Ceylon: Government Press, 1957).

Saw Swee-Hock, *Singapore Population in Transition* (Philadelphia: University of Pennsylvania Press, 1970).

Saw Swee-Hock, *Construction of Malayan Abridged Life Tables, 1956–1958* (Hong Kong: Department of Statistics, University of Hong Kong, 1970).

Saw Swee-Hock, *Estimation of Interstate Migration in Peninsular Malaysia, 1947–1970* (Singapore: Institute of Southeast Asian Studies, 1980).

Saw Swee-Hock, *Changing Labour Force of Malaysia* (Manila: Council for Asian Manpower Studies, 1984).

Saw Swee-Hock, *The Labour Force of Singapore* (Singapore: Department of Statistics, 1985).

Silcock, T.H. and E.K. Fisk (eds.), *The Political Economy of Independent Malaya* (Canberra: Australian National University Press, 1963).

Smith, T.E., *Population Growth in Malaya* (London: Oxford University Press, 1952).

Taiwan, *1973 Taiwan Demographic Fact Book* (Taipei).

Tregonning, K.G., *A History of Modern Malaya* (London: University of London Press, 1964).

United Nations, *Age and Sex Patterns of Mortality: Model Life Tables for Under-Developed Countries* (New York: Department of Social Affairs, 1955).

United Nations, *The Ageing of Population and Its Economic and Social Implications* (New York: Department of Economic and Social Affairs, 1956).

United Nations, *Manual III: Methods of Population Projections by Sex and Age* (New York: Department of Economic and Social Affairs, 1956).

United Nations, *Handbook of Population Census Methods, Volume II: Economic Characteristics of Population*, Series F, No. 5, Rev. 1, Studies in Methods (New York, 1958).

United Nations, *Recent Trends in Fertility in Industrialized Countries* (New York: Department of Economic and Social Affairs, 1968).

United Nations, *Manual VI: Methods of Measuring Internal Migration* (New York: Department of Economic and Social Affairs, 1970).

United Nations, *Conditions and Trends of Fertility in the World*, Bulletin No. 7 (New York: Department of Economic and Social Affairs, 1976).

Voules, A.B. (compiler), *Laws of the Federated Malay States, 1877–1920* (London, 1921).

World Health Organization, *Mortality in South and East Asia: A Review of Changing Trends and Patterns, 1950–1975* (Geneva: World Health Organization, 1982).

Windstedt, R.O., *A History of Malaya* (London: Malayan Branch of the Royal Asiatic Society, 1935).

Articles

Abdul Razak bin Hussein, "Government Policy on Birth Control in Malaysia", *Kajian Ekonomi Malaysia*, Vol. 3, No. 1, June 1966.

Ahmad bin Mohamad Ibrahim, "Developments in Marriage Laws in Malaysia", *Malayan Law Review*, Vol. 2, No. 2, December 1970.

Azizah Kassim, "Women and Divorce Among the Urban Malays" in Hing Ai Yun, *et al.* (eds.), *Women in Malaysia* (Kuala Lumpur: Pelanduk Publications, 1984).

Blythe, W.L., "Historical Sketch of Chinese Labour in Malaya", *Journal of Malayan Branch of the Royal Asiatic Society*, Vol. 20, Part 1, June 1947.

Caldwell, J.C., "Fertility Decline and Female Chances of Marriage in Malaya", *Population Studies*, Vol. 17, No. 1, July 1963.

Dixon, Ruth B., "Explaining Cross-Cultural Variations in Age at Marriage and Proportion Never Marrying", *Population Studies*, Vol. 25, No. 1, July 1971.

Dobby, E.H.G., "Settlement Patterns in Malaya", *The Geographical Review*, Vol. 32, No. 2, April 1942.

Golstein, Sydney, "Urbanization in Thailand, 1947–1967", *Demography*, Vol. 8, No. 2, May 1971.

Gordon, Shirle, "Malay Marriage/Divorce in Eleven States of Malaya and Singapore", *Intisari*, Vol. 2, No. 2, n.d.

Hajnal, John, "Age at Marriage and Proportion Marrying", *Population Studies*, Vol. 7, No. 2, November 1953.

Jones, Gavin J. and Manjit S. Sidhu, "Population Mobility in Peninsular Malaysia", *Development Forum*, Vol. 9, No. 2, December 1979.

Jones, Gavin, "Trends in Marriage and Divorce in Peninsular Malaysia", *Population Studies*, Vol. 34, No. 2, July 1980.

Kernial Singh Sandhu, "Emergency Settlement in Malaya", *Journal of Tropical Geography*, Vol. 18, 1964.

Labrooy, Joan R., "Estates and Family Planning", *Proceedings of the First National Family Seminar, 10–12 June 1968* (Kuala Lumpur: National Family Planning Board, n.d.).

McTaggart, W.D., "The Distribution of Ethnic Groups in Malaya, 1947–1957", *Journal of Tropical Geography*, Vol. 26, June 1968.

Mohamed Din bin Ali, "Malay Customary Law and Family", *Intisari*, Vol. 2, No. 2, 1965.

Mohamed Khir Johari, "National Family Planning Board: Chairman's Inaugural Address", *Kajian Ekonomi Malaysia*, Vol. 3, No. 1, June 1966.

Purcell, Victor, "Chinese Settlement in Malacca", *Journal of the Malayan Branch of the Royal Asiatic Society*, Vol. 20, Part 1, 1974.

Rafiah Salam, "The Legal Status of Women in a Multi-Racial Malaysian Society" in Hing Ai Yun, *et al.* (eds.), *Women in Malaysia* (Kuala Lumpur: Pelanduk Publications, 1984).

Ravenstein, E.G., "The Laws of Migration", *Journal of the Royal Statistical Society*, June 1979.

Saw Swee-Hock, "A Problem of Estimating a Contingency Table Arising in Demographic Analysis", *Population Studies*, Vol. 19, No. 3, March 1966.

Saw Swee-Hock, "Malaya: Tables of Male Working Life, 1957", *Journal of the Royal Statistical Society*, Series A, Vol. 128, Part 3, 1965.

Saw Swee-Hock, "State Differential Mortality in Malaya", *Population Review*, Vol. 10, No. 1, January 1966.

Saw Swee-Hock, "Sources and Methods of Labour Force Statistics in Malaya", *Ekonomi*, Vol. 3, No. 1, December 1966.

Saw Swee-Hock, "Errors in Chinese Age Statistics", *Demography*, Vol. 4, No. 2, 1967.

Saw Swee-Hock, "Fertility Differentials in Early Postwar Malaya", *Demography*, Vol. 4, No. 2, 1967.

Saw Swee-Hock, "The Structure of the Labour Force in Malaya", *International Labour Review*, Vol. 98, No. 1, July 1968.

Saw Swee-Hock, "Family Planning Knowledge, Attitude and Practice in Malaya, 1966–1967", *Demography*, Vol. 5, No. 2, 1968.

Saw Swee-Hock, "Birth Control Use at Eve of the National Action Programme in West Malaysia", *Journal of Family Welfare*, Vol. 16, March 1970.

Saw Swee-Hock, "Patterns of Urbanization in West Malaysia, 1911–1970", *Malayan Economic Review*, Vol. 17, No. 2, October 1972.

Saw Swee-Hock, "Increasing Life Expectancy in Singapore during 1969–1981", *Singapore Medical Journal*, Vol. 25, No. 3, June 1984.

Sendut, Hamzah, "Patterns of Urbanization in Malaya", *Journal of Tropical Geography*, Vol. 16, October 1962.

Smith, Peter C., "Asian Marriage Patterns in Transition", *Journal of Family History*, Vol. 5, No. 1, 1980.

Tsubouchi, Yoshihiro, "Marriage and Divorce Among Malay Peasants in Kelantan", *Journal of Southeast Asian Studies*, Vol. 6, No. 2, September 1975.

Tungku Shamsul Bahrin, "Indonesian Labour in Malaya", *Kajian Ekonomi Malaysia*, Vol. 2, No. 1, June 1965.

Tungku Shamsul Bahrin, "The Pattern of Indonesian Migration and Settlement in Malaya", *Asian Studies*, Vol. 5, Part 2, August 1967.

United Nations, "The Situation and Recent Trends of Mortality in the World", *Population Bulletin of the United Nations*, No. 6, 1962.

Other Publications

Kok Kim Lian, *Levels, Trends and Patterns of Urbanization in Peninsular Malaysia, 1957–1980*, Mimeograph.

MacAndrews, C., *Mobility and Modernization: A Study of the Malaysian Federal Land Development Authority and its Role in Modernizing the Rural Malays*, Ph.D. Thesis, Massachusetts Institute of Technology, 1976.

Maeda, Narifumi, *The Changing Peasant World in a Melaka Village: Islam and Democracy in the Malay Tradition*, Ph.D. Thesis, University of Chicago, 1974.

Saw Swee-Hock, *The Demography of Malaya, with Special Reference to Race Differentials*, Ph.D. Thesis, London School of Economics and Political Science, 1963.

Annual Report of the Family Planning Association of Selangor (Kuala Lumpur).

History and Activities of the Federation of Family Planning Associations, Federation of Malaya, 1958-1965, Ref. F.F.P.A. General 24 (Kuala Lumpur: Federation of Family Planning Associations, 1965).

Netherlands Indian Labourers Protection Enactment, 1909.

Asian Wall Street Journal.

Asiaweek.

Eastern Sun.

Malaysian Business.

Malaysian Business Times.

Singapore Monitor.

The Malay Mail.

The New Straits Times.

The Star.

The Straits Times.

INDEX

Abortion, 184
Abridged life tables, *see* life tables
Abridged male working life tables, *see* working life tables
Administration of Islamic Law Enactment, 1955, 146
Administration of Muslim Law Enactment, 1962, 146
Administration of Muslim Law Enactment, 1965, 146
Age pyramid, 74–75
Age-specific death rates, 126–28, 131–33, 138–40
Age-specific fertility rates, 184–87, 193–96, 202, 206
Age-specific labour force participation rates, 226–31
Age-specific loss rates from working population, 256–58, 295–96
Age-specific retirement rates, 257–58
Age-specific standardised death rates, 128, 135–37
Age structure, 72–77, 266–68
Agriculture, 5–6
Aliens Ordinance, 1933, 15–17, 40, 325
Annual average births, 178–79
Annual average deaths, 122–23
Annual rate of natural increase, 52–53
Annual rate of population growth, 49–56
Average life expectancy, *see* life expectancy
Average working life expectancy, *see* working life expectancy

Babas, 198
Bangkok, 92
Bangladesh, 135
Bangladeshis, 64
Beri-beri, 123

Births and Deaths Registration Enactment, 1920, 323
Births and Deaths Registration Ordinance, 1957, 323
Birth control, 172–78, 204–205
Birth rates, *see* crude birth rates
Birth registration, 9, 322–24
Blythe, W.L., 21–22
Braddell, Thomas, 7, 318
Bugis, 37
Bumiputra, 219, 238

Census, 7–9, 318–22
China, 11, 14, 16, 20, 22, 42, 46, 50
Chinese
 age at first marriage, 151–57
 age structure, 76–78
 citizenship, 81–82
 divorce, 164
 fertility trends, 189–98
 future population, 265–66
 industrial structure, 238–40
 internal migration, 116–20
 international migration, 11–22
 labour force, 219–22, 226, 229–31
 marriage, 147–49
 mortality trends, 130–35
 occupational pattern, 246–50
 population distribution, 63–64
 population growth, 53–56
 sex composition, 69–70
 urbanisation, 95–101
 working life pattern, 258–59
Chinese Immigration Ordinance, 1877, 13, 325
Chinese Protectorate Office, 13, 16, 325
Christian Marriage Enactment, 1915, 147
Christian Marriage Ordinance, 1898, 147
Christian Marriage Ordinance, 1940, 147

338

www.ingramcontent.com/pod-product-compliance
Lightning Source LLC
Chambersburg PA
CBHW021544260326
41914CB00001B/152